Transformation
Through Myth & Metaphor
— the personal hero's journey

by Vic Shayne

Transformation
Through Myth & Metaphor
— the personal hero's journey

© 2019 Vic Shayne

Published by
Creative Bureau Enterprises, Inc.
Niwot, Colorado

ISBN: 9781089176343

Table of Contents

Some helpful terms 3

Embarking on the Journey into Myth and Metaphor 11

Writing on Myth and Metaphor 17

Myth is Metaphorical 21

The Creation of the Egoic Mind 25

What does a person have to do with myth? 35

Why do we need Myth? 47

Expressions on Myth and Metaphor 51

Jung at Heart 59

Examples of Archetypes 63

The Part is the Whole 67

The Hero's Journey 73

Death and Rebirth 81

Personal Myth 93

Koan and Myth 97

Ritual, Myth, and Rites 101

A Medley of Mythical Motifs 111

Self Enquiry and the Myth of the self 121

Youtube videos 125

About the Author 126

Transformation Through Myth & Metaphor
— the personal hero's journey

by Vic Shayne, PhD

"Dreams are real as long as they last.
Can we say more of life?"

—— *The Upanishads*

Some helpful terms

Archetype

noun

1. 'archetypes' from 'arche' meaning primordial, and 'typos' meaning typical. Archetypal images embody the most essential elements of the human experience and drama.
2. a very typical example of a certain person or thing.
3. a recurrent symbol or motif in literature, art, or mythology.
    "mythological archetypes of good and evil"

4. Joseph Campbell noted that "an archetype is a constant form, a basic fundamental form which appears in the works of that person over there, and this person over here, without connecting them. They are expressions of the structure of the human psyche."

Belief

noun

1. an acceptance that a statement is true or that something exists
2. something one accepts as true or real; a firmly held opinion or conviction
3. a religious conviction
4. trust, faith, or confidence in someone or something

Connotation

noun

1. an idea or feeling that a word invokes in addition to its literal or primary meaning.

"the word "discipline" has unhappy connotations of punishment and repression"

Denotation

noun

1. the literal or primary meaning of a word, in contrast to the feelings or ideas that the word suggests."beyond their immediate denotation, the words have a connotative power"

2. the action or process of indicating or referring to something by means of a word, symbol, etc.

3. In PHILOSOPHY: the object or concept to which a term refers, or the set of objects of which a predicate is true.

Consciousness

noun

1. the state of being awake and aware of one's surroundings.

2. "she failed to regain consciousness and died two days later"

3. the awareness or perception of something by a person.

4. the fact of awareness by the mind of itself and the world.

Consciousness can also be defined, according to ancient Eastern tradition, as the totality of all that exists, including creation, action, destruction, the mind, all forms and expressions, phenomena, and the potentiality of existence.

Egoic self

noun

1. the sense of "I," the persona, the self, the center, all of which are created by an accretion of thoughts. The egoic self is created when the mind is conditioned by myriad psychological influences such as parents, teachers, authority figures, religion, society, and more. The egoic self is the persona that identifies and associates with a name, gender, the body, and titles, accolades, successes and failures, wins and losses, memories, friends, relatives, sports teams, job positions, and so on.

4

2. the egoic self is not the Self of consciousness; the egoic self is consciousness that is focused upon the beliefs of the conditioned mind so that it believes itself to be an individual apart from the totality of life and reality.
3. The false ego or false self is the individual that the mind considers itself to be.

Figurative

adjective

1. departing from a literal use of words; metaphorical.

"gold, in the figurative language of the people, was "the tears wept by the sun.""

Koan

noun

1. a paradoxical anecdote or riddle, used in Zen Buddhism to demonstrate the inadequacy of logical reasoning and to provoke enlightenment.

Language

noun

1. the method of human communication, either spoken or written, consisting of the use of words in a structured and conventional way."a study of the way children learn language"

Literal

adjective

1. taking words in their usual or most basic sense without metaphor or allegory; "dreadful in its literal sense, full of dread"

If you are being literal, then you are explaining what something is. For instance, you may say, "The dog is exhausted." Or you can not be literal and instead be metaphorical and use a figurative explanation. For example, "The dog is a lump of clay."

Metaphor:

noun

1. a figure of speech in which a word or phrase is applied to an object or action to which it is not literally applicable. "Her poetry depends on suggestion and metaphor"

2. a thing regarded as representative or symbolic of something else, especially something abstract."the amounts of money being lost by the company were enough to make it a **metaphor for** an industry that was teetering"

Mind

noun

1. the element of a person that enables them to be aware of the world and their experiences, to think, and to feel; the faculty of consciousness and thought. "as the thoughts ran through his mind, he came to a conclusion"

2. a person's intellect

Myth:

noun

1. a traditional story, especially one concerning the early history of a people or explaining some natural or social phenomenon, and typically involving supernatural beings or events.

Joseph Campbell, author, researcher, and professor of Mythology, said, "**Myths** are clues to the spiritual potentialities of the human life."[1] Myth, he explained, "is the field of reference...metaphors for what is absolutely

---

[1] PBS series Joseph Campbell on The Power of Myth with Bill Moyers

transcendent." Myths are the guidebooks for life itself, with all its beauty and mystery. They reflect the concept of transcending duality (because while things do come in pairs and everything has its opposite, there can be no good without evil). Myths are the keys to understanding the whole of human experience.[2]

Ontological

adjective

1. relating to the branch of metaphysics dealing with the nature of being: "ontological arguments"
2. showing the relations between the concepts and categories in a subject area or domain: "an ontological database"

Personification

noun

1. the attribution of a personal nature or human characteristics to something nonhuman, or the representation of an abstract quality in human form: "His religion tells him he cannot drink wine."

Religion:

noun

1. the belief in and worship of a superhuman controlling power, especially a personal God or gods."ideas about the relationship between science and religion"
2. a particular system of faith and worship
3. a pursuit or interest to which someone ascribes supreme importance: "Science is the new religion"

Simile:

---

[2] Loar, Christel, The Meaning of Life: Joseph Campbell on The Power of Myth with Bill Moyers, popmatters.com, Oct 28, 2010

noun
1. a figure of speech involving the comparison of one thing with another thing of a different kind, used to make a description more emphatic or vivid (e.g., *as brave as a lion, crazy like a fox*). The use of simile."His audacious deployment of simile and metaphor"

Transformation

noun
1. a thorough or dramatic change in form or appearance
2. a change in focus or attention that takes place due to the realization that one is not the egoic mind with all of its beliefs, associations, and identities
3. the reconditioning of the conditioned egoic mind to a new state of understanding and feeling

"Human beings cannot live without challenge. We cannot live without meaning.
Everything ever achieved we owe to this inexplicable urge to reach beyond our grasp, do the impossible, know the unknown.
The Upanishads would say this urge is part of our evolutionary heritage, given to us for the ultimate adventure: to discover for certain who we are, what the universe is, and what is the significance of the brief drama of life and death we play out against the backdrop of eternity."

— The Upanishads

Embarking on the Journey into Myth and Metaphor

This book is about myths, metaphors, the conscious mind, and consciousness. Most of all, it's about transformation.

Like any useful myth, it is my hope as the author that you won't take anything you read as the truth, but will instead consider what is written and then take it inside of you. Digest the words and imagery, and observe your sense of self to find your own Truth. This is the only way transformation happens. It's a personal hero's journey into the depths of the Self.

Included in this book are the ideas of me the author, Vic Shayne, as well as notable figures who understand myth and metaphor as a pointer more than a guide, map, or morality play.

Every good book needs to have a strong theme that is an overarching statement about his or her work. The theme of this book is spiritual *transformation through myth and metaphor*. The word spiritual is used to be clear that we are not speaking of the physical, mental, or emotional aspects of a person. Spiritual implies some state that is not limited to the mind and body.

Everywhere we turn we hear myths. This is the only way we can communicate the complexity of ideas, experiences, and all else that is somewhere inside of us yearning to be conveyed to others. If you listen, you will hear them for now on.

I encourage you, the reader, to keep in mind the importance of regarding myth, religious teachings, and communications as metaphors, because when imagery is taken literally it is soulless and usually an incredible story that is fundamentally unable to pierce the armor of the egoic self to find what is waiting beyond.

Myth, and life in general, is the play between the egoic self and the one and only consciousness that is the wholeness of life — the singular interconnected network of movement, creation, potential, destruction, action, and so on. It's about the little self and the greater Self. This has been described many ways, including as Carl Jung's conscious mind and the collective unconscious. In religion it is referred to as the human being and God. In Vedanta philosophy it is the self and the Self, differentiated by the lower case and upper case "s."

Myth is about transformation, which is the death of the egoic self that gives rise to the rebirth, or realization of, the greater singular consciousness. It is a symbolic death.

Death gives way to something new and awe-inspiring.

The sage teachings of the *Upanishads* tells the myth of a boy named Nachiketa who meets the Lord of Death, Yama. When Nachiketa arrives at Yama's house, the Lord of Death is not home and the boy waits for him for three nights. When Yama returns he apologizes, and to make up for his inhospitality, he grants the boy three wishes. Nachiketa's third one is to ask what happens when we die. This is how the story unfolds:

> *Nachiketa looked Yama in the eye and said, "I want to know what happens when a person dies. Some say he continues to exist, some say not. Tell me what is the truth. That is my third wish.'*

> *Yama was shocked. 'This question has haunted even the gods of old. The secret of Death is hard to know. Please ask for something else. I will give you*

all the riches in the world and fulfill your every worldly desire. I will give you the power to dominate the world; powers beyond the confines of time and space and the ability to live a thousand years.'

Nachiketa did not waver. 'All of this is but passing joy. How can I rejoice in any of it when I know death awaits me as it does every mortal,' he replied. 'Dispel this doubt oh great King, does a person live after death or does he not?'

Having tested Nachiketa, Yama found him worthy of such instruction. 'I offered you everything a man could desire and you have wisely turned it down, so listen...

The wise men know that true Self is eternal.

There are two selves within. One is the ego and the other is the indivisible Atman. When a person rises above, I, me and mine, the Atman is revealed as one's real Self.

'However, the Self cannot be known through study of the scriptures, nor through the intellect, nor through hearing learned discourses. It must be experienced,' Yama answered.

Yama gifted Nachiketa with the Om, the symbol of the formless, changeless and omnipresent Self. Yama said those in whose hearts Om reverberates know the Self. They see the one indivisible Self in all.'

'Hidden in the heart of every creature is the same Self. Subtler than the subtlest, greater than the greatest. Formless in the midst of form, changeless in the midst of change. Omnipresent and supreme.

And the wise know that the Self was never born nor will it die. Beyond cause and effect, the Self is eternal, unchangeable. The eternal Self slays not, nor is it ever slain. We live not by the breath that flows in flows out but by the one who causes the breath to flow in and out.'

'Know that Self,' said Yama.' Your pure and immortal Self.'

And so Nachiketa having learned the truth from the King of Death, freed himself from all separateness became one with the eternal.[3]

In myth, death is not the finality of the biological body. It is about what comes next — a metaphorical rebirth. But the hero must push through and face this death, often risking his physical body, daring to go where his sense of a personal self is uncomfortable, afraid, or resistant to go. But once he or she steps onto the path, this is the beginning of a very personal hero's journey.

---

3 Gupta, Anuradha, Death the Ultimate Teacher, All About Hinduism, http://www.allabouthinduism.info//?s=death&search=Go, July 13, 2015

*"Enlightenment, joy, and peace
can never be given to you by another.
The well is inside you."*

— *Thich Nhat Hanh*

Writing on
Myth and Metaphor

It's no easy task to find book authors who truly understand the depths of myth as much as the late mythologist and professor Joseph Campbell did. He was the guru, the expert, the guide who fully realized what myth teaches by way of metaphor and the inward journey. It is through myth that Campbell had a full realization of who he was beyond the egoic self and as the totality of consciousness.

It is apparent that many who have written about the meaning of myth really don't "get it." They can speak and write about myth from an intellectual or pedagogical perspective, but when it comes to understanding the transformation of the egoic self to the greater Self of consciousness, they fail to realize and embody the full implications. As the writer of this book, I have searched for authors with Campbell's insight, but the search has been difficult to say the least. Like any sage, Campbell was one of a kind. So I have leaned heavily on his decades of research and teachings in this little book. Though not authors, fortunately there are a number of people who have a lot to contribute to this topic of the penetrating and transformative messages of myth and metaphor, and I have included what some have expressed in their articles and reflections.

Myths are the result of social, psychological, cultural, and even physical evolution. Mirroring the human psyche, they seem to be one thing but are actually something much deeper. In psychology as well as the arts, we are familiar with the idea of the conscious and unconscious minds and their role in relating to, and navigating through, the world around us. These are two currents through which we perceive and navigate what is inadequately called reality. The conscious mind is shaped by psychological factors that condition it into the individual sense of self, the

"I," or the one you call "me." But much deeper, there is another kind of "I" that is the stream of consciousness; it is universal. It is this deeper stateless state from which myth arises. This is what makes myth powerful — it can move one beyond the conscious and into the great expanse of the unconscious. To the conscious mind, myths are stories that seem fanciful, unrealistic, harsh or embracing, and so on. But to the unconscious mind, myth makes sense and speaks to it through metaphor. When this can be known as an absolute fact, a light goes on because the one who is the seer becomes enlightened — transformed — by it. The seer and the seen are one nondual entity. And this realization is what made Joseph Campbell so uniquely special in his field.

From ancient India there have been gurus and sages who have guided people over the millennia into the Self by way of inner work, introspection and self-enquiry. This inner Self is the Self of consciousness, while the outer self, the conscious one, is the self of the egoic mind.

*"Someone who wants to attain enlightenment
must be brave.
He must rush into the crowd of enemies with a dagger.
In the practice of Zen,
enemies are our delusive thoughts and passions."*

— *Koun Yamada*

Myth is Metaphorical

It is problematic that, on the whole, we human beings, especially from the Western tradition, move through our days — and entire lives — without contemplating the essence of mythology and metaphor that shapes our every step and thought. And, in general, relatively few people question their own sense of self beyond the conscious mind.

The meaning of the word "myth" is practically unknown, and those who do offer a definition usually equate it with a lie. The misrepresentation of the word has been used so often that even the common dictionary lists "a lie" as one of the definitions. We see this misuse all over our advertising messages and articles so that we are further and further removed from the absolute richness of the concept of myth and how it affects us at the very core of our beingness.

The late great Joseph Campbell said, "Whether one thinks of mythology in terms of the affirmation of the world as it is, the negation of the world as it is, or the restoration of the world to what it ought to be, the first function of mythology is to arouse in the mind a sense of awe before this situation through one of three ways of participating in it: by moving out, moving in, or effecting a correction."

A university professor, world traveler, speaker, and prolific writer, Campbell spent his life in pursuit of the meaning, depth, breadth, application, and significance of mythology. From his teachings, writings, study, and realization of myth, he brought forth a little sentence that still echoes throughout world cultures: "Follow your bliss." You may ask how Campbell gleaned this message from the topic of myth. He realized that people are always looking for the meaning of life — the purpose for why things are the way they are. But this is looking in the wrong direction.

Instead, he showed, we are best served looking for the meaning *in* life. One little preposition makes a world of difference.

Life is here, and we are experiencing it as well as creating it. When we find meaning in it then we are in accord with it. If we do not then we live in conflict and pain. It sounds simple, yet there is one stumbling block, one obstacle, that gets in the way: The egoic mind.

"Metaphor as a figure of speech has intrigued and stimulated scholars for thousands of years.
Aristotle considered metaphor a sign of genius,
believing that the individual who could make unusual connections was a person of special gifts.
From that ancient tradition has emerged a working definition of metaphor: the capacity to perceive a resemblance between elements from two separate domains or areas of experience and to link them together in linguistic form."

— *Howard Gardner*

The Creation of the Egoic Mind

The egoic mind is the sense of self, the persona, or that which we call "me" or "I." This egoic mind is created when consciousness is focused upon, or attending to, all of the things of the self — identities, progress, relationships, associations, worries, fears, achievements, losses, gains, failures, successes, and above all, the pursuit of pleasure and avoidance of pain.

The ego is your idea of your face to the world, the person you presume yourself to be.

Though Sigmund Freud may have been maligned for many of his ideas, and conclusions, his descriptions of parts of the mind are still accepted as valid and useful. He spoke of the Id, ego, superego, unconscious (subconscious), and conscious mind. In brief, the Id is the little devil in us, like a spoiled child, who wants to do whatever it desires, irrespective of what is socially acceptable. The superego, on the other hand, is the little angel who wants to do the right thing and hopes that the rest of the world sees what a wonderful person we are. The ego is defined as a person's sense of self-esteem or self-importance.

**Why is the ego so important,
and how did it come to be that way?**

We all accept that the brain is a biological, physical organ that has something to do with thinking, nerve transmission, and other functions. But what is unclear and in debate is the mind — is it physical or not? Does it arise from the brain, or is it separate? Materialists argue that the mind, like everything else that exists, is the result of chemistry. Their belief is that there is nothing more to life than what you see, and the only mystery is a chemical process that is just not yet understood. On the other hand, there are many people, including a good number of philosophers and even scientists, who argue that the mind is a product of consciousness, and neither of these are dependent upon, or arise from, the brain and physical world.

In any regard, the mind is an instrument that is essential for navigating through life. With the mind you remember where you live, how to drive a car, who your relatives are, what time it is, what you have to do, how to open the refrigerator, how to eat with a spoon, and on and on. The mind, in this sense, is a practical instrument. But when the mind comes into contact with certain strong ideas, it forms a sense of self. This self is also called the egoic mind, the center, "I," "me," and other terms, such as Tasha, Janice, Robin, Josh, Harish, Mary, Bharat, Omar, and so on. Carl Jung called it the *persona*. There are billions of these selves who are running around in a big metaphoric play that we call life.

The egoic mind is created by psychological conditioning. We can each know this simply by observing ourselves —— the way we think, act, relate, interact, respond, create, and destroy; as well as how we think, why we think certain things, how we have been influenced, and what we tend to think about. The egoic mind is constructed out of the ideas of psychological conditioning from authority figures who shape the functional mind — parents, religious leaders, neighbors, friends, relatives, society, culture, teachers, and so on. Therefore, the egoic mind —— what we take ourselves to be —— is merely an accretion of thoughts; it is a belief of who we are.

If, by example, a man says, "I am a professor," this is not really true. He is playing the role of a professor, but if he were to look inside of himself for something called a professor, he would not find one. And if a woman says, "I am a Druid," this cannot be true, because there is nothing found

26

in the biology or the mind that is a Druid. A belief is not a person or a physical thing, yet it is part of the complex that we call the individual, the egoic self.

To use a metaphor, the egoic mind is a mask that is worn by consciousness. There is an adage spoken by a clever anonymous person that states, "If you wear a mask long enough, you begin to forget who you are beneath it."

Writer Nikki Sapp explained, "The ego is based in concepts, in belief systems, in the 'idea of,' not on anything real or tangible. It quite literally depends on our belief in it for its survival. So what happens when we stop believing in it? When we start to become more in tune with our true self, which is the part of us that OBSERVES the ego —not the ego itself — we realize that a state of peace lies within us. This peace transcends all concepts and ideas of who we think we should be. The more a person becomes rooted in this part of themselves, the more they realize that everything they believed to be true about themselves or about others or about life in general, was all based in illusion."[4]

Perceived as an independent, single unit, we may say that the sense of self, or that which we consider "me," is actually no more than a belief. It does not exist in that it is not tangible, it is subject to change, it evolves, it cannot be located, it has no location, and it is not biological. We even have terms to describe the mutability of the egoic mind, as we say, "I no longer believe in that," or, "I used to be afraid of heights," or, "I'm a changed woman," or "Today I am a university graduate." Who is this "I" that changes, and who (or what) remains that has not changed yet knows of the change?

---

[4] 4 Sapp, Nikki, The Mask of Ego: How Attached are You to Yours? Fractal Enlightenment online, fractalenlightenment.com/31345/life/the-mask-of-ego-how-attached-are-you-to-yours, Jul 2019

The sage Nisargadatta said, "There is no such thing as a person. There are only restrictions and limitations. The sum total of these defines the person. You think you know yourself when you know what you are. But you never know who you are. The person merely appears to be, like the space within the pot appears to have the shape and volume and smell of the pot. See that you are not what you believe yourself to be. Fight with all the strength at your disposal against the idea that you are nameable and describable. You are not. Refuse to think of yourself in terms of this or that. There is no other way out of misery, which you have created for yourself through blind acceptance without investigation. Suffering is a call for enquiry, all pain needs investigation. Don't be too lazy to think."

We'll get to the suffering issue further ahead, because it is the driving force for seeing beyond the egoic self.

In an effort to stay in force, this sense of a self — the person — is preoccupied with two things: the pursuit of pleasure and the avoidance of pain. Bouncing between the two opposites, we move through the day in a state of hoping, dreading, wishing, fearing, desiring, lusting, repelling, dreaming, and lamenting.

This desire of the egoic mind, the sense of self, is all about perpetuation of the "I." In the world of Freud, it is the ego that is self-important. It has learned — it has been taught — that it is important and that it is attached to a body and all sorts of identities and associations, and these are precious to it. It's afraid to lose what it believes are vital parts of itself. The conscious mind is selfish, self-centered, self-absorbed. When it recedes into the background, something else emerges that is compassionate and altruistic. This is the Self of unalloyed consciousness.

But consciously, even the most so-called altruistic among us is ego-driven because the conditioning of the mind is unavoidable. What we do is for the satisfaction, protection, and perpetuation of the egoic mind — unless what we do is unconscious, which is where the idea of myth and the hero comes in.

Myth gets the egoic self to step aside.

In the Eastern tradition from India, where sages have contemplated the nature of the mind and consciousness for thousands of years, there has arisen the idea of enlightenment. Enlightenment is when a person realizes that he/she is not the persona, but rather some essence that pre-exists the egoic mind, the rational mind, the body, all forms and expressions, nature, objects, phenomena, and even the sense of reality. Myth speaks to this pre-existent Self, which is also called consciousness. Myth has the power to enlighten, which is an awakening to the true essence of all that is.

As the enlightened person looks out onto the world, he/she understands life to be a sort of play wherein the characters, stage, props, scenery, and so on are temporary expressions of consciousness. Even more importantly, the enlightened one knows that he/she is actually this consciousness itself; and, as consciousness, we all create the world, reality and all that happens. When this is known, there is *moksha*, or liberation — freedom from the illusion that, as the egoic mind and the individual, we are the effect of life. The realization of liberation is that we are life itself. Thus, consciousness is the totality of all that is, including action, destruction, creation, phenomena, objects, nature, movement, and potentiality. Everything that exists is an expression of consciousness. As consciousness we are all the source of the same movement of consciousness. There is not *your* consciousness and *her* consciousness, or higher consciousness and lower consciousness; there is just consciousness.

There are varying levels of awareness, but consciousness just *IS*, without quality or quantity. The body and mind is an expression of this singular source. The only difference between the enlightened being and everyone else, according to the sages of the Eastern traditions such as Hinduism, Taoism, Buddhism, or Vedanta, is that she/he has realized this truth while most others have not.

When it is realized that you are consciousness, the totality of all there is, then there is no longer the belief of "the other." Jesus said, "Love thy neighbor as thyself." How could you do otherwise if you were to realize that your neighbor *IS* you? And all that exists in nature, from the most intelligent animals to the grains of sand — these, too, are you.

From the world's oldest religion, Hinduism, the *Upanishads* have brought forth teachings from sages about the nature of all of us as consciousness. Hindu scholar Anuradha Gupta explained that the teachings of the sages "place us in a compassionate universe where nothing is 'other' than ourselves — and they urge us to treat the universe with reverence, for there is nothing in the world but That."[5] Overflowing with metaphor, the *Upanishads* teach:

> *The Self is the sun shining in the sky,*
> *The wind blowing in space: he is the fire*
> *At the altar and in the home the guest;*
> *He dwells in human beings, in gods, in truth,*
> *And in the vast firmament; he is the fish*
> *Born in water, the plants growing on the earth,*
> *The river flowing down from the mountain.*
> *For this Self is supreme!*

---

5 Gupta, Anuradha, *Upanishads* Part 4, http://www.allabouthinduism.info/tag/sat-chit-ananda/, Aug 9, 2013

Myth offers transcendence

In his series *Myth as Metaphor*, Jack Meier explained, "A religious tradition severed from its archetypal roots, its mythologic grounding, becomes a set of signs or rituals without depth. Rather than rest everything on the uniqueness of a religion, one might better argue for the ways in which it taps the same mythic sources that undergird every other religion."[6]

Myth offers a metaphor on how to reestablish the perceived fragmented self as the Self of consciousness. It does so by way of stories, but to take these stories to be literal historical events is to miss the meaning completely. Likewise, to criticize these stories as meaningless because they seem so fanciful, impossible, or supernatural, is also to miss the power of myth. Thus, we can witness literal religious minds and literal scientific or skeptical minds both missing the boat with great enthusiasm and arrogance.

It is often helpful to consider the microcosm of this idea of being consciousness... Psychologists have long taught that dreams are metaphors to help understand who we are. But who is the dreamer, and where does the dream come from? It comes from the recesses of the mind, often called the unconscious. The dreamer is creating the dream, all the characters, and all of the action. It all seems so real, sometimes scary, sometimes funny, sometimes sexual, sometimes violent, often disjointed, and so on. But the dreamer is the creator.

In the macrocosm of the dream world, consciousness is the Great Dreamer, and we are this consciousness. The reason why people may not know this is because consciousness is focused upon the complex of beliefs

---

6 Meier, Jack, Metaphor as Wisdom, Jan 2016, https://jackmeier.wordpress.com/

that comprise the egoic mind. Out of this attention on the false self comes the idea forwarded by Indian sages that is called *maya*.

Joseph Campbell wrote, "Maya is the field of time and space that transforms that which is transcendent of the manifestation into a broken up world."

When the attention is removed from the egoic mind then something awesome takes place. This is a common occurrence, often accidental or ephemeral, but how often do we reflect upon what has happened? In sports we call this attention-off-the-egoic-self as being "in the zone." The famous psychologist Abraham Maslow called it "the peak experience." He said that peak experiences are "rare, exciting, oceanic, deeply moving, exhilarating, elevating experiences that generate an advanced form of perceiving reality, and are even mystic and magical in their effect upon the experimenter."[7]

We use the metaphor of "losing ourselves" when the attention is fully disengaged from the egoic mind and its encrustation of beliefs and associations. What we are losing is our "selves" — our egoic selves — in favor of being in the moment. This happens in the midst of great danger, as well as during the experience or creation of art, dance, music, and even science. The egoic mind gives way to the moment of experience without regard to its self-importance. In moments of extreme danger or tragedy it is often reported that time stands still. And we have seen complete strangers risking their lives without any personal reflection in order to save another human being or animal. This is the surrender of the ego. It happens in the heat of a battle, when a puppy is stranded in the middle of an icy lake, when a person races into a burning house to save his neighbor, when a woman jumps in front of another person to

---

[7] Corsini, Raymond J. (1998). *Encyclopedia of Psychology*. United States: John Wiley & Sons.

shield him from harm, and so on. The fragmentation of the egoic mind can disappear in a flash under the right conditions.

Campbell pointed out that the Eastern gurus, "in their full-fledged teaching mode," "speak as though they are themselves what they are speaking about; that is to say, they have in their minds identified themselves with a mode of consciousness that then speaks through them."[8] "That message from India," Campbell wrote, "electrifies us, but sadly, the churches are not preaching it."[9]

---

[8] Campbell, *Thou Art That,* p.19

[9] ibid, p. 20

*"The metaphor is perhaps one of man's
most fruitful potentialities.
Its efficacy verges on magic, and it seems a tool for creation which
God forgot inside one of His creatures when He made him."*

— *Jose Ortega y Gasset*

What does a person
have to do with myth?

Myth is the metaphor that explains the workings of consciousness so that we may come to know who we are and what constitutes our world and experience. We are the infinite. We are the mystery. Myth shows us this in the art and language of metaphor. But the egoic minds of most people have been so conditioned that they are prone to take the words of myth and language to be literal. This is the most original sin of all, because it is the very obstacle to knowing oneself as consciousness. (The word "sin" here is being used to denote a wrong turn, an error or omission in thinking and teaching.)

In most religious traditions, teachings and teachers tend to reinforce the literal while ignoring the metaphorical. This inadvertently, and ignorantly, prevents people from knowing and understanding who they are and how life works. It keeps them from the totality that governs all existence and establishes all of life firmly in the one and only consciousness.

While many may be incapable of, or resistant to, accepting the metaphors of their religion, those who open up to them may find a great sense of wonder, awe, appreciation, meaning, and even transcendence. Instead of perceiving the trials and tribulations of Jesus as a literal historical event, for example, to know it as a metaphor brings power and meaning to it. It turns the story from a troubled and improbable historical occurrence into a beautiful, breathtaking, and inspiring metaphor meant to penetrate the egoic mind and touch the heart.

Joseph Campbell said that there are four functions of mythology, with the first being that of reconciling consciousness to the preconditions of its own existence — that is, of aligning waking consciousness to the *mysterium tremendum*[10] of this universe, as it is. "The second function of a traditional mythology," he wrote, "is interpretive, to present a consistent image of the order of the cosmos. At about 3200 BC, the concept of a cosmic order came into being, along with the notion that society and men and women should participate in that cosmic order because it is, in fact, the basic order of one's life."

"The third function of a traditional mythology is to validate and support a specific moral order, that order of the society out of which that mythology arose. All mythologies come to us in the field of a certain specific culture and must speak to us through the language and symbols of that culture. In traditional mythologies, the notion is really that the moral order is organically related to, or somehow a piece of, the cosmic order. Through this third function, mythology reinforces the moral order by shaping the person to the demands of a specific geographically and historically conditioned social group."

Lastly, said Campbell, "The fourth function of traditional mythology is to carry the individual through the various stages and crises of life — that is, to help persons grasp the unfolding of life with integrity. This wholeness means that individuals will experience significant events, from birth through midlife to death, as in accord with, first, themselves, and, secondly, with their culture, as well as, thirdly, the universe, and, lastly, with that *mysterium tremendum* beyond themselves and all things."

Joseph Campbell said, "The life of a mythology springs from, and depends on, the metaphoric vigor of its symbols. These deliver more than just an intellectual concept, for such is their inner character that they provide a sense of actual participation in a realization of

---

10 awe inspiring mystery

transcendence. The symbol, energized by metaphor, conveys not just an idea of the infinite, but some realization of the infinite. We must remember, however, that the metaphors of one historically conditioned period, and the symbols they innervate, may not speak to the persons who are living long after that historical moment and whose consciousness has been formed through altogether different experiences."[11]

In his book *Thou Art That*, Campbell wrote, "A mythology may be understood as an organization of metaphorical figures connotative of states of mind that are not finally of this or that location or historical period, even though the figures themselves seem on their surface to suggest such a concrete localization. The metaphorical languages of both mythology and metaphysics are not denotative of actual worlds or gods, but rather connote levels and entities within the person touched by them. Metaphors only seem to describe the outer world of time and place. **Their real universe is the spiritual realm of the inner life.** The Kingdom of God is within you."

The 20th Century sage Nisargadatta Maharaj said, "Wisdom is knowing I am nothing, Love is knowing I am everything, and between the two my life moves."

Myth is metaphor without specific definition
Myth excites and pushes the egoic mind to turn in on itself. It speaks to that "something" that appears hidden and yet in plain sight. Myth calls out to the listener or reader to step out of the way and let this "something" shine forth. There are hundreds or thousands of myths that are all doing the same thing in guiding or pushing the egoic mind to enquire as to its true nature as consciousness, and to contemplate that a "something" lies beyond the world of words, images, collective sense of

[11] Campbell, Joseph, *Thou Art That*

reality, and all other senses. This "something" is you as consciousness, as well as all others who are expressions of this same consciousness. But breaking this consciousness down into pieces for the sake of trying to understand it is an error. Once we begin to name it or speak about it, it is tainted, distorted, and misrepresented. It cannot be understood by the limited mind; it cannot be described. Whatever is described is surely not it. Myth is saying, "I'll give you a hint with inappropriate imagery, and you take things from here." Metaphor is saying, "I'll call it something, but surely this is not really what it is." In contrast, philosophy and all other schools of thought are handing us more and more information to process and retain about consciousness without ever coming close to saying what it actually is. But myth is telling us to set this knowledge free; let it go and let the feeling penetrate the mind.

One of the great myths in the world of motion pictures is embodied in Stephen Spielberg's *Indiana Jones and the Last Crusade*. Spielberg's hero is the swashbuckling professor of archaeology Indiana Jones who sets out to rescue his father and then go on to find the Holy Grail. But it is what our hero learns on his journey that transforms him, not what he finds. In fact, at the end of the movie, when the world is caving in around Indiana Jones and his father is holding his slippery hand as he is falling into an abyss while attempting to reach the Grail on a precipice, a three-word metaphor is uttered. In the midst of the great chaos and destruction, Henry Jones softly says to his son, "Let it go." What needed to be let go was the Grail that in this case represents the hero's egoic, conscious mind. The father is telling the son that it is not the object that is of value, but rather the lesson that there is no object that is more valuable than transformation of the self.

The Self beyond words

Karl Renz, philosopher and teacher, said, "...whatever you can define, whatever you can perceive, whatever you can take as a sensation, cannot be what you are…" Renz was speaking of the essence that lies beyond the egoic self. He said, "This is the final discrimination that you cannot be what you can perceive. And then finally you see, even the perceiver is part of the perception. So even the perceiver you can perceive. So you can't be the perceiver. So, even the I-thought as perceiver becomes a fiction. And then you see, you are the only real thing that is. You are Reality itself. Because whatever you can perceive is not real. Because it depends on you to exist. And this pure existence is the very ground of existence. And whatever is dancing on this ground is not the ground. It's merely a dance, of life, of existence, of dreamlike sensations, fleeting shadow."[12]

There are no words to describe what we are at the core, yet we try anyway. And we have tried since our species could share ideas. But we continue to fail over and over again, because the word is not the thing. The best we can do is create myth and metaphor to paint an attractive picture. We look at this picture, listen to it, feel it, taste it, and smell it, and then we take it into the heart to internalize it. The myth moves past the gates of the "I am" and into a territory where the self does not dwell.

Peter Russell, mathematician and philosopher, explained, "My ego, personality, my beliefs and views, and other personal characteristics may change over time, but the sense of 'I' that is aware of them never changes. In that respect I am the same 'I' that knew my experiences yesterday, last year, and as far back as I can remember. It is my true essence. When I stop identifying with my thinking and other mental qualities, and drop back into the Self, I find that familiar sense of 'I am.' Not I am this or that, but simply 'I am.' More accurately, since there is no

---

[12] /www.spiritualteachers.org/karl-renz/

longer a sense of individual identity, simply 'am'. Or, as I like to put it, 'am-ing', which is the first-person experience of 'being.'"[13]

What is the 'I am'?

There is a phrase that is used billions of times a day all over the world by human beings — "I am."

Renz said, "I say, out of this unfolding 'I' as awareness comes as a thought the 'I am', and out of the 'I am' comes the 'I am an object, in time'. And all this is part of the unfolding."

Let's look deeper into what Renz is getting at, because it's a primal, ancient teaching...

Consciousness is. We cannot really say more than this, and even this statement is limited by a concept; we're putting something that is beyond words into words. To say that something "is" already places it in the field of time and space, but consciousness is not in anything. Rather, all is in consciousness. We have repeatedly tried to reduce the nameless into something that can be named. Why do we do this? Because consciousness is attending to the conditioned sense of self posing as individuals. As individuals we need to find out that we are not really not individuals at all, but rather the totality of all that is. But consciousness cannot realize what it is without being in a body. This is a catch-22, a paradox.

The individual is, to use a metaphor, a little tide pool of water trapped by a ring of rocks at the shore. When the ocean tide rises over the rocks, the little pool of water and the ocean are indistinguishable. The water of the tide pool was always the ocean but appeared as separate from it. The "I am" that says, "I am a little pool of water" appears as an individual apart

---

from the ocean. But it is really the ocean and has always been the ocean all along.

Think of all the objects that we put on the end of the "I am" every day, including in our thoughts and communications — I am a woman, I am a man, I am a dog-lover, I am a Turk, I am an American, I am a plumber, I am a student, I am an insurance salesman, I am a husband, I am a wife, I am a worried person, I am nervous, I am a silly billy… The list is unending. It all begins with "I am." This "I am" stands on the edge of a cliff about to jump into the things of personhood. Another metaphor.

Goddesses and gods

In mythology we have goddesses and gods. These are metaphorical beings; they cannot be otherwise. Consciousness is the totality of all that is, and as such, words cannot say what it is. The mind must wrestle with what it perceives to be aspects of it. So, in mythology these aspects are given names — goddesses, gods, angels, trees, dogs, crosses, demons, boats, rivers, lakes, and so on.

The palette, the painter, the paints, the brushes, the rags, the paint thinners, and the canvas are all consciousness. But we cannot know these parts without the mind, so we break the whole of consciousness into these parts so that those of us who are yearning to know what the whole is can use the parts to find the whole. It all seems quite complicated and unnecessary, but this is only because words, language, and ideas are onerous and insufficient.

Myth may use a god or goddess to represent the creator or creative force, but since consciousness is actually one single, dynamic, complex, and comprehensive "thing," it would be a mistake to think that the god is a literal being. The lesson is, don't worship and fixate upon the god, but instead find out how the god or goddess is you, as consciousness. You are

41

the god as well as everything he or she does. Gods and goddesses are mirrors to, and of, your Self.

Let's take one example of a Greek myth and see how this applies — the myth of Sisyphus who was a Greek king who was punished. His eternal sentence was that he had to push a large rock up on a steep hill, only to find it rolling back on nearing the top. When it fell back to the bottom, he repeated the process. He does this for eternity. He's still doing it! Metaphorically, Sisyphus may be you or someone you know. We work and struggle, which causes great pain. It seems like there is no purpose or end to it. Life is a terrific burden and no matter how much we don't like it, it continues on this aweful path. We have sayings for this sort of experience: "I'm in a dead-end job," or "I just can't catch a break," or "My life has no meaning, I just work, eat, sleep and then repeat over and over again." And we say, "I am in a rut." The myth of Sisyphus is telling us to take a look at ourselves by way of an exaggerated story of a poor guy — a king, because this can happen to anyone regardless of social or financial standing — who just struggles all the time without any hope in sight.

While the Sisyphus story may be interpreted as a message that we have to keep on going , a story about fortitude, this hardly seems plausible for the mere fact that Sisyphus reaps no reward or satisfaction. It seems there is something deeper to the myth than this. It is a wake-up call for those who contemplate it. Sisyphus is damned to eternity, but are you? We have to see what's going on in our lives by Sisyphus' example so we can make a change and find meaning in what we do. It's better to do something enriching. And this thing that we do is not necessarily the enactment of a physical change; it could mean a change in attitude as well — to find a way to make what we do enjoyable, rewarding, or even a way to enrich the lives of others.

Sisyphus, like other myths, is a mirror to ourselves. It tells us to look at ourselves carefully and see what is going on. Unless a myth can do this, it is not a useful metaphor. Thanks, Sisyphus, because after watching you push that rock up the hill so many times, I get the message. I'm going to do something I really love instead of performing this same task over and over again without any mental or spiritual reward.

Time for one more Greek myth. This one involves a fellow named Icarus who became known for flying too close to the sun. He is the son of the master craftsman Daedalus, the creator of the Labyrinth — a complicated irregular network of passages or paths in which it is difficult to find one's way; a maze. Icarus and his father plan to escape from Crete by means of wings that his father constructed from feathers and wax. Icarus' father warns him first of complacency and then of hubris, telling his son that needs to pay attention not to fly too low or too high, so the sea's dampness won't clog his wings and the sun's heat won't melt them. But being a careless and capricious youth, Icarus is overcome by the giddiness of flight. He soars into the sky, but in the process comes too close to the sun, which melts the wax and causes him to fall into the sea and drown in the area which today bears his name, the Icarian Sea, which is near Icaria, an island southwest of Samos. From this myth we are left with the metaphorical warning "don't fly too close to the sun." But what the heck is this telling us?

Myth is about pointing, not about educating

Myth is a metaphorical story that points us inward to look at our own lives. One interpretation of the Icarus myth is that one should heed the wisdom of our elders. Another comes from someone on an online forum who wrote, "life is a gift, and maintaining a balance with everything in moderation will ensure a long one. The wings represent the father giving his son life; the ocean and the sun represent the extremes of denying and overindulging yourself; flying in between is the answer."[14] Have fun, be free, but also be responsible. Or, with freedom comes responsibility. But these are morals, and myths are not morality plays, they are about messages that lead to transcendence. So let's take a closer look at this story.

If transcendence is our goal, we may interpret the Icarus myth as a pointer for us to contemplate whether we have a tendency to get caught up in mindless sensations that keep us from focussing instead on the deeper goal of spiritual freedom.

Another question that comes to mind regarding the Sisyphus myth is whether we should focus only upon Icarus. What does the father's role in this story have to do with us? Daedalus tells his son not to fly too high nor too low. In other words, take the middle path. Further, what is the father-son relationship all about, and what can we find in ourselves that relates to this relationship? Here we have a father who does not have the hubris or daring of youth. He warns his son not to fly too close to the sun, because he has wisdom and insight. In the end, it is up to each person to use a myth to dive deep to find meaning. Otherwise it's no more than a story with a moral; but myth is so much more than this — it is more like a key to which each person must find the lock and then open the door into the unknown.

There are, of course, thousands of myths from all over the world still waiting to be explored and interpreted. There is no need to begin evaluating them in this particular writing that you are reading. In fact, the more we discuss them the less personal they become for you. The main point is to first realize that myths contain life lessons — spiritual

---

[14] Milshire, mythology.stackexchange.com/questions/1664/what-is-the-moral-of-the-myth-of-icarus, Oct 13, 2018

lessons that urge the listener to go within. So when you read them and keep this in mind then they may be transformative stories for you. Otherwise they are morality lessons, and this is a superficial way to regard them.

Beyond all of this, several scholars have noted that myths are time- and space-bound. Some mythical stories may have been poignant for a certain time, period or place, but are not as relevant today. And so new myths evolve to meet the needs of modern peoples. Instead of sitting around a campfire telling stories of gods and goddesses in the starry sky, we may sit in a dark theater and watch the *Star Wars* trilogy, *A Room With A View*, *The Razor's Edge*, or *Joe Versus the Volcano*. Or we can stare at a Van Gogh painting, a modern artist's work in a museum, or listen to profoundly moving music over the internet. The medium, setting, and characters change with the times, but the purpose always remains the same — to lead your thoughts inward past the conscious mind so you can find what lies prior to the egoic self.

"All things are metaphors."

— *Johann Wolfgang von Goethe*

Why do we need Myth?

If not for the fragmentation caused by the mind, there would be no need for myth, because myth is a tool to realize wholeness.

When the mind is conditioned by psychological factors to form the egoic mind, this sense of being an individual self leads to suffering. This is because it fragments the totality of consciousness into individual pieces, precisely because it fails to perceive the totality. The irony is that the mind must fragment the totality of consciousness in order to perceive, understand, communicate, use the senses, interpret, judge, create, destroy, and interact; however, it is due to fragmentation that the individual suffers. This is because with fragmentation the mind has a desire for wholeness, so it is constantly searching for answers, trying to be happy, looking for purpose, seeking pleasure, and fearing change and death. So, on one hand, fragmentation is necessary to perceive and navigate this world of form, but on the other hand the egoic mind misbelieves that fragmentation is the natural way of things.

The mind is conditioned by an array of psychological factors — beliefs, ideas, memories, teachings, fears, and so on — and therefore it believes that it is an individual apart from the whole; it does not realize that it is consciousness itself. This leads the conditioned mind, the egoic self, to believe that it needs to obtain and attain something in order to feel satisfied and whole. It often senses that something's missing, but rarely sees that it is the actual problem.

The egoic mind it is never really satisfied because it is stuck in an unending cycle of pursuing pleasure and avoiding pain. This cycle of desire is what causes the suffering that Hinduism, Taoism, Vendanta, Buddhism, and other Eastern traditions refer to as the prime problem inherited by the egoic mind. Simply, if you desire something then you feel you are not complete and not happy. Once you get what you want, then you fear you may lose it or not have it again, so you once again become obsessed with desire.

The nature of the egoic mind is replete with all the ills that have been contemplated since the beginning of humankind — jealousy, anger, attachment, envy, greed, fear, violence, frustration, and so on. All of these are both the cause, and effect, of desire and suffering. And because desire and suffering of the petty egoic mind exists, there is a fundamental need for myth. The mind desires answers to the most puzzling, pressing, and spiritual questions. Myth offers a way out — a way to bypass the egoic mind and to reach the ground of all being, which is consciousness.

If the mind encounters the language of myth, which is metaphor, as being literal, then it stops or misses the myth's function, which is to awaken the mind to consciousness. But if a person regards the language of myth as metaphor then something entirely new happens — a journey is initiated into the depths of the Self as consciousness.

"As long as there is the center as the me, every action must be distorted. Acting from a center you're giving a direction, and that direction is distortion."

— *Jiddu Krishnamurti*

Expressions on
Myth and Metaphor

As noted, we communicate our ideas in metaphors. There is no actual way to download the information from one person's mind into another's, keeping intact all the sensations, feelings, ideas, memories, images, emphases, and intonations. So metaphors are exchanged. They begin with an attempt to convey thoughts through words, actions, gestures, dance, art, and so on. Myths are metaphors ⸺ stories that represent some grander and cohesive idea in the form of language. Following are the expressions of several people on the topic of myth and metaphor.

PBS documentarian Michael Wood explained, "The subjects of myths reflect the universal concerns of mankind throughout history: birth, death, the afterlife, the origin of man and the world, good and evil and the nature of man himself. A myth taps into a universal cultural narrative, the collective wisdom of man. An excellent illustration of the universality of these themes is that so many peoples who have had no contact with each other create myths that are remarkably similar. So, for example, cultures worldwide, from the Middle East to the distant mountains of South America have myths about great floods, virgin births, and the afterlife…

"…Myths are also pervasive in the arts and advertising, for a very simple reason. From film to cars to perfume, advertising uses visual metaphors to speak to us. While artists of every generation reinterpret myths, the same basic patterns have shown up in mythology for thousands of years. A name, phrase, or image based on a familiar myth can speak volumes to those who have been absorbing these mythic tales since birth. When we hear the expression, 'Beware of Greeks bearing gifts' or when we see a television commercial featuring a wooden horse full of soldiers, we recognize the reference to Odysseus, who tricked the Trojans into admitting an army into their city this way…

"When Jacqueline Kennedy referred to her husband's tenure as a new Camelot, we understand that she meant it was a golden age, like that of King Arthur. When the Greek government dubbed a campaign to rescue ethnic Greeks from behind the walls of the Iron Curtain "Operation Golden Fleece," we understood that they were invoking an ancient name to communicate that these people belonged to them. Each generation of storytellers adds another layer of fact and fiction to the myths, such that the themes and characters of myths are timeless, and endlessly relevant, as they are reinvented and reapplied to the lives of each new generation."[15]

"As soon as people became aware of their own mortality," wrote Karen Armstrong, author of *A Short History of Myth*, "they created stories that gave their lives meaning, explained their relationship to the spiritual world, and instructed them on how to live their lives…" Armstrong explained, "Human beings have always been mythmakers. Archaeologists have unearthed Neanderthal graves containing weapons, tools and the bones of a sacrificed animal, all of which suggest some kind of belief in a future world that was similar to their own. The Neanderthals may have told each other stories about the life that their dead companion now enjoyed. They were certainly reflecting about death in a way that their fellow-creatures did not. Animals watch each other die but, as far as we know, they give the matter no further consideration. But the Neanderthal graves show that when these early people became conscious of their mortality, they created some sort of counter-narrative that enabled them to come to terms with it. The Neanderthals who buried their companions with such care seem to have imagined that the visible, material world was

---

[15] https://www.pbs.org/mythsandheroes/myths_what.html

not the only reality. From a very early date, therefore, it appears that human beings were distinguished by their ability to have ideas that went beyond their everyday experience…

"We are meaning-seeking creatures. Dogs, as far as we know, do not agonise about the canine condition, worry about the plight of dogs in other parts of the world, or try to see their lives from a different perspective. But human beings fall easily into despair, and from the very beginning we invented stories that enabled us to place our lives in a larger setting, that revealed an underlying pattern, and gave us a sense that, against all the depressing and chaotic evidence to the contrary, life had meaning and value."[16]

Karen Armstrong explained, "In our scientific culture, we often have rather simplistic notions of the divine. In the ancient world, the 'gods' were rarely regarded as supernatural beings with discrete personalities, living a totally separate metaphysical existence. Mythology was not about theology, in the modern sense, but about human experience. People thought that gods, humans, animals and nature were inextricably bound up together, subject to the same laws, and composed of the same divine substance. There was initially no ontological gulf between the world of the gods and the world of men and women. When people spoke of the divine, they were usually talking about an aspect of the mundane. The very existence of the gods was inseparable from that of a storm, a sea, a river, or from those powerful human emotions — love, rage or sexual passion — that seemed momentarily to lift men and women onto a different plane of existence so that they saw the world with new eyes."[17]

[16] AUTHOR INTERVIEWS: Karen Armstrong: Myths and the Modern World; November 7, 200512:00 AM ET, Talk of the Nation, National Public Radio

[17] ibid

On Medium (medium.com) Geoff Ward who wrote about Bernardo Kastrup's views on myth, truth, and belief. Ward noted, "The philosopher-scientist Bernardo Kastrup, in his book *More than Allegory: On religious myth, truth and belief* (2016), tells the reader that his intent 'is to help you see beyond the dull, superficial cultural dialogue reigning in society today', this aim being, one might say, crucial to his remarkable and inspiring *oeuvre*." Ward continued, "To Kastrup, any interpretation of (any) images is to be (re-)defined as myth. His new and broader definition, his sought-after metamorphosis of myth, revitalises the ancient concept: he sees myth as the code we all use, whether we're aware of it or not, to interpret life in the world. It allows the events of consensus reality to mean something to us. But because of its very nature in this respect, there are no arbiters of mythical veracity other than intuition, and it can be argued that, appropriately, a philosophy of intuition would be a positive existentialism. Kastrup urges us to see that religious myths, the validity of which cannot be decided by the intellect, point to transcendent truths through symbolic stories, that these myths are 'more than allegory'."[18]

Terrance McKenna, the 1960s-70s guru of hallucinogenic drugs and philosophy, who died before the internet really took off, as well as far before the idea of artificial intelligence and the full spectrum of virtual reality began to blossom, said, "There is something about the formal dynamics of information that we do not understand. Something about how we process language holds us back. That's why I encourage everybody to think about computer animation, and think about it in practical terms. Because out of that will come a visual language rich enough to support a new form of human communication."

---

[18] Ward, Geoff, Truth, belief, the metamorphosis of myth and a 'trip into transcendence,' on Bernard Kastrup, medium.com/@geoffjward/truth-belief-the-metamorphosis-of-myth-and-a-trip-into-transcendence-a117192722a7, Jan 16, 2019

"In McKenna's mind," wrote *Wired* magazine, "we are not just conjuring a new virtual language. We are also, in good old shamanic style, conjuring the ineffable Other. McKenna argues that the imagery of aliens and flying saucers — which spring up in numerous tripping reports as well as in pop technoculture — are symbols of the transcendental technologies we are on the verge of creating. In other words, we are producing the alien ourselves, from the virtual world of networked information. 'Part of the myth of the alien,' says McKenna, 'is that you have to have a landing site. Well, I can imagine a landing site that's a Web site. If you build a Web site and then say to the world, "Put your strangest stuff here, your best animation, your craziest graphics, your most impressive AI software," very quickly something would arise that would be autonomous enough to probably stand your hair on end. You won't be able to tell whether you've got code, machine intelligence, or the real thing.'"[19] McKenna predicted this trend ahead of his time.

"In the end, all McKenna is asking anyone to do is to become a shaman, journey to the numinous, and draw their own conclusions," says Mark Pesce. Even if the invisible landscapes one discovers hold no more reality than dreams or VR worlds, the trip itself forces a direct confrontation with just how weird life is. And how deeply, profoundly weird dying may prove to be."

McKenna said, "We are on the brink of a posthuman existence. What's it gonna feel like?" He said, "Taking shamanic drugs and spending your life studying esoteric philosophy is basically a meditation on death." McKenna calls death the black hole of biology. "Once you go over that event horizon, no messages can be passed back. It represents a limit case in the thermodynamics of information. So what is it?..."The best answer

---

[19] *Wired* magazine, TERENCE MCKENNA'S LAST TRIP, www.wired.com/2000/05/mckenna/, May 1, 2000

I've gotten yet is out of Don DeLillo's *Underworld*, where the nun discovers that when you die you become your Web site."[20]

Donald Kalsched and Alan Jones wrote this introduction to Jungian psychology as a companion to a photographic exhibition at The Hofstra Museum, New York City, November 15 – December 19, 1986: "Mythology is the most archaic and profound record we have of mankind's essential spirit and nature. As far back as we are able to trace the origins of our species, we find myth and myth-making as the fundamental language through which man relates to life's mystery and fashions meaning from his experiences. The world of myth has its own laws and its own reality. Instead of concepts and facts that make logical sense, we find patterns of irrational imagery whose meaning must be discerned or experienced by the participant-observer. Discovering these patterns of meaning is what Jung meant by the *symbolic* approach to religion, myth, and dream."[21]

Kalsched and Jones continued, "The comparative method is the basic key to a symbolic understanding of mythology. Through it we discover certain patterns which recur in widely varying cultures separated by an immensity of both distance and time. Jung called these underlying patterns 'archetypes' from '*arche*' meaning primordial, and '*typos*' meaning typical. Archetypal images embody the most essential elements of the human experience and drama. They manifest both as powerful images, and as dynamic behavioral patterns. They are a repertoire of instinctive human functioning, analogous in our species to the instinctive impulse that impels, say, the Baltimore Oriole to build a beautiful teardrop nest, or Salmon to return to the streams of their birth. The generality of these

---

20 *Wired*, ibid

21 Kalsched, Donald and Alan Jones, Myth and Psyche: The Evolution of Consciousness, CG Jung Foundation for Analytical Psychology, www.cgjungny.org/d/d_mythpsyche.html

images result from recurrent reactions of human beings to situations and stimuli of the same general order, repeated over thousands of years…

"The archetypal images represent several basic stages of the life drama symbolized by the Hero myth. They lead from an initial stage of unconsciousness before the ego has awakened, through various stages of heroic struggle, to a final state of 'wholeness' or integration when life has reached its full potential and a relationship between the human and divine has been reestablished. Jung called this process 'individuation,' the process of becoming the true individual that one really is. This 'true self' Jung felt to be the dynamic factor in the unconscious of each individual. It represents the central archetype of order and wholeness among the other archetypes. Jung called it the Self."[22]

Joseph Campbell said, "An archetype is a constant form, a basic fundamental form which appears in the works of that person over there, and this person over here, without connecting them. They are expressions of the structure of the human psyche."[23]

---

[22] ibid

[23] Moyers, Bill, Ep. 6: Joseph Campbell and the Power of Myth – 'Masks of Eternity,' June 26, 1988

"The archetype concept derives from the often repeated observation that myths and universal literature stories contain well defined themes which appear every time and everywhere. We often meet these themes in the fantasies, dreams, delirious ideas and illusions of persons living nowadays."

— Carl Jung

Jung at Heart

Carl Gustav Jung was a Swiss psychiatrist born in 1875 who influenced a great number of disciplines such as archaeology, psychology, literature, philosophy, and religious studies. He developed now-famous theories including those about synchronicity, archetypal phenomena, the collective unconscious, the psychological complex, and extraversion and introversion.

Jung's arsenal of psychological jargon defined:[24]

Archetype – a concept "borrowed" from anthropology to denote supposedly universal and recurring mental images or themes. Jung's definitions of archetypes varied over time and have been the subject of debate as to their usefulness.

Archetypal images – universal symbols that can mediate opposites in the psyche, often found in religious art, mythology and fairy tales across cultures

Complex – the repressed organization of images and experiences that governs perception and behavior

Extraversion and introversion – personality traits of degrees of openness or reserve contributing to psychological type.

Shadow – the repressed, therefore unknown, aspects of the personality including those often considered to be negative

Collective unconscious – aspects of unconsciousness experienced by all people in different cultures

Anima – the contrasexual (a portion of a person's psyche, hypothesized by Carl Jung, that has characteristics of the opposite gender) aspect of a

---

24 These terms are from the Wikipedia entry on Carl Jung: https://en.wikipedia.org/wiki/Carl_Jung#Key_concepts

man's psyche, his inner personal feminine conceived both as a complex and an archetypal image

Animus – the contrasexual (a portion of a person's psyche, hypothesized by Carl Jung, that has characteristics of the opposite gender) aspect of a woman's psyche, her inner personal masculine conceived both as a complex and an archetypal image

Self – Jung's term for the central overarching concept governing the individuation process, as symbolized by mandalas, the union of male and female, totality, unity. Jung viewed it as the psyche's central archetype.

Individuation – In Jungian psychology, also called analytical psychology, individuation is the process where the individual self develops out of an undifferentiated unconscious – seen as a developmental psychic process during which innate elements of personality, the components of the immature psyche, and the experiences of the person's life become, if the process is more or less successful, integrated over time into a well-functioning whole

Synchronicity – an acausal principle as a basis for the apparently random simultaneous occurrence of phenomena.

"The mind must be utterly silent.
Not asking, not hoping for experience.
It must be completely still.
Only then is there a possibility
of that light which will dispel our darkness."

— *Jiddu Krishnamurti*

Examples of Archetypes

There three main categories of archetypes that include archetypes, archetypal motifs, and archetypal events.

Here are some examples:

Archetypal events: birth, death, separation from parents, initiation, marriage, the union of opposites

Archetypal figures: great mother, father, child, devil, god, wise old man, wise old woman, the trickster, the hero

Archetypal motifs: the apocalypse, the deluge, the creation.

Although the number of archetypes is limitless, there are a few particularly notable, recurring archetypal images, "the chief among them being," according to Jung "the *shadow*, the *wise old man*, the *child*, the *mother* ... and her counterpart, the *maiden*, and lastly the *anima* in man and the *animus* in woman."[25]

The **Self archetype** designates the whole range of psychic phenomena in man. It expresses the unity of the personality as a whole.

The **Shadow archetype** is a representation of the personal unconscious as a whole and usually embodies the compensating values to those held by the conscious personality. The shadow often represents one's dark side, the aspects of oneself that exist, but which one does not acknowledge or with which one does not identify.

The **Anima archetype** appears in man and is his primordial image of woman. It represents man's sexual expectation of women, and is a

---

[25] Jungian archetypes, *Wikipedia*, https://en.wikipedia.org/wiki/Jungian_archetypes#cite_ref-11

symbol of a man's possibilities, his contrasexual[26] tendencies. The animus archetype is the analogous image of the masculine that occurs in women.

The *Wikipedia* entry on Jung's archetypes aptly explains, "The confusion about the essential quality of archetypes can partly be attributed to Jung's own evolving ideas about them in his writings and his interchangeable use of the term 'archetype' and 'primordial image.' Jung was also intent on retaining the raw and vital quality of archetypes as spontaneous outpourings of the unconscious and not to give their specific individual and cultural expressions a dry, rigorous, intellectually formulated meaning."[27]

---

[26] Contrasexual: a portion of a person's psyche, hypothesized by Carl Jung, that has characteristics of the opposite gender

[27] ibid

"We've strengthened in our consciousness,
through great development of skill, the structure and the nature
of the self. The self is violence, the self is greed, envy and so on.
They are the very essence of self. As long as there is the center as
the me, every action must be distorted.
Acting from a center you're giving a direction, and that direction
is distortion. You may develop a great skill in this way but it is
always unbalanced, inharmonious.
Now, can consciousness with its movement undergo a radical
transformation, a transformation not brought about by will. Will
is desire, desire for something and when there is desire there is a
motive, which is again a distorting factor in observation.

—— J. Krishnamurti

The Part is the Whole

The part is the whole, but just doesn't know it yet.

In Jung's psychological theory, which is not necessarily linked to a particular theory of social structure, the *persona* appears as a consciously created personality or identity, fashioned out of part of the collective psyche through socialization, acculturation, and experience. In the book *Collected Papers on Analytical Psychology*, the editors noted that Jung applied the term *persona* explicitly because, in Latin, it means both personality and the masks worn by Roman actors of the classical period, expressive of the individual roles played. The persona, he argued, is a mask for the "collective psyche," a mask that "pretends" individuality, so that both self and others believe in that identity, even if it is really no more than a well-played role through which the collective psyche is expressed. Jung regarded the "persona-mask" as a complicated system which mediates between individual consciousness and the social community: it is "a compromise between the individual and society as to what a man should appear to be."[28]

Jung explicitly explained that the persona is, in substance, a character mask in the classical sense known to theatre, with its double function— to make a certain impression on others, and to hide (part of) the true nature of the individual. The therapist then aims to assist the *individuation* process through which the client (re)gains his or her "own self." This occurs through the liberating of the self as the deceptive cover of the persona, and from the power of unconscious impulses.[29]

---

[28] Jung, CG, *Collected Papers on Analytical Psychology*, p. 472

[29] *Wikipedia* entry on Carl Jung, ibid

Individuation

In Jungian psychology, also called analytical psychology, *individuation* is the process where the individual self develops out of an undifferentiated unconscious – seen as a developmental psychic process during which innate elements of personality, the components of the immature psyche, and the experiences of the person's life become, if the process is more or less successful, integrated over time into a well-functioning whole.

Jung's ideas about individuation closely resemble the idea of shedding the egoic mind that is formed by way of impressionable psychological influences that cause a person to believe that he/she is distinct from the whole of consciousness.

In some Eastern philosophies, such as Vedanta, the idea of enlightenment or becoming awakened has to do with the realization that there really is no individual, because all that exists is of the same fabric of consciousness; and as people, places, objects, and phenomena, we are all merely expressions of one and only consciousness. Individuation, then, is a process of realizing that one is actually the wholeness rather than the individual.

Jung's theories explain a great deal about myths, because he shows the relationship between the egoic self, which is conscious, and the deeper sense of Self that lies behind what he called the persona (egoic self). In therapy, the therapist's role (if the patient is fortunate enough to have a therapist who is actually aware of this fact) is similar to the role of myth — to move past the persona and into the deeper states of consciousness.

The collective unconscious

Another very important idea that Jung forwarded was that of the *collective unconscious*. Now the backbone of Jungian psychology, the idea is that the collective unconscious is the part of the unconscious mind that is derived from ancestral memory and experience, and it is common to all humankind, as distinct from the individual's personal unconscious. The collective unconscious is sometimes referred to as the objective psyche — the idea that a segment of the deepest unconscious mind is genetically inherited and is not shaped by personal experience. However, it remains debated whether this inheritance is physical or has more to do with a mind that is not an artifact of the brain and body.

Figuring into the idea of the collective unconscious are several other ideas that Jung forwarded that we have touched upon thus far in this book, including archetypes, the Self, wholeness, and the individuation process. He also spoke of the sage and dreams, along with symbols common to all people. Carl Jung's findings support the idea that myths are the metaphors that touch us on a level much beyond the conscious mind.

Carl Jung Resources, a group that teaches Jung's psychological theories online, explained:

> Jung's concept of collective unconscious was developed at the time when he was working with schizophrenic patients in Burgholzli psychiatric hospital. Though initially Jung followed the Freudian theory of unconscious as the psychic strata formed by repressed wishes, he later developed his own theory to include some new concepts. The most important of them is the archetype. Archetypes constitute the structure of the collective unconscious - they are psychic innate dispositions to experience and represent basic human behavior and specific situations. Thus mother-child relationship is governed by the mother archetype. Father-child - by the father archetype. Birth, death, power and failure are controlled by archetypes. The religious and mystique experiences are also governed by archetypes. The most important

of all is the Self, which is the archetype of the Center of the psychic person, his/her totality or wholeness. The Center is made of the conjunction of consciousness and unconscious reached through the individuation process. Archetypes manifest themselves through archetypal images in all the cultures and religious systems, in dreams and visions. Therefore a great deal of Jungian interest in psyche focuses on interpretation of dreams and symbols in order to discover the compensation induced by archetypes as marks of psyche transformation. The word "compensation" refers to what Jung believes to be the psychic version of homeostasis, that is the ability of the body to maintain a certain equilibrium and stability. Thus archetypes are related to the basic functioning of our psyche. The collective unconscious is an universal datum meaning that every human being is endowed with this psychic archetype-layer since his/her birth. One can not acquire this strata by education or other conscious efforts because it is innate. We may also describe it as a universal library of human knowledge, or the sage in man, the very transcendental wisdom that guides mankind.[30]

The collective unconscious includes mythological motifs or primordial images that comprise the myths of all peoples, both culturally and personally. Psychologists from the Carl Jung Resources group note that the whole of mythology "could be taken as a sort of projection of the collective unconscious... We can therefore study the collective unconscious in two ways, either in mythology or in the analysis of the individual." (From *The Structure of the Psyche*, CW 8, par. 325.) This is an important concept, because it is saying that the microcosm is a reflection

---

[30] As a point of clarification, readers and listeners of Jiddu Krishnamurti and theoretical physicist David Bohm will be familiar with different uses of the word "Center." When used by these two men in their discussions, the word "center" refers to the self (lower case "s") that is also called the egoic mind. And the word "Self" (upper case "S") that is used in Vedic philosophy as well as by various sages refers to consciousness and not the egoic mind.

of the macrocosm, or the other way around. This is also reflected in the study of DNA as well as fractals. Therefore, in agreement with the sages of ancient history, in order to understand life in general, all that is necessary is to understand oneself first. Or, in the jargon of the gurus, the answers to life are all within you.

"Every religion is true one way or another. It is true when understood metaphorically. But when it gets stuck in its own metaphors, interpreting them as facts, then you are in trouble."

— *Joseph Campbell*

The Hero's Journey

From myth we derive something that has been called the *hero's journey*. This is a significant concept, because it places both the protagonist of the myth and the person who is touched by the myth in the seat of thought, contemplation, deliberation, hesitation, action and transformation.

Through the hero's journey the hero realizes that he/she is something special; and that "something" is potential. This is a key idea, because ultimately consciousness is the entire field of potential. We often speak of the hero's newfound potential, but if it is meant as a mirror for those who are touched by the myth to reflect upon our own ability to move from the state of nothingness, then into the state of potential, and then into the state of actuality.

Vic Shayne's book, *Consciousness: The Potentiality of All Existence*, explores this idea of potentiality and reality. The message is simple, but mostly overlooked because people are so absorbed with struggling, suffering, and being distracted by life that they do not stop to find silence. In the dead of silence, prior to any movement or thought, is nothing but potential. What is going to happen next? And, where will the action come from?

As consciousness, like the mythic hero, we are all this powerhouse of potentiality. In our modern culture there are many mythic movies that revolve around this idea, including *The Matrix* and most superhero films in which the hero discovers that he has the potential to use a secret superpower. And the most astute moviegoer will ask him/herself: What is my superpower and how do I harness and release it? Do I use it for the benefit of humankind?

We find this motif of the embodiment of potentiality in the teachings of enlighten sages as well.

Speaking of potentiality, Nisargadatta, the 20th Century sage of Bombay, said, "You are the maker of the world in which you live, you alone can change it, or unmake it." And he said, "You are the infinite potentiality, the inexhaustible possibility. Because you are, all can be. The universe is but a partial manifestation of your limitless capacity to become." He also said, "You are the maker of the world in which you live, you alone can change it, or unmake it."

Compare Nisargadatta's teaching with what the hero Neo discovered in the movie *The Matrix*. Leadership expert and author Robin Sharma explained that the hero has been confronted with the fact that the world he thought was reality is nothing more than an illusion. The "matrix" in the movie represents "the dominant value and beliefs that the world had put around this guy Neo" who took the red pill and woke up to reality. "The reality was that he was full of potential," explained Sharma.

The hero's journey is imbued with potential all the way through. We may be moved to ask all sorts of questions that hinge on what may potentially happen: Will the hero "accidentally" meet someone or do something that threatens to change the status quo? Will the hero then follow the next course of events out of curiosity or duty? Will the hero refuse the call to act? What will the hero do even though he or she lacks the physical skills or knowledge to be successful? Will the hero exercise self control with his newfound power? On and on, the hero is buffeted by the forces of the universe that work for and against him/her. What might happen? What is the risk? These are all matters of potentiality that exist in the larger container that we call consciousness, which is the totality of all that exists.

In a myth, the hero arrives at a point in his journey where there is no turning back. Perhaps you remember this point in movies you have seen or in books you've read. Indiana Jones in *The Last Crusade* movie has to risk his life in the face of the impossibility of getting through all the obstacles in front of him; otherwise his father will die. There is no going back for him.

In the classic movie *Casablanca*, Rick must give up the woman he loves and lose her to another man so that the world will have a chance to defeat the Nazis in the Second World War. In *Star Wars*, the hero Luke Skywalker cannot return home because his house has been burnt to the ground. In our own hero's journey, we experience the same sorts of points of no return. We can get fired from our job, lose our home, be deported or flee from our country of birth, get divorced and have to start our lives over again, and so on. The universe seems to be kicking us in the rear end and into a new experience that we would ordinarily resist on the most conscious level.

Myth touches us in yet another way. When things happen "to us" that we do not want, we are witnessing the eternal and ubiquitous struggle of the egoic mind. The egoic mind, which is also the sense of "I," "me," the person you think you are, desires stability and order. But the universe is chaotic and is not contained within the egoic mind. So there is inherent conflict within us. The universe cannot be understood or controlled by the mind. For this reason, from the unwillingness to change or move from the status quo, we resist the call to action until we can resist no longer. We require a push, physically or psychologically, that collapses the metaphorical bridge behind us so that we just can't go back to the way things were.

A personal account of a hero's journey

Several years ago I, the author of this book you are reading, wrote a biography about a Holocaust survivor named Martin Small. The book is entitled *Remember Us*. As a young man living in a Russian-Polish border town in 1942 Martin (his post-war Americanized name) was taken away by the German occupying forces to a labor camp as an enemy of the Nazi state. He longed to return home to his family and his way of life. One day one of his Polish neighbors, a childhood friend, came to find him at the place where he was being forced to work. His neighbor brought him the sad news that Martin's entire family, including 84 members — cousins, mother, father, sisters, grandparents, uncles, and aunts — were all taken to the edge of their village and murdered by gunfire and thrown into a mass grave. Now there was no going back to the Martin who had existed prior to the war. The loved ones who comprised his old world were gone, and that world no longer existed. He could have fallen into despair and given up, but something inside of him that was part nature and part upbringing made him go on and survive. As the war progressed, Martin escaped a forced labor camp, was shot in the arm and treated without anesthesia or medical equipment by another escapee who happened to be a doctor, lived through the Siberian winter with a thousand refugees in the forest, and then was eventually captured with members of the Polish resistance and sent by train to Mauthausen death camp in Austria. Somehow Martin survived even this harrowing reality. Barely.

When all hope was gone for the remaining survivors of Mauthausen, the United States Army rolled in with their jeeps, trucks, artillery, medics, and tanks and liberated the death camp at the end of the war. Unconscious, Martin Small was carried out of the camp in a state of severe starvation and deterioration and taken to an army hospital with little chance to survive. But he did survive. When he recovered months later, he knew there was no going back to the life of his childhood and his family that existed before the war. In his little village there were no relatives or friends left alive. The traditions and warm memories had been taken from him. And all of the homes of his people were now being occupied by new residents who simply claimed them as their own. Martin had to start all over.

If you read this book about Martin Small's turbulent life, you will see the story of the hero as it plays out.

Nowadays we seem to use the word hero much too flippantly. We confer status on a person for a brave or daring act. But if you were to talk to one of these everyday heroes you would likely discover that they do not even perceive themselves as heroes — they insist they were just doing what they had to do.

If you do a google search for "hero…just doing my job," you will find a number of examples of people who society calls heroes, but that's not how they refer to themselves. Firefighters, security guards, soldiers, police officers, mothers, fathers, teachers, school children, and others act out of instinct, fear, training, or a maybe a little of each, and in the end, they protect the lives of others for which they are labeled heroes. Sometimes people are called heroes simply because they survive against great odds or because they merely react in a positive manner and (even in their own estimation) just get lucky.

But the hero of myth is a hero because he or she set out on a journey reluctantly, faced all sorts of obstacles and rejections, discovered something about themselves by way of struggle, and emerged transformed. This type of hero is not necessarily the same as the one on the nightly news who rescued a cat from a tree.

Life presents situations and then those who manage to transform themselves and others are called heroes once the journey has been made. Like all heroes, Martin Small returned from a crucible and tremendous loss, not to his ancestral home, but to a life of normalcy. He eventually made it to America and started a family that still thrives to this day, years after his death at the ripe old age 91. His family is his legacy as a survivor who lived an extreme example of the hero's journey. Martin was transformed by the most horrific of experiences in a period of history that cost the lives of more than fifty million people worldwide.

The hero's journey is real. It is the stuff of myth, but it happens to real people. Some journeys are more exciting, dangerous, and thrilling than others. But at the core there is something that emerges out of them — transformation. When we read a myth, the story is talking to us on a very personal level if we care to notice. It is reminding, or encouraging, us about our own journey as well as the stages to expect along the way.

"Wit invents; inspiration reveals.
The inventions of wit are conceits
— metaphors and paradoxes —
that discover the secret correspondences that unite beings and
things among and with themselves;
inspiration is condemned to dissipate its revelations
— unless a form can be found to contain them."

— Octavio Paz

Death and Rebirth

David L. Miller, professor of religion, Syracuse University, explained that death is a motif in a myth that is an indication that change is taking place. It does not necessarily mean there is a biological death. He said, "No death, no life. No death, no transformation. No death, no change."[31]

Although death in myth does not necessarily mean a biological death, even the death of the physical body is a metaphor as well.

One of the most enduring themes of mythology is death and rebirth. This is not to be taken literally, but as a metaphor. Something dies (not necessarily biologically) and something new comes out of the death. What is it? For some it is the death of a belief, for others it is the death of a job or a marriage. For some there is a death of a way of life or the death of a role that had been played, such as when a person retires and is now without his subordinates or workmates. Death is symbolic.

In Christianity we find this metaphor of death in a very striking lesson about the death of the egoic mind that gives way to rebirth as consciousness, as God. Similarly, Siddhartha died and became the Buddha when he dropped his egoic mind and was reborn as universal consciousness.

In human history's earlier myths, the motif of death and rebirth was experienced in nature as a miraculous occurrence — nature's life forms died in the winter and returned in the spring. A revered buffalo died in its role as a buffalo but was reborn in a strong warrior who ate it and was

---

31 Joseph Campbell The Hero's Journey documentary, youtube, www.youtube.com/watch?v=T3LozCNO30w

nourished by it. In this latter type of myth, life feeds upon life, which is how life is perpetuated.

The *Upanishads* teaches that every living being is a "food body." The philosophy regarding food bodies is simple yet hardly recognized in our modern society. It states that life lives on life, and that is the natural cycle keeping nature in balance, sustaining and perpetuating all of existence as we know it here on our delicate planet. The body of a plant feeds on animals, and animals feed on plants and on the bodies of other animals. Insects, micro-organisms, and plants feed on the the bodies of all forms of life, keeping everything in balance. In essence, then, each living being feeds off of other living beings, and each being has something else feeding off of it. We as human beings are a part of this process.

The cycle of death and rebirth has been woven into early myth by way of the observation of nature.

What's in a name?

In the movie *The Matrix*, the protagonist Thomas A. Anderson dies and is reborn as Neo (which actually means "new"). We are speaking of a symbolic death. To a much lesser degree, not quite as exciting, there are many people who simply change their names because they want to change their lives — to be reborn as someone new. Maybe you know someone personally who has done this. Celebrities do it all the time. Stefani Joanne Angelina Germanotta became Lady Gaga, singer Katheryn Elizabeth Hudson became Katy Perry, musician David Becker became Elton John, boxer Cassius Clay became Muhammed Ali, actor Nicolas Cappola became Nicholas Cage, Maurice Joseph Micklewhite became actor Michael Caine, Eric Marlon Bishop became comedian/actor Jamie Foxx, and Peter Gene Hernandez became the pop star Bruno Mars.

When a baby is born, or shortly thereafter, he or she receives a name. One day there is just a nameless baby who is born into this world, and the next day there is little Mary or Anthony. The parents decide "from this day forward, you will be Mary," and the baby has no choice but to go along in this direction, starting off with one of a string of conditioned identities to come. There is a metaphorical death of a nameless being and the rebirth as a family member with a name. Quite often this new beginning is accompanied by a ritual such as a christening or baptism.

In many Native American traditions, a name is given early in a child's life, but then the child comes of age and must head out on a vision quest to test his mettle and face the elements to realize his place in the universe. When he returns he does so as a new man with a name to match his experience. According to Native American philosophy, "Those of us on a spiritual path and more specifically on a Vision Quest believe that we are put on this earth for a special reason, but that reason is not always clear to us. We want to know what we need to accomplish in life for our highest benefit, and, in turn, the benefit of the world. The quest can reveal our life's purpose, but it is an arduous journey into the core of our being that we should only embark upon with sincerity. William Walk Sacred cautions, "It's very important for people to realize that this is not fun and games. Going into the spiritual world is very serious. If the intent isn't clear, the spirits will not give the vision. The most important thing is being clear in your heart as to what you are seeking for yourself and the people of the world."[32]

In her article for *Psychology Today*, Elisabeth Pearson Waugaman wrote that Wompsi'kuk Skeesucks) Brooke, a Mohegan, "notes that in the Native American naming tradition, names should change. Children receive names that are descriptive, they may be given new names

---

[32] www.native-americans-online.com/native-american-vision-quest.html

at <u>adolescence</u>, and again as they go through life according to what their life experiences and accomplishments are. Society bestows a new name—a new name is earned. W.S. Brooke explains, 'Some people are like lakes. They change very little as they age. (...) Some people are like rivers. When you trace the Mississippi, or any other river at its source, it can be very small. Later on it can be wide and strong. When it meets the ocean, it spreads out.' In other words, names should change as the individual changes."[33]

Waugaman wrote that "Native American tribal names represent a much larger concept than most family names in Europe and America. Clan names still carry this broader concept of the human family although these names are still much more specific than what [Phil] Konstantine [americanindian.net] describes — i.e., tribal names that represent 'us.' Imagine the psychological impact of growing up with a name that means 'mankind' instead of 'me.'"[34]

African traditions have also built rituals around naming. In his article "7 Most Fascinating Traditional African Baby Naming Ceremonies," Mark Babatunde wrote, "In traditional African society, the naming ceremony announces the birth of a newborn, introduces the child to his or her extended family and the larger community, and above all, it confers on the child a name. The name given to a baby can have an enduring influence on their personality and upbringing…The Akan people of Ghana name a newborn child on the eighth day after they're born. The new born child is usually named after relatives (dead or alive), or the circumstances surrounding his or her birth. The Akan traditionally leave the naming ceremony until the eighth day as a way to confirm that the

---

[33] Waugaman, Elisabeth Pearson, *Psychology Today*," Names and Identity: The Native American Naming Tradition, Native American naming traditions can enrich your sense of self," Jul 08, 2011

[34] ibid

child has come to stay and will not be returning to back to the world of the ancestors. It's also common for the Akan to name a child after the day of the week that they were born."[35] There is an array of baby-naming rituals in Africa, depending upon the peoples, but they all intend to send the infant into the world with a new persona, predetermined by tribe and tradition.

From the moment of birth, usually beginning with a new name, human beings continue to collect identities and associations, and these are part of the formation of the egoic self, which suggests, "I am this" or "I am that." In a few ancient Indian philosophies there is a recognition of this process and a method of returning to the original "I am" that is prior to the inculcation from the psychological influences of life. This return is not effected through a name change, ritual, or any act performed by the mind or body. In the Vedic tradition, which predates Hinduism, the method begins with the basic question, "Who am I?" A person may also ask "What is this sense of 'I' or self?" In the end, if the person is successful in exposing the egoic mind for what it truly is, there is the transformation from the self of the person to the Self of consciousness. Teachers of this tradition say that we all have the potential to realize this transformation from self to Self; it is inherent in us as expressions of the same and only consciousness.

Author-biologist-physician Robert Lanza wrote, "…[P]hysics tells us that energy is never ever lost, and that our brains, minds, and hence the feeling of life operates by electrical energy, and therefore this energy like all others simply can't vanish, period. The biocentric view of the timeless, spaceless cosmos of consciousness allows for no true death in any real sense. When a body dies, it does so not in the random billiard-ball matrix

35 Babatunde, Mark, 7 Most Fascinating Traditional African Baby Naming Ceremonies, https://face2faceafrica.com/article/7-fascinating-traditional-african-baby-naming-ceremonies, Oct 13, 2016

but in the all-is-still-inescapably-life matrix…"

Lanza continued, "The Eastern religions have of course argued for millennia that birth and death are illusory. When a person strictly identifies his only existence with his body and is certain the universe is a separate, random, external entity, then saying "Death isn't real" is not only ludicrous, it's untrue. His body's cells will all indeed die. His false and limited sense of being an isolated organism — this will end, too. The concept of death has always meant one thing only: An end that has no reprieve or ambiguity. That fine wine glass you inherited from your grandmother can have a death when it falls and shatters into a dozen fragments; it's gone for keeps. Individual bodies also have natal moments, their cells destined to age and self-destruct after about 90 generations, even if not acted upon by outside forces. Stars die, too, albeit after enjoying lifespans usually numbered in the billions of years."[36]

The argument that Lanza and many others forward is that we are all the movement of a singular energy. Some call it consciousness, others call it God or the Tao, and still others may call it the universe, consciousness, or the Self.

The struggle to know death and life

Elisabeth Kübler-Ross, American-Swiss psychiatrist renowned for working with dying patients, was a pioneer in near-death studies and the author of the groundbreaking book *On Death and Dying*, where she discussed her theory of the now famous five stages of grief, known as the Kübler-Ross model. She noted, "The most beautiful people we have known are those who have known defeat, known suffering, known struggle, known loss, and have found their way out of those depths."[37]

---

[36] Lanza, MD, Robert, The Myth of Death, *Psychology Today*, Dec 22, 2013

[37] Kübler-Ross, www.brainyquote.com/quotes/elisabeth_kublerross_553966

And she said, "Consciously or not, we are all on a quest for answers, trying to learn the lessons of life. We grapple with fear and guilt. We search for meaning, love, and power. We try to understand fear, loss, and time. We seek to discover who we are and how we can become truly happy."

The mind is conditioned to think of death as finality, but when we look at it as metaphor then we see that even physical death is not, in a greater sense, the end of life. Death is a phase, a transition that occurs prior to the next phase to come. This is not a matter of belief even though this idea is indeed part of some belief systems. Death as a transition is a matter of physics as well as neuroscience. Because the mind is a limited instrument that cannot comprehend the whole movement of consciousness and therefore cannot realize all of its complexity, it can also not perceive the absolute "now" in which both death and life appear to exist. And, the mind cannot perceive the great movement and complexity of consciousness that underlies life and death. For this reason, death remains as much of a mystery as life.

Death is a metaphor for the ending of something and the beginning of something else. What happens after death absolutely requires death to occur; it's as crucial as opening a door so you can pass through it and into the next room, or out of the house.

If a new breeze is to blow in through the bedroom window, there must first be stillness; the breeze comes out of stillness. If this were not true then there would be no cessation of the breeze; it would be constant. So, in our language we say that the breeze has died down and then it picks up again. This is the cycle of death and rebirth. Out of the stillness comes something new; out of the ending of one thing comes the new thing. This is much more difficult to accept in Western culture when applied to the life and death of people and animals. The reason for this is, as Robert Lanza and others suggest, we have been conditioned to associate the energy, or consciousness, with the body. We mistakenly accept the two as inseparable and the same. Instead of regarding the body as being contained within the greater energy, we tend to be body- and mind-centric, or egocentric.

Robert Lanza speaks a great deal about biocentrism, a way of thinking in which all life deserves equal moral consideration or has equal moral standing. Biocentric ethics calls for a rethinking of the relationship between humans and nature. Lanza's philosophy is that we are all — at the core and independent of the body and mind — the same source of energy. He wrote, "If we're only our bodies, then we must die. But if one pins things down, the "alive" feeling, the sensation of "me" is, so far as science can tell, a sprightly neuro-electrical fountain operating with about 20 Watts of energy. Now the skeptical might argue that this internal energy merely "goes away" at death, and vanishes. But one of the surest axioms of science is that energy can never die, ever. Energy is known with scientific certainty to be deathless; it can neither be created nor destroyed. It merely changes form."[38]

Lanza's words may be meditated upon: Energy merely changes form. But how do we know that we are this energy or consciousness and not actually a physical organism confined to a body? As Lanza argues, everything is energy and therefore you are also energy. And energy is deathless; it merely changes form. Next, there are two ways that we come to know something. The first is through secondhand knowledge, and the second is through direct observation without judgment. Most of what we claim to know is from secondhand knowledge; we study, read, listen to experts, and accept the beliefs of others as truth. Scientists do this as well

[38]Lanza, ibid

as religious people. We often call this secondhand knowledge "truth," but it is not our truth unless it is from direct observation.

When the mind is applied to observing consciousness, the importance of death becomes as apparent as that of life. A powerful myth leads a person to this sort of introspection. If you want to know what is in that dark and foreboding cave, you have to go in there yourself and find out. If someone else tells you what's in there, you will never be certain that this is the truth and you can have no personal transformation from the secondhand knowledge. You have to do it yourself. Even as you read these words you should take care not to accept them as truth, otherwise it will be a case of the mind getting out of one trap and into another. This path of life, myth informs us, is a personal journey, not a spectator sport.

It's best to listen to an idea and then, if moved to take action, do your own observation to see whether it personally rings true. But in this process of persistent observation, the egoic mind must be left out of the equation. The egoic mind has a propensity for judging, drawing conclusions, using points of reference for understanding, overanalyzing, studying, and so on. But these must be abandoned in the observation process. Just observe.

Wisdom from Watts
Alan Watts was a British philosopher who interpreted and popularized Eastern philosophy for a Western audience. Born in Chislehurst, England, he moved to the United States in 1938 and began Zen training in New York. He spoke a great deal about consciousness, as well as birth and death. Watts said, "Without birth and death, and without the perpetual transmutation of all the forms of life, the world would be static, rhythm-less, undancing, mummified."

And Watts said, "If you awaken from this illusion, and you understand that black implies white, self implies other, life implies death — or shall I say, death implies life — you can conceive yourself. Not conceive, but feel yourself, not as a stranger in the world, not as someone here on sufferance, on probation, not as something that has arrived here by fluke, but you can begin to feel your own existence as absolutely fundamental. What you are basically, deep, deep down, far, far in, is simply the fabric and structure of existence itself. So, say in Hindu mythology, they say that the world is the drama of God. God is not something in Hindu mythology with a white beard that sits on a throne, that has royal prerogatives. God in Indian mythology is the self, Sat-chit-ananda. Which means sat, that which is, chit, that which is consciousness; that which is ananda is bliss. In other words, what exists, reality itself is gorgeous, it is the fullness of total joy."

Another thought on death from Alan Watts: "The death of the individual is not disconnection but simply withdrawal. The corpse is like a footprint or an echo — the dissolving trace of something which the Self has ceased to do."

When the ego mind dies then death occurs; there is a fall into silent stillness, a nothingness. Potential is at this starting point. And then from the stillness arises a new "something."

Watts said, "What we see as death, empty space, or nothingness is only the trough between the crests of this endlessly waving ocean. It is all part of the illusion that there should seem to be something to be gained in the future, and that there is an urgent necessity to go on and on until we get it. Yet just as there is no time but the present, and no one except the all-and-everything, there is never anything to be gained—though the zest of the game is to pretend that there is."

"In Hinduism, Shiva is a deity who represents transformation. Through destruction and restoration, Shiva reminds us that endings are beginnings, and that our world is constantly undergoing a cycle of birth, death and rebirth"

— *Karen Salmansohn*

Personal Myth

Myth is personal. It doesn't seem this way, but it is. If myth was not personal it would have no reason to exist; it would serve no function. It is personal in that it is meant to transform the person who takes in the metaphors and applies them to his or her own life and situation. It's often been said that myths are maps to the unconscious mind, but this is not quite it. There is no map at all. There is just a sign pointing inward.

We are again reminded of what Jiddu Krishnamurti declared as he embarked on his 70-year career of public speaking on matters of the mind and consciousness: "Truth is a pathless land." No map. Truth is always right here and right now, so it is not a matter of working to find it, but rather waking up to the fact that it's been here all along. Myth mirrors human experience in a multitude of ways, including that we humans think we have to have a long, arduous, perilous experience in order to find something great. At the end, however, the realization is that we are what is great, but we just didn't know it.

Joseph Campbell said, "Your own path you make with every step you take. That's why it's your path." And he said, "If the path before you is clear, you're probably on someone else's." No map.

It cannot be overstated that myths are metaphors, and those who take them to be literal accounts are missing the purpose and power of them. If a myth resonates with you it wakes you up — to yourself. It is all about penetrating the conscious mind to stir and awaken the awareness to what lies deep within you. How much more personal can myths get than that?

Reality exists as stories within stories, and pieces within pieces. The parts contain the whole, and the whole contains the parts. Therefore, a mythical story is a reflection of you, and your life is a mythical story. Can you see it this way? If you were to think about it, you could plot out segments of your own life and be aware of your personal version of the hero's journey. Perhaps you are right in the middle of a journey as you read this. Chances are that this is what is happening in your life.

The mythic story speaks of stillness, potential, movement, action, creation, destruction, death, and rebirth, which is not an all-inclusive list. This cycle occurs not only over the course of a lifetime, but also every single day. It begins with the awakening in the morning and it ends in the deepest of sleep at night — the birth of a new day and the death of an old one. All that happens in between is the story of you. It is up to you to recognize myths as metaphors and then use them to help you figure yourself out.

Sometimes, as myths go, you enter your potentiality for transformation through a gentle nudge or from something you read or hear. At other times you are thrown with great force into a new direction, perhaps through tragedy or loss. When you set out on your journey, you are the heroic character of your own personal myth. And when it has played out, you look back and see all the turning points; and you are a changed person.

It is because we can say that we have changed that we know we are not the egoic mind, the sense of a person, at our core. It is the egoic mind that changes, not the essence of who we are, which is consciousness. But the egoic mind must move out of the way for a realization to occur — this is the way of transformation. The word transformation means a thorough or dramatic change in form or appearance. The egoic mind appears to change, yet what really happens is that it is pierced or realized to be no more than a mirage. On the surface, the egoic mind, which is the conscious mind, becomes reconditioned to accept a new attitude,

94

belief, value system, etc. But beneath the surface is where the real transformation occurs.

To be specific, it is not the ego that transforms through myth. And it is not consciousness that is transformed. What is called transformation is actually the shifting of focus of consciousness from the egoic self to the Self of consciousness.

"Thought is constantly creating problems...and then trying to solve them. But as it tries to solve them it makes it worse because it doesn't notice that it's creating them, and the more it thinks, the more problems it creates."

— *David Bohm*
theoretical physicist

Koan and Myth

People from the Zen Buddhist tradition are familiar with the term *koan*. A koan is a paradoxical anecdote or riddle that demonstrates the inadequacy of logical reasoning and to provoke enlightenment. In this light, a koan is perhaps a distant cousin of a myth, because myth is not meant to be explained as a moral, nor does it have a clear and overt meaning. Instead, it is designed to inspire and provoke the individual to delve into his own sense of being, past the conscious mind and through to the wholeness of consciousness.

An example of a koan, as you've probably heard, is "What is the sound of one hand clapping?" Of course there is no logic or reasoning to this, because it is quite clear that, literally, one hand cannot clap. So we have to move past the literal and into the metaphorical. In this sense now, the question does not have be taken as having a rational answer. It is up to each person to follow the course of observation provoked by the koan. Myth works the same way, except that myth is in the form of a story rather than a simple question or a short anecdote. Both myth and koan lead you on an inner journey.

John Tarrant, author and director of the Pacific Zen Institute, explained, "A koan is a little healing story, a conversation, an image, a fragment of a song. It's something to keep you company, whatever you are doing. There's a tradition of koan study to transform your heart and the way you move in the world. The path is about learning to love this life, the one you have. Then it's easy to love others, which is the other thing a practice is about. Koans don't really explain things. Instead, they show you something by opening a gate. You walk through, and you take the ride. Before anything is explained, there is the sky, the earth, redwood forests, pelicans, rivers, rats, the city of San Francisco. And you are part of all that. We're all part of that. In the land of koans, you see that everything that happens in your life is for you. There is no one else it can be for. Your life counts."[39]

Tarrant wrote, "Those who have used koans have described them as a poetic technology for bringing about awakening, a painful but effective gate into the consciousness of the Buddha, an easy method of integrating awakening into everyday life, the most frustrating thing they have ever done, an appalling waste of time, a tyranny perpetrated by Zen masters... Well, you get the idea — about koans, opinions differ."[40] In this way, like a myth, a koan makes little sense when taken literally. The mind does not usually like to be provoked out of its comfort zone by being challenged. However, when the mind is ripe, then the challenge is not only welcomed, but it is also sought after.

Zen teacher Suzuki Roshi said, "From the Buddha's time to our age, human nature has been nearly the same. We live in the world of time and space, and our life does not go beyond this limit. To live in the world of time and space is like putting a big snake into a small can. The snake will suffer in the small can. It does not know what is going on outside of the can. Because it is in the can, it is so dark he cannot see anything, but he will struggle in the small can. That is what we are doing. The more we struggle, the greater the suffering will be. That kind of practice will not work. Putting yourself in a small can and sitting day after day in a cross-legged position is worse than a waste of time. Do you understand? Sometimes our practice is something like this. We don't know how much our understanding is limited. That is why you have to study koans. Koans will open up your mind. If you understand your way of life more objectively, you will understand what you are doing."[41]

---

[39] Tarrant, John, How to Practice Zen Koans, www.lionsroar.com/how-to-practice-zen-koans/, Lions Roar online, Sep 7, 2018

[40] Tarrant, John, The Power of Koan Practice, Pacific Zen Institute, www.pacificzen.org/the-power-of-koan-practice/

[41] Tarrant, ibid

The koan in which a person asks, "Who am I?" may seem on the surface to be a simple question with a simple answer. For example:

Question: "Who am I?"
Answer: "I am Dave, an accountant, father of two, president of the Lion's Club, and an avid fan of the Dodgers."

But Dave's answer is superficial. If Dave realized that he is actually a metaphor, because the persona is no more than a belief that is created as an accretion of thoughts to which he feels attached or identified, then his answer might be quite different. For example:

Question: "Who am I?"
Answer:

That's right, you're not reading a typo. There is no answer given, because Dave is very busy observing his true nature beyond the superficial idea that his egoic mind believes he is. Maybe after a few years Dave will return to the question and his answer will be different. For example:

Question: "Who am I?"
Answer: "No one, nothing. There is no 'I.'"

Perhaps one day Dave will have a realization that there is really no "I" or persona, but the word "I" is only a metaphor used by consciousness that is expressed as someone named Dave. Maybe Dave will realize that Dave is just an idea.

"Meditation is the dissolution of thoughts in Eternal awareness or Pure consciousness without objectification, knowing without thinking, merging finitude in infinity."

— *Voltaire*

Ritual, Myth, and Rites

A ritual is often the personal enactment of a myth in which the individual physically acts in order to bring the mind, body, and spirit into play. A ritual does not always fit this model, but it does so in the practice of religion and spirituality.

All religions have rituals, and the purpose for them is often lost to history and culture so that they are often performed as superficial exercises devoid of meaning or transformation.

Each year in the Philippines, women and men relive the suffering and crucifixion of Jesus that culminates with participants actually being nailed to a cross and then uprighted to hang for hours in agony. One such man has done this for 33 years in a row. Writing for CNN, Doug Criss explained, "Since the 1980s, Ruben Enaje, 58, has portrayed Jesus Christ's crucifixion and death on Good Friday in front of crowds of locals and tourists in a village north of Manila. During these realistic crucifixions actors drive four-inch nails into both his hands and feet and lift him on a wooden cross for around five minutes. Enaje, who is Catholic, said he continues the tradition to remind the world about the plight of Jesus Christ, but he added he has decided to stop participating in the crucifixions after next year…In addition to the Good Friday crucifixions, other believers drag heavy crosses or crawl on bloodied hands and knees in cities and towns across the country. Others, dressed as Roman centurions, aid the voluntary crucifixions."[42] This is a unique example of a ritual — in an attempt to embody the suffering of Jesus. However, it remains a personal matter whether the participants in this extreme act realize the deeper meaning of the metaphor of the story of Jesus, or whether they are merely copying what they perceive as an

---

[42] Criss, Doug, Every year a Filipino man marks Good Friday with an actual crucifixion. He just did it for the 33rd time, CNN report, April 19, 2019

historical event of persecution and execution. Only the individual knows for certain.

Generally, rituals are highly symbolic. It is not necessary in this book to go into detail listing all the different rituals that are performed by Jews, Muslims, Christians, Zoroastrians, Hindus, Jains, Buddhists, Shintoists, Zen Buddhists, Wiccans, and others. What is more significant to this study is the "why" aspect of ritual — what is it for and what is gained from it.

A ritual in the context that we are exploring in this book is a religious or solemn ceremony consisting of a series of actions performed according to a prescribed order. Joseph Campbell said, "A ritual is the enactment of a myth. And, by participating in the ritual, you are participating in the myth. And since myth is a projection of the depth wisdom of the psyche, by participating in a ritual, participating in the myth, you are being, as it were, put in accord with that wisdom, which is the wisdom that is inherent within you anyhow. Your consciousness is being re-minded of the wisdom of your own life. I think ritual is terribly important."[43]

Author Elizabeth Gilbert wrote, "This is what rituals are for. We do spiritual ceremonies as human beings in order to create a safe resting place for our most complicated feelings of joy or trauma, so that we don't have to haul those feelings around with us forever, weighing us down. We all need such places of ritual safekeeping. And I do believe that if your culture or tradition doesn't have the specific ritual you are craving, then you are absolutely permitted to make up a ceremony of your own devising, fixing your own broken-down emotional systems with all the do-it-yourself resourcefulness of a generous plumber/poet."

Author CS Lewis wrote, ""The modern habit of doing ceremonial things unceremoniously is no proof of humility; rather it proves the offender's

---

[43] Moyers, Bill and Joseph Campbell, Ep. 3: Joseph Campbell and the Power of Myth – 'The First Storytellers,' billmoyers.com, June 23, 1988

inability to forget himself in the rite, and his readiness to spoil for every one else the proper pleasure of ritual."

And author Michael Pollan wrote, "People have traditionally turned to ritual to help them frame and acknowledge and ultimately even find joy in just such a paradox of being human - in the fact that so much of what we desire for our happiness and need for our survival comes at a heavy cost. We kill to eat, we cut down trees to build our homes, we exploit other people and the earth. Sacrifice — of nature, of the interests of others, even of our earlier selves - appears to be an inescapable part of our condition, the unavoidable price of all our achievements. A successful ritual is one that addresses both aspects of our predicament, recalling us to the shamefulness of our deeds at the same time it celebrates what the poet Frederick Turner calls 'the beauty we have paid for with our shame.' Without the double awareness pricked by such rituals, people are liable to find themselves either plundering the earth without restraint or descending into self-loathing and misanthropy. Perhaps it's not surprising that most of us today bring one of those attitudes or the other to our conduct in nature."[44]

Susan Cain, author *Quiet: The Power of Introverts in a World That Can't Stop Talking*, said, "Purification and redemption are such recurrent themes in ritual because there is a clear and ubiquitous need for them: we all do regrettable things as a result of our own circumstances, and new rituals are frequently invented in response to new circumstances."

Perhaps one of the great irony of rituals is that they are often performed in group or social settings. This is ironic because spiritual transformation is individualistic and personal. Of course there can also be social transformation, but the effects of ritual on each individual within the group may be varied or even nonexistent. In group settings, rituals are led by a chosen individual such as a priest, rabbi, minister, shaman, or other person. It is up to the insight and ability of such representatives as

---

[44] Pollan, Michael, *A Place of My Own: The Architecture of Daydreams*, 2008

to whether they will act as guides for personal transformation or whether they will serve only to dictate the performance of actions and words for others to blindly repeat at their command. Consider for a moment, for example, a priest who leads a mass in Latin and faces his congregation as if it was filled with students listening quietly and obediently to a teacher and then repeating his instructions. Compare this scenario to one in which the priest faces in the same direction as his congregation (with his back to them) while conducting his service. In the latter example, the priest is metaphorically heading in the same direction as his congregation, leading them, guiding them, toward a greater sense of being.

Some of the oldest surviving rituals are still practiced in India. In his article, "Harnessing the Power of Vedic Rituals," Roger Gabriel wrote, "India pulsates with rituals and sacred ceremonies, many dating back thousands of years into Vedic times. The Vedas themselves are filled with mantras, chants, and rituals for just about any purpose you can imagine. These sacred rituals are an integral part of Indian life, used before any new undertaking and to:
- Mark rites of passage.
- Change a situation.
- Give thanks.
- Honor the beginning or ending of the day"[45]

While there are untold different rituals performed by billions of Hindus, of note is the spirit in which they are carried out. The ultimate goal is to bring oneself into *at-one-ment* with beings and states of beings that transcend the human experience. For example, there is the Hindu ritual of *Aarti*: "Every morning and evening in India, the ceremony of *Aarti* (offering light) is performed in temples, shrines, ashrams, and on the banks of sacred rivers. This beautiful ritual involves the devotional waving of lamps (usually containing burning ghee or camphor) before the

---

45 Gabriel, Roger, Harnessing the Power of Vedic Rituals, The Chopra Center online, chopra.com/articles/harnessing-the-power-of-vedic-rituals

image of the presiding deity, guru, or a sacred aspect of nature. The image or guru represents the Immortal Soul, while the lamp represents the individual soul seeking Oneness with the Divine. The ritual is usually accompanied by sacred chanting, singing songs of praise, offering flowers and incense, and the ringing of bells and blowing of conches."[46]

Common to a great many rituals is the use of light. We see this in the Jewish lighting of candles to remember an historic triumphant battle after which the celebration of Chanukah (which means dedication) was created. The ritual is meant to bring Jews in touch with the spirit of their ancestors and their sacrifices, as well as the rededication of their Holy Temple in Jerusalem in service of God. Also in the Jewish tradition is the lighting of candles in a ritual called Yahrzeit in remembrance of relatives who have died so that the survivor may experience solidarity and a connection with the deceased despite the separation caused by biological death.

In Indian traditions, it is also common to light candles to remember loved ones, including personal gurus, in a ceremony called a *puja*. Author and Siddha Yoga meditation teacher Swami Shantananda explained, "We express gratitude to the guru who awakens us to the splendor of our own Self and guides us on the path to which we attain oneness with the Self."[47]

In the Vedic tradition of India, "*Puja* is a ritualistic form of worship that has been used throughout the temples of India for thousands of years. The word *puja* comes from two Sanskrit words which together translate as 'to create purification of the mind and to acquire virtuous qualities while removing bad qualities or karma.' Thus the act of performing a puja brings to us positive energies while simultaneously dissolving the ill effects of our negative actions…A puja also includes a fire ceremony called a

---

46 Gabriel, ibid

47 Swami Shantananda, siddhayoga.org/practice/puja/exposition-guru-puja, 2019

homa. This fire ceremony forms an integral part of the puja rituals with fire used to represent the concept of God, which may otherwise be too abstract for us to visualize. During the *homa*, prayer requests, beautiful garments, various metals and other substances are tossed into the fire as an offering to God and an indication of the release of our desires."[48]

Tibetan cultural tour guide Catherine Jigme noted, "It is said that there are five offering rituals in Tibetan Tantric Buddhism: pasting incense to the body, offering flowers, burning incense, sacrificing food, and lighting lamps. The spiritual meaning of fire offering can be summarized as 'burn a big fire to end all sufferings so that the soul could transcend the endless hardship in this life.'"[49]

There are also various Christian rituals connected with candlelight rituals. For example, NBC News reporter Alexey Eremenko wrote, "On the eve of Orthodox Easter for the past 12 centuries, candles placed by the Church of the Holy Sepulchre in Old Jerusalem light up by themselves, an annual miracle shoring up faith with material evidence. Or so the believers say…The Holy Fire has been recorded since the 9th century at the Church of the Holy Sepulchre, where Christian tradition holds that Jesus was crucified, buried and resurrected. It is witnessed only by the Orthodox Patriarch of Jerusalem. The cleric is locked up in a chapel after being stripped of his outer layer of clerical garments and sometimes searched. Believers observe only flashes of blue light inside the room, until the Patriarch emerges with burning candles."[50]

And each Olympic Games ceremony is started and ended in a ritual involving firelight. The Olympic torch relay begins in Olympia, Greece,

[48] Vedic Healing Institute, "PUJA CEREMONIES: Traditional Vedic Prayer Events Using Meditation, Mantras & Rituals," vedichealinginstitute.com/puja-ceremonies.html, 1999

[49] Fire offering ceremony in Tibet, www.tibettravel.org/news/fire-offering-ceremony-in-tibet.html, July 28, 2016

[50] Eremenko, Alexey, Holy Fire: Millions of Russian Christians Embrace Ritual, NBC News online, May 2, 2016

the historical birthplace of the international games, to the stadium housing the current games Quite ironically, the relay was first performed in Nazi Germany at the 1936 Berlin games and has taken place prior to every Games since. The light of the Olympic flame transcends the sense of individual athletes and individual nations in favor of uniting all the peoples of the planet as a single world culture. Again, the ironic may not be lost on some people who could argue that sports represents competition, which is inherently a conflictual enterprise that pits one person against another to create winners and losers. Not all rituals are coherently sensible.

On the subject of ritual and meaning, NYU psychiatrist Abigail Brenner explained, "Self-created ceremonies give meaning and order to our personal lives….By creating and performing personally expressive rituals for our selves we move freely into our own spiritual lives, taking charge of marking and honoring the transitions, the special moments in our lives that we find significant, in the ways we deem meaningful. Rituals are tools that give us the freedom to take responsibility for the direction and purpose of our lives. Our task is to seize and shape this freedom— consciously, deliberately, and joyfully."[51]

Regarding light as a metaphor, then through the rituals using fire and candles, we find a sense of en-lightenment — waking up to a transcendent fact. This may be recognizing that life goes on without us, that there is something greater than the physical, biological body that exists in perpetuity, that the sense of self is but a small spark in a reality of blinding light, that the ego must be burnt away to reveal the totality of consciousness beneath it, and so on. Many rituals use fire as a way to symbolically destroy memories as a means of transcending death and suffering, so that people can move forward from the past.

Brenner wrote, "Rituals afford us a sense of belonging. When we engage in the ritual process we are, in essence, connected to "original time."

---

[51] Brenner, Abigail, 11 Ways Rituals Help Us Celebrate Our Lives, *Psychology Today*, Aug 26, 2015

Rituals awaken that which is eternal within us and show us how our individual lives are part of a much grander design. Rituals connect us with nature and the seasons. The ongoing transitions that occur in nature provide the prototype for change. By watching the constant shifts and turns in nature we recognize our own cycles of life, our own rhythms as humans. Rituals remind us of the interconnectedness of all of life."[52]

[52] Brenner, ibid

"Rituals remove us from the ordinary flow of life and place us in sacred space. It is out of the realm of ordinary space and time that rituals create their magic through the mysterious and mystical language of symbolic reenactment."

— *Abigail Brenner*

A Medley of Mythical Motifs

There are many mythical motifs. These are distinctive features or dominant ideas in artistic or literary compositions, including a myths. A motif can be an animal, a person, a place, and so on. These motifs are often found in dreams and have been recognized as *archetypes* by Carl Jung.

The longer we study myths and motifs, it becomes apparent that they center upon the eternal juxtaposition and struggle between the conscious and unconscious mind — the superficial and the deep, so to speak. The conscious world is perceived as safe and reliable, because it is known and relatively uncomplicated. But the unconscious reality, like a cave in a myth, is deep, dark, often disturbing, chaotic, uncomfortable, and unfamiliar. The question remains as to whether the conscious mind will concede to the unconscious — whether it will turn in on itself in order to realize a transformation. Getting the conscious mind to do this is no easy feat, and in the iconic hero's journey we usually find that the confrontation between the conscious and the unconscious is facilitated by accident or force. The hero is reluctant to heed the call to go bravely into the unconscious.

In the Eastern traditions of philosophy from whence we have received the practice of meditation, the push for the conscious to know the unconscious is a deliberate action borne of curiosity, suffering, or even a deep desire to "find one's true nature." In this case, we have a scenario wherein the goal is to get the egoic mind — the persona — to yield to what has always been present (the greater consciousness of totality) yet has been unknowable due to the attention that consciousness has been placing on the thoughts, identities, beliefs, and associations of the egoic mind.

111

Swami Rama, writing for *Yoga International*, explained, "From childhood onward, we have been educated only to examine and verify things in the external world. No one has taught us how to look within, to find within, and to verify within. Therefore, we remain strangers to ourselves, while trying to get to know others. This lack of self-understanding is one of the main reasons our relationships don't seem to work, and why confusion and disappointment so often prevail in our life. Very little of the mind is cultivated by our formal educational system. The part of the mind that dreams and sleeps — the vast realm of the unconscious which is the reservoir of all our experiences — remains unknown and undisciplined; it is not subject to any control…The goal of meditation is to go beyond the mind and experience our essential nature— which is described as peace, happiness, and bliss. But as anyone who has tried to meditate knows, the mind itself is the biggest obstacle standing between ourselves and this awareness. The mind is undisciplined and unruly, and it resists any attempts to discipline it or to guide it on a particular path. The mind has a mind of its own. That is why many people sit for meditation and experience only fantasies, daydreams, or hallucinations. They never attain the stillness that distinguishes the genuine experience of deep meditation."[53]

Regarding what Swami Rama has written, why try to quiet the mind at all? Teachers of self-enquiry in which the mind challenges itself, tell us that the mind is unruly, distracted, noisy, and unsettled, so let it be what it is — don't try to make it quiet or control it. Instead, just observe it; pay attention to it, and find out what it is, and eventually you will realize that you are not it, because you are that which is aware of it. If you are aware

---

[53] Swami Rama, The Real Meaning of Meditation, *Yoga International*, https://yogainternational.com/article/view/the-real-meaning-of-meditation, Aug 2019

of the mind, then you must not be the mind. The silent watcher of thoughts does not change, yet the mind does change. So which are you?

Myth is a story that challenges the egoic mind. It is attempting to show us the relationship between the egoic (conscious) mind and the unconscious mind. In a myth's bag of tools are myriad metaphorical images to facilitate this. Here are a few of them...

The cave

From the University of Michigan's Dictionary of Symbolism, we learn that the cave is thought to be closely related to the symbolic heart, and is often a place where the self and ego unite. Caves can be secret passageways to an underworld, places in which to make contact with the powers and forces which will eventually make their way into the world of light. In popular legend, caves usually house gnomes, spirits, dragons, and treasure; they are often the site for initiation ceremonies. Psychologists interpret a dreamer's dangerous passage through caves as symbolizing the search for the meaning of life in the deep strata of the "maternal unconscious." In Carl Jung's world, the cave represents the security and the impregnability of the unconscious. Entering the cave is considered re-entry into the womb of Mother Earth and is, in general , a symbol of containment.[54]

Going into a cave may represent a deep descent into the psyche, as the mythic hero overcomes trials, and experiences moments of tremendous insight. Eventually the hero's previous self begins to disintegrate, giving way to transformation. In myths, this stage is symbolized as death and rebirth in which the hero enters a dark area such as the belly of a whale,

[54] Brown, Geoff, Jamie Smith, Eric Jaffe, Dictionary of Symbolism, University of Michigan, http://umich.edu/~umfandsf/symbolismproject/symbolism.html/C/cave.html, 1997-2001

a tomb, or dark cave, and emerges from it reborn.[55]

Joseph Campbell succinctly said, "The cave you fear to enter holds the treasure you seek.

In the movie *Indiana Jones and the Last Crusade*, the hero reluctantly enters a cave in search of the Holy Grail. He not only risks his life and his father's life, but also all of humanity is at stake.

When the hero enters the cave there is no turning back. He is in fear, but knows that he must push forward at great peril. He is going into darkness where the scary things are and even his own appearance disappears in the absence of light — his superficial personhood vanishes before his eyes.

Writing about the cave motif, Deb Peterson explained "The hero has adjusted to the special world and goes on to seek its heart, the inmost cave. She passes into an intermediate zone with new threshold guardians and tests. She approaches the place where the object of the quest is hidden and where she will encounter supreme wonder and terror...She must use every lesson learned to survive."[56]

The dragon

The dragon (European dragon, not the Asian dragon) is a powerful metaphor in myth associated with greed. Joseph Campbell explained, "The European dragon guards things in his cave, and what he guards are heaps of gold and virgins. And he can't make use of either of them, but he just guards. There's no vitality of experience, either of the value of

---

[55] Joseph Campbell and the Myth of the Hero's Journey, https://academyofideas.com/2016/06/joseph-campbell-myth-of-the-heros-journey/, June 16, 2016

[56] Peterson, Deb, The Approach to the Inmost Cave in the Hero's Journey, https://www.thoughtco.com/inmost-cave-the-heros-journey-31347, March 8, 2019

the gold or of the female whom he's guarding there. Psychologically, **the dragon is one's own binding of oneself to one's ego**, and you're captured in your own dragon cave. And the problem of the psychiatrist is to break that dragon, open him up, so that you can have a larger field of relationships…. The real dragon is in you….That's your ego, holding you in."[57]

A body of water

"Water," wrote Carl Jung, "is the commonest symbol for the unconscious…Psychologically, water means spirit that has become unconscious…The descent into the depths always seems to precede the ascent…The unconscious is commonly regarded as a sort of incapsulated fragment of our most personal and intimate life…" On the other hand, he noted, consciousness sees everything "separately and in isolation, and therefore sees the unconscious this way too, regarding it as outright *my* unconscious. Hence, it is generally believed that anyone who descends into the unconscious gets into a suffocating atmosphere of egocentric subjectivity, and in this blind alley is exposed to the attack of all the ferocious beasts which the caverns of the psychic underworld are supposed to harbour. True, whoever looks into the mirror of the water will see first of all his own face. Whoever goes to himself risks a confrontation with himself. The mirror does not flatter, it faithfully shows whatever looks into it; namely, the face we never show to the world because we cover it with the *persona*, the mask of the actor. But the mirror lies behind the mask and shows the true face. This confrontation is the first test of courage on the inner way, a test sufficient to frighten off most people, for the meeting with ourselves belongs to the more unpleasant things that can be avoided so long as we can project everything negative into the environment. But if are able to see our own shadow and can

---

57 Moyers, Bill, Ep. 1: Joseph Campbell and the Power of Myth – 'The Hero's Adventure,' June 21, 1988

bear knowing about it, then a small part of the problem has already been solved; we have at least brought up the personal unconscious."[58]

In the Greek myth of Narcissus, the hero stares into a body of water and is enamored with his own beauty. He is seeing a reflection of his face just upon the surface of the mirror-like water. But Narcissus does not realize that it is his own face that he is staring at and falls deeply in love with it, as if it is somebody else. Unable to leave the allure of his image, he eventually realizes that his love will not be reciprocated and he melts away from the fire of passion burning inside him, eventually turning into a gold and white flower. In this myth we have a metaphor for one who is unaware, superficial, and thinking only of the conscious mind.

As explained by psychiatrist Neel Burton, upon staring into his reflection for quite some time, "Narcissus grew ever more thirsty, but would not leave or disturb the pool of water for fear of losing sight of his reflection. In the end, he died of thirst, and there, on that very spot, appeared the narcissus flower, with its bright face and bowed neck."[59]

Since myth is intended to lead one inward into his/her own psyche, what is the point of the myth of Narcissus? The way to know ourselves beyond superficiality — beyond the conscious, egoic, mind, is to enter the depths of the unconscious. We have to go into that dark, unknown territory of water rather than staring only at its surface, enamored by all the distractions of the superficial life and self.

---

[58] Jung, CG, *The Archetypes and the Collective Unconscious*, Routledge, p. 18-20, Dec 18, 2014

[59] Burton, MD, Neel, Who Was Narcissus? The story of Narcissus and its meaning, *Psychology Today*, Mar 22, 2018

Death

Krishnamurti said, that death "is like a vast river in which man is caught with all his worldly goods, his vanities, plans, and knowledge. Unless he leaves all the things he has accumulated in the river and swims ashore, death will always be at his door, waiting and watching."

Death is the end of the way things were, but this ending is always a segue into rebirth. When the individual faces death, the egoic mind is in fear because it resists yielding to the totality of consciousness. Like Narcissus, the egoic mind is in love with its own illusion. This is because it has been conditioned, trained, to perpetuate itself. It is resistant — it does not want change or to be sacrificed to something greater. The egoic mind struggles to exist and persist, and even though the struggle may be painful, the mind is nevertheless in fear of annihilation. It prefers the known over the unknown.

Death is not a symbol of biological death, but rather a transition from one state to another state. One of the most enduring examples of this is the metaphor of Jesus dying on the cross. His death is a transformative experience that stands as an example to others. If you take this story literally you see one of torture and suffering, but if you take it metaphorically, you find a hero's journey in which the egoic mind dies to rebirth as the consciousness.

The wise old man

The wise old man, or sage is typically represented as a kind and wise, older father figure. His wisdom and experience imbues his stories and teachings with mysticism. From his words comes guidance that impresses upon the hero a sense of who he is as well as his potential. He is a mentor who is often depicted as being foreign — perhaps from a different culture, nation, or occasionally, even a different time, from those he advises. In extreme cases, he may be a liminal being such as Merlin, who was only half human.[60]

The circle

The circle is a profound symbol found in many myths around the world. It is a metaphor for the entire hero's journey, from start to finish, as the hero starts off here and then returns to the same place, now transformed. It also represents the circularity of life, events, and nature.

Carl Jung noted, ""The circle is one of the great primordial images of mankind, that in considering the symbol of the circle, we are analyzing the self."

While interviewing Joseph Campbell, journalist Bill Moyers said, "And I find you, in your own work throughout the course of your life, coming across the circle, whether it's in the magical designs of the world over, whether it's in the architecture both ancient and modern, whether it's in the dome-shaped temples of India or the calendar stones of the Aztecs, or the ancient Chinese bronze shields, or the visions of the Old Testament prophet Ezekiel, whom you talk about, the wheel in the sky. You keep coming across this image."

Joseph Campbell answered, "Yes, it's an ever-present thing. It's the center from which you've come, back to which you go. I remember reading in a book about the American Indians, called *The Indian Book*, by Natalie Curtis, it was published around 1904, her conversation with a chief. I think it was a chief of the Pawnee tribe. And among the things he said was, 'When we pitch camp, we pitch the camp in a circle. When we looked at the horizon, the horizon was in a circle. When the eagle builds a nest, the nest is in circle.' And then you read in Plato somewhere, the

---

[60] Wise old man, *Wikipedia*

soul is a circle. I suppose the circle represents. totality. Within the circle is one thing, it is encircled, it's enframed. That would be the spatial aspect, but the temporal aspect of the circle is, you leave, go somewhere and come back, the alpha and omega. God is the alpha and omega, the source and the end. Somehow the circle suggests immediately a completed totality, whether in time or in space…You experience it in the day and the year, just as we've said, and you experience in leaving home, going on your adventure, hunting or whatever it may be, and coming back to home. And then there's a deeper one also, that mystery of the womb and the tomb. When people are buried it's for rebirth, I mean, that's the origin of the burial idea, you're put back into the womb of Mother Earth for rebirth."[61]

---

61 Moyers, Bill, Ep. 6: Joseph Campbell and the Power of Myth – 'Masks of Eternity,' June 26, 1988

"Fire is His head, the sun and moon His eyes, space His ears, the Vedas His speech, the wind His breath, the universe His heart. From His feet the Earth has originated. Verily, He is the inner self of all beings."

— *The Upanishads*

Self Enquiry and
the Myth of the self

In 1902, Philosophy graduate-turned-revenue officer M. Sivaprakasam Pillai traveled to Virupaksha Cave on Arunachala Hill in Southern India to meet a sage named Ramana Maharshi. Like thousands of others up until Ramana's death in 1951, Pillai was in search of his own true nature beyond the egoic self, so he put this simple question to Ramana: "Who am I?" The question is the cornerstone to what is now called *self-enquiry*, an investigation into the self that is known as the first step to realizing oneself at the deepest level. Here is the exchange between Pillai and Ramana:

QUESTION: Who am I?

ANSWER: The gross body which is composed of the seven humours (*dhatus*), I am not; the five cognitive sense organs, viz. the senses of hearing, touch, sight, taste, and smell, which apprehend their respective objects, viz. sound, touch, colour, taste, and odour, I am not; the five cognitive sense organs, viz. the organs of speech, locomotion, grasping, excretion, and procreation, which have as their respective functions speaking, moving, grasping, excreting, and enjoying, I am not; the five vital airs, *prana*, etc., which perform respectively the five functions of in-breathing, etc., I am not; even the mind which thinks, I am not; the nescience too, which is endowed only with the residual impressions of objects, and in which there are no objects and no functionings, I am not.

QUESTION: If I am none of these, then who am I?

ANSWER: After negating all of the above-mentioned as 'not this', 'not this', that Awareness which alone remains — that I am.[62]

You may notice that Ramana never told Pillai the answer to his question "Who am I?" Instead, he systematically went down a list of negations. This is because the true Self of consciousness cannot be known by the mind. It cannot be explained in words — words, images, descriptions, and all else must be eliminated in order to find what remains after they are gone. If you were to go through this process of elimination through observation of yourself and thoughts, then eventually you may come to find that *what you are is what you are not.*

What you are   is what you are not.

This may be the ultimate of all koans!

---

62 Ramana Maharshi, *Who am I?* The Teachings of Bhagavan Sri Ramana Maharshi, Translation by Dr. T. M. P. Mahadevan, Sri Ramanasramam Tiruvannamalai, South India, 1902

*"What you are
is what you are not."*

— *Vic Shayne*

"To be specific, it is not the ego that transforms through myth. And it is not consciousness that is transformed. What is called transformation is actually the shifting of focus of consciousness from the egoic self to the Self of consciousness."
— *Vic Shayne*

Youtube videos

Campbell, Joseph

4: 22 minutes

https://www.youtube.com/watch?v=VgOUxICCHoA

Krishnamurti, Jiddu

Beyond Myth & Tradition 10 - Death: leaving the stream

28:44 minutes

https://www.youtube.com/watch?v=X0B0gOKb1Vs

Campbell, Joseph

Joseph Campbell The Hero's Journey documentary

1:24:25

https://www.youtube.com/watch?v=T3LozCNO30w

About the Author

Vic Shayne's work spans myriad areas of interest, yet his prevailing study is in the area of the mind and consciousness, and how one may uncover the wholeness that exists behind the limited sense of the egoic self. He has been a professional writer for more than 40 years, with more than 500 articles and several books to his credit, including a best-seller on the *New York Times*, *Wall Street Journal* and amazon.com lists. He is a practitioner and teacher of mind-body therapy modalities, as well as meditation and self-inquiry.

Made in United States
Orlando, FL
09 May 2022

17692882R00081

WALTER
GEORGE
SMITH

Walter George Smith

WALTER
GEORGE
SMITH

Thomas A. Bryson

THE CATHOLIC UNIVERSITY OF AMERICA PRESS
Washington, D. C.
1977

Library of Congress Cataloging in Publication Data

Bryson, Thomas A   1931-
    Walter George Smith.

    Bibliography: p.
    Includes index.
    1. Smith, Walter George, 1854-1924. 2. Lawyers—
Pennsylvania—Philadelphia—Biography. 3. Politicians—
Pennsylvania—Philadelphia—Biography.
KF373.S58B78   340'.092'4 [B]   77-9967
ISBN 0-8132-0539-5

iv

CONTENTS

Preface   viii

The Years of Preparation   1
    Antecedents and Early Education   1
    The Move to Philadelphia and College   4
    Law School   10

A Philadelphia Lawyer   13

    First Disappointments and Successes   13
    Professional Associations   17
    A Democrat in Politics   19
    The Rising Young Lawyer: Grant, Twain, Davis   23
    Marriage to Elizabeth Drexel   29

Profile of a Catholic, Philadelphia Progressive   37

    The Turn of the Century Progressive   37
    The Legal Reformer   42
    The Educator and Religionist   46

The Political Reformer 51
The Committee of Nine 57
Smith and the Uniform Divorce Law 62
Smith and Uniform Commercial Law 71
Reform Politics, Post-World War I 73

Journey to the Middle East 79

Smith and ACRNE: Constantinople 81
The Trip to the Caucasus 85
Back in Constantinople 92

The Paris Peace Conference 98

The Reorganization of ACRNE 99
Armenian Repatriation 101
British Evacuation of the Caucasus 108

An Advocate for Armenia 118

The Williams Resolution 120
The Armenia-American Society and Near East Relief 122
Armenia and the League of Nations 125
A New Armenian State 128
Financial Support for Armenia 134
France, Cilicia, and the United States 138
The Treaty of Lausanne 144

The Washington Naval Conference 149

The Advisory Committee 150
The Subcommittee on Naval Limitation 153
Pacific and Far East Questions 157
Land Armaments 158

Pleading for the Pueblos 162

The Board of Indian Commissioners 164
Smith Among the Pueblos 166

The Report on the Pueblos   169
Smith's Last Journey   171

The Summing Up   174

Notes   182

Bibliography   205

Index   214

Preface

I first became familiar with Walter George Smith's role in American history while completing a doctoral dissertation on the Armenian mandate question, a topic in American diplomatic history, at the University of Georgia in 1965. From Smith's manuscript collection to which I gained access, I learned that he was among that small but articulate group of American Armenophiles who kept the problem of the "starving Armenians" before the American public during the period 1915 to 1927. I decided that at some future date I would investigate the possibilities of examining Smith's career.

The chief problem for the biographer of a minor figure is to assess the auxiliary role of his subject in history. He should not be primarily concerned with the minutiae of daily life; rather, he should deal with those areas where the subject touches the society in which he moves, interacts, and to some degree modifies, stimulates, or alters its goals. Indeed, the writer's main task is to determine whether society is the better or worse for his subject's efforts.

This study explores the connection between Walter George Smith and the movements he worked for between 1898 and the immediate post-World War I era. In the main, this is the story of Smith's public career, the career of a Catholic, Philadelphia lawyer and a conservative progressive, one who combined the qualities of a Philadelphia aristocrat with those of the reformer sincerely interested in urban good government, efficiency, and social cohesion. The study is somewhat less and somewhat more than a biography. It tries to describe the context in which Smith moved; for that reason, the subject is absent from portions of the narrative. It does not treat Smith's personal life from birth to death.

Walter George Smith's life spanned the Civil War, the Gilded Age, the Progressive Era, World War I, and the time of America's flirtation with internationalism following that war. In his lifetime he pursued three "careers": Philadelphia lawyer,[1] progressive reformer, and international humanist. Smith's talent as a lawyer placed him in a position to embark on the second and third careers, and tended to overlap with the others in time, but underlying all three are two unmistakable themes. First, Smith, a staunch Roman Catholic, sought to move toward and interact with the dominant white, Anglo-Saxon Protestant element in American society while at the same time retaining his Catholic identity. Second, Smith associated with those interested in progressive reform, and the theme of progressivism—the desire to reform, rationalize, uplift, and organize—was a major force in the three phases of his life. As one who strove to impose order on his surroundings and to direct change along constructive lines, his progressivism might be styled "a rather conservative sort of thing."[2] But it was closely linked to his training as a lawyer.

Smith's legal career began in 1877 when he graduated from the Law School of the University of Pennsylvania. Although he started his profession under serious handicaps, Smith made several important contacts among members of the Philadelphia legal fraternity and soon found his practice expanding. In addition to the WASP Syndrome, progressivism also motivated Smith's legal career. Like other professional men, he joined local, state, and national bar associations to improve the content of legal procedures, to raise the standards for legal education, and to protect the profession from the unfit and unethical who sought to enter its ranks. At the time of his marriage in 1890, at age 36, he had established himself in his profession and was on the road to becoming one of the most successful members of the Philadelphia bar, a bar dominated in the main by scions of old line, Protestant, Philadelphia families.

As with many professional men in the Northeast, marriage proved a boon to Smith's professional life. His marriage to Elizabeth L. Drexel, a daughter of wealthy Philadelphia banker Francis Drexel, was fortunate. By his own admission his marriage opened new doors to him. The assurance of his acceptance in the upper levels of Philadelphia society, dominated for the most part by Episcopalians, and his membership on many influential boards of directors and trustees, stem as much from his marriage as from his native ability. His wife's death within a year of their wedding caused Smith great anguish. In the period following her death he sought new pursuits, some in the direction of reform.

The decade of the 1890s witnessed the beginning of the progressive era, a period when Americans felt a sense of crisis and became conscious of the need to preserve order by reforming existing political, social, and economic institutions. Smith's law career provided him with the steppingstone to a career as a progressive reformer.

The young attorney's proclivity for reform took essentially two major directions. First, his interest in Philadelphia politics had developed in the 1880s. A staunch Democrat, he realized that popular participation in local government in his adopted city was futile because a Republican machine dominated the local political process. He associated with the city's Protestant-led aristocracy in the attempt to achieve urban reform. Second, although he devoted himself to the cause of municipal good government, Smith's most extensive work as a reformer came with his advocacy of uniform state divorce and commercial laws, non-political goals often overlooked by students of the progressive era.

Smith's progressivism also compelled him during the 1920s to join other reformers in their attempt to preserve the American Indian's cultural uniqueness and to protect his rights to tribal lands. As a member of the Department of the Interior's Board of Indian Commissioners, Smith did his utmost to defend the Indian from those who would obliterate cultural particularism and to safeguard the title of Pueblo Indians to lands in Arizona and New Mexico long held by tribal right.

Smith's other career as an international humanist also stemmed from his prominence as a lawyer. As in the earlier and the later phase of his life, the progressive theme was present. Smith the progressive pursued a domestic mission to impose order on his social, political, and economic surroundings; Smith the internationalist joined those men and women who sought to bring order to the world scene by means of international organization and legal instrumentalities. Motivated by the same humanitarian sentiment that stimulated his penchant for local philanthropy, Smith associated with the American Commission for Relief in the Near East, traveled to the Middle East, and took part in the massive endeavor to speed relief supplies to the starving refugees cast adrift by the World War. Because he was anxious that order be restored to the Middle East, Smith attended the Paris Peace Conference. There he made special representations on behalf of the Armenians, who were then seeking the fruits of self-determination. Smith labored for the realization of an American mandate for Armenia. An American presence there, he reasoned, would help to realize peace in that region of the world and would offer the United States the mission of using its power and wealth to bring progress, order, and efficient government to the chaotic Armenian scene.

Smith was an advocate for the League of Nations and world peace. He eschewed isolation and urged upon the United States an international role. He attended the opening of the League of Nations as a prominent internationalist to advocate the Armenian cause, hoping the League would take responsibility for preserving the territorial integrity of the Armenian state by preserving peace in the Transcaucasus. For similar reasons he later accepted appointment to the Advisory Commission for the American Delegation to the Washington Naval Conference. He took his task seriously, believing that the Conference would produce treaties that would realize world disarmament as a step toward ensuring world peace.

In this study of Walter George Smith I have made extensive use of his papers, a collection hitherto unknown and unused by scholars. Some parts of the collection have been destroyed or lost but the residual offers a substantial quantity of material and, when supplemented by other manuscript collections, provides rare insight into the evolution of the public career of a prominent American lawyer, reformer, and citizen-diplomat.

No writer is without debt to others, and in this respect I am no exception. I am obliged to Sister M. Francisca, S. B. S., Mrs. Jean Bullit Darlington, Mr. Hubert Horan, Mr. Charles J. Biddle, Miss Flora O'Malley, Mrs. Kate Loughran Sands, Miss Constance

O'Hara, and Mr. William Barclay Lex for sharing with me their remembrances of Walter George Smith. I am obliged to Mr. A. J. Drexel Paul of Philadelphia for directing me to various sources of legal information in the Philadelphia area. I am grateful for the assistance rendered by Nicholas Biddle Wainwright of the Historical Society of Pennsylvania; by Professor Raymond H. Schmandt, former editor of *Records of the American Catholic Historical Society of Philadelphia;* by James Tashjian, editor of the *Armenian Review;* by Moreau B. C. Chambers of the Catholic University Library; by Miss Marti Shaw, Houghton Library, Harvard University; and by various persons at the libraries of Rollins College, the Catholic Archdiocesan Center in Baltimore, the University of Pennsylvania, Emory, Princeton, Columbia, and Yale Universities. Mrs. Lilla Hawes, director of the Georgia Historical Society Library, and Stephen T. Riley, director of the Massachusetts Historical Society, were both very helpful.

I wish to express my thanks to Mrs. Charles MacNeal of Hightstown, N.J. for permitting me to see the diary of her father Charles Trowbridge Riggs. John McDonough of the Manuscript Division, Library of Congress, has been most helpful, as have Handy B. Fant and Mark Eckhoff of the National Archives. Professor J. Chal Vinson, department of history, University of Georgia, directed me to several valuable collections relative to the Washington Naval Conference. Members of the West Georgia College Library staff, particularly Mrs. Betty Jobson, Mrs. Sarah Rigg, and Miss Jan Ruskell, and Mrs. Jane Hersch, performed many valuable services.

A special note of thanks is due my colleague Gordon E. Finnie, who encouraged me to write this book and gave valuable criticism at every stage of its development. A world of appreciation is also due colleagues Mary Anne DeVillier, whose critique of the manuscript greatly improved its readibility, and to Richard A. Folk and Mollie Camp Davis for their helpful suggestions. Joseph L. Grabill of Illinois State University gave me a keen insight into the character of my subject, while Joel Mustin of Western Reserve University supplied me with a better understanding of the intricacies of Philadelphia politics during the progressive era. James Gidney of Kent State University deserves a note of thanks for reading and criticising the manuscript. The Reverend Fathers Edmund Halsey, O.S.B., John J. Shellem, and the late Bartholomew Fair, all associated with the American Catholic Historical Society of Philadelphia, were most helpful and kind. Indeed, without the charity of Father Fair this study would not have been possible. Publication of this study was assisted by grants from the West Georgia College Faculty Research Council, the Alexander Manoogian Cultural Fund, and the National Association for Armenian Studies and Research. Finally, I must also thank my wife Anne who daily encouraged me in the completion of this work.

Thomas A. Bryson
Carrollton, Georgia

CHAPTER 1

The Years of Preparation

Walter George Smith, born in 1854, was much too young to take an active part in the Civil War, but events of the era stamped an indelible imprint upon his mind.[1] Despite his youth he was a member of the war generation, and participated emotionally in the four-year drama that threatened to rend the nation asunder. He knew at first hand the years of loneliness of a boy whose father was absent from home, serving with the Union Army in the West. His early heroes were men like Generals Ulysses S. Grant, William Tecumseh Sherman, and of course his father, Thomas Kilby Smith, a man accustomed to associating with the nation's leaders by virtue of both his talents and his ancestral background.

ANTECEDENTS AND EARLY EDUCATION

Descended on both sides of his family from professional men, many of them lawyers, judges, physicians, and clergymen, Walter George Smith could claim an ancestry made up of persons who fitted into the nation's dominant Anglo-Saxon Protestant socio-economic class. The first of his paternal forebears to reach American shores was Gottfried Christian Schmidt, a physician who migrated from Ger-

1

many in 1752 to Boston, where he joined the British Army as a surgeon. After service during the French and Indian War he settled at Newburyport, Massachusetts, where he married Hannah Calef in 1764 and devoted himself to the practice of medicine. George Smith, youngest of the seven children of Gottfried and Hannah, was born in Boston in 1782.

After a lengthy career at sea this grandfather of Walter George settled in Boston, where he married Eliza Bicker Walter on January 31, 1817. Her ancestray included many Congregational and Episcopalian clergymen, a president of Harvard College, and two chief justices of the Massachusetts Bay Colony. Thomas Kilby Smith, born on September 23, 1820, was the first surviving child of this marriage between George and Eliza. The family resided for a time in Quincy, where it became intimate with the illustrious Adams family, and Thomas Kilby recalled listening to stories at the feet of old John Adams. But Captain Smith did not remain in the Northeast. Failing in business and lured by tales of growing opportunity in the burgeoning West, he moved his family in 1829 to Cincinnati.

He sent his son Thomas Kilby to Woodward High School, where he associated with many students who would later become outstanding leaders in Ohio. The captain then placed the young man in the law office of Salmon P. Chase, a future republican governor of Ohio from 1856 to 1860 and Chief Justice of the United States from 1864 to 1873. After reading law young Smith was admitted to the bar in 1846 and remained in the office of the future Chief Justice for several years. But he found hunting and fishing more to his liking. Following an outing in 1847 Donn Piatt, a young Cincinnati lawyer, invited Smith to visit his home at Mac-O-Cheek. There he met his future wife, Elizabeth Budd McCullough. She—following her mother's death—had been reared at Mac-O-Cheek, the Logan County, Ohio home of her grandparents, Judge Benjamin M. and Elizabeth Piatt. Because the judge's wife had been converted to Roman Catholicism, Elizabeth was brought up in that faith. She was married to Thomas Kilby on May 2, 1848, by the Right Reverend J. B. Purcell, Bishop of the Diocese of Cincinnati, in the old log chapel which Elizabeth Piatt had erected near the family home.[2]

Thomas Kilby settled his bride in Cincinnati and continued to practice law with varying success until 1853, when he moved his wife and two daughters, Betty and Arabella, to Washington to accept a political appointment in the Post Office Department. In 1854 Elizabeth returned to Mac-O-Cheek where she gave birth on November 24, 1854, to her eldest son, Walter George. She returned to Washington early in 1855 at a time when the slavery controversy raged across the nation. In 1856 Thomas Kilby resigned from the Post Office Department and removed his family to Cincinnati where he assumed a position as Deputy Clerk of the Court of Hamilton County.

Shortly after arriving in Cincinnati Walter George's parents began his training. Thomas Kilby hired Miss Kate Carville to teach the boy and his sisters the rudiments of reading, writing, and arithmetic. In summers the boy's mother took the children to Mac-O-Cheek where he experienced the discipline and rigors of rural life. His elders taught him to care for horses, work in the garden, feed the livestock, and to do odd chores about the house, instilling a deep sense of responsibility. His mother was a devout Catholic and saw to his early religious training, which included a thorough grounding in the catechism. But the boy's early training was soon disrupted with the outbreak of war in April, 1861.

The furor between Blue and Grey soon swept Walter George's father up into the conflict, a conflict that would require him to be absent from home for four long years. Offering his services to the Union cause, Thomas Kilby soon received command of the 54th Ohio Volunteers. Following a six-month period of training at Camp Dennison, Ohio, the Colonel marched away to the war in the West. Leaving behind a family that included his wife, daughters Betty and Arabella, and sons Walter George, Dehon, and Adrian.

With the approach of summer Walter George's mother determined to move her family to Yellow Springs, a small village that proved an ideal locale to spend the war years. So strong was her moral and spiritual guidance in these years that he would later write that "it would be a difficult thing to place limitations upon the influence of her life and character upon mine, but whatever good there may be in my nature has been stimulated and strengthened by her teaching and example." Elizabeth continued the education of her son and his brothers and sisters, sending them to the juvenile school connected with nearby Antioch College. The three-year sojourn at Yellow Springs was a happy period for Walter George, who enjoyed new friendships in the rural environment.

But in addition to the practical education learned in the rural surroundings of Ohio, the formal education obtained in the classroom, and the moral and spiritual precepts absorbed at his mother's knee, tales of the hardships and sadness that accompany war also broadened young Smith considerably. Soldiers stopped off at Yellow Springs frequently. Eager to hear of the war, the boy pressed them for stories of battle and army life. The youngster never tired of reading press accounts of the ebb and flow of battle, and he daily rode to the village to pick up the mail and the Cincinnati newspapers. The boy also heard about the war from his father's many letters home, for Colonel Smith had asked that his mother read his letters to the children against the day when he would return and be able to regale them with stories of his campaign in the South. These letters provided Walter George early lessons in place geography, for the Colonel advised his wife to trace on the map for the children the course of his travels. How happy the boy must have been when his father, now a Brigadier General,[3] returned home in the fall of 1864 to recover from a sun-stroke incurred during the course of the war, and happier still when the soldier presented him with a piebald Comanche pony and a single barrel gun acquired from the Shiloh battlefield.

The lad also learned of conditions in the war-torn South by personal observation. Following a second visit to Yellow Springs in February, 1865, General Smith decided to take his wife and eldest son with him to New Orleans. As they coursed down the Mississippi on their steamboat, the lad could view evidence of the conflict waged to gain control of the Mighty Father of Waters. Their stay in New Orleans was cut short because the army ordered General Smith to proceed at once to Mobile in order to join the Union forces besieging the city. Elizabeth and her son returned to Yellow Springs to await the end of hostilities and the return of the general.

THE MOVE TO PHILADELPHIA AND COLLEGE

The war over, General Smith reached home early in September. He held several family conferences to decide upon the location of their new home. Ultimately, the presence in Philadelphia of friends, of his cousins George W. Hunter and George Budd, and of his mother's sister led the elder Smith to move his family to that city. He was concerned about the religious and educational needs of his children; after learning that the religious order of the Sacred Heart operated a school for girls, Eden Hall, at Torresdale, he decided to move his family to that suburb, which is located on the Delaware River about ten miles upstream from center city. Accompanied by his mother, daughters, and son Dehon, the general departed for Philadelphia in September, 1865, leaving his wife, sister, and sons Adrian and Walter George to close the Yellow Springs house and follow at a later date.

Thus in late 1865 General Smith brought his family to Philadelphia, one of the nation's largest urban centers. He settled them in a three-story brownstone house in fashionable Torresdale. The social climate into which he had moved his family was somewhat incongruous: he was a professional man and an enthusiastic Democrat who had located his Catholic family with its love of literature and the arts in the midst of a community largely Episcopalian, rock-ribbed Republican, and devoted in the main to sports, to commerce, and to finance.

For Walter George the arrival at Torresdale meant the beginning of a new, more sophisticated way of life. He soon fitted comfortably into a clique consisting of the sons of older, more established residents. That he learned early to adapt himself with ease to the ways of Philadelphia's more prominent citizens was to his advantage. This pattern of behavior was also somewhat prophetic for, in attaining success in his profession and national acclaim as a man of affairs, Smith would spend the remainder of his life interacting with the American Protestant elite, at the same time maintaining his identity as a prominent, devout Roman Catholic.

During the initial years at Torresdale, the Smith family experienced great sorrow over the loss of two of its members and great joy over the birth of four babies. The drowning of Arabella, called Belle, in August, 1868, caused Walter George considerable grief. The death of this older sister affected his personality, giving him an introspective disposition and deepening his religious faith.[4] In the following year the boy grieved over the death of his grandmother Smith. But if the Smith's knew sorrow, they also knew happiness. The birth of Helen Grace in 1865 was soon followed by the arrivals of Caroline (Caleen) in 1867, William Duncan in 1868, and Thomas Kilby in 1871.

The education of this large number of children proved no problem to the general. He consigned his daughters to the care of the sisters at nearby Eden Hall, where the family attended mass in the stranger's chapel, and enrolled his sons in Episcopal Academy in Philadelphia, long associated with its Anglo-Catholic gentry. Daily, Walter George and his brother Dehon made the long trip. Smith enjoyed his course of study at prep school since he was a bookish type and learning came easily to him. Concerning his attitude toward study, he later wrote: "from my childhood I had always been fond of reading and literary pursuits." Probably aware of this tendency, his father had advised him to study history and to improve himself by reading and research.[5] The lad pursued the classical course and learned his Latin and English well enough to return later to the Academy as a teacher.

But the youngster realized that all learning was not confined between the covers of books. He met at the Academy many students who had substantial impact on his development. His father had counseled him to "learn the art of making friends."[6] He followed his father's advice and increased his circle of acquaints, who considerably widened his perspective. First, most of his new friends and associates were Protestant. This gave him a social and educational milieu broader than that of any youth confined to the Catholic ghetto with its many restrictions. Second, many of Smith's young cohorts at the Academy were to become the future leaders of Philadelphia. From them he began to acquire many of the social attitudes, assumptions and values current among the elite, attitudes that would later enable him to move with ease among the city's leading lights at board meetings and among the nation's diplomatic and military leaders at international conferences.

Accepted by his peers, young Smith felt free to invite them to visit him at the Torresdale home, which was already a gathering place for the friends of the younger members of the family. General Smith enjoyed his eldest son's companions and often talked to them of public affairs and politics, in which he was deeply immersed.

His father's interest in public affairs—particularly national politics—made a lasting impression on Walter George, who later was convinced that his own interest in this subject was a result of his father's guiding hand and example. On this point he noted that he was greatly "stimulated by the teachings of my Father who had been in public life during the greater part of his career." Further, his father's example "stimulated my ambition to attain what is known as success among public men."

Unfortunately, the general enjoyed little success in national politics, a fact that had a negative influence on Walter George. The boy's father failed to attain immediate political preferment on arriving in Philadelphia, but his luck soon turned. Within a year, he accepted an appointment at Panama as American consul. The general left his family at home due to unsanitary conditions in Panama. After a stay of two years, the general returned home in the summer of 1868 to attend a mass political meeting of Democrats in New York. He invited his eldest son to attend. There Walter George, now a precocious fourteen, had his first experience of a national political gathering. He was impressed at the sight of former Confederate and Union officers mixing in a spirit of comradeship and joining together in a common cause to nominate General Winfield Scott Hancock as Democratic candidate for the presidency. The effort failed. The boy returned to Philadelphia, the father to Panama.

The general soon lost his post and his fortunes steadily declined. In spite of his failure in the political world, the former soldier nevertheless left an important legacy to his son, because his ventures in politics and others phases of public life had a decisive effect. First, through his father, the boy saw and met many local, state, and national leaders. It was this kind of exposure that led to his ease, in later years, in talking with diplomatic, religious, military, business and political leaders. Second, the father's failure in politics deterred the son from seeking to exercise the family proclivity for public life to the exclusion of all else. Although Walter George would run for Congress in 1886 and for Register of Wills in Philadelphia in 1917—unsuccessfully in both cases—his law practice was always his prime concern. Third, the general's poor health and his failure to secure a permanent position through his political efforts left the Smith family in straitened financial circumstances, necessitating Walter George's early assumption of responsibility for the family's well-being. It was under considerable hardship that the General's eldest son completed his education.

Walter George finished his preparatory schooling at Episcopal with a diploma in classics in June, 1869, and prepared to enter the University of Pennsylvania in the autumn. Placed on the roll of the

Class of '73 as "Smith #VII," one of a class of sixty-six, Walter George attempted to pursue his degree under very unfortunate circumstances, that called forth all his tenacity and forthrightness of purpose. Although well grounded at the academy, his preparation for the university was hurried and there were gaps in his training. To compound his problem his father, wanting his son to complete his education as soon as possible to conserve limited family financial resources, implored university officials to admit young Smith to the sophomore class. Permission was fortunately denied. As it was he was compelled to press himself to his fullest capacity to complete the degree requirements. Plagued by anxieties at home over the lack of money, he frequently attended class without textbooks, not having the wherewithal to purchase them. He often learned his lessons by paying close attention to the recitations of his classmates. Not until his last year was he able to implement his meager resources by tutoring. No doubt the boy had to contribute some of his earnings to help meet the annual tuition of $150.00.

Smith took the classical course which included French, Greek, Latin, rhetoric, logic, English, mathematics, physics and chemistry. Since he believed them to be prerequisite to entering public life he also took courses in history, international law, and public speaking. Scholarship was the point of emphasis in those days; the student was not distracted by the all-absorbing atmosphere of athletics that would later invade the university campus. *The University Record*, as the University of Pennsylvania yearbook is called, noted that although a crew, a baseball nine, and a cricket eleven were active, athletics was not the outstanding pastime.

At the university Smith began to develop abilities that made for a more effective, better rounded personality. At his father's suggestion he elected courses in public speaking and composition. These disciplines added immeasurably to his skill to communicate from the podium or from the printed page. As time passed he gained poise, assurance, and effectiveness both as a public speaker and as a publicist.

Furthermore, Smith made numerous contacts at the university that prepared him to work with all sorts and conditions of men. He studied under professors who brought to the classroom not only values and ideas that broadened his outlook but also expertise in their respective fields that developed his latent talents. His association with these scholars added considerable breadth to Smith's character.

The young student also made many life-long friends while at the university. He joined the Phi Kappa Sigma fraternity, the Zelosophic Literary Society, and the Latin Club. He became intimate with Theodore B. Stork, Randall Morgan, Samuel T. Bodine, and Joseph S. Neff, adding them to his coterie of close, life-long friends. Other students whom he liked were H. R. Wharton, Robert Meade Smith, Henry Pleasants, and Charles P. Keith. As is so often the case, these associations were important because in later life, as Smith wrote, the strongest influence in his life, aside from his home environment, was "the companionship formed while at college."

His finances circumscribed by the reverses suffered by his father, his time consumed by the long journey to and from the university and by the added responsibility of tutoring, Smith had few spare hours for extracurricular activities. Several afternoons a week he went to the home of Mr. and Mrs. Rodman Abbott to tutor their son Louis in the finer points of Latin grammar. The fees thus earned were his first, and without them he could hardly have met his expenses. The Abbotts not only invited Smith to tutor their son, but they also accepted him socially and often invited him to dine with them. This was later to prove most fortunate for the aspiring young man.

A member of the class of '73, Smith was one of "66 members all told—short, tall, fat, thin, bold, serious, good, naughty fellows."[7] These fellows thought well enough of Smith to elect him their class president. One member later remarked: "We were always at loggerheads in our class, but there was one thing on which we were at one and that was that Walter should be our President." As class president Smith had an opportunity to develop the arts of presiding over public meetings and making public speeches, talents that would serve him well in the later years of his life. *The University Record* observed that Smith presided at Class Day ceremonies and conducted the festivities with considerable aplomb. He also presided over Ivy Day activities at which the class of '73 revived the old custom of planting a sprig of ivy, an event still marked by a marble slab fixed in the wall of College Hall bearing the inscription: "Ivy planted by the class of '73, June 7th, 1873."[8] On this occasion Smith also presented to W. Wilkins Carr the "wooden spoon," an award given the most popular man in the class. He received his degree on

June 26, 1873, and, as class president, made one of the numerous speeches that usually accompany commencement.

LAW SCHOOL

The Class of '73, the first to graduate on the West Philadelphia campus, numbered only thirty-six out of the initial sixty-six that had matriculated four years earlier. The class regarded as its strong points its "gentlemanliness" (a trait often attributed to Smith in later years), and its belief in "progress." Of the thirty-six who graduated, the majority entered the professions of law, medicine, engineering, the clergy, and teaching and became leaders of the community.

Smith was not quite twenty years old when he made the decision, with the aid of his father, to study law. His father, who had begun a small practice in Philadelphia, introduced him to Furman Sheppard. This eminent lawyer, who had twice served as District Attorney of Philadelphia, agreed to act as the younger Smith's preceptor. The study of law was a natural goal for Walter George, in light of the long line of attorneys on both sides of his family tree. But it soon became evident that pursuit of a law degree would have to be postponed. The family's straitened financial circumstances demanded that the young university graduate contribute to its support.

With the aid of a relative of his father Walter George obtained an appointment as clerk in the office of G. Clinton Gardener, General Superintendent of the Pennsylvania Railroad at Altoona. Early in September, 1873, Smith reported for his job, which paid him $45.00 per month.

The Altoona phase of his life was dull and uneventful. The chief clerk assigned him to work in the Department of Conducting Transportation. Assistant to a typical clerk of the old school, Smith had the task of adding up long columns of figures, a task for which he considered himself "utterly incompetent." His "abominable handwriting" must certainly have been a handicap. But with practice the work became easier and Walter George quickly fell into a routine that was none too taxing. What proved to be the only interesting interlude of the Altoona period was a visit to the nation's capital, where Walter George attended a White House reception given by President Grant, his father's old commander.

After his brief holiday in Washington Smith returned to his

work-a-day position in provincial Altoona, but not for long. He soon recognized that this job held no future, because his liberal arts education had not fitted him for a career with the railroad. Most of his peers in the company were graduates in mechanical or civil engineering. Smith soon concluded that he should renew his application to Dr. James W. Robbins, headmaster of Episcopal Academy, for a post on the school's faculty. This position would enable him to study law. It seems that Robbins had offered him such a position prior to his taking the clerkship at Altoona but, feeling honor bound to accept the railroad post, he had then turned down the teaching job. Dr. Robbins renewed the offer of a mastership and Smith promptly accepted.

He was only twenty-one when he returned to Philadelphia in early 1875 to assume his post at the Academy. Smith would remain there until June 30, 1879, when he was ready to resume preparation for his life's profession. These days were busy ones for the young man. He spent his mornings teaching elementary English and Latin at the Academy and his afternoons either attending lectures at the Law School or tutoring. His meager earnings were now supplemented by a small legacy from his Uncle Walter George, so that he was able to help out his family and at the same time pursue his legal studies at the University of Pennsylvania Law School. He was always deeply grateful to Dr. Robbins, whose friendship and offer of a job made his study of law possible.

Although he became a student of several branches of the law and was eventually awarded two honorary doctor of laws degrees, Smith later concluded that he had achieved only a bare minimum foundation in law at law school. He came to his law lectures after spending five hours teaching at the Academy, and simply lacked the physical stamina to do the necessary work that would enable him to obtain depth in his studies. Reading long court decisions, written in the tortuous, discursive style of the lawyer, required a fresh mind. He maintained that his work in the law school fitted him only "superficially" for the bar and that he got by in class by utilizing his "perceptive powers." He lacked the time to study his class notes at home and usually made up for this omission while traveling across town on the street car.

Smith's hours were indeed precious, but he did take time out to enjoy some social activities during the great Centennial Exhibition in

1876. In company with his father, he attended a reception in honor of Emperor Dom Pedro of Brazil. He also found the time to join the Philadelphia Law Academy and to participate in its activities. With a group of his fellow students who had also associated with this organization Smith was instrumental in forming a Constitutional Club, which met periodically for the purpose of arguing questions on constitutional law. To facilitate the passing of bar examinations the group also organized a quiz class. During the summer of his final year in law school Smith spent his vacation with his brother Dehon, who was then preparing for the day when he would enter the religious life as a Passionist. The break from his duties was indeed welcome. With the coming of autumn Smith resumed his responsibilities, but he did find time to campaign for Samuel J. Tilden, the Democratic nominee for president in 1876.

In his final year in law school Smith's classmates elected him president of the class. At the suggestion of a classmate Smith delivered the Law Oration at commencement exercises on June 28, 1877. Taking as his subject "The Individual Responsibility of the Lawyer," he delivered an address that was well received. Chief Justice George Sharswood, who was present to address the class, praised Smith's efforts. From that time until his death in 1882 he was the younger man's friend and adviser.

A few days following commencement the twenty-two-year-old Smith was admitted to the bar. Now the years of preparation were over. Walter George Smith was ready to assume his dual responsibility as a citizen and a Philadelphia lawyer.

CHAPTER 2

A Philadelphia Lawyer

In 1877 Walter George Smith began his career as a Philadelphia lawyer with a number of disadvantages.[1] Roman Catholic in a city dominated by Episcopalians, Democrat in a center largely directed by staunch Republicans, rural Ohio-born in a metropolis in which the legal profession consisted largely of native-born Philadelphians—all of these increased for Smith the difficulties in getting a start. His father had not succeeded in the practice of law and had but few connections in that profession in the city. But Smith had inherited his mother's disposition, with its combination of ambition, self-abnegation, piety, patience, and industry. He was aware that he had chosen a vocation for which he deemed himself well-suited, unlike his father, and he began the practice of the law with firm determination to succeed. That he earned his place in his chosen profession—a profession for which Philadelphia has been so highly regarded—was because of his own talent, hard work, and several strokes of luck.

FIRST DISAPPOINTMENTS AND SUCCESSES

One of these good turns of fortune came while visiting the Abbotts,

13

whose son he continued to tutor. Asa Israel Fish was an elderly lawyer who frequented the Abbott home, and in 1875 Smith met the older man. Fish was favorably impressed with this young man who had the ability to study law and at the same time teach classics at the Academy. Two years later, following Smith's admission to the bar, Fish offered him a desk and a room in his small law office in the old Mercantile Library Building on Library Street.

Despite Fish's generosity the next two years were discouraging ones for Smith. The invalid condition of his father required the young lawyer to continue the support of his family, a responsibility that necessitated his retaining his mastership at the Academy. He supplemented his income by giving lessons in the afternoons and reporting for the Weekly Notes of Cases in the Court of Common Pleas No. 1. The one hundred dollars per month he earned just barely enabled him to meet family obligations. Since there seemed no escape from his salaried position, he had been unable to follow the advice of Judge Sharswood to open his own office and enter private practice. To a young lawyer bursting with ambition and with the desire to practice the profession for which he had been trained, such a situation must have been indeed frustrating.

His first fee of six dollars came from George Jackson, a Torresdale storekeeper who had given him a judgment to enter. With the help of George Stehr, Mr. Fish's assistant, and the Prothonotary's Office, Smith—as he put it—"managed the task." He commented that he felt some pride as he "jingled the statutory fee" in his pocket. His income was soon implemented when Judge Craig Biddle of the Court of Common Pleas No. 1 named him examiner of an equity case. Fees for additional equity cases followed. But Smith's fortunes soon rose even higher.

The death of Mr. Fish in the spring of 1879 was a mixed blessing for Walter George. Fish's demise cast him adrift, for the older man's office was then closed. On the other hand, luck came his way a second time. It was customary for members of the bar to hold a meeting in memory of a deceased member, and one was held for Fish. Facing the members of the bar with some trepidation, Smith paid tribute to the man who had been his friend and benefactor. Among those in the audience was Francis Rawle, an ambitious young lawyer who, in addition to holding the post of librarian at the Law Association Library, shared an office with Samuel Robb.

Rawle was impressed with young Smith and asked Smith's friend Bayard Henry for some details about him. Henry complied and later escorted Smith to Rawle's office at Fourth and Walnut. In their conversation Rawle advised him to give up his teaching post and offered him a desk in his office.

Francis Rawle, a member of an old Philadelphia family long connected with the bar, greatly influenced the course of Smith's career. He had a rather large general practice and although he could spare nothing from his own earnings he thought something could be done to increase Smith's prospects for increased income and a steady practice. Smith accepted the generous offer; at the conclusion of the schoolyear he resigned his teaching post and found himself established in the office of a man destined to be one of the city's most distinguished attorneys. Not only did Rawle obtain for him the sum of five dollars per month for reporting for the *American Law Review*, but he also engaged Smith to help him make his first revision of *Bouvier's Law Dictionary* (1883).

One of the founders of the American Bar Association, Rawle served as treasurer of that body from its inception in 1878 to 1902, when he was elected its president. In 1882 he introduced Smith into the association, an association of which he too would one day serve as president. At first Smith acted as a clerk for Rawle but he soon found himself "in the full tide of practice in all of the courts." Smith regarded Rawle as a "good business getter," since he had graduated from Harvard College and Law School and had numerous classmates in New York and elsewhere. These connections brought in additional clients from cities other than Philadelphia. Thus Smith not only tried cases for Rawle but also obtained some of his own.

In the early days before turning to corporation law, Smith developed an expertise as a trial lawyer with a specialty in homicide cases. Two cases are mentioned here because they indicate the social consciousness of the future progressive, eager to secure equal justice for all regardless of economic condition. To help him prepare his defense in the first case in 1879, he took as his associate Hampton L. Carson, a future attorney general for the Commonwealth of Pennsylvania. He and Carson, who would later be elected president of the American Bar Association and also gain a reputation as one of the city's leading attorneys, ably defended their client, Dennis O'Sullivan, and became fast friends.

O'Sullivan had lost a leg at the battle of Gettysburg and was now a hatter employed by the Stetson factory. That he had murdered his wife with a razor was an undisputed fact. Nevertheless Smith and Carson attempted to reduce the degree of murder by showing that it was not a deliberate, premediated act but one committed in a fit of rage by a man whose mind had deteriorated. A key point was their attempt to prove that the defendant was shaving with a razor at the time of the act. In a case fraught with high tension and emotion, Smith escorted the defendant's little girl to the stand where she testified that she had witnessed the deed. She added that her father had been shaving at the time of the murder and that he killed his wife after she had enraged him.

The case was successfully concluded; as Smith and his associate had hoped, the jury rendered a verdict of murder in the second degree.[2] The favorable conclusion of this case led to a friendship between Smith and James Ludlow, the presiding judge, and to a second murder case for Smith.

Judge Craig Biddle appointed Smith in late 1879 to defend Joseph McGurk, indicted for murder committed in the act of robbery some ten years earlier. Smith regarded the case as one of his most important because it involved the making of new law. He requested and obtained the assistance of his friend Effingham B. Morris, a young attorney who would soon be elected president of the Girrard Trust Company, one of Philadelphia's leading banks. Although Smith and his associate defended their client competently, a guilty verdict seemed virtually certain. However, Judge Thomas Elcock made a procedural error when charging the jury and Smith and Morris were therefore able to secure a new trial. But the district attorney set no specific date.

Aware that a statutory provision required the trial of all alleged criminals indicted for felony within two terms of court, Smith warned the district attorney that if the trial did not take place within the time specified by law he would seek a writ of *habeas corpus* and request the prisoner's discharge. His theory was that since the court had granted a new trial, the prisoner stood in the eyes of the law as though he had never stood trial. When the district attorney refused, Smith argued the case for discharge in court, but the judge ruled against his motion. Undismayed, Smith turned to the Supreme Court of Pennsylavania. Chief Justice Sharswood issued a writ of *certiorari,* calling the case up for review. At length Associate Justice Ulysses Mercur rendered the decision of the court, holding that a prisoner awaiting a new trial could be held in confinement indefinitely. In doing so, he made new law.

Although Smith was unsuccessful in his appeal to the Supreme Court, he and Morris, by showing that the murder was not a deliberate, premeditated act were able to get McGurk's charge reduced to second degree murder when the new trial came up in the spring of 1880. Thus Smith's second important criminal case was concluded in a relatively successful manner.[3]

Smith's able defense of O'Sullivan and McGurk not only acquainted him with the plight of Philadelphia's urban poor, it also brought him into contact with Judges Biddle, Ludlow, and Elcock, three of the city's most prominent jurists, and cemented his friendship with Carson and Morris, two men who would be among the city's leaders in future years. While these two cases enhanced his career, Smith also attributed some part of his later success to the prominent members of the bar whom he met through his association and participation in the activities of the Law Academy and other associations.

PROFESSIONAL ASSOCIATIONS

Membership in the Law Academy proved a vehicle for Smith's advancement. Peter S. Duponceau had founded the academy in 1829, making it one of the oldest legal associations in the nation. Eminent judges and leading members of the bar acted as Provost and Vice-Provost. The academy frequently held moot courts before which law students and young members of the bar argued cases prepared by the Argument Committee. Smith joined this institution and attended its meetings with great regularity during his early years at the bar. There he met the city's most distinguished attorneys: George W. Biddle, Richard G. McMurtrie, Peter McCall, John C. Bullitt, Samuel Dicksen, William Henry Rawle, Richard Vaux, and John Graver Johnson. In the politics of the academy in those days there was a clear line of demarcation between the students and lawyers who had come out of the more prominent law offices, and the others. Generally, the men who dominated the politics of the academy in the 1880s had received their training under the leading members of the bar. Smith aspired to political leadership in this organization, realizing it would further his badly handicapped start in the profession. Too, he hoped for social acceptance by the old line, prominent Philadelphia attorneys. After several setbacks Smith finally defeated his friend Bayard Henry in 1880 for the academy presidency. This stroke of fortune gave him a substantial boost in the profession and indicated a turn for the better in his career.

Smith's membership in the Lunch Club was also an indication of his growing status within the legal profession and of his social acceptance. Consisting of a group of older, prominent men and a small group of younger attorneys who would later achieve distinction, the Lunch Club was a meeting place for a small, select coterie of men who enjoyed each other's company. After serving themselves at the sideboard, members sat around a long table chatting about various topics, depending on the humor of those present. For example, they might "talk shop"; William H. Rawle, who had written on several law topics, or Stuart Patterson, professor at the Law School, might explicate on a point of law. On another occasion jest might be the order of the day, and Joseph C. Fraley or Charles Biddle, two of the wittiest members of the club, might regale their colleagues with funny stories. If religion were under discussion, Walter George or his friend Percy Keating might be holding forth at length on some point of Catholic dogma.[4] Smith enjoyed the comradeship of the club, and associating with distinguished members of the bar such as William H. Rawle, Bayard Henry, Galbraith Ward, Charles Biddle, J. Rodman Paul, Richard Cadwalader, and Sussex Davis. These associates undoubtedly furthered his career.

His affiliation with the Law Association of Philadelphia, as the Philadelphia Bar Association was then known, also helped him professionally. Organized in 1802 as the Law Library Company, it could lay claim to being one of the oldest legal associations in America. The first chancellor was the distinguished lawyer William Rawle, an ancestor of Smith's law partner. In the early days it existed to provide members with the facilities of a law library, but in 1827 it became known as the Law Association of Philadelphia and began offering greater services. Smith believed that local and state bar associations were necessary to developing a young lawyer and to raising the standards of the legal profession. He joined the movement to form a state bar association, a movement that came to fruition in the following decade when he became a charter member of the Pennsylvania Bar Association.

Just as membership in the Law Academy introduced him to the leading members of the Philadelphia bar, so his joining the American Bar Association in 1882 made it possible for him to meet and know many of the great lawyers in the United States. During the more than forty years that he was a member of the association, Smith attended the majority of its annual meetings and knew all of its presidents, "most of them on intimate terms." His affiliation with the association would have a marked effect on his career.

A DEMOCRAT IN POLITICS

Although he devoted much of his time to professional associations and directed most of his energy toward professional advancement, Smith from time to time in his career drifted into politics. The year 1880 marked one of the highpoints of his activities in national politics. He associated with a group to form the Young Men's Democratic Association in Philadelphia, a company he described as the "most virile Democratic Club known in many years." As a member of this political organization he worked with his father in campaigning for General Winfield Scott Hancock, the Democratic nominee for the presidency. He made a number of speeches that were well received, particularly one given to a meeting of veterans in Baltimore. But his efforts went for naught; Scott lost the election. Smith reminisced years later that his "disappointment was great" and that he "never felt the same enthusiasm for any political candidate." This statement apparently did not apply to his own candidacy, for in 1886 he ran a heated race for Congress in attempting to wrest the seat from a long-term Republican incumbent. Although an unsuccessful bid, the race indicates the political philosophy that the young lawyer later carried when he joined the ranks of Philadelphia's progressives.

On September 30, 1886, the nominating committee of the Democratic Convention for the 5th Congressional District advised Smith of his nomination to run for Congress. The *Philadelphia Public Ledger* noted that Smith, a member of the Young Men's Democratic Association, had been selected. The young attorney, it was observed, had served his party well by frequently presiding over Democratic meetings and by speaking on behalf of Democratic candidates for public office. Concerning his decision to run for election, Smith later concluded that "it was futile. The Democratic party in Pennsylvania was composed in its leadership of men without political vision, and with no principles beyond the acquisition of office. Of course there were exceptions, but I refer to the practical man."

Late in the summer of 1886, the outlook for the Democrats was very grim indeed. The party was split into various factions and could achieve no real harmony. Indeed, one faction frequently supported the Republican machine in order to win place and privilege. Corruption in government met the eye on every hand as the Republican network ran the city and state to suit the interests of machine members. Labor troubles and strikes abounded on all sides in the Friendly City. But realizing the party's dire need and aware of the depths to which American political life had dropped, Smith answered his party's call. In his letter of acceptance to 5th District headquarters, Smith revealed some important tenets of his political creed.

He announced that he stood for "honest enforcement of the Constitution and the laws of the Commonwealth. If elected," he asserted, he "would work to secure enactment of such laws as will protect the interests of working men from the encroachment of class legislation . . . and from hasty and ill-considered attempts to settle by law great social problems." Smith expressed the view that "the relations between capital and labor are to be settled upon a basis that will recognize their equal rights under the law." He affirmed his belief that it was "the duty of every patriotic citizen to discourage and denounce any infringement of the rights of property," and that "it is equally his duty to assist by every means in his power to elevate and advance the conditions of the wage worker." Smith concluded: "While I do not believe that legislation has ever been, or, in the nature of things, can be a universal remedy for the evils which arise in our social system, and which are brought painfully to our attention by the increasing number of strikes, lockouts and contentions between the laboring man and his employer, I am satisfied that much can be done by Congress and the State Legislature to change the conditions which produce or tend to produce these baleful consequences."[5]

Smith's decision to seek a better deal for the working man was well taken, for the city of Philadelphia, like many cities in the country, was beset with strikes. There were approximately 4,000 idle workers at the time and the city's major newspapers were full of stories of labor unrest. He made several speeches to large rallies, notably at the Academy of Music on October 9 and again on the last day of the month. His theme was the same as that expressed in his letter of acceptance cited above. He feared that the violence accompanying the growing industrialization of the country would lead to cataclysmic changes in the social, political, and economic fabric of the nation. The young lawyer believed an attorney had a place in politics because, as he would later assert: "Lawyers, as their name implies, are the only elements in the community who are expected to know the history and philosophy of law and legal institutions. They know the danger of sudden change. On them rests the duty of exercising a conservative influence at times when apprehension of danger excites the emotions."[6] But his effort was in vain, for Republicans were too well-entrenched. The voters went to the polls on November 2 and cast 23,488 votes for A. C. Harmer, the Republican incumbent, 13,306 votes for Smith, who ran second, and about 4,000 votes for the last place candidate.

The election can be summed up simply. Democrats were feuding, Republicans marched together. The democratic strategy of appealing to the vote of the common laboring man failed. The order of the day was protection for private property and protection for American industries. The election of 1886 was the first effort that Smith made to seek public office, but it would not be the last try for political laurels. In the following decade Smith, the 1880-style Mugwump, would join the ranks of Philadelphians bent on progressive urban reform.

The future progressive was not only unsuccessful in furthering his career in the political arena, he also failed to achieve advancement by political appointment, a step not infrequently followed by reform-minded citizens interested in municipal good government. During the decade of the 1880s Smith had hopes of preferment as a result of a fortuitous turn of state and national politics. Following the election of Robert E. Pattison as Democratic governor, he hoped for an appointment to the Court of Common Pleas Bench No. 3 when a vacancy occurred due to the death of his friend Judge James Ludlow in 1886. Since he had served the party well by making speeches and by running a vigorous campaign for Congress in 1886, an appointment seemed probable. Letters from Furman Sheppard, J. Sergeant Price, and Samuel Robb, all members of the bar in good standing, testified to Smith's qualifications. Price noted that Smith "was one of the brighter of the younger members of the Bar" and would in his opinion "make an excellent judge." Robb asserted that Smith's "industrious habits, attractive manners, and great pride in his profession," plus "his patience to listen" and his "courage in making decisions," were all traits of character that should qualify him for a judgeship. Furman Sheppard, his old preceptor, regarded him highly, writing that since his admission to the bar he had never ceased to be a student of the law.[7] But Smith had stiff competition, with five others mentioned as candidates for the judgeship. In 1886 the governor selected for the office Smith's friend Henry Reed, who later sent him many appointments to equity cases, the fees of which helped meet family obligations.

Although disappointed by Governor Pattison, Smith retained his hope for a place on the bench,[8] and many years later almost realized this ambition. His friend F. Amadée Bregy, the President Judge of Common Pleas No. 1, tried to obtain an appointment in his court for him; but Smith's opposition to the 1906 election of Republican Governor Edward B. Stuart made such an appointment impossible. While ardently desiring a judgeship and convinced he would "have made eventually a good judge," he nevertheless accepted his lot as a practicing lawyer. Smith's failure to obtain the much-desired judgeship did not really hurt him. Actually, it freed him to engage in many activities which eventually led him to receive national recognition.

National politics also worked to Smith's advantage in the 1880s. Following Grover Cleveland's election to the White House in 1883, there seemed a chance the young lawyer might obtain an appointment as United States District Attorney for Philadelphia. His uncle, Donn Piatt, a lawyer by profession, worked for the position for Smith. Piatt had given up his Cincinnati law practice and moved to New York City to assume the editorship of *Belford's Magazine*. Piatt had used an acid pen to good effect in excoriating the reconstruction policies and political scandals of the Grant administration, and had gained the admiration of many Democrats in Congress. He not only had influence in the national legislature, where fear of his pen created respect, but also among Cleveland's cabinet members. In 1888 Piatt tried to help the advancement of his young nephew by gaining the support of the President's Postmaster General D. M. Dickinson, of the Attorney General A. H. Garland, and of William E. Dorsheimer, a former congressman from New York and personal friend of Cleveland. His efforts were to no avail. The President selected John R. Read, assistant to District Attorney Henry S. Hagert, who had bettered Smith in the first McGurk case. Smith enjoyed a good relationship with Read, who later offered him a place in his office which Smith did not accept. As a consolation, he did receive a personal letter from Cleveland assuring him of his best wishes. This was the last time that Smith actively sought political appointment. Unlike his father, he realized that professional achievement was the road to success for him.

THE RISING YOUNG LAWYER: GRANT, TWAIN, DAVIS

Although he failed to obtain a position on the bench or in the district attorney's office, Smith advanced professionally, for in 1885 he was admitted to practice before the United States Supreme Court by Justice John F. Dillon. While associated with Rawle he had the chance to appear before that body in the case *Stephenson v. Brooklyn Cross-Town Railroad Co.*, a case involving patent infringements. John Stephenson had brought suit against the railroad company, Smith and Rawle's client, seeking to restrain it from a violation of patents on street cars. The two attorneys won their case before Judge William Butler in the United States District Court in Philadelphia and successfully represented their client before the Circuit Court for the Eastern District in New York, which dismissed the appeal. The high court upheld the Circuit Court's action.[9] It must have been gratifying to Smith to appear before Justice Stanley Matthews, a friend and schoolmate of his father who was then a very ill man.

Despite this achievement, Smith suffered great personal loss when his father died on December 14, 1887, in New York City. General Smith had not been successful in obtaining a permanent position following release from his post at Panama, forcing his eldest son to shoulder many of the family burdens. The general had thought of practicing law again, and at the suggestion of David Paul Brown, a prominent Philadelphia attorney, was admitted to the Bar of the Supreme Court of Pennsylvania on January 14, 1871. The general did not open an office, however, and beyond transacting some business before the United States Court of Claims he did not assume the responsibilities of an active lawyer. Walter George's brother Dehon, now Father Maurice of the Passionist order, celebrated the Requiem Mass at St. Dominic's Church, Holmesburg, the Smiths' parish church; and the general was buried in the churchyard. The death of his father, who had converted to the Catholic faith sometime before his death, caused Walter George much personal grief. He observed that "no man is just the same after he has lost his father." Losing what he considered a "guiding hand," Walter George was now aware that he must "stand on his own feet and become a center of strength to himself and others." He was only too well aware of his father's inadequacies and sought to profit from this knowledge. He commented that his father had "no real aptitude for the drudgery" of the law profession and that he always tried "to obtain success at a bound." This was why the general had "immersed himself in politics without a constituency at his back." Smith believed his father would have been far happier as a farmer or as a member of the regular army.

If the year 1880 had marked the turning point of Smith's career, certainly the years 1886-89 constituted the period when he began to prosper in his chosen profession. A rising young Philadelphia lawyer soon to make his mark on the American legal profession, Smith had the good fortune to become involved in two cases that greatly enhanced his legal career. The first concerned the sale of the memoirs of General Ulysses S. Grant, former United States President, while the second involved litigation between ex-President Jefferson Davis of the Confederate States of America and D. Appleton Company, the publisher of his book *The Rise and Fall of the Confederate Government*. Smith's partial success in the first case led to his appointment in the second.

In the Grant memoir suit Smith and his partner Francis Rawle represented Charles L. Webster and Samuel L. Clemens (Mark Twain), the owners of the copyright of General Grant's memoirs. They made an effort to restrain John Wanamaker, the Philadelphia merchant prince, and his partners Thomas Wanamaker and Robert G. Ogden, from selling the work.[10] Smith and his associate claimed that it was a subscription book and that Wanamaker had neither the right nor the title to sell it.

The former President had failed to win a third nomination in 1880. He then decided to enter the world of finance, a venture that ruined him. Grant had been compelled to sell much of his and his wife's property to repay his debts and was in straitened circumstances. To recoup his fortune Grant, like other war heroes before and after, turned to the pen. He completed his memoirs and arranged with Charles L. Webster and Co. to sell the work by subscription. It earned $450,000 in royalties. Grant died knowing his family was provided for by virtue of his success as an author. The general could hardly have foreseen that four lawsuits would result from his book.

Walter George was involved in three of these cases related to the book by Grant, who had known the young attorney and his family. It was a penurious, poorly attired twenty-year-old young man full of self-doubt who had met the President of the United States at the White House reception on that cold day in 1875. No longer shy and awkward, but on the threshhold of a brilliant law practice, it was a poised, self-assured Smith who took the initiative and commenced work on the case while his partner was absent on vacation. On Rawle's return the two lawyers worked out a plan of action. Their strategy was to obtain an injunction against the defendants to stop them from selling the book, pending the final decision of the court. Since the case involved parties from different states, it had to be brought before a federal court. Accordingly, on July 22, 1886, Smith and Rawle made application to Judge William Butler in the United States District Court in Philadelphia on behalf of Webster and Clemens, for a preliminary injunction to restrain Wanamaker and partners from selling the book.[11]

Public interest ran high in this case, and Smith and his associate argued on August 3 before a courtroom crowded with lawyers and bookdealers. Mark Twain appeared in court in a light grey suit, carrying a high white top hat in his hand. There was a swing in his step as he swaggered over to the table and took a seat beside his two attorneys. With his long, droopy moustache, the writer must have been an impressive sight. However, he did not seem impressed as Smith opened the case, for he tipped his chair back and soon fell asleep.

On August 9 Judge Butler rendered his decision. His denial of the application for the injunction meant loss of the case against Wanamaker.

Although he lost the case against the Philadelphia merchant, Smith personally achieved three valuable ends: first, the case gave him the opportunity to work with the prestigious New York law firm of Alexander and Green; second, he had the opportunity to test his forensic talent before his peers at the Philadelphia bar and increase his good repute among members of the city's legal fraternity; and third, the trial gave him maximum exposure to the press which spread his name across the nation. The press covered the case from start to finish. On August 3 at least nine stories covering the petition for preliminary injunction appeared in the Philadelphia *Evening Bulletin, Evening Star, Herald, News, Press,* and *Telegraph* as well as in the New York *Post, Record,* and *Tribune.* On the following day no less than ten other newspapers ran the story: the Philadelphia *Inquirer, Press, Public Ledger, Record, Times,* the *New York Star, Times, Tribune, World,* and the *St. Louis Globe Democrat.* From August 5th to 7th five more newspapers carried accounts of the case: the *Philadelphia Inquirer, Savannah Morning News, Chicago Herald, Albany Argus,* and the *Pittsburgh Dispatch.*[12]

Smith was quite disappointed in the outcome of the case with the Philadelphia merchant. Not only was Wanamaker free to dispose of the two hundred books remaining in his possession for the price of $5.50, or $1.50 below the subscription price of $7.00 but, as Smith wrote, "Wanamaker having done the mischief went scot-free of liability. It was a foolish and destructive act on his part." George W.. Childs, part-owner and publisher of the *Philadelphia Public Ledger,* disclosed to Smith that he "had pleaded with him [Wanamaker] not to renew the sale of the books but to no purpose." Concerning Wanamaker's conduct Smith left this estimate: "The character of this merchant prince has been the subject of much praise and animadversion. In recent years I have seen him often in action. There is predominating his subconsciousness the natural result of the years he has spent in commercializing every emotion and every event or desire by publicity, a feeling hard to describe. He is," Smith continued, "very kindly, he is not ungenerous, but one always doubts the sincerity of him 'who doth protest too much.' He is now a very old man and his constructive work is done. I think the verdict will be that he has never successfully entered other fields than those connected with his great business."

Smith and Rawle represented Mark Twain in two other suits involving Grant's book. On July 24, 1886 the two attorneys brought action against Joseph M. Stoddart Co. for $13,302.43. In a third case they filed suit against Hubbard Brothers for $30,630.25. It appears that the two agents had contracted with Webster & Co. to sell books only to subscribers, but then violated the contract by selling to bookdealers as well. The cases were both decided for Mark Twain, the court awarding $13,200.73 in the Stoddart case and $31,433.33 in the Hubbard case. Ironically, the latter two cases did not receive as much publicity as the Wanamaker suit, and the writer did not take the interest in them that he took in the Wanamaker case.[13] At all events, Smith's legal career was enhanced and he was later recommended to represent Jefferson Davis in a suit of a similar nature. But during the interim between the two suits Smith's status changed. Rawle decided to sever their relationship late in the summer of 1889. Smith had found their association perfectly acceptable, for he had advanced from the position of a "sort of managing clerk" to that of "partner on a division of fees in the proportion of two-thirds to him and one-third to me." Smith desired to retain the partnership since he reasoned they could have continued their association and in a few years have built up a thriving practice. Smith made no complaint but apparently there was some hard feeling. At any rate, Smith observed that "the bar at large with whom he [Rawle] was not popular, were indignant. From all sides came evidences of goodwill and substantial aid."

Smith formed an association with Charles Biddle and William Rudolph Smith. They joined Henry Austie Smith, the younger brother of William Rudolph and took offices at 505 Chestnut Street. Charles Biddle was a grandson of Nicholas Biddle of the United States Bank and a son of Colonel Charles J. Biddle of Andalusia, a man whom Walter George visited at his ancestral home as a boy to hear tales of the Mexican and Civil Wars. Charles Biddle had studied law in the office of George W. Biddle, to whose firm he later returned and became a senior partner. William Rudolph Smith remained associated with Smith until his own death in 1922.

This change in Smith's partnership with Rawle occurred just at the time circumstances converged to make possible his involvement in the Davis case.[14] Smith had related his experience in the Grant suit to his Uncle, Donn Piatt, who was still the editor of *Belford's Magazine*. In addition to being on friendly terms with many Southern politicians, Piatt also knew Jefferson Davis and had agreed to publish one of Davis's articles concerning the Civil War. Davis was successful as a storyteller, and he later decided to write a book defending his role in the Confederacy. He hoped to replenish by it his badly depleted financial resources which, like those of General Grant, had been lost in a business venture. In April, 1875, he accepted the offer of Major W. T. Walthall, an ex-Mississippi soldier who had exhibited some skill at writing about the war, to aid him in the preparation of his book. Walthall concluded an arrangement with D. Appleton Publishing Company for the publication of the work, which was completed in 1881.

However, the book did not net Davis the high return that he had anticipated and, in pecuniary difficulties, jealous of the success of Grant's book, and disenchanted with D. Appleton, he sought legal advice as he suspected his publisher was not abiding by their contract. Davis consulted Piatt, who had experience in the legal and publishing worlds, and the former attorney suggested that he retain George Hoadly, a former governor of Ohio then practicing law in New York as a member of the wellknown firm of Hoadly, Lauterbach, and Johnson. Piatt recalled his young nephew's experience in the Grant case and suggested to Davis that he also retain Walter George Smith.

As in the Grant case, Smith acquired further experience by representing Davis. In working with Governor Hoadly he was associating himself with a lawyer of good repute. Hoadly had been a partner of Salmon Chase in Cincinnati, where he had worked with Walter George's father. Smith made numerous trips to New York to confer with the elderly attorney. Although the Davis case did not attract the attention of the press to the extent that the Grant case did, it nevertheless aroused considerable public interest, giving Smith further exposure to the public and to the legal community.

Smith and Hoadly drew up a plan of action which called for an examination of the accounts of the publisher and the initiation of an arbitration proceeding, the normal step in such cases. In this way Davis could confront D. Appleton with any violation of the contract. Smith's role in the case was to examine D. Appleton's account books to determine if it owed Davis any royalties. He soon discovered that Appleton owed the former Confederate president the sum of $8,134.98. But before he and Hoadly were able to initiate arbitration proceedings Smith had to withdraw from the case in order to marry and take an extended wedding trip.

The young lawyer returned to the case in the autumn of the following year to learn from his associate that the arbitration had gone against Davis, who had died at the end of 1889. But that did not end the litigation, for in the latter part of the year Hoadly obtained evidence indicating conclusively that D. Appleton owed Mrs. Davis approximately $5,000.00.

In 1890 Smith's law practice was on a sound footing, and he had every expectation of a successful career. It is now necessary to explain the events that transpired between January and September, 1890, when Smith temporarily absented himself from the Davis case. In this interim period he married and took an extended wedding trip with his bride Elizabeth L. Drexel, a daughter of Francis Anthony Drexel, a member of the illustrious House of Drexel, the premier Philadelphia banking establishment.

MARRIAGE TO ELIZABETH DREXEL

Smith's romance with Elizabeth had ripened slowly. Now a mature man, he had found the woman he thought suitable to be his wife, but felt that he could not in good conscience ask for her hand in marriage until he had attained some degree of success in his profession.[15] The Grant and Davis cases and his newly-formed legal association with Biddle and the Smiths apparently convinced him that he had achieved sufficient professional status to propose marriage.

A portrait made about this time indicates that he was a man of large stature. Actually, although standing above six feet in height, he was slender. He resembled his mother in appearance; dark hair, a high, broad forehead, a well-shaped head, a firm chin, and a prominent, acquiline nose. The strong jaw, the firm set of his lips, the thick black eyebrows, and the fixed gaze of his deep set eyes gave him an air of determination. His dress was sober but fashionable. Overall, his appearance was commanding. The serious countenance denoted the man of reflection and intelligence. He has been described by those who knew him as having a "dignified, distinguished bearing," an "elegant nonchalance," a "scholarly appearance." Certainly, he was a man of confidence. In the middle years he had the sort of quiet arrogance that results from self-assurance. Indeed, he has been called a "proud man." In later years this quality would mellow and the appearance of arrogance, pride, and self-assurance would give way to one of dignified compassion. The Philadelphia lawyer had the quiet, courtly manner of a gentleman, and a sense of *noblesse oblige*.

Although blessed with many virtues, Smith was not without faults. He possessed an exceedingly perceptive mind and was quick to exhibit impatience with those who did not understand the problem at hand as quickly as himself. He was aware that success in life went to those perceptive, intelligent people who had the right contacts for advancement. Smith was readily liked by older, successful men who frequently offered to help him, and made it his purpose to meet and cultivate those who could aid him to achieve his goals. He was also possessed of a physical ailment, a chronic respiratory condition that plagued him throughout his life.

To his marriage Smith brought rare personal qualities which, like fine steel, had been tempered by the fires of adversity and shaped by the hammer of the world's hard realities. Years of caring for his family had given him a sense of responsibility; striving for an education in the face of hardship added character; seeking success in a profession fraught with innumerable handicaps gave determination; being well-born and well-connected in Ohio made him all the more determined to gain social and professional acceptance in Philadelphia.

Smith had known his intended for almost twenty years—perhaps from the day when Elizabeth's father first brought his family in June, 1871, to St. Michel, the Drexel summer home at Torresdale. A wealthy banker, Drexel had purchased a farm of about ninety acres located on the Red Lion Road not far from the Smith home. Shortly after that the younger generation of Smiths at St. Helen's, as the Smiths called their home, and the Drexel girls from St. Michel became close friends.[16] In those days the Drexels did not go often to town during the summer; but as the Franco-Prussian War was still going on, Mr. Drexel traveled daily to his office on the eight o'clock boat and returned at four. No doubt when Smith returned to classes in the autumn he frequently accompanied the older man whose daughter he would one day marry.

Elizabeth Drexel grew up in a happy, deeply religious environment. Emma Bouvier Drexel saw to the upbringing of the three girls, treating all alike; and she was accepted by the older girls as their own mother. Elizabeth attended the convent school run by the Religious of the Sacred Heart, duly made her First Communion at age twelve and, for some unexplained reason, made her debut belatedly in 1876 at the time of the Centennial celebration. Hers was a life of servants, governesses, travel to Europe, and fine clothes; but religion was a strong undercurrent running through her life. Although a young lady of wealth and privilege, Elizabeth's parents encouraged her from an early age to serve God and to utilize her bountiful wealth for helping the less fortunate.

Francis Drexel, a widower since 1883, died in 1885 and left Elizabeth and her two sisters a considerable fortune. The girls received in three equal shares the proceeds from a trust of about $14 million. Walter George's fiancée was a wealthy woman, for her annual income amounted to about $190,000.

The year 1889 brought about changes in the lives of the three Drexel girls. Louise married wealthy Edward Morrell, a prominent Philadelphia attorney, Katherine made the decision to enter the religious life, preparatory to founding her own religious order, while Elizabeth became engaged to Walter George.

The couple approached marriage with maturity and a clear idea of its obligations. Walter had selected for his wife a woman of thirty-four. A marble bust of Elizabeth in the possession of the Sisters of the Blessed Sacrament, the order founded by Katherine Drexel, reveals her to have had a certain patrician air, with a strong nose, gentle chin, and a long and graceful neck. A more revealing full-length photograph shows her as a lovely and warm person—sweet and affectionate looking—with doe-like blue eyes and full lips. She was tall and slim, with her long blond hair upswept at the back of her neck.

Although anticipating his marriage, Smith nevertheless experienced considerable anxieties lest the Drexel family not accept him. He wrote Sister Katherine, saying, "You will be glad to know that all of your relatives beginning with your Uncle Anthony have given me the kindest welcome. Elizabeth said to me once that I was a proud man, and perhaps you have thought so too. Never have I felt so proud and at the same time so humble, as I do to receive such a trust in such a way."[17]

Their engagement was the coming together of two kindred spirits. George W. Childs, the Philadelphia newspaper publisher and honorary "uncle" of the Drexel girls, wrote Kate at Christmas that Walter and Elizabeth were "most happy, and they seem so well suited to each other."[18] Elizabeth herself had written just previous to this: "The world has changed its aspect considerably for me and for Walter . . . and you would scarcely believe how used we have gotten to each other, how much we feel and judge alike on many subjects, and how happy we are in the prospect of each other's support and companionship through life. We seem to have pleased all the world and ourselves besides."[19] The bride-to-be followed with another letter to Kate giving an excellent picture of her intended: "It is a gloomy Sunday, and Walter is easily stretched in a chair opposite me hunting through the Sunday Times and Press for some small notice of our united names. He is at the same time smoking and whistling quietly to himself." She closed with the comment: "Altogether, Kitten mine, I think you would have the greatest difficulty in reconstructing out of the frivolous lightminded gentleman in the easy chair, chuckling over the silly Sunday paper jokes, our elegant, nonchalant, classical friend of former days. Louise and I have puzzled over the attempt in vain."[20] While the two sisters may have puzzled over the change in Walter, there is really little cause to wonder. His lightheartedness stemmed from his satisfaction and from his anticipation of a life with his beautiful and desirable heiress. On the other hand, Elizabeth too had cause for satisfaction for Walter was a handsome man, one of character and of proven ability to succeed in his profession. Though lacking in wealth, his many fine qualities made him a good catch.

Walter George Smith and Elizabeth Langstroth Drexel married on January 7, 1890, in St. Dominic's Church with Archbishop Patrick J. Ryan presiding. The bride was attended by her sister Louise and given away by her uncle Anthony Drexel. The groom was attended by his brother Adrian as best man. A nuptial mass was celebrated by Father Maurice, brother of the groom, after the marriage ceremony. Then the wedding party and guests, consisting of some of Philadelphia's oldest and most prominent families, traveled via carriage to St. Michel for the reception. Following the reception the couple departed for an extensive wedding trip.

Elizabeth treated her little-traveled husband to the type of European tour taken by fashionable Americans in the late 19th century. Elizabeth's letters and Smith's "Autobiography" provide an interesting journal of their jaunt. The sea voyage from New York to Le Havre afforded him the opportunity to indulge his weakness for associating with the wealthy, the important, the wellborn. Stops at

Paris, Lourdes, and Biarritz permitted him to enjoy a life of ease and to make a pilgrimage at the wellknown shrine. From Nimes Elizabeth wrote Grace Smith a prize verbal picture, depicting her fastidious husband, attired in a newly acquired smoking jacket, seated at a writing table with a cigar in one hand and a pen in the other, busily writing.[21] They broke their journey on the Riviera to stay a few days with Junius S. Morgan, the head of the House of Morgan. At Monte Carlo the couple visited Anthony Drexel, Elizabeth's cousin. They traveled via San Remo and Genoa to Florence where the pregnant Elizabeth required rest and medical care. Her letters show Smith to have been a willing servant and "a faithful nurse" during her illness.[22] When his wife's recovery was assured Smith made a fleeting trip to Rome, there to tour the Eternal City and obtain a private audience with Pope Benedict XV. On his return to Florence in mid-July the Smiths began to think of the return home. Elizabeth wrote the faithful Miss Cassidy to prepare St. Michel, which she had purchased from the Drexel estate for herself and Walter, for their arrival in September.[23] They traveled elegantly and leisurely via Milan, Interlaken, and Paris to England, where a sojourn at Royal Leamington Spa gave Smith the opportunity to visit the famous Bodleian Library at Oxford.

Their tour over, they sailed for home on August 30 and arrived on September 7 at Torresdale. Elizabeth and Walter apparently approached the sloping landscape and beautiful gardens of St. Michel with great anticipation, ready to settle down to a life they hoped would soon be blessed with the birth of Elizabeth's baby, due in about three months.

The first few days at home were taken up with unpacking, distributing gifts, entertaining relatives, and picking up the threads of life. Elizabeth had purchased St. Michel so that she and Walter could live there, and her time was consumed with putting the large house in running order. Smith was confident that she was receiving excellent treatment at the hands of her physician, and he returned to his law practice.

But all was not well with Elizabeth. On September 24, following a walk to the nearby estate of San José, the Morrell home, she complained of discomfort. The next day her physician called and expressed the opinion that she should have no cause to worry. Shortly afterwards the expectant mother was "seized with violent convulsions." No doubt the attack led on the next day to the premature birth of her baby. On the 26th Elizabeth was delivered of a still-born son and she expired shortly after.

The death of his beloved wife of a few short months stunned Smith. The loss of a woman with all of the desirable qualities that a man of his station in life could desire—only to have her taken from his grasp at the very moment when his life was to be fulfilled with the birth of a son—must have doubled the magnitude of his loss.

On October Father Maurice, who a few short months before had celebrated the couple's nuptial mass, sang the requiem at the funeral in the chapel at Eden Hall. Elizabeth was interred in the crypt beneath the Lady Chapel at Eden Hall.

The full extent of his loss came to him only after the funeral. His letters to Sister Katherine reveal his depression. While still at St. Michel he wrote: "I have been much troubled of late, and it seems almost harder to bear my loss than at first, but I feel hopeful that I may be strengthened."[24] While they comforted him, his letters to Sister Katherine indicate that he was still confused and emotionally distraught.[25] His sister Betty (Mrs. E. B. Esler) came to comfort him. He did not plan to remain at St. Michel, even though Elizabeth had willed it to him, because Louise Morrell wished him to give up the property. In exchange for St. Michel, the executors of the Drexel estate presented Smith a handsome, red brick town house at 1814 Spruce Street, valued at $18,000; in addition, as provided in Elizabeth's will, he was paid a sum equal to the appraised value of the St. Michel estate. This figure amounted to $100,000.[26] Smith returned to live with his family in the Torresdale house.

Contrary to what might be expected, Smith did not inherit a vast sum from his wife. Francis A. Drexel's will had left a sum of approximately $14 million in trust for his three daughters, each to receive one-third of the income after deductions for numerous charities. Article VI of the will provided that should a daughter die without issue her portion would then revert to the estate and be divided between the remaining sisters. Since her son was born dead, Elizabeth's income from the estate was divided equally between Louise and Katherine.[27] Elizabeth had also spent much of her income on numerous charities, the most noteworthy being St. Francis's Industrial School at Eddington, Pa. Smith, therefore, received nothing directly from the Drexel estate but he did inherit approximately $118,000 from Elizabeth's property.

While Elizabeth's death caused Walter great anguish, his marriage to her had nevertheless brought him a measure of security hitherto unknown. More important, it had opened many doors for him both socially and professionally. On this point Smith left a brief but revealing statement: "Looking back on this period of my life, I believe I could have continued to support my family on the proceeds of my practice, but it is not likely I should have attained any pronounced success, since I lacked the background of family influence or political strength or commercial value, any one of which would have pushed me indefinitely." Remarking on his background he observed, "I was not a Philadelphian by birth, was a Catholic in religion, without Irish blood, and had no commercial connections." Yet Smith was convinced of his own talent as a lawyer and of his ability to get on: "On the other hand, though of delicate physique, I was in good health, comparatively young for a professional man, being then thirty-six. I knew the bar and the bench and counted many friends among them." While the Drexel family might not properly be styled "old" Philadelphia, it certainly fitted into that important category of "proper" Philadelphia, and his marriage into that family provided him with the opportunity that would lead him to pronounced success in his profession and, like his late wife and many reform-minded Americans, to useful service for his fellow-man.

Although Smith's grief over Elizabeth's death apparently was very deep and lasting, he gradually recovered from his loss. Encouraged by a marble bust of Elizabeth which he kept at his bedside, he and his family moved into the newly-inherited house on Spruce Street where he lived for the next ten years, going to Torresdale only for the summer months. He did not remarry; as was often the case in that day he choose to bring his brothers and sisters about him and to find familial warmth within the confines of those for whom he had long felt a lasting responsibility. He was now ready to enter that phase of his life which would be most productive and would see him pursue new interests. Almost prophetic about his new way of life, he had written Sister Katherine: "Doubtless new interests, new influences will distract a mind that seems now capable of but one sorrowing habit."[28]

During the period following his wife's death, Smith experienced greater success in his law practice. Although he was not a member of one of the old, established firms of Philadelphia, he nevertheless enjoyed a good reputation among lawyers at the bar. In addition to expanding his practice he worked for higher ethics in his profession and for the improvement of justice in several areas of the law, for Smith had a high sense of the lawyer's public responsibility. He viewed the attorney as a member of a conservative profession who should not only uphold the law but act "as a barrier against ill-judged visionary and hasty schemes for settling the inevitable evils arising from the conflict of human passions."[29]

In an address entitled "The Lawyer as a Citizen," delivered to the Rhode Island Bar Association in 1912, Smith observed: "Obviously, the man whose whole life is devoted to the practical application of the law to the conduct of affairs, is best fitted to be the representative of a law-abiding people—to interpret the existing law and to expand its fundamental principles to new emergencies." He was aware of the growing discontent in the nation with the American political system and of increasing attacks on it from every hand, and suggested: "In such a struggle the lawyer's only duty as a citizen is plain. Learned in the history of his profession, knowing that justice is the aim of all well ordered government, convinced that the principles of the bill of rights are immutable, let him meet the modern heresies with sound and patient argument and he will be following worthily the example of those great men who have made an enduring fame, not alone as lawyers, but as patriots and lovers of mankind."[30] This sense of responsibility propelled Smith into the struggle to right the evils in American social, economic, and political institutions during the progressive era.

CHAPTER 3

Profile of a Catholic, Philadelphia Progressive

During the decade following his wife's death Walter George Smith joined the ranks of Americans devoted to the reform of social, political, and economic institutions. This was in response to the sense of crisis that pervaded the nation during the closing years of the 19th century.[1] The sense of impending crisis produced a widespread reaction. Muckrakers focused the attention of the populace on the ills of American social, political, and economic institutions that could no longer meet the needs of a growing, urban-industrial society. Little wonder that the cries of reform heard on every hand induced a large number of men and women—styled progressives—to heed the call. Who were these progressives?

THE TURN OF THE CENTURY PROGRESSIVE

Historians are engaged in a continuing debate about the biographical background of these reformers, their values, and the content of their program. An older group of historians of the progressive era has tried to demonstrate that it is possible to draw a profile of the progressive reformer. They maintain that he was urban, Protestant, middle class, college educated, professional, economically secure, under forty, and new to politics.[2] Ultimately, George E. Mowry and Richard Hofstadter devised the theory of the "status revolution", a thesis that attributes the progressive era to the old urban middle classes trying to preserve their position against the rising plutocrats and workers.[3]

Subsequent historians questioned the validity of the progressive profile and the "status revolution" thesis. Samuel P. Hays, for example, asserted that the "source of support for reform in municipal government did not come from the lower or middle classes, but from the upper class."[4] Otis L. Graham, Jr. found that many urban reformers were from the ranks of the "very rich" and that many had been reared on farms.[5] These studies argued historian Peter Filene, indicated variations of the progressive profile rather than outright rejections. But he also cited evidence that tends to undermine the "status revolution" thesis. He showed that a number of biographies of progressives contain profiles with traits identical to those of non-progressives.[6] Thus Filene concluded it is no longer possible to offer a simplistic interpretation of the progressive era as one in which the middle class seeks to protect its status from the plutocrats and the laboring masses.[7]

It is not only difficult to place progressives in a typology, it has also been demonstrated that progressives pursued no predetermined program, a factor that further weakens the progressive profile. It had normally been thought that progressives uniformly were interested in a wide spate of social, political, and economic reforms. But Filene has observed that these progressives in fact had many different goals. Since they frequently disagreed on aims, he has found that it is difficult to characterize the progressive phenomenon as a monolithic movement. Rather, he has shown that what has been described as a progressive movement was no movement at all but an amorphous, multi-faceted phenomenon. Moreover he has determined that many progressives actually opposed a number of reforms usually associated with the progressive program: labor legislation, women's suffrage, and prohibition.[8]

Filene has also suggested that the progressive profile loses further acceptance to the extent that progressives were actually motivated by different sets of values.[9] There is much to be said for this observation. On the one hand, historian Robert H. Wiebe viewed the progressive mind as optimistic, determined to effect rapid change through reform, and to achieve efficiency and order by expertise and improved administration.[10] On the other, George E. Mowry described the progressive as plagued by ambivalence: "at once nostalgic, envious, fearful, and yet confident about the future."[11] Richard Hofstadter, however, depicted the progressive as a socially genteel person who was anxious about the rapid pace of change because of his fondness for the past.[12]

An examination of Smith's profile and a further contrast of that one with those offered by other historians demonstrates the futility of attempting to place him into any limited typology. But it does permit one to draw some interesting conclusions about a Catholic, Philadelphia progressive whose profile includes several novel characteristics. In many respects Smith's background fits the progressive profile found in California, Baltimore, Iowa, Washington, and Massachusetts.[13] He had an urban Philadelphia background, was native-born of a good Protestant New England family that had associated with the Adams of Quincy, had a university and professional education, was young (under forty), and new to politics. But Smith's Catholic faith and his membership in Philadelphia's genteel elite set him apart from the progressive profile. As a Catholic, this conservative Philadelphia progressive provided a variation.

Smith's values also make it difficult to apply the profile to him. On the one hand, he was defensive and anxious about accomplishing too much change. This associate of genteel Philadelphia aristocrats wanted to participate in the process of change, to direct or control its direction, and to avoid excesses of any kind. Yet he was quite willing to make certain changes. He advocated urban political reform, the passage of uniform state commercial laws in the interest of greater efficiency in the transaction of interstate business, the passage of uniform divorce legislation to maintain social control and social cohesion, and higher education standards for the legal profession to keep out the unfit. Here is a paradox. How could Smith combine the genteel, defensive, slightly conservative values assigned by Hofstadter to the progressive with those assigned by Robert Wiebe, who claimed that the progressive mind was marked by an emphasis upon efficiency, expertise reform, and administration?

First, Smith was influenced by his times. There were ample grounds for his being able to combine seemingly diverse characteristics. There was a feeling of fear in his city of Philadelphia where urban disorders increased as the endless flow of immigrants continued to flood the industrial areas of the city. The conditions of life among the city's laboring masses were harsh. During the 1880s and 1890s Smith was aware of the threat of riot and violence that accompanied the increasing number of strikes plaguing Philadelphia's large industrial plants. He feared that a radicalized mass of workers would seize political power to close the ever widening economic gap between worker and manager. He was only too well aware that the city political machine, based on the vote of the countless thousands of ghetto dwellers, posed a threat to political institutions in Philadelphia. Smith was convinced of the necessity of leaving the comfortable confines of his law office to join those seeking political reform that would end the corruption and inefficiency in municipal government and replace it with a more centralized administration combining expertise with honesty.

Second, Smith felt that his status as a well-established lawyer was somewhat threatened. On the one hand, he resented the growth of commercialism in the legal profession which produced lawyers who tended to overshadow the old, established members of the legal fraternity. On the other hand, he was appalled at the influx of poorly educated, improperly prepared young lawyers then entering the profession. Both of these eventualities he regarded as bad since they led to a lowering of ethics and standards. Like many professional men in his day he participated in local, state, and national professional organizations to ensure high levels of expertise and to direct the future course of the profession.

Third, religion played a part in shaping Smith's attitudes and actions during the progressive era. As a practicing, intelligent Catholic, he recognized that increased pressures brought on by industrial growth posed a distinct threat to the cohesive structure of the nation's social fabric. Divorce, alcoholism, vice, and crime threatened to undermine the American family. He worked for the cause of the uniform state divorce law movement, a movement largely initiated by Protestant clergy and supported by Protestant laymen, because he perceived that the industrial revolution placed such strains on the family that divorces increased at geometrical rates as families sought to reduce the pressure. He believed that uniform state divorce laws would ensure a greater measure of social control over the family. While recognizing that social control was necessary,

Smith also hoped to raise the level of morality of the family that it might meet the increased strains and stresses of the industrial society. Needless to say, Smith's Catholic faith played no small part in motivating him to participate in this anti-divorce movement, since the Catholic Federation of which he was a leading member frequently exhorted members to combat the divorce evil.

Fourth, Smith had a profound respect for the growth of American industrialism. Indeed, his stock portfolio contained securities in some of the best American corporations. He firmly believed that American society as a whole benefited most when the business-industrial community prospered. he realized that American business had outgrown its local and state confines and that it now conducted business on a national scale. Aware that the nation's legal system was composed of many diverse state and commercial laws that hindered interstate commerce, Smith worked to rationalize the American commercial law system by the passage of uniform state laws.

Fifth, Smith's membership in the legal fraternity gave him the lawyer's conservative nature that aimed at preserving existing institutions and at retaining some control over the forces making for rapid change. His fears of the violence resulting from mass discontent with many of the prevailing social, political, and economic institutions led him to join those progressives in the 1890s with a fervent desire to control the forces of change. He believed that the privileged classes in American society must take responsibility for directing change and preventing excesses.

Sixth, with a Protestant, New England family background that included many leading lights in that region during the 17th and 18th centuries, Smith was motivated by the psychological desire to join with the American, Anglo-Saxon, Protestant elite in every phase of his life, a social drive that also held true during the reform period. To overlook his quest for association with this elite in the progressive era would be a failure to understand a strong factor behind his drive for reform.

But to characterize Smith as a reformer who sought rapid change would also be an error, for his progressivism was conservative. Like other Eastern conservative progressives he attempted to direct change along constructive lines that would prevent excesses. In this respect he is typical of Richard Hofstadter's description of the conservative Eastern progressive whose progressivism was a "mild and judicious movement."[14] Certainly, no one could construe elitist-sponsored urban reform, the uniform state law movement, the raising of legal education requirements—the two last both having the *imprimatur* of the American Bar Association—as radical. Yet these goals all fitted within the spectrum of legitimate, progressive aims.

Like many progressives, a large number of whom were attorneys, Smith developed a keen sense of social responsibility, and he avidly pursued a wide range of interests in education, religion, business, history, and literature—all of which indicate his place in Philadelphia's aristocracy—in addition to reaching out to new areas in his own profession. An examination of his varied pursuits enables one to draw an interesting profile of a certain type of "conservative progressive." But no description of the man would be complete without sketching Smith's legal career during the middle years.

THE LEGAL REFORMER

As was the case with many progressives, Smith's profession fitted him neatly into the ranks of the reform element in American society. His peers at the Philadelphia bar regarded him as an excellent lawyer. Indeed William Barclay Lex, a well-known attorney who worked with Smith on several cases, Hubert Horan, admitted to the Philadelphia bar in 1911 and practicing successfully before becoming a prominent bank president in later years, and Charles J. Biddle, the son of Smith's onetime partner who was admitted to the bar in 1914 and became a senior member of the established firm of Drinker, Biddle, and Reath, all attested to Smith's great esteem among lawyers in a city known for the high quality of its legal fraternity.[15]

During his early career he gained a good name defending homicide cases and developed notable forensic skill in the courtroom. He did not follow the new trend around the turn of the century and specialize in one area of the law. There was hardly any field in which he did not acquire some degree of expertise. During his later years he largely withdrew from the excitement of jury trials. A profile of his practice indicates that Smith never ceased to play the lawyer's role and his early practice was real and considerable. He was retained not only in corporation and real estate litigation but also in patent and admiralty law cases, and in those involving decedent's estates. He practiced in all of the courts in Philadelphia. He was admitted to practice before the Supreme Court of Pennsylvania and also before the United States Supreme Court. But in later life "he confined his professional activities to the business and office side of his profession and gave most of his energy to other fields."[16]

Although he deplored the decline of the legal profession's image because of the growing commercialism which resulted from the tendency of the lawyer to become the servant of the corporation, Smith nevertheless recognized that the corporation was a permanent reality in the American economic structure and that the health of the nation's economy depended in large measure on the smooth functioning of the large business enterprise. He believed that "commerce is a great civilizing influence" and that its growth and development must be aided through the establishment of a new uniform system of commercial law.[17] To that end he worked unceasingly and successfully to promote the adoption of a more rationalized system of commercial laws to facilitate the transaction of business across state lines.[18]

Smith's untiring efforts placed him in the elite of the nation's legal fraternity. One might well ask the question: How did Smith, a Catholic, achieve eminence and reach the heights in a profession which was predominantly Protestant? Smith realized that historically the law had been a vehicle by which a man would rise to the ranks of what Alexis de Tocqueville called the closest thing to an American aristocracy, and he did just that. He was not simply a token Catholic admitted to the ranks of leadership in the nation's legal profession. He earned his place in that Protestant-dominated elite group by his native ability, by making a fortunate marriage, and by winning the acclaim and respect of his colleagues in the local, state, and national bar associations in which he participated, as made clear in the last chapter.

He served on the American Bar Association's Committee on Legal Education[19] and worked diligently to improve legal ethics and to raise the standards of education for the attorney[20]. In 1912 Smith's committee issued a report that recommended the acceptance of a three-year period of study, based on the case method, in an accredited law school, as necessary to the preparation of the well-trained lawyer. In the year 1913 Smith, as chairman of the Committee on Legal Education, addressed the general meeting of the American Bar

Association on September 13. He seconded the substance of the 1912 committee report, remarking that the "prosperous law schools" bore the responsibility for preparing a knowledgeable bar. While he recognized that higher standards would work to the disadvantage of the "poor youth" and the immigrant, Smith said that these would reduce the public's "general accusations" that the bar lacked "general education" and that some of its members were guilty of "ignorance of their profession."[21]

He also achieved the respect of his peers as chairman from 1901 to 1910 of one of the association's most important standing committees, the Committee on Uniform State Laws. The association also formed and financed the Conference of Commissioners on Uniform State Laws. The work of this conference has been described as its main accomplishment during its first generation. Assignment to this conference was given only to those who had the "time to do considerable uncompensated work."[22] Smith, who had sufficient private means to take time from his practice, also attained national eminence when the members elected him president on September 11, 1917, at the annual meeting at Saratoga Springs, New York. By this time the association had grown in numbers and become more national in scope.[23] As a ranking member Smith knew many of the nation's best lawyers and all of the association's presidents, a number of them on fairly intimate terms: Francis Rawle, elected in 1902, Frank Kellogg in 1912, William H. Taft in 1913, Peter Meldrim in 1914, Elihu Root in 1915, George Sutherland in 1916, Hampton Carson in 1919, and Charles Evans Hughes in 1924.

Smith was also active in legal circles at the state level. In the early days he enjoyed a good relationship with Chief Justice Sharswood, one of Pennsylvania's most illustrious jurists during the late 19th century. He was a charter member of the Pennsylvania Bar Association, and served for a number of years as one of that body's Commissioners on Uniform State Laws and as chairman of its committee on legal education in 1899.

With respect to Smith's legal career two further questions must be raised: first, how could a progressive become president of the ultra-conservative American Bar Association; second, how could a progressive actively seek to restrict admission to the bar only to those who had graduated from well-known law schools—an eventuality that would hurt the ambitious poor and the newly-arrived immigrant, many of whom were actually members of the Catholic community like himself? The times give the answer to this question. The progressive era is earmarked by the wide-spread frequency of professional men organizing to control professional standards and pursue reforms. Historians of the period are in agreement that it was an "Age of Organization," as Robert Wiebe described it, when men in the professions organized to cope with the challenge of the times and the increased rate of change.[24] Smith might well be criticized for trying to achieve higher standards, a reality that imposed difficulty on the immigrant Catholic. But he was a creature of his times. Like other progressive professional men he did not give much thought to the immigrant in his determination to raise the standard in his profession in order to protect his hard-won status from the poorly trained.

In summerizing Smith's participation in local, state, and national bar associations, it can be said that he affiliated with these organizations for two reasons. First, it was for him a means of advancement in the legal profession. Second, it seems quite evident that he desired to join with those in his profession who were anxious to maintain high professional standards of education and ethics, thus exerting a measure of control over members of the profession and maintaining the lawyer's status in the community. These men also hoped to achieve legal reform.

To achieve this latter end Smith also took an interest in the technical side of the law. As one writer said of him: "Mr. Smith's best professional work was done, not in the ordinary course of practice, but in the efforts to improve the administration of justice as a member of the Conference of Commissioners on Uniform State Laws and a member of the Divorce Commission."[25] The achievement of uniform state legislation was one of the progressive goals sought after by the American Bar Association.

Finally, Smith himself attributed his success to a fortunate marriage which enabled him to achieve a measure of success over and above what his native ability would have gained for him. Association with the Drexel family gave him entrée that might ordinarily have been denied him.

For his high place in the legal profession Smith received several honors. For example, the Catholic University of America in 1915 and Grinnell College in 1920 conferred upon him the honorary degree of Doctor of Laws. Little wonder that honors came his way, because his greatest service to his profession was not rendered in court or chamber—efforts leading to pecuniary reward—but in his efforts to improve the administration of justice in the areas of divorce and commercial law.

THE EDUCATOR AND RELIGIONIST

Although active in many facets of his profession, Smith also had other interests. As was the case with many progressives he took an active role in education, but unlike the vast majority of them he had a conservative outlook. Progressive educators generally aimed at improving society by removing the "old, rigid, classical curriculum in favor of an education relevant to life and directed toward freeing the creative potentialities of the student."[26] Smith opposed the trend toward technical education and favored the retention of classical, liberal arts curricula.[27] Indeed, this conservative educational philosophy provided the intellectual framework through which he viewed his responsibilities as a member of the Board of Trustees of the University of Pennsylvania.

Between 1891 and 1909 Smith sat on the University of Pennsylvania's highest governing body, a board of trustees that Digby Baltzell described as consisting of "wealthy fashionable citizens."[28] During the time of his tenure on the board he served with numerous members who were leading citizens—socially and professionally—in the city of Philadelphia: Samuel Dickson, whom he styled "my friend," was an "eminent lawyer" associated in practice with John C. Bullitt and Richard C. Dale; Randal Morgan, "my chum from college days," had become vice president of the United Gas Improvement Co. and had donated $250,000 to the university to build a new physics building; Dr. S. Weir Mitchell, a true renaissance type characterized by Smith as an "old-school gentleman" who "thought a great deal of the niceties of life" and "made for himself a very high place in his profession and no mean one in literature", invited him to dinner on "several occasions"; Henry Galbraith Ward had been a groomsman at his wedding and soon became a federal judge; J. Levering Jones, a prominent member of the Philadelphia bar, was Smith's fellow member of the lawyer's Lunch Club; Charles S. W. Packard was his colleague on the board of the Philadelphia Contributionship, one of the nation's oldest fire insurance companies; and Governor Samuel Pennypacker, who later thought well enough of Smith's talents as an attorney to appoint him to a position on a national organization that aimed at reform of existing state divorce laws.

But Smith's tenure on the board, as will be seen, ended in 1909 when he resigned over a matter on which he would not compromise his strict adherence to the teachings of his Church. Although he disassociated himself from the University of Pennsylvania, Smith nevertheless remained active in the field of education.

Officials of the Drexel Institute, founded by his wife's uncle Anthony Drexel, named him to its Board of Managers in 1901. He remained active in this capacity until 1920. Even though he had obtained his education at private institutions Smith served the interests of public education, because in 1916 city fathers approved his membership on the Board of Public Education of the city of Philadelphia. During his tenure on the board he served as chairman of the Committee on High Schools and Discipline and vitally concerned himself with the question of higher salaries for teachers. This illustrates the inescapable fact that progressives often acted inconsistently with respect to progressive goals: Smith, who would later oppose women's suffrage and prohibition, goals highly valued by most progressives, worked assiduously and successfully on the Board of Education to obtain equal salaries for women school teachers.

Although interested in the advancement of public education, it appears that in the years following his break with the University of Pennsylvania Smith's greatest efforts in education were directed to furthering the expansion of the Catholic University of America in Washington, D.C. For many years he worked closely with its rector, the Right Reverend Thomas J. Shahan, on a variety of matters pertaining to curriculum, new buildings, fund-raising, budgetary matters and library acquisitions.[29] Needless to say, the bishop greatly appreciated Smith's conservative views on education. But Smith's zeal in furthering Catholic education comes as no surprise, for he was known as one of the outstanding Catholic laymen in the country, a fact that in 1923 earned for him the Laetare Medal, an honor bestowed annually by Notre Dame University on an American Catholic for "services in behalf of God, Church, and country."

Smith participated in organized religion like the overwhelming number of progressives, the vast majority of whom were members of the Protestant faith.[30] But his Roman Catholic faith and strict adherence to its conservative teachings set him apart from his progressive colleagues, most of whom professed a faith considerably modified by the liberal forces of modernism and secularism. Although his faith seems to have been first instilled by his mother at a tender age, his earliest formal activity on behalf of the Church seems to have stemmed from his relationship with the Drexel family in general and with Katherine Drexel in particular.

Following his wife's death Smith continued his close relationship with Sister Katherine, a relationship that involved him in the work of the religious order that she founded. He was present in Pittsburg on February 12, 1891, the day on which she took her vows as a Sister of Mercy and also founded the Congregation of the Blessed Sacrament for Indians and Colored People. As its duly appointed Mother Superior she set up her temporary convent and novitiate at St. Michael until the new convent could be constructed. Located at Cornwells Heights, it would be called St. Elizabeth's in honor of his late wife.

He assured Mother Katherine, from whom he derived great spiritual strength, of his willingness to "do what I can to aid you in the mission you have so well begun. I cannot tell what way may be opened to me, but I hope you will feel that it is your right to call upon me and my privilege to respond."[31] The many letters from Smith to his sister-in-law indicate that he worked diligently on behalf of her religious order in drawing up deeds, handling real estate transactions, drafting articles of agreement between sisters and the order, helping in the writing of the order's constitution, and in advising on a large number of miscellaneous matters.[32] For the remainder of his life he aided her in a professional way and charged no fee of any kind,[33] and was thus involved in helping one who would one day be considered for sainthood by the Roman Catholic Church. In aiding her apostolate among the Negroes and American Indians, two minority groups then seemingly overlooked by many progressives in their quest for social justice, Smith undoubtedly became sufficiently informed about the plight of the American Indian to warrant his later selection as a member of the Department of the Interior's Board of Indian Commissioners in 1923.

As was the case with many non-clerical progressives, Smith's interest in church affairs brought him into contact with many prelates and princes of the Church. He developed lasting friendships with them and good working relationships—relationships indicating Smith's conservative outlook and his high social standing among his co-religionists. Smith counted among his correspondents James Cardinal Gibbons of Baltimore, Dennis Cardinal Dougherty, Archbishop Patrick J. Ryan of Philadelphia, Bishop John Ireland of St. Paul, and Bishop James McFaul of Trenton.[34] The content of these letters indicates that Smith was conservative and a loyal and obedient son of the Church. Because of his devotion Archbishop Ryan appointed him in 1893 to represent the Philadelphia Archdiocese at the Catholic Congress at Chicago. Another occasion indicating Smith's loyalty to the episcopate occurred in 1921 when Cardinal Dougherty returned from Rome to Philadelphia with the red hat. Representing the laity at a pontifical mass, Smith said "we welcome you, we pledge you again and again our dutiful allegiance."[35]

Like many progressives, Smith was a publicist. While his father seems to have stimulated his interest in history and law, his mother gave him a flare for writing and a love of literature. His writings and speeches are many and he covered a wide variety of subjects such as education, government, law, history, religion, and literature. [36] Wherever he traveled he sought out the company of scholarly men. If in Rome it would be Francis Cardinal Gasquet, the eminent historian of medieval English monasticism. If in Great Britain it would be the poet Aubrey de Vere or the biographer Wilfrid Ward. As he enjoyed the company of men of letters beyond Philadelphia, so he also enjoyed the company and approval of members of Philadelphia's literary set—a group highly esteemed for its literary talent as well as for its high social standing. He was frequently at the home of Dr. S. Weir Mitchell, perhaps Philadelphia's most talented citizen since Benjamin Franklin. He also knew Agnes Repplier, the city's well-known Catholic essayist who was also a friend and correspondent of Grace Smith. He was on friendly terms with Horace Howard Furness, the Shakespearean scholar, and knew Owen Wister, the lawyer-turned-writer and author of *The Virginian*. [37]

Just as his educational, religious, and literary affiliations placed him in good standing with proper Philadelphians, so his business associations also found the stamp of approval of the city's elite.

Boardsmanship, always popular among the upper element of the city's professional and entrepreneurial men, was important to a man of Smith's caliber. The Philadelphia lawyer held directorships on the Beneficial Saving Fund Society, the Philadelphia Company for Guaranteeing Mortgages, and the Philadelphia Contributionship for the Insurance of Houses from Loss by Fire.[38] Discussion of his association with the latter will suffice for the purpose of establishing Smith's identity with the upper echelon of Philadelphia's proper financial institutions.

Founded in 1752 by Benjamin Franklin, the Philadelphia Contributionship was known simply as the Contributionship or referred to by its nickname the Hand-in-Hand. It was long directed by the city's "dominant Quaker elite," but in later years it became "virtually an Anglican gentleman's club which it has continued to be to the present day."[39] Smith became a member of this select board on January 20, 1904 and associated there with many of the leading business and professional men in Philadelphia. Regarding his service on the board J. Rodman Paul the board's chairman, wrote that he was "diligent in the performance of his duties as Director and brought to the consideration of all questions that highminded intelligence for which he was distinguished."[40]

No biography of Smith would be complete without a brief word about his Torresdale home—a home that Maisie Ward, the English Catholic writer and publisher, later compared to an aristocratic English country house of the Edwardian era.[41] Smith believed in the solidarity of the family, a virtue possessed by many progressives. He was a patriarch in his own home which housed his unmarried brothers and sisters Grace, Duncan, Caleen, and Kilby. With Smith as head of the household the atmosphere was formal and elegant. A staff of four servants and a housekeeper saw to the needs of the family. A perfectionist, Smith liked order in the Torresdale brownstone. Though mild-mannered and even-tempered, he could on occasion lose his temper. One evening at dinner a sharp family disagreement caused his brother Duncan to exclaim profanely, at which Walter George slammed his hand on the table and loudly asserted in a fit of anger: "I am the head of the house. I have kept you all here, and I want peace."[42] As mainstay of the family, responsible for the education of his younger brothers, Smith felt he could demand obedience. Doubtless the success of Adrian, educated as an architect, and Kilby, educated as a lawyer, depended on him. Adrian had obtained the commission to design and build the new wing at Eden Hall and also St. Francis's Industrial School at Eddington, while he brought Kilby into his law practice in 1898.

His family described as aristocratic, his home compared to that of a fashionable English country house, little wonder that Smith achieved membership in the best Philadelphia men's clubs. Although not a native Philadelphian he gained entry into the select company of the Philadelphia Club, the city's most exclusive social organization, in 1913. He was also a member of the Rittenhouse, Penn, Legal, and University clubs. That Smith had made his way socially in the city long noted for its emphasis on family and social connections there can be little doubt. And so it was that Walter George Smith approached the progressive era with the best social and professional credentials—credentials that placed him, indeed, in the ranks of Philadelphia's aristocrats.

THE POLITICAL REFORMER

During the last decade of the nineteenth century urban Americans experienced growing concern about the corruption in government at the local, state, and national levels. Although the war with Spain had been successfully concluded many citizens felt aprehension and pessimism, believing that a crisis had arrived in the nation's history that might well spell disaster for its political, social, and economic institutions. For over a decade there was a growing fear that the radicalism of the lower classes posed a threat to the system.

Of the major American cities Philadelphia had the dubious distinction of being the most corrupt. Lincoln Steffens, the urban muckraker without peer, wrote of the Quaker City's reputation: "Other American cities, no matter how bad their own condition may be, all point with scorn to Philadelphia as the worse—the 'worst-governed city in the country.'" In analyzing the city's plight Steffens wrote: "The Philadelphians are 'supine,' 'asleep'; hopelessly ringruled, they are 'complacent'! "[43]

While the political apparatus of many cities was the well-oiled machine of the Democratic party, Philadelphia's was Republican. Clinton Rogers Woodruff, the Philadelphia urban reformer, called it a "Republican Tammany". Over the years Philadelphia advocates of good government had enjoyed but small success. They elected Samuel King as Democratic reform mayor in 1881 and obtained the Bullitt Bill, a forward-looking municipal charter in the 1880s, but, by and large, Philadelphia remained under the heel of the Republican machine. This machine, Woodruff claimed, maintained its power by the dual force of patronage and corrupt voting practices.[44] To give the machine its due, it did obtain much of its support at the ward level by providing service to voters. While party stalwarts could expect place and privilege as the result of political victory, the average voter could expect service as the reward for supporting the party at the polls. Even so corruption at the polls made many Philadelphians feel literally disfranchised. To compound the felony and add insult to injury, they did not even enjoy a self-governing machine, for theirs had been successively the property of politicians Simon Cameron, J. Donald Cameron, and U.S. Senator Matthew S. Quay. But for a time during the 1890s Quay had his troubles in Philadelphia and throughout the state as insurgents tried to oust the machine.[45]

Quay had chosen David Martin, who had come up the hard way, as his lieutenant in Philadelphia, but Martin asserted his independence of the boss when in 1895 he refused to nominate Boies Penrose, Quay's choice for mayor of Philadelphia.[46] Martin, no friend of reform and the possessor of his own machine in Philadelphia, gave the nod to John F. Warwick instead. Quay then named Israel Durham to be his henchman in Philadelphia. It was not until 1899 that Durham regained control of Philadelphia for Quay with the election of Samuel H. Ashbridge as the city's mayor. After getting rid of Quay's heavy hand in 1895, reform-minded Philadelphians waited patiently to find some vulnerable chink in Quay's armor, hoping to strike him down. The senator soon obliged them. Quay and many of the state's politicians had been speculating with the funds of the People's Bank of Philadelphia. In return for large, no-interest loans without collateral he and his cronies were accustomed to placing large state deposits in the bank. News of the speculation with state funds leaked out. Realizing that Quay was off balance, reformers decided to try him for conspiracy in 1898. The year 1898 was the time Philadelphians hoped to shake free from the onerous political clutches of Boss Quay. Spirits ran high during the summer as the country was at war with Spain. Just as red-blooded

American soldiers and sailors wrested victory from corrupt, jaded Spain, so Philadelphians hoped to wrest political freedom from Quay. Pennsylvanians looked to Philadelphia for leadership. John Wanamaker, the Philadelphia merchant prince, carried one of the banners of reform. Since he had almost defeated Quay's man Boies Penrose for the Senate in 1896, Wanamaker was one of the centers around which reform elements coalesced. Soon two reform elements—one pro-Wanamaker, the other anti-Wanamaker— emerged.

Many citizens felt that "Pious John" made such a good showing against "Big Grizzly" in '96 that he was the man to run against Quay's candidate for governor, William A. Stone, in the upcoming Republican party convention. Wanamaker also had the support of many business and corporate leaders in Philadelphia;[47] but he did not get the nomination, for the delegates named Quay's man. Wanamaker chose to support Charles W. Stone, an anti-Quayite who ran on an independent ticket. Dr. Silas Swallow, a Methodist book publisher from Harrisburg, carried the second banner of re- form. He was anti-Wanamaker and had the support of the Honest Government Party. In the ensuing race Wanamaker made many anti-Quay speeches. Ironically enough these helped Swallow. Wanamaker was not only trying to remove Quay's influence from the governor's mansion, but he was also trying to remove Quay from the Senate by helping to elect a state legislature opposed to his re-election. As reformers sought to defeat Boss Quay on the state level, so they also hoped to attack him in Philadelphia, the location of the People's Bank. Judge James Gay Gordon, Smith's good friend and one of the most respected jurists in Philadelphia, made available to District Attorney George S. Graham evidence of Quay's misuse of state funds deposited in the Philadelphia bank. Graham decided not to seek re-election in 1898. A group of men who included Judge Gordon and Colonel Alexander S. McClure, the publisher of the *Philadelphia Times*, put forward the mane of P. F. Rothermel, Jr., the Philadelphia attorney who had been Wanamaker's personal counsel in opposition to Smith in the Grant memoir case some years earlier. As a member of the Wanamaker team that aimed to bring down Quay, Rothermel enjoyed the support of Philadelphia business in- terests. P. A. B. Widener, president of the Philadelphia Traction Co., and William Lukens Elkins, president of the Pennsylvania

Globe Gas Light Co., endorsed Rothermel, as did the Businessmen's League. In describing his law practice the *Philadelphia Evening Bulletin* noted that Rothermel was counsel for "many of the largest corporations in the city and state and his knowledge of mercantile law and customs has made him the counsel of several of our leading mercantile houses."[48] At the Republican convention on September 21, this representative of progressive mercantile interests received the nomination over his competitors Dimner Beeber and John L. Kinsey. Needless to say, Wanamaker used his influence to bring about this nomination.[49]

Although Smith had been on the opposite side of the courtroom in the Grant memoir case and was not of the same party as Wanamaker and Rothermel, he nevertheless gave them his support. While Smith had refused to support William Jennings Bryan in the 1896 election, he was a staunch Democrat. Even so, in 1898 he consented to support two Republicans in the name of good government because he felt that the Republican machine represented a threat to the function of democracy in Pennsylvania.

As early as 1886, when he ran for Congress on the Democratic ticket, Smith had evinced real fear of the "evils which arise in our social and political system." Not only was he aware of the danger that a dissident labor force posed to the capitalistic system, he was also acutely concerned that the American political system was being subverted by a combination of politicians and business men. Concerning the state of political life in the decade of the 'nineties, Smith observed: "There are many matters of public interest and public policy in the affairs of Pennsylvania which appeal to me as of the most serious import." He deplored the fact that both Republican and Demoratic parties were machine-dominated and that a small element in the latter frequency supported the former, thus ensuring the continuation of Republican ascendancy. Of the plight of his own city, Smith declared: "In Philadelphia we see where all the forms of law are observed with a Mayor, Chambers of Common and Select Councils, and all of the evidence of popular government, but as the Roman Senate became under Caesar a mere form of body to register the will of the reigning pronce, so, though of course, not to such an extent, the Councils of Philadelphia register the will of the head of the political organization without debate."

Continuing his criticism of government at the state level, Smith noted: "What is said of municipal government may be said also with certain very distinct limitations with regard to the legislative government of the State, and the people are being gradually educated to look upon elections as a matter of form. The parties are ruled in the same way, conventions meet, but there is no struggle of opposing candidates. In the private office of the leader and his advisers a slate is made up and the convention meets to register the decree of the leader." In summing up his criticism Smith concluded: "If nothing can be done to break up this system, which is aided by cumberous and unfair election laws, patriotic men will lose faith in the possibility of successful popular government and the hopes of the founders of the republic and their political teachings, which were accepted as axioms in other days will have been shown to be impossible of permanent fulfillment."

In supporting the Wanamaker-Rothermel effort to defeat Quay at the polls and thus remove him from the political element that enjoyed the backing of many of Philadelphia's Protestant upper class entrepreneurial, professional, and industrial leaders. These men desired first, to achieve the downfall of an inefficient, alien political group and, second, to obtain power and use it to achieve the goals of good government. This is not to say that all upper class Philadelphians were reform-minded. Indeed, Digby Baltzell has accused this social element of apathy in the face of machine rule.[50] But many of them did support reform.

In the election of 1898 Rothermel's opposition came from John M. Campbell, the Democratic nominee, and James M. Beck, the United States District Attorney in Philadelphia who carried the anti-Wanamaker banner of reform. The Municipal League and Herbert Welsh, Philadelphia's perennial reformer and the editor of *City and State*, supported Beck. Welsh maintained that Beck was the true reformer and that Rothermel would merely do the bidding of business and corporate interests.[51] Although Rothermel carried the pro-Wanamaker reformers, many other reformers supported Beck. The election was hotly contested. Rothermel was victorious, carrying all but one of the city's wards. His victory was largely due to a split in the Demoratric Party, many of whose supporters voted for Rothermel.[52] Rothermel served as district attorney from 1899 to 1901 and did a commendable job in trying Boss Quay. But he failed to win a conviction; Judge Craig Biddle decided that the statute of limitations ruled out the evidence needed to convict. Even so, his work gained the plaudits of muckraker Lincoln Steffens, who compared Rothermel to Joseph Folk, the crusading district attorney of St. Louis.[53] And Clinton Rogers Woodruff, counsel for the Philadelphia Municipal League, the organization which had opposed Rothermel's ekection in 1898, wrote that Rothermel had served "with great distinction for three years" by handling his job with fairness and obtaining a larger number of convictions for violations of the election code and liquor law than any of his predecessors. Woodruff concluded that Rothermel represented the people and not the machine.[54] However, Republicans criticised Rothermel on the ground that his failure to prosecute cases readily resulted in a long backlog. Referring to an editorial in *City and State* in praise of Rothermel, George Wharton Pepper wrote to Herbert Welsh charging Rothermel, with a lack of promptness in attending to the affairs of his office.[55]

In 1901 the Republicans in Philadelphia chose not to nominatee Rothermel for re-election. This led to a revolt and the emergence of an anti-machine group known as the Union Party.[56] By 1901 Quay had regained control in Philadelphia, where Isreal Durham did his master's bidding. When questioned about the renomination of Rothermel Durham said: "The man we nominate must be a man we can control."[57] Obviously Rothermel, the district attorney who dared to try Boss Quay, was not the man. On June 19 at the Republican party convention in Philadelphia George Wharton Pepper nominated John Weaver to run for Rothermel's post.[58]

Irate at this callous treatment of Rothermel, reform-minded citizens held a mass meeting at the Academy of Music on June 27. The hall was crowded from "pit to dome." Undeterred by record-breaking heat, progressive Philadelphians organized a town meeting for the purpose of putting Rothermel's name in nomination for district attorney. They selected Edward Shippen as chairman of the meeting and of the organization that ultimately became the Union Party. After Rothermel's formal nomination Shippen announced that he and other leaders would soon appoint a committee of nine citizens to handle Rothermel's campaign. The next day Rothermel accepted the nomination.[59]

THE COMMITTEE OF NINE

On July 18 Shippen announced the membership of the Committee of Nine: Samuel Clement, second assistant district attorney under Rothermel; John H. Bromley, carpet manufacturer; Nathan T. Folwell, drygoods executive; Franklin L. Sheppard, stove manufacturer; Charles W. Potts, financier; John Birkenbine, civil engineer; Albert D. Ladner; Walter George Smith; and William Stenger, deputy attorney general under Governor Robert Pattison.[60] Shippen reported that every member accepted his appointment "cheerfully because of the hopefulness of the contest.[61] Smith thus associated with the leaders of urban reform in Philadelphia, in the vanguard of Americans interested in the improvement of municipal government. He approached his task firmly convinced that advocates of good government must succeed in their task in order to preserve the American democratic system of government.

Support for the Committee of Nine was soon forthcoming. The *Public Ledger* endorsed the Nine, saying it was composed of "men of high character and business ability," six Republicans and three Democrats, none of whom had been conspicuous in the reform movement before this time. The editorial noted that the Nine lacked practical political experience but said that they truly represented the revolt of Philadelphians against both Republican and Democratic machines.[62] Although opposed to Rothermel's successful bid in 1898 for election, Herbert Welsh of *City and State* now announced his support for the campaign of the Committee of Nine, saying: "it is composed of men of high standing in the community whose characters are a sufficient guarantee that the Rothermel campaign will be prosecuted with the utmost vigor."[63]

The Committee of Nine became affiliated with the Union Party during the summer and wasted little time in drawing up a plan of campaign. The group met on the evening of July 22 at the Lafayette Hotel where it elected Bromley as chairman, Folwell as treasurer, and Clement as secretary. As the first order of business the group drew up a four-point program: first, it appointed a subcommittee on fraud for the purpose of ensuring a fair election; second, it agreed that steps must be taken to arouse public sentiment; third, it recognized that an effective campaign required the immediate organization of ward committees; and fourth, it made plans to solicit the aid of other reform-oriented organizations in the city.[64]

Uppermost on the committee's program was the appointment of the sub-committee on fraud. Too many elections in the past had gone to the machine due to deception at the ballot box.[65] Eventually, the committee announced the membership of this subcommittee: Rudolph Blankenburg, chairman;[66] George S. Graham; Hampton Carson; Charles Biddle; Judge James Gay Gordon; William Sellers; George Burnham, Jr; Thio. Justice; Robert J. Linden; Clarence Harper; Frank Leake; Joseph DeF. Junkin; J. Hampton Barnes; William Tilden; and Harold Goodwin.[67] The dual purpose of this subcommittee was to examine the lists of election officials to ensure their fitness to serve and to check voting lists for accuracy.

Blankenburg, a Philadelphia merchant long active in reform circles, spurred his subcommittee to action. It diligently performed its duty by locating many padded voting lists. the chairman duly notified the Board of Tax Assessors, whose responsibility it was to maintain accurate lists, that steps must be taken to remove the names of persons no longer eligible to vote.[68]

Herbert Welsh kept a close watch on the efforts of the Committee of Nine and commended it for taking the practical step to organize a subcommittee on fraud. In late October, just prior to the election, Welsh reported that the Blankenburg group had actually achieved a modicum of reform by having authorities strike names from padded lists and getting the appointment of competent overseers for the election.[69] The Committee of Nine felt that a successful reform movement depended on the work of the Blankenburg subcommittee, because it believed that popular sentiment strongly favored its goal of a fair election.

The committee made a poignant appeal to the public for support of its candidate. It pointed to Rothermel's three-year record with pride and averred that he was well qualified to continue in office. It raised the question: "Shall the bosses or the people rule?" The committee declared its intention to represent the will of citizens indignant at the inefficiency and corruption of machine rule. It blamed both Democratic and Republican politicians for ineptitude; the Nine called for a "Union" of all elements of the populace who favored "good government" over government by boss.[70]

To apprise the public of its goals the committee made a strong effort to organize the city's wards, hoping thereby to contact voters at the grassroots level. Between late July and mid-October it achieved an effective structure in many of the city's forty-eight wards.

In addition to appealing for popular support, the Nine also sought the co-operation of other reform-oriented groups. This quest was successful. The Municipal League, the Allied Organizations for Good Government, the Jeffersonian Society, and the Young Democracy all threw their support to Rothermel. Labor organizations such as the Machinists Union openly endorsed him. The Businessmen's League gave its stamp of approval. And a large number of outstanding lawyers such as George Tucker Bispham, who lectured on equity at the law school, and John Graver Johnson, one of the nation's outstanding coporation lawyers, gave their support to Rothermel.

During the summer anti-machine, reform-minded men, following the leadership of Colonel Alexander S. McClure, organized the Union Party. Its leadership, moved rapidly and by August 1st the party had representatives in fifty-one counties across the state. By mid-August party officers, in compliance with state law, circulated petitions in all of the state's counties for the purpose of calling a state convention.[71]

The Union Party, of which the Committee of Nine was now an integral part, held a convention in the Academy of Music on September 24, 1901. Party leaders included Democrats, Republicans, and Municipal Leaguers. Men such as Walter George Smith, Judge James Gay Gordon, and ex-Governor Robert E. Pattison of the Democratic Party mixed with George Burnham, H. B. French, and Clinton Rogers Woodruff of the Municipal League, and both of these made common cause with reform-minded Republicans. Union Party leadership centered on Colonel McClure, Judge Gordon, and John Wanamaker.[72] Several thousand citizens attended the convention and doubtless enjoyed the excitement produced by banners, bands, processions, and all the antics that accompany American political conventions.

Convention delegates wasted no time in getting to work. They elected Frank M. Riter, former Public Safety Director, as chairman of the party convention and selected Colonel McClure as state party chairman. The "Goo Goos," as cynics called the Union Party members, based their appeal to the people on a platform calling for election reform, tax reform, and better fiscal control of public expenditures. The platform criticized both parties for inefficiency and urged the election of men who would administer the machinery of government with "honesty and efficiency."[73] The party ticket included Rothermel for District Attorney; Judge Harmon Yerkes for Supreme Court; Simon Gratz and R. A. Lukens for Board of Revision of Taxes; G. H. Davis and Henry Budd for Court of Common Pleas; and J. M. Walton for Controller. Smith of the Committee of Nine played a role in the convention, nominating the independent Republican E. A. Coray for Treasurer. In a "carefully studied speech," Smith exhorted his listeners to cast aside party feeling and "rally under a non-partisan banner."[74] Although his nominating speech did not greatly arouse those assembled, it did nevertheless emphasize the theme of the party—unity and non-partisanship. Non-partisanship was definitely the secret, and the Union Party ticket included five Republicans and four Democrats.

In spite of the enthusiasm created at the convention and the apparent rising tide of reform sentiment in Philadelphia, Union Party leaders realized the need to broaden their base by fusion with the Democrats. But fusion between the Union and Democratic parties was not possible; the two were unable to come up with a ticket mutually agreeable to both.[75]

The election was ardently contested. Colonel McClure described it as one of "unusual activity and bitterness.[76] The fervently Republican *Philadelphia Inquirer* declared that Rothermel was merely the "personal attorney of Wanamaker" and would do his bidding. Congressman Henry Burk, the third district representative and member of Durham's organization, claimed that Rothermel had not performed his duties effectively. Burk said he left many cases untried because he spent too much of his time seeking re-election.[77] Republican machine hacks made an effort to break up a Union Party meeting on Saturday evening, November 2 in the Academy of Music, where some 5,000 people had gathered to hear Union Party orators extol the virtues of party candidates. Police Chief Edgar told a *Public Ledger* reporter that on the night of the meeting he "had 400 men" in his charge and was "instructed to let the Penrose Club [a Republican political organization] march up and down Broad Street and do all they could to detract from the meeting.[78] Outside the music hall "drunkenness and lawlessness were rampaging," reported the policeman. In front of the Penrose Club building across Broad Street from the music hall, members erected a stand on which men and boys stood to set off fireworks.[79] The Republicans were indulging in what William Vare, Republican candidate for Recorder of Deeds, called "an old-fashioned campaign with mass-meetings in every part of the city."[80]

In the face of intense opposition from the Republican machine, the Union Party worked diligently to put together an organization that could compete with the long-entrenched Republicans. A straw vote conducted by the *Inquirer* on October 22 showed Republican candidate John Weaver out front with 282 votes, with Rothermel running a respectable second at 208 and W. Wilkins Carr, the Democratic hopeful, trailing far behind at 18 votes. But given the political situation in Republican Philadelphia, this poll indicated that the reformers were working hard. Remarking on Union Party efforts, Herbert Welsh observed: "It seems as if the Union Party with its reform allies had done all an organization of this kind could do."[82]

The poll indicates that Weaver was definitely the leader, and thus it becomes hard to explain why J. Hampton Moore, Weaver's campaign manager, was unable to arrange a debate between the two contestants. Generally speaking, the candidate reputedly in second place is only too willing to debate the front-runner. But Rudolph Blankenburg replied to Moore's invitation to debate by saying that Rothermel considered "it improper in a candidate for a quasi-judicial position to appear on the stump."[83]

But in spite of the enthusiasm for reform candidates, the November 5 election marked another victory for Republican stalwarts who gave Weaver 138,120 votes. Rothermel finished second with 94,453, while Carr trailed far behind with only 7,252 votes. Of the Union Party candidates in Philadelphia only Henry Budd, Smith's cousin, was elected.[84]

The outcome of the election was not wholly discouraging. Welsh of *City and State* commented on the results and observed that although the Union Party did not win, "it at least secured undisputed recognition as the minority party," as it was able to carry the Nineteenth, Twenty-second, Twenty-third, Twenty-fourth, Thirty-second, Thirty-fifth and Forty-first wards. But Welsh pointed out that the machine relied on intimidation and fraud at the polls and on the support of the Donnelly-Ryan faction of the Democratic Party for delivering many votes to the Republicans. On the subject of election fraud Colonel McClure wrote: "the most colossal frauds ever practiced in Philadelphia were exhibited in the returns." As an example, he noted that in some wards larger majorities were returned against Rothermel than there were legal voters in those wards.[85] The *Public Ledger*, an unbiased, independent Republican journal, found the election results encouraging, noting that advocates of reform should be stimulated to keep up their efforts. "Instead of being discouraged," the editorial ran, "the friends of good government should be inspired by the splendid exhibition of industry given on Tuesday, and should prepare for future contests."[86] Giving the Union Party's 1901 endeavor its proper place in the early twentieth century reform movement in Philadelphia, Colonel McClure wrote: "the battle left the vital embers of revolution in Philadelphia which, four years later, led to the hurricane and disaster that overwhelmed the organization leaders in both city and state."[87]

A future political contest was not long in the making. The 1901 Union Party effort to unseat the machine was but a dress rehearsal for the year 1905 when Philadelphia insurgents and their allies mounted an all-out attack on the Republican organization under the aegis of the City Party, an amalgam of the city's various reform elements.[88] But by 1905 Smith had turned his reforming zeal in a new direction. Although he supported the City Party, 1905 found him much more interested in combating the rising rate of divorce, a phenomenon that increasingly claimed the attention of many progressives who viewed divorce as a major threat to the American family.[89]

SMITH AND THE UNIFORM DIVORCE LAW

In the western world divorce was rare until the middle of the nineteenth century. The incidence of divorce began to increase at that time. After the American Civil War the occurrence of divorce became more common. No longer was it confined to the upper class. Now all strata of society began to feel that divorce was a proper remedy for the family that had suffered too many strains and stresses as a result of the complexities of American industrial society.

Reaction to this social phenomenon was not long in coming. By the 1880s sociologists, church leaders, lawyers, and other socially conscious persons began to look upon divorce as an evil that threatened the most basic social institution—the family. This reaction took three responses: on the one extreme were the traditional-conservatives like James Cardinal Gibbons who absolutely opposed divorce; at the other extreme were the sociologists like Dr. James P. Lichtenberger who felt that divorce was desirable in the industrial society of modern America. In the middle were those like Episcopal Bishop Henry Potter who condoned divorce for certain just causes.[90]

One of the foremost opponents of divorce was the Reverend Dr. Samuel W. Dike, a Congregational minister who had lost his parish in 1877 when he refused to marry an influential divorced parishioner. He then turned his attention to the full-time study of the divorce question and in 1882 formed the New England Divorce Reform League. Well-informed on his subject, Dike viewed the industrial revolution as the force that placed such heavy burdens on American families that many couples finally sought divorce to reduce the pressure. His organization began to attract many outstanding men, a number of whom viewed the divorce problem as directly proportional to the laxity of state divorce laws. One of these was Walter George Smith, who first developed an interest in the anti-divorce movement in the late 1890s.[91]

Smith was a conservative moralist on the divorce issue. He associated with Dr. Dike for many years in an effort to combat the divorce evil. His views on this matter were well defined, because his Catholic faith and his practice of law gave him a definite frame of reference. In writing to Dike Smith clearly enunciated the Catholic position to which he strictly adhered: "What I object to, speaking generally, is the idea that modern society is getting any better conception of the Kingdom of God by its own inherent intelligence, or education, or strength of development. Christianity rests upon Revelation, and while we may aid ourselves to believe by a study of all the wonders of science, whether of biology or sociology, because the nearer we get to any ultimate knowledge on any subject, the nearer it brings us to a proper conception of what is truth, yet we are in danger when we dwell on these arguments." In conclusion he warned: "We are in danger when we vary from the commands of the church.[92] In an article on the subject of divorce in the *Catholic Encyclopedia* Smith, adhering to the Church's teaching, wrote that marriage is a "sacramental union," one that is as indissoluble "as that of soul and body, which can be dissolved only in death."[93]

As a progressive, Smith looked upon divorce as a threat to the family and as ultimately an "agent that threatens the country."[94] He suggested that some form of social control was necessary, and it was as an attorney that he arrived at what he thought was the proper solution. In his professional capacity Smith rejected federal divorce legislation or an amendment to the Federal Constitution as a practical means of social control. He suggested that the only feasible remedy, given the American system of government, was the passage of uniform state legislation.[95] In his view the lack of uniform marriage and divorce laws caused "results which are illogical and confusing." This situation, he maintained, frequently resulted in a divorce granted in one state not holding up in another.[96]

But Smith also went beyond measures of social control that might be achieved by the legislative process. He urged a higher morality, a sense of duty, as most effective in eradicating an evil that struck at the family, and hence at the core of society. Addressing a woman's club in Philadelphia, Smith declared: "The divorce evil does not so much need remedial legislation as good, pure, sensible women, who will realize that in marriage the guiding star should be duty and not selfishness. The evil itself," he conldued, "will never be eradicated until the hearts of the people are turned back to a higher conception of the meaning of matrimony."[97] While urging the return to a higher morality, Smith, ever the pragmatist, realized that only uniform state divorce and marriage legislation had a chance of altering the rising divorce index.

The most significant means of fighting the divorce evil was the movement toward uniform state laws that resulted in the National Divorce Congress in 1906, which Smith attended. Since he had accepted appointment to the American Bar Association Committee on Uniform State Laws in 1897, it was only natural that he should represent his state at the Divorce Congress. The movement came to fruition when the Pennsylvania state legislature on March 16, 1906, passed an act authorizing Governor Samuel Pennypacker to appoint a three-man commission, with himself as an ex officio member, "to examine and codify the laws of the state relating to divorce, and to report the results of their efforts to the governor for submission to the legislature." The legislature further authorized the governor to communicate with the governors of the other states, territories and the District of Columbia, requesting them to send delegates to a national congress in Washington in February of 1906 for the purpose of drafting a model uniform state divorce law. The legislature appropriated the sum of $10,000 for defraying the expenses of this meeting. In 1905 the governor appointed C. La Rue Munson, a Williamsport lawyer, as chairman of the special commission, William H. Staake as secretary, and Walter George Smith as the third member.

Along with Governor Pennypacker these men made up the Pennsylvania delegation to the National Divorce Congress which convened in the nation's capital on February 19, 1906. The delegates to the meeting, by and large conservative lawyers and clergymen, came from 42 of the 45 states, but the delegation from the keystone State easily dominated the congress. William Staake was the Chairman of the Provisional Committee on Arrangements and called the meeting to order, whereupon the delegates elected Governor Pennypacker as President. Walter George Smith served as chairman of the all-important Committee on Resolutions which had the responsibility of drafting the model law. He had come to Washington well prepared for the task at hand as he had received and digested a mass of statistics and other data relevant to divorce sent him by Dr. Dike.[98]

As Chairman of the Resolutions Committee, Smith conducted the main business of the meeting. The *Proceedings* indicate that he played a commanding role in accomplishing its primary work.[99] The congress completed its task smoothly because conservatives like Smith were in control of the machinery of the meeting and the delegates were generally in agreement on most issues. Under Smith's chairmanship the resolutions went through pretty much as drawn up in committee. There was some disagreement over a statement on causes for divorce and on the matter of migratory divorce. Dissenting factions reached a compromise on the first point, while conservatives voted down the liberalizing amendment on the latter point. The congress rejected a federal solution to the divorce question, and the original resolution submitted by Smith calling for the adoption of a uniform state divorce bill was passed by a vote of 26 to 4.

John C. Richberg, delegate from Illinois, submitted a resolution calling on the Chairman of the Resolutions Committee to draft a model divorce law based on the resolves passed by the congress assembled at Washington and to advise the Governor of Pennsylvania when the statute was drafted that he might reconvene the congress to consider the model statute. This measure was adopted, and the full Committee on Resolutions thereupon delegated the preliminary work of preparing such a uniform statute to a subcommittee consisting of the Pennsylvania delegation (Smith, Staake, and Munson) and John R. Emery of New Jersey.[100]

This special subcommittee, with Williamsport lawyer William D. Crocker acting as special secretary, held frequent sessions from March to July, and drafted a comprehensive law covering questions relating to annulment and divorce proceedings, property rights, alimony, rights of children and the effect of foreign decrees. The full Committee on Resolutions met at St. Paul, Minnesota, during the last week of August, 1906, in connection with the meeting of the American Bar Association. The subcommittee, of which Smith was a member, presented its draft of a uniform statute to the full committee. After a discussion that lasted through several sessions, the committee decided to eliminate only a number of details related to forms of procedure. The committee notified Governor Pennypacker that it had drawn up a model statute and he sent out a call for a reconvened session of the Divorce Congress to meet at Philadelphia on November 13.

Governor Pennypacker called the adjourned session of the Divorce Congress to order at Philadelphia's Hotel Bellevue-Stratford on November 13, 1906. Twenty-one delegations were present at this session. As the chairman of the Committee on Resolutions, Smith reported that the committee had complied with the wishes of the Richberg resolution by drafting a model statute, "embodying the principles formulated by the Congress" in the initial session at Washington.[101] As before, Smith presided. He "conducted the session and he skilfully pushed the bill through exactly as written."[102] After some debate on the matter of granting foreign decrees, the session closed on a favorable note with leaders confident that the states would adopt the uniform statute. The major provisions of the model law were as follows: a bona-fide two-year residence of either plaintiff or the defendant in the state in which suit is brought; the defendant should be given adequate notice of date of trial that he might have his day in court; trials should be open; no remarriage for one year following the final decree of divorce.

Like other conservative opponents of the divorce evil, Smith felt confident that the work of the congress and the adjourned session would surely bear fruit. On returning home from the second session he participated in the work of annotating the proposed uniform divorce bill for presentation to the Pennsylvania state legislature. He had high hopes that his home state would lead the way with passage of the uniform divorce law. His hopes would soon be dashed.

In just two short years the third meeting of the American Sociological Society at Atlantic City, New Jersey, on December 28-30, 1908, provided the conservative opponents of divorce with an indication that their efforts to curb it would not be accepted by the sociology profession. Certainly this was a harbinger of the ill reception the state legislatures would give the uniform state divorce law. Smith attended this meeting, as he had received an invitation from Professor C. W. A. Veditz of the political science department of George Washington University. Convention planners requested Smith to present the Catholic position on divorce.[103]

The sociologists focused their attention on marriage and the family. Several scholars presented papers attacking the traditional father-dominated family. Professor George E. Howard's paper enlivened the meeting because it aroused interest and brought about a sharp exchange on the subject of divorce in the modern, industrial society. Howard cautioned that the traditional patriarchal family was no longer the norm; with the rise in the status of women there was a corresponding decline in the status of men. He observed that the "old patriarchal bonds have not yet been adequately replaced by spiritual ties." The professor noted that divorce was due to the ills of society and he concluded that the "freer granting of divorce is not a social evil. Rather, divorce is merely a healing medicine for marital ills."[104] Dr. Dike and Rabbi Krauskopf of Philadelphia followed Howard, with the former opposing and the latter supporting his position. Also substantiating Howard's argument, Dr. James P. Lichtenberger, author of *Divorce: A Study in Social Causation*, presented a paper that would have an important bearing on Smith's membership on the board of Trustees at the University of Pennsylvania.

In discussing marriage and law, the sociologist said that matrimony "is dependent upon law neither for its institution nor for its perpetuation." On divorce and religion the Assistant Professor at the

New York School of Philanthropy declared: "The time-honored landmarks of religious authority have been obliterated." In words that must have caused Smith further discomfort, Lichtenberger concluded; "The increasing disruption of the family is a clearly recognized evil, but the necessary readjustment of the legal and social status of persons whose marriage relations have broken down, which we call divorce, is necessary and moral. Until the new family finds its equilibrium in the changed economic, social, and religious environment, a high rate of divorce is inevitable, and is an index of progress rather than a sign of social disintegration."[105] Smith replied specifically to Howard, but his remarks might also be applied to Lichtenberger. The Philadelphia Catholic decried the former's seeming approval of the social revolution that was altering the relationship of man and wife in the family: "he is expressing satisfaction with a gradual social revolution that fills my mind with alarm." Smith presented the Catholic position: "Professor Howard and men of his school are at the opposite pole from men who look upon the marriage relation as a sacrament, as a relation that rises so high above a civil contract that the state is guilty of usurpation in attempting to dissolve it." Concerning the equality of man and woman, Smith warned: "The attempt to individualize so as to give to man and woman the same sphere of action is going contrary to nature. The attempt to establish an equality that results in comradeship, that endeavors to ignore the relative strength, mental and physical, of the male and female . . . I must conclude is founded upon fallacy."[106] Howard replied by saying that Smith had set forth "brilliantly" the Church of Rome's views on the position of "indissoluble wedlock." He declared that he had respect for this position but that "progress cannot be won by clinging to the authority of ancient ideals in social questions." Referring to natural law, the basis of the Church argument, Howard asked: "May it not be possible that natural law now guides social evolution?" He concluded with a thesis that was more and more gaining acceptance in academic circles: "It is high time to cease the appeal to mere authority, and to accept marriage, the home, and the family as purely human social institutions to be freely dealt with by men according to human needs."[107]

The meeting must have shaken Smith. He certainly must have realized that the traditional, conservative position on marriage and the family had suffered a severe blow. Writing Dike following the meeting, he said: "Judging from the attitude of the leading members and their vigorous applause," ideas that "were uttered diametrically and defiantly in the face of the Christian teaching of any denomination" seem to have greater currency.[108] The convention of sociologists had an important bearing on Smith. It marked the beginning of his breach with Dike and his National League for the Protection of the Family, and it would also eventually result in the severing of his relationship with the Board of the University of Pennsylvania.

Dike began to forsake the conservative position on marriage and divorce shortly after the American Sociological Society's 1908 meeting. In a letter to him two weeks after the meeting Smith wrote: "I can only regret that while our positions are so close yours is not identical with mine."[109] A little over a year later Smith told Dike that he could not "very readily subscribe further to the National League for the Protection of the family." He said that Dike had essentially compromised his position by accepting that of "those gentlemen of the American Sociological Society" which he could not accept.[110]

In addition to severing his relationship with Dike, Smith also terminated his membership on the Board of Trustees at the University of Pennsylvania. A short while after attending the 1908 convention of sociologists, Smith wrote Provost Charles Harrison of his opposition to the appointment of Dr. James Lichtenberger to an assistant professorship in the university's Wharton School.[111] Smith opposed the appointment because he believed that Lichtenberger's remarks on marriage and divorce at the Atlantic City conference were deleterious to the welfare of university students. Harrison acknowledged Smith's letter, saying he had examined the papers presented at the conference by Howard, Smith, and Lichtenberger, and could find nothing that would disqualify him from a position on the faculty. He told Smith that he was appointing Lichtenberger to the position.[112] Smith promptly tendered his resignation on May 26, giving as his reason the inability to approve in good conscience Lichtenberger's appointment.[113] After the June meeting of the board Harrison communicated to Smith the news that board members had voted unanimously to appoint a committee consisting of Randal Morgan, J. Levering Jones, ex-Governor Pennypacker and Harrison to meet with him to try to persuade him to withdraw his resignation.[114] In the autumn, the committee, less Morgan, called on Smith who agreed to review the facts of the case and reconsider his resignation. After some reflection Smith, unwilling to compromise his principles, wrote the provost that he had gone over in his mind the pertinent facts but could not alter his decision to resign.[115] The following day Edward Robbins, assistant secretary, wrote Smith that the trustees accepted his resignation "with very sincere regret."[116]

The press had been kept in the dark during the six-month exchange between Smith and Harrison and now made, in Smith's words, "a great to do." The *Philadelphia Evening Telegraph* carried the announcement of Smith's resignation on December 3rd, saying it was due to the "privately expressed opinion of one of the professors in regard to the teaching of free love.[117] The press reported a statement made by Bishop James McFaul of Trenton about certain university professors who were guilty of teaching doctrine contrary to the Church's teaching. This had caused Smith to look into Lichtenberger's appointment.[118] The following day Lichtenberger, who enjoyed the support of the university faculty, denied teaching "free love."[119]

For his stand Smith received many letters congratulating him on the position he took. Notable among those were expressions from Bishops Shahan and McFaul, and a note from George Wharton Pepper. Smith had confided in his friend Archbishop Ryan, who advised Rome of his stand in the matter; in the following year the pope honored Smith by making him a Knight of the Order of St. Gregory the Great. The archbishop gave Smith permission to have a private oratory in his Torresdale home, where Mass was frequently said by one of the Fathers from the Order of the Holy Ghost.[120]

Smith's attendance at the meeting of the American Sociological Society, his break with the university, and his disassociation with Dr. Dike's movement must have been very disconcerting to one dedicated to the Catholic Church's position on marriage and divorce. He was not only beginning to realize that the universities were now accepting the teaching of liberal professors on the divorce question, but he was also becoming aware that the uniform state divorce law movement was not succeeding. By 1914 he acknowledged the movement's failure: "If there were any real, strong, popular discontent with existing conditions [pertinent to state marriage and divorce laws], these reasonable attempts to obtain uniformity would long since have met with approval, but so far only the states of Delaware, New Jersey, and Wisconsin had adopted the uniform act. Even Pennsylvania, whose initiative brought about the Congress of 1906, has persistently refused to accept the proposed act." Smith then commented on futile attempts to amend the Federal Constitution to bring about divorce law reform at the national level and concluded: "The fact is that outside the large body of Catholics, the masses of the people do not look upon existing conditions with any real appreciation of the dangers connected with them, being more concerned that the unhappiness arising from the frequent mismating of married couples shall be cured by what is called 'the surgery of divorce,' than with the injury entailed upon the morals of the community at large."[121]

Although Smith was able to achieve success in drawing up a uniform divorce law, its rejection by most of the states resulted in the movement's failure. However, he was able to obtain a larger measure of success in the drive to draft uniform commercial instruments, a non-political, progressive goal often overlooked by historians of the progressive era.

SMITH AND UNIFORM COMMERCIAL LAW

Historian Samuel Haber has said of the period of reform that the "progressive era is almost made to order for the study of Americans in love with efficiency. For the progressive era gave rise to an efficiency craze—a secular Great Awakening, an outpouring of ideas and emotions in which a gospel of efficiency was preached without embarrassment to businessmen, workers, doctors, housewives, and teachers, and yes, preached even to preachers."[122] Further, Otis L. Graham, Jr. has observed that Americans in the progressive era "in numbers which allow us to speak of a mass movement, turned to . . . rationalize disorderly and unpredictable business . . . practices, and pursue a vision of an expanded role of society."[123] Smith's efforts to effect a number of uniform commercial laws was nothing more than a response to the business community's demand that the lawyer, the servant of the corporation, work to achieve rationalized state commercial laws that would facilitate the efficient transaction of business across state lines.

Smith's success in the uniform commercial law movement largely resulted from his serving from 1909 to 1912 on the Conference of Commissioners on Uniform Laws as conference president, a position that gave him leverage in directing the movement. The aims of this movement found greater acceptance among state legislatures across the nation. During the three-year period of his presidency no less than thirty bills passed through his hands, many of which were adopted by the various states. These included the bill of lading act, the negotiable instrument act, the limited partnership act, the fraudulent conveyance act, the sales act, the stock transfer act, and the warehouse receipts and workman's compensation acts. The experitse and comprehension required to grasp the legal technicalities involved in drafting these acts, as well as the persuasive powers necessary to secure their adoption by several of the states, denotes a high order of skill and persistence.

In making his initial presidential address to the Conference of Commissioners at Washington, D. C. on January 17, 1910, Smith briefly set forth the history, motives, and goals of the conference. He pointed out that the conference had become a reality in 1890, following an initial impetus given it by the American Bar Association and the New York State legislature. With regard to the motivation behind the founding of the conference, Smith asserted that the needs of the business community must be met: "Obviously, if your system of government is to be preserved, and at the same time the legitimate demands of the business world are to be heeded, there must be one law on those subjects that affects business interests for all of the states, or loss, irritation and serious injury to the prosperity of the country which have already ensued will be continued, and eventually the remedy, probably more fatal than the disease, will come in an all-embracing centralization of power in the Federal government."

Smith opposed an amendment to the Federal Constitution for the purpose of securing uniform commercial codes. He said it was the goal of the conference to pass a series of uniform laws that would be adopted by the various states to remedy the "uncertainties, inconvenience and dangers arising from the divergencies of the commercial laws of the different states." For, Smith observed, "Our dual system of government, under which there exists side by side courts of the United States and courts of the states, exercising jurisidction over many identical subjects, led naturally to a diversity of the laws."

He then pointed out the benefits that accrued following passage of the uniform negotiable instruments bill: "As a result of the adoption of this law in so many different jurisdictions, merchants whose business extends beyond their own State lines need no longer apprehend the danger arising from divergent decisions and statutes, but have a reasonable certainty that the provisions of the law relating to commercial paper in all its forms are not alone identical in letter but are likely to receive substantially the same interpretation in case of litigation in an overwhelmingly preponderating majority of the American courts."[124]

Over the years the Philadelphia attorney continued to support the movement for uniform commercial laws. He made a number of speeches to various bar associations for the purpose of publicizing the work of the commissioners. These speeches were based on three premises: first, that the dual system of commercial laws is both inconvenient and inefficient; second, that the business community required a more rational system of commercial law; and third, that a uniform state law was preferable to an amendment to the Federal Constitution.[125]

REFORM POLITICS, POST-WORLD WAR I

Smith's advocacy of uniform state laws and his participation in the urban good government movement in Philadelphia earned for him the badge of the progressive, but his subsequent political behavior—desertion of Woodrow Wilson in the 1916 presidential election at a time when many Republican progressives flocked to the Democratic banner—detracts from his earlier progressive record.

In the 1916 election Woodrow Wilson gained reelection. His victory was in large measure due to the support that Republican progressives gave him; but Smith, unlike most progressives who voted for Wilson, deserted the Democratic fold and cast his vote for Charles Evans Hughes, the Republican candidate. To be sure, Hughes had earned the progressive stamp of approval by his investigation of the New York insurance industry, but in the 1916 election Wilson, not Hughes, was the darling of progressives. Smith gave as his chief reason for opposing Wilson the passage of certain pieces of legislation closely associated with the Democratic president. Smith declared that the income tax provision contained in the Underwood

Tariff was "so clumsily drawn as to be unfair and burdensome in the extreme. The theory upon which the income tax is based is fair and just," Smith conceded, "but the present law is obnoxious as class legislation and is so devised as to throw its burden almost entirely upon a part of the citizenship." Smith also opposed the Adamson Act which provided the eight-hour day for railroad workers, and the Keating-Owen child labor act. In addition to opposing these pieces of domestic legislation, all three highly esteemed by many progressives, Smith abhorred Wilson's Mexican policy, claiming it was a "hopeless" and "blundering" policy which led to "anarchy." He also found fault with his "spineless attitude toward Germany" following the sinking of the *Lusitania*."[126]

While he opposed several measures of Wilson's progressive domestic program, in 1917 Smith found himself back in the vanguard of those Philadelphians striving for good municipal government. Between 1901, the time of Smith's work with the Union Party and the Committee of Nine, and 1917, when he returned to an active role in reform politics, reformers in Philadelphia had made appreciable gains. In 1905 they organized the City Party and effectively upset the schemes of the machine. This new reform drive was the initial effort of a decade of reform activity in both the city and the state. This 1905 movement culminated in 1911 in the election of the Keystone Party candidate Rudolph Blankenburg as reform mayor of Philadelphia. The last of the big city reform mayors before World War I, Blankenburg gave the city four years of honest and efficient government.[127] Unfortunately, Republican stalwarts in the city councils often blocked Blankenburg-sponsored reform measures. Frustrated with the obstructive tactics of Republicans and tired of reform, Philadelphia liberals voted the crusaders out in 1915 and the Republicans returned to power.

In 1916 the Republicans were once again securely ensconced in City Hall. Thomas B. Smith, a former postmaster of the city and a staunch Republican, was mayor. The days of reform activity seemed to be over as liberals returned to the Republican fold. But an incident in the fifth ward in the 1917 primary rekindled the fires of the anti-machine reformers.

The "bloody fifth," as it was called, was the location of Independence Hall (the State House), the Liberty Bell, and other historical sites, but it was also the scene of a political battle between the followers of Edwin H. and William S. Vare, bosses of Philadelphia, and those of Boies Penrose. This resulted in the murder of a city detective on the morning of September 19. An irate citizenry blamed Mayor Smith who knew of the impending violence but did little to avert bloodshed.[128]

Violence in the fifth ward aroused Philadelphia "Goo Goos." They organized the Town Meeting Party on September 27. Indicative of the interest and intensity of those present, Rudolph Blankenburg observed in his address: "I have never seen such crowds. It means that Philadelphia is thoroughly awake, and that the Day of Redemption has come."[129] Shortly after that H. R. Sheppard, the Town Meeting chairman, announced on October 11 a slate of officers to oppose the well-entrenched Smith-Vare "50-50" ticket. As reformers chose Republican Rothermel in 1901 to be their candidate for District Attorney, so it was that in 1917 Samuel P. Rotan, the Republican District Attorney since 1905, received the reform party's nod as the candidate to succeed himself. Thomas F. Armstrong, a Republican and former president of the Common Council, accepted the party tap as the candidate for Receiver of Taxes. The reformers put up Walter George Smith to run for Register of Wills. William R. Nicholson, a Republican and president of the Land Title Company, was the Town Meeting candidate for City Treasurer, while the party chose the following to stand for magistrates: William Eisenbrown, Edward R. Borie, J. J. Grelis, and James S. Boyle.[130] The ticket represented a fusion of the two major parties because Smith, Eisenbrown, Borie, Grelis and Boyle were Democrats while the others were reform-minded Republicans.

The Philadelphia press was disgusted with the Republican machine and covered Town Meeting activities with zest. The *Evening Bulletin* reported on October 12 that workers had started immediately to obtain signatures on nominating petitions, which by law must equal at least two percent of the highest vote given at the last general election to any candidate.[131] The *Inquirer*, traditionally a Republican paper, endorsed the Town Meeting slate of candidates and wrote: "These candidates all own themselves. There is not a stench of bossism, about them. No one need go to the polls and hold his nose while voting for them. They represent democracy, not political slave drivers of the contractor-boss sort. They stand for freedom, for common decency, for liberty of individual action."[132]

Even Boies Penrose, a man in whom muckraking elicited only "cynical disgust," endorsed the Town Meeting Party.[133]

Smith accepted the Town Meeting nomination as a "matter of duty. It is many years," Smith said, "since I have been active in political affairs. I had not expected to be drawn into them at this crisis, but since you have concluded that I can aid the cause of good government by entering this contest, I acquiesce in your decision." He decried corrupt election practices and asserted that "Either the citizens of Philadelphia will shake themselves clear of the unscrupulous men who are responsible for the mis-government under which we are now living, or life, liberty, and property will be at risk wherever opposition is made to a tyrranous machine. The Republic," Smith continued, "is engaged in a great war to make the world safe for democracy. In the conduct of that war we have pledged to the President of the United States our whole-hearted support. We shall be false to that pledge, even though the flower of our youth offer their lives on the battlefield, if we permit the fountainhead of democracy to be corrupted at home." Smith closed his letter of acceptance by saying: "Realizing that the purpose of your Committee is to organize all liberty-loving citizens, irrespective of political affiliations, for the vindication of the principle of honest government in Philadelphia, I am ready to do my utmost to aid you to bring about the success of the cause."[134]

In spite of his more than three-score years Smith campaigned with a will against James B. "Fee Grabber" Sheehan, the Republican incumbent, and John P. Brown, the Socialist candidate. At a rally at Town Meeting headquarters at 1527 Chestnut Street on October 22, all of the candidates appeared to make short speeches. Smith "created the wildest enthusiasm" when he announced that if elected he would not accept the fees that accrue to the register but would be content with the $10,000 salary. He closed with a ringing denunciation of the administration that had permitted politics to reach a low ebb in the fifth ward.[135]

Smith carried his campaign to the people. Dora O'Malley, the family housekeeper who doubled as chauffeur, drove him out into the highways and byways to issue his appeal. In an effort to attract Republican votes Smith frequently told his hearers of his family association with General Grant, saying that the general, under whom his father had served, had had a great admiration for General

Smith and for his fine stallion Bellfounder. As a memento, Grant had presented Smith with a military cap.[136] But campaigning was not always pleasant because prospective voters, prodded by the machine, frequently heckled Smith, saying that he was too honest or too old to be seeking public office. On one occasion Smith's detractors said he was running for office primarily to protect Drexel family interests. On another, "Fee Grabber" Sheehan said that Smith was "sissified" because he wore a wristwatch—this at a time when most men still carried a pocket watch in a vest pocket. Rising to the occasion, Smith rebutted: "My opponent has said one thing about me—he has accused me of wearing a wrist watch." Hitching his sleeve to show a wrist bare of a watch, Smith exclaimed in grim rejoinder: "If I did wear one, I'd be in the same class with those young men who have just been selected for duty in the trenches. They were drafted for public service. So were we. I think I'll buy a wrist watch."[137]

Town Meeting Party candidates created a wide tide of enthusiasm among voters, Party chairman H. R. Sheppard noted that party workers had worked diligently to eliminate erroneous names from voting lists and looked forward to manning polling booths on election day, predicted a victory at the ballot box.[138]

But as usual in Philadelphia victory went to the machine. Of the Town Meeting candidates only Rotan won election, and this was only a partial victory for he had remained on the Republican ticket. Sheehan received 106,874 votes to 103,204 for Smith and thus only narrowly defeated the elderly attorney. The Socialist candidate received a scant 3,000 votes in the race for register of wills.[139]

In this election machine candidates won by a very close margin. Town Meeting chairman Sheppard charged election fraud; he maintained that a fair count would give his party's candidates a clear victory across the board.[140]

Along with Thomas F. Armstrong and William R. Nicholson, Smith presented on the 29th a petition calling on the court to order a recount.[141] Three days later the court granted the petitioners' request. A recount showed that fraud was present but, while it narrowed the margin between Town Meeting and machine candidates, it did not produce the desired victory.[142]

The 1917 venture in politics was Smith's last. Although Democratic party leaders mentioned his name as a possible candidate to run for the seat of Peter E. Costello, the Republican from the 5th Congressional District who declined to seek reelection, nothing came of this. Smith no longer had time to devote to urban reform. As president of the American Bar Association he was frequently away from home delivering addresses to various bar associations. When he made his presidential address to the Association's annual meeting in August, 1918, the World War was entering its final phase. After the war Smith accepted membership on the American Committee for Relif in the Near East and thus embarked on the third career of his life, that of internationalist, a phase of his life in which he would attend three international conferences.

CHAPTER 4

Journey to the Middle East

World War I cast millions of human beings adrift as refugees, and many Americans responded by offering their gold and their services to alleviate this suffering. Smith joined them in a leadership capacity. His response to the call for assistance was motivated by a progressive humanitariansim, a sense of mission, and an awareness of the need to restore order to the chaotic Middle East. The humanistic, progressive drive that led him to urban reform and Catholic philanthropic work in Philadelphia was a nautral antecedent for international relief work. He simply translated this humanistic concern for his fellow man to the world scene, and in early 1919 affiliated with the American Committee for Relief in the Near East to help the suffering in the war-ravaged lands of the Ottoman Empire where thousands of Armenians and others were starving and homeless.[1] As much of his charitable work in Philadelphia had been for Catholic orphans, so his work for ACRNE, as the relief organization was abbreviated, would be among the Armenian orphans of the Middle East. It is this that makes Smith a humanitarian progressive, for his work in overseas relief was a natural complement for his progressivism; he thereby joined the ranks of Charles R. Crane and Cleveland H. Dodge, two better known progressives who engaged in both domestic reform and overseas philanthropy.[2]

Of his motivation for pursuing philanthropy, Smith wrote that his father "had stimulated my ambition to attain what is known as success among public men, but as years . . . passed . . . the truth has been more and more borne in on me that the only success worth having is that which follows the unconscious performance of one's duty in whatever relation of life he may have been placed." The Philadelphian noted that "from my experience and observation I am of the opinion that true success in life is not based upon notoriety that comes from ephemeral wealth or by the reputation for wealth; that, while wealth may be and should be earnestly and manfully sought after, it should always be considered a means and not an end." Smith concluded, saying that wealth should not be expended "upon luxurious living," but rather it should "liberate its possessors to work for the benefit of society." Inherited wealth enabled Smith to fulfill the role of philanthropist.

While motivated by altruistic considerations, Smith also had personal motives for joining ACRNE. Like his father, he possessed a desire to associate with important men of national affairs, a happy turn of events that was his lot after enrolling in the ACRNE leadership. Many of the officials of ACRNE were Protestant clergymen and laymen whose entrée at the White House and State Department had enabled them to influence American Middle Eastern policy for years. President Wilson, the son of a Presbyterian clergyman, was particularly influenced by these men. Association with this Protestant elite placed Smith in the vanguard of the nation's philanthropists, gave him access to the sources of power in the United States Government, and made it possible for him to have some influence in shaping American policy in the Middle East between 1919 and 1924.

Although many of the committee's officials and founders were Protestant clergy, missionaries, and wealthy business men, it required leadership representative of the broad spectrum of American religious groups. Therefore the American Committee chose Smith for membership because of his Catholic background. To his membership in this philanthropic organization he brought a wide range of talent that included the ability to make persuasive public speeches, a keen executive aptitude, a gifted faculty for using the written word with telling exactness, and a poise and grace acquired from association with important religious, political, financial, and military personages.

SMITH AND ACRNE: CONSTANTINOPLE

Viewing with compassion the chaotic world situation at war's end, leaders of ACRNE launched a fund-raising drive to collect $30 million from private sources to meet the needs of the vast number of refugees. In addition, relief officials determined that a fact-finding mission should be dispatched to the Middle East to learn the extent of human suffering and to study ways and means for its alleviation. Members of this mission would be selected from the various religious faiths.

ACRNE authorities selected Smith because his Catholic background would enable him to work effectively with the large numbers of his co-religionists among the destitute. Others chosen were Harold A. Hatch. New York businessman; Arthur Curtis James, New York philanthropist and business man; Professor Edward C. Moore of Harvard; Dr. J. H. T. Main, president of Grinnell College in Iowa; Dr. Stanley White, secretary of the Presbyterian Board of Missions; Rabbi Aaron Teitlebaum of New York; Dr. George H. Washburn, director of medical relief; and Dr. William W. Peet, member of the American Board of Missions in Turkey. The chairman of the commission was Dr. James L. Barton, secretary of the American Board of Commissioners for Foreign Missions and chairman of the National Committee of ACRNE.[3] The majority of the members of the Barton Relief Commission, as the group soon became known, departed for the Middle East in early January, 1919. But Smith, accompanied by his sister Grace (who frequently acted as his secretary) and Dr. White sailed for LeHavre on the 18th of February.

Following an uneventful crossing, Smith repaired at once to Paris, where Arthur C. James, the ACRNE liaison man, gave him further instructions. After a brief visit to the battlefields and a tour of an American cemetery, the Smiths departed for Rome.

They arrived on the 9th of March in the Eternal City, where Smith was particularly eager to interview Roman Catholic and Armenian religious leaders about his mission to the Middle East, a subject that proved of spcial interest to them. Accordingly, an audience was arranged with Pope Benedict XV. The Pope was intensely interested in Eastern affairs and told Smith of his own concern about the treatment of Eastern Catholics. Smith advised His Holiness that he expected to visit Syria while in the East and hoped to find out more about the status of Catholics in that area. After receiving the papal blessing, the Smiths departed.

At the conclusion of his audience, Smith conferred with Cardinal Gasparri, the Papal Secretary of State, regarding the condition of Catholics in the Levant. The Cardinal was familiar with the situation and filled Smith in on what to expect. He also conferred with prelates who had traveled in the East, because there were rumors that Protestant missionaries and relief workers had discriminated against Catholics in the distribution of relief supplies. He talked too at some length with Cardinal Merry del Val and also with Cardinal Bourne, the Archbishop of Westminster, who had just returned from the East where he had been investigating charges of French maltreatment of Catholics.

As his mission vitally concerned the Armenians, Smith also called on Armenian religious leaders who were familiar with conditions in the East. He visited Paul Pierre XIII Terzian, the Armenian Catholic Patriarch,[4] who was most interested in the thrust of his mission. He thanked Smith for making the call and gave him cards and letters of introduction to a number of Eastern prelates.

Having achieved the dual purpose of his visit to the Roman capital—making transportation arrangements to the East and ascertaining the state of affairs among Catholics and others in that region—Smith and his sister departed. They arrived in the Turkish capital on March 24, having traveled via train to Taranto, and from there by ship via Salonika, the Aegean Islands, and Gallipoli.

The Smiths went ashore and were conducted to Constantinople Women's College, where they were warmly greeted by Dr. Mary Mills Patrick, a long-time resident in the Middle East and the college president. Located about one hour's train ride from the city, the college was situated on a hill commanding a magnificent view of the Bosporus. Dr. Patrick and the faculty made them feel quite at home. But even with the very cordial reception and the beautiful scenery, the two hour's daily commuting soon led Smith to search for quarters more accessible to Bible House, the Stamboul location of ACRNE headquarters in Constantinople. Much of Smith's efforts were spent in obtaining a grasp of the complicated conditions in the Middle East and of the intricacies of detail related to the process of getting relief supplies to the interior. He was even compelled to forego one of his favorite pastimes—sightseeing in one of the most fascinating cities in the world. Daily he made the long journey to Stamboul station, and then through the narrow, tortuous streets—a trip that he found nerve-wracking and energy-depleting. On April 4 he declared to his brother Kilby that he had been pressed for the ten days that he had been in the East, trying to make order where there was none, attempting to streamline where there were only rough edges. All of his talent gleaned from years of boardsmanship in Philadelphia, all of his executive ability developed by years of directing the affairs of others, were brought to bear on the task. He and Dr. E. C. Moore, the Harvard faculty member, spent countless hours working on matters of organization.

At the outset Smith and Moore worked with Dr. Peet, Rabbi Teitlebaum and Dr. White. They were assisted by Charles Riggs, who worked as local treasurer of the Barton group, and by George White of Anatolia College who served as personnel director.[5] Other members of the commission were busy elsewhere: Dr. Main was at Batoum; Barton was in Egypt; Washburn had led a group to Konya; Hatch was returning home ill; James remained in Paris. Ultimately when Dr. White departed for Beirut, Teitlebaum for Palestine, and Moore went down to the warehouse facility at Derindjé, Smith was left to carry on alone, because Peet devoted most of his time to the affairs of the American Board of Missions.

One of the biggest problems confronting the Commission was the helter-skelter condition that obtained at the relief organization's warehouses at Derindjé, located on the Bay of Ismet some forty miles from Constantinople. Unfortunately, the warehouses were in poor order because, in unloading the ships, naval officers had dumped cargoes into the facility in an arbitrary fashion; this unhappy turn of events required Smith to make an inspection tour to ensure that steps were taken to correct the fault.

In addition to inspecting the warehouses and reshuffling the Commission's work in Constantinople, Smith also did some private relief work of his own to alleviate the distresses of orphans and refugees. For example, the Apostolic Delegate, Monsignor Dolci, had managed to save the lives of many Armenian children, and he maintained an orphanage with one hundred and ten little Armenians, all of them needing clothing and other necessities. Smith visited the orphanage, ascertained their needs, and saw to it that they were supplied with clothing, shoes, soap, and sugar from the ACRNE warehouse stores.

But Smith did not permit his private relief efforts to hinder his main purpose, in the accomplishment of which he found social functions very helpful. At a dinner given by Dr. Patrick on March 29 for Admiral Mark Lambert Bristol, United States Navy, the American High Commissioner at Constantinople, Smith had an opportunity to meet the man who would be of such great assistance to ACRNE in getting supplies and relief workers to the various part of the old Ottoman Empire. At a subsequent dinner given by Dr. Patrick for a Turkish senator and several Turkish officials, Smith discussed relief problems with the Admiral, who proved to be most receptive to Smith's presentation. Smith also met Howard Heinz, a member of the Heinz Catsup family who had formerly served as Federal Food Administrator for Pennsylvania. Heinz was then serving as Herbert Hoover's Director of American Relief Administration for Southeastern Europe, with headquarters in Constantinople. He and Heinz talked at length about their mutual problems. At one of Dr. Patrick's social functions, Smith also met Dr. Caleb Gates, the president of Robert College. Through Gates he met members of the college faculty such as Dr. and Mrs. George Huntington. Mrs. Huntington was a daughter of Cleveland Dodge, who was on good terms with President Wilson and one of the most active supporters of education in the Near East as well as backer of the work of ACRNE. These contacts made at dinners proved of value to Smith in conducting commission affairs.

Smith had early recognized that government aid would be necessary to facilitate the work of ACRNE, and for this reason he frequently sought out Admiral Bristol, finding him to be most accomodating in supplying his ships and staff members to aid the work of ACRNE. In fact, Admiral Bristol believed that assistance to relief workers was one of the most important tasks confronting the American Navy in the Near East. Smith also worked with the special Advisory Commission established by Admiral Bristol to take care of immediate relief problems in the Constantinople area. The Admiral's diary indicates that he gave much of his time to Smith.[6]

Smith also managed to spend much time with Heinz. At length, at Heinz's invitation, Smith made arrangements to accompany the ARA official on a fact-finding tour of the Transcaucasus to determine the needs of the Armenians in that area. This trip proved of great importance to Smith, because it provided him with a first-hand knowledge of conditions in Armenia, a knowledge that would later enable him to take part in deliberations at the Paris Peace Conference.

THE TRIP TO THE CAUCASUS

On April 20th, the day appointed for his departure with Heinz, Smith arose at 5:30 A.M. after a wretched night caused by a bad cold. Worried about her brother's condition and aware that the intended trip to Armenia would certainly be an arduous one for a man of sixty-five suffering from a cold, Grace thoughtfully packed a flask of cognac and one of ginger in Smith's bag. Although feeling some distress, Smith, accompanied by Grace and Colin Campbell Clements, a young Catholic Relief worker, went to early Mass at the Pensionate St. Elizabeth, as it was Easter Sunday. After breakfast, Smith made arrangements to sublet the suite that he had taken in Pera. Grace returned to the College, to remain there in his absence, and Smith repaired to his club for a light meal before meeting Heinz. The latter called for him promptly at 11:00, and together they motored to the dock and boarded the *U.S.S. Noma*, a converted yacht formerly belonging to Vincent Astor, the son of financier John Jacob Astor.

The ship got underway shortly after noon and soon passed through the Bosporus into the Black Sea. Although Smith continued to suffer some discomfort, the calm sea, the beautiful, clear blue sky, and the good weather acted as a tonic, and by late afternoon he felt greatly improved. "Luxuriously quartered" with a Lieutenant Heins of the United States Army bound for duty in the Transcaucasus, he enjoyed the two-day voyage to Batoum, the port of entry for the region. A good night's sleep in a comfortable bed, his cabin bathed by the cool sea breezes and, on arising, a warm bath followed by an excellent breakfast, all did wonders to restore Smith's vitality. On the second day out, the weather continued fine; and Smith, soon to become one of the nation's leading advocates for the Armenian cause, enjoyed a relaxing day reading late newspapers and chatting with his fellow passengers Louis Edgar Browne, a correspondent for the *Chicago Daily News;* Captain V. Rugovitch, an officer in the anti-Bolshevik Russian Volunteer Army; and Lieutenant (junior grade) Preston Lincoln, a member of Admiral Bristol's staff assigned to secure information for the purpose of writing an intelligence report on the Transcaucasus. Smith also talked with the ship's officers and larned that the *Noma*, attached to anti-submarine warfare units during the war, had destroyed one enemy submarine. But even with the delightful company, Smith, ever the lover of beautiful scenery, did not miss the enchanting sight of the Turkish shoreline. As he sat on deck on the starboard side of the ship he record in his "Journal" that the day "is fine and as we coast along, the massive mountains of the Asiatic shore rise in misty blue." He could not help musing that the people and the land probably did not differ greatly from the time when they were described by Xenophon in the *Anabasis*.

The following day was overcast and Smith spent much of the time in the ship's wardroom exchanging pleasantries with his fellow travelers and reading some of the Philadelphia and New York newspapers, complements of Howard Heinz. Feeling much better physically, Smith lounged in his cabin and spent the early afternoon reading Thucydides. However, he came on deck at mid-afternoon as the ship began her approach to Batoum. In the afternoon light, he beheld a spectacle that he deemed second in grandeur only to the approach to Constantinople. Although the day was a little hazy, he nevertheless had a magnificent view of the Gateway to the Caucasus, the great snowcapped Caucasus mountains rising high in back of the city.

Late in landing, Smith had little opportunity to see much of the Georgian port city. He was curious, for instance, about the Baku-Batoum pipeline. As a native of Philadelphia, a great oil refining center, Smith had heard of the pipeline that terminated in Batoum, whose point of origin was Baku, the refining center on the coast of the Caspian Sea. He had also hoped to view some of the Russian Orthodox churches, but time did not afford him the opportunity. At 9:45 P.M. he and the members of his party boarded a shabby, second-class railroad car pulled by a special engine and headed for Tiflis, the capital of Georgia. The night journey was uncomfortable, but Smith managed a fitful sleep. Early morning found them in the mountains. At breakfast they could look out the windows and observe the countryside, which Smith described as "splendid." That the Georgia peasants plowed with oxen and a "crooked stick" impressed him. With their sheepskin caps and coats, the inhabitants looked rough, and he observed that the people were little changed from ancient times.

The train reached Tiflis about noon, and Smith gladly left the dirty railroad carriage to enter the city, a well-built capital with broad streets and a surprising, up-to-date appearance. He met for the first time his fellow-commissioner Dr. John H. T. Main, and gleaned from him details about the ghastly conditions in the Caucasus. As Smith had been instructed to look to ACRNE affairs in Constantinople, so Dr. Main had been assigned the task of investigating conditions in the Caucasus, the region hardest hit by the war. He also had the ancillary duty of putting aright the ACRNE organization in that region. Smith's vicarious experiences in the Civil War did not prepare him for the appalling conditions in the Transcaucasus. In company with Main, he visited orphanages and hospitals in the Tiflis district; these were a part of the total work of the relief committee, which then maintained some thirty-odd orphanages, hospitals and communicable disease centers. During the year 1919-1920, the committee expended about $11 million in relief funds in Armenia and the remainder of the Transcaucasus. Even with such a large outlay, Smith concluded that private relief efforts were not sufficient for the task, and that vast outlays of federal relief funds were necessary to remedy the sad plight of the countless thousands of diseased, starving peoples.

At midnight on April 25 Smith and Heinz bid Dr. Main goodbye and boarded a train for Erevan, capital of the Armenian Republic. They spent a good night on the train. Smith rose early, washed and shaved at a fountain alongside the railroad line, reboarded the train and had breakfast. All day the train passed through mountains. The frequent stops gave Smith an opportunity to visit the huts in villages along the way. He found them to be low, one-story structures with no opening but door and chimney. They frequently stopped at stations, all of which were cluttered with refugees. After much stopping and starting, they finally reached Alexandropol about midnight. The next day Smith saw that Alexandropol, like Kars, was one of the fortified cities built by the Russians during the war with the Turks almost a hundred years earlier. He walked about the city the next morning and was greatly distressed by collections of ill-fed Armenian children and adults. He endeavored to distribute some biscuits to them and was almost mobbed. After he returned to the train, the party set out for Erevan, where they were met by Dr. C. C. Ussher, a medical missionary, and by members of the Armenian Provisional Government.

The Armenian Republic was formerly part of the Russian Empire. But in 1919, the Armenians, Georgians, and Azerbaijanis—the three predominant peoples of the Transcaucasus—united in the Transcaucasian Federative Republic. The effort proved futile, for the Turks compelled the Republic to cede the three districts of Kars, Ardahan, and Batum to the Ottoman Empire. Without these districts there could be no independent Transcaucasian Republic. Subsequent Ottoman demands for additional territory in pursuit of Pan-Turanian goals made it all the more apparent that the federation could not survive. In less than one year events forced the three peoples to go their own ways in May, 1919, and where there had been only one republic, there were now three: Georgia, Azerbaijan, and Armenia.

The establishment of the Armenian Republic had not been anticipated by Armenian leaders, for it was a goal they had not sought.[7] As a consequence, the demise of the Transcaucasian Federation and the emergence of an independent Armenia caught the Armenian leadership unprepared to deal with the problems brought on by the chaos that accompanied the war. The little Republic consisted of some 4,400 square miles. But the weak, tragic Armenian Republic existed more as a client of the Ottoman Empire than as an independent, sovereign entity. Like the Georgians who sought the protection of the Germans and the Azerbaijanis who drew closer to the Turks, the Armenians eschewed protection from the Turks whose past history belied any good intentions the Ottomans might have toward the Armenians. Looking to the West, the Armenians threw in their lot with the Entente Powers, hoping one of them would give aid and comfort. When the war drew to a close, the Armenian Republic sent delegates to the Paris Peace Conference, hoping the conference would assign to one of the powers the responsibility for protecting Armenia until such time as conditions in the Caucasus should stabilize.

And so it was that when Smith and the members of his party met with Hovhannes Kachaznuni, the Premier-President, and with the members of his cabinet—making up what is called the Provisional Government of the Armenian Republic—the question of a mandatory power for Armenia arose. Smith concluded that the Armenian people had the stamina to recover from the ravages of massacre, famine, and war and the ability to govern themselves once a stable political climate was restored. But he felt they needed a protector. He wrote his sister, Mrs. E. B. Esler, on May 6: "I believe the Armenians are capable, under reasonable tutelage, of self-government. At this writing 200,000 people are on the verge of starvation. . . . But with it all, give these people half a chance and they will rise again." To his brother Kilby he wrote on April 25 that he had been in consultation with the members of the Provisional Government and was "favorably impressed by their beginnings of National political existence. All depends on the outcome at Paris." Smith also noted that "My conclusions as to the worth and endurance of the Armenians are borne out by the study of others more competent. It will be a shame if the Paris Peace Conference does not aid them to renew their national existence with boundaries on the Black Sea, the Caspian and the Mediterranean." He was making implicit in his letter to his brother that the *sine qua non* for the continued life of the Republic was a protectorate by one of the powers assembled at Paris.

Smith was absolutely right in his estimate of the great need for an Armenian mandatory power, because the postwar problems were simply too complicated, too numerous, and too far-reaching for the Armenian Provisional Government to solve without the assistance of one of the Great Powers. Famine, heavy debts, a vast number of refugees and the hostility of the Georgians, Kurds, Turks, Azerbaijanis, and the Bolsheviks were beyond the capacity of the Provisional Government to manage. Smith's estimation of the situation was shared by his fellow commissioner. Together they would later testify before a special Senate Foreign Relations subcommittee hearing on the Armenian question and reiterate at that time their conclusions that the Armenian Republic could survive, provided a mandatory power gave it protection.

After talking with the Armenian government officials, the party drove across the plain of the Araxes to the ancient Armenian religious center of Etchmiadzin. There the members of the investigating team interviewed the Catholicos, the spiritual head of the autocephalic National Armenian Church, and the famous Armenian military hero General Andranik Ozanian, considered by some to be the Armenian George Washington. The visit included a tour of the ancient cathedral, which dates from the fourth century.

From the holy city of Etchmiadzin, the party drove on to Igdir, where truly appalling sights met their eyes. Here the ends to which starving people will go to assuage their ravening hunger reached the ultimate degree, for here Smith obtained irrefutable evidence of acts of cannibalism. Of conditions at Igdir he wrote his brother Kilby on April 30: "The sight of human suffering and death I hope I shall never have to see equalled. All that has been written is not an exaggeration. I spared myself unnecessary trial, but I saw enough of starvation of children and the aged, death and utter hopeless misery." He noted hopefully that "relief supplies are going in. Conditions are not as bad as they were, but at least these wretched fugitives can dig the roots and plants and get the genial warmth of the sun."

Smith returned that evening to Erevan, feeling completely drained by the horror of human suffering that he had seen at Igdir. Of their visit to that pitiful town, John Elder, the ACRNE relief worker who escorted them there, observed: "We have been having some distinguished visitors. One was Mr. Howard Heinz, the head of the great Heinz Pickle factories . . . and with him Mr. Smith, president of the American Bar Association. I took them down to Igdir," Elder continued, and "what they saw they will not forget in a hurry. We just went from house to house asking how many lived there and how many there had been when they just came back shortly before. Not a house had less than two dead, some eight or ten."[8]

The next morning Smith and Heinz inspected several ACRNE orphan asylums and various clothing factories. Smith was quite pleased with the work done by John Elder and James Arroll, the two relief officials in charge at Erevan. Toward late morning Smith and Heinz again conferred with members of the Armenian Provisional Government. As a representative of the American Relief Administration, Heinz could promise aid from this government-sponsored relief body; but in exchange for their proffer of immediate aid, he extracted a promise from the Armenian leaders to repay the American Government. After the conference luncheon was served at the house of the Armenian Archbishop of Erevan. Later in the afternoon the visitors were treated to a review by about 150 Armenian soldiers.

They took their leave of the Armenian capital, a city Smith described as a "sad place," and proceeded by train to Alexandropol, which they reached early in the morning of April 29. This fortress city, like Kars, was in shambles because the Turks had blown up an ammunition dump following their evacuation. Smith walked about the city and saw countless sights of great misery among the populace. The sight of a woman dying while her daughter looked on hopelessly touched him deeply. Along the railroad siding he looked into the box cars loaded with refugees, and saw pitiful sights of human suffering among those being brought in from the South. However, the train on which Smith had arrived brought in sixteen car loads of flour, enough to reduce the human suffering greatly. In many of his letters Smith contrasted the natural scenery and the quality of life in Asia with the horror and human misery. To his niece Bettina Eshleman he wrote on May 8: "It was fine to be in Russia and to hear Russian music in the Church at Tiflis, and the natural scenery is magnificent. But the spectacles of horror, death and starvation will not easily fall away from my memory." Later that afternoon Smith and Heinz conferred with Lieutenant M. M. Mitchell and Mrs. Martha McNeille, two relief workers assigned to assume control of a relief hospital and orphanage in the area. Satisfied that ACRNE affairs were in good hands, they had a long interview with General Sir Francis Milne, the commander of British forces in the Near East, and with his subordinate, Lieutenant General Sir William Thomson, in charge of British troops in the Transcaucasus. Smith was concerned lest the British withdraw their troops from the region and leave American relief workers to the mercy of the brigands. He requested the British officers to retain their troops in the region, pointing out that the only railroad line to the interior ran from Batoum to Tiflis and on to Alexandropol, with branches to the east to Erevan and to the West to Kars. This was the main artery of transportation to the interior, and over it traveled the supplies so badly needed by the destitute Armenians. British troops guarded this vital link. Without them, all would be lost. Smith pointed out this important fact. He also asked the British to continue to provide guarantees of safety for the American relief personnel. This was granted, with the stipulation that no personnel should go beyond the old border of Imperial Russia.

Their mission completed, Smith and Heinz left with J. O. Arroll for Erevan, where they returned to their vermin-infested second-class railroad car and departed for Tiflis about 1:00 P.M. They reached the Georgian capital early in the morning of April 30th, "after five strenuous days and but one night with clothes off." This was how Smith described his tour of Armenia. They returned to their former lodgings and Smith had a welcome shave and a good breakfast. The pair bade goodbye to Dr. Main. They had accomplished the purpose of their mission, and the information gathered would shortly serve an important purpose. Smith then took the opportunity to see some Armenian art work and to visit a Russian Orthodox Church, where he heard Russian religious music.

BACK IN CONSTANTINOPLE

Smith and Heinz departed Tiflis at 7:00 P.M. They traveled through the night, arriving at Batoum the next morning about 5:30. The *Noma* was a welcome sight. A hearty breakfast, a bath and a shave, and Smith felt greatly refreshed after his travel.

The ship sailed at 10:30 and made good time to the port of Trebizond. Smith went ashore and interviewed the Reverend Doctor Robert Stapleton, an old missionary who had been working among the Armenians for twenty-five years. He had been present at Trebizond during the deportations and massacres of 1915. He was now in charge of the ACRNE relief facility. Stapleton averred that of the peoples of the Transcaucasus, the Armenians were by far the "keenest"; but he cautioned that he did not think they could assume the awesome responsibility for self-government, for they were much too given to carrying on feuds among themselves. Conditions at Trebizond, Smith noted in his "Journal," were far better than in the interior. The *Noma* departed Trebizond on May 2 and immediately ran into foul weather. The wind blew rain in great torrents across the deck and over the bridge, while the tumbling sea tossed the small ship about as she made her way to the Bosporus. They reached the waterway early in the morning of May 4. Landing, Smith drove at once to the Embassy. Following lunch at his club, he called on Dr. Moore, whom he found ill and about to return to the United States. He then attended a meeting at the Embassy with Heinz and Peet and Major Davis G. Arnold, the U.S. Army officer retained by Arthur Curtis James for the purpose of serving as manager-director of ACRNE operations in Constantinople. Afterward, he drove out to the college, where he was welcomed by Grace, Dr. Patrick and the members of the faculty. For the remainder of his stay in Constantinople, Smith and his sister lived at the college.

The tour of Armenia greatly fatigued Smith, but he remained in

Constantinople to work with Dr. Peet, because Dr. Washburn was still in the hinterland, Dr. Stanley White had gone to Syria, and the other commissioners were scattered widely over the Middle East. Fortunately, much of the administrative work was now taken up by Major Davis Arnold, a former American soldier; but Smith, as a result of the absence of the other commissioners, was compelled to spend much time at Bible House or at the Embassy conferring with various people about the relief problem in the interior. In a long consultation with Dr. Peet, Major Arnold, and Dr. Moore, it was determined that relief work in the Transcaucasus would require more than private relief efforts could provide. The conclusion was reached on the basis of suggestions put forward by Smith and seconded by Main, whose deposition Smith had taken.

The Heinz-Smith Mission to the Caucasus had important results because, as will be shown, the matter of relief in that region was taken under consideration at a later date at the Paris Peace Conference. It should also be noted that Heinz had filed a report with Herbert Hoover in which he related the "distressing situation" that obtained in Armenia, where starvation, disease and lack of shelter were taking a toll, and that private relief measures needed to be supplemented. Heinz reported that much food had been landed at Batoum, but that ACRNE was failing to get it to the Armenians. He said that corruption had penetrated the relief operation. ARA officials, Hoover learned, had discovered that two relief workers and several native workers had been selling supplies for personal gain. Heinz recommended that the ARA assume responsibility for all relief efforts in the Transcaucasus.[9] As a result of the knowledge Smith gained on the trip to Armenia, conference officials would later request him to participate in talks at Paris relative to the Armenian situation.

The remainder of Smith's time in Constantinople, until he departed for a brief sojourn in Athens, was taken up with a great many conferences related to his work. He met constantly with Heinz, Moore, Arnold, and Peet. Eventually, Heinz went to Paris, where Smith would later confer with him; Dr. Moore returned to the United States. That left Smith and Peet in Constantinople. But much of the commission's work devolved upon Smith, because Peet continued to devote most of his time to the activities of the American Board.

In carrying on ACRNE work, Smith was somewhat shocked to

learn that American businessmen were not wholly sympathetic with the activities of the Protestant missionaries and relief workers in the Middle East. Meeting Oscar Gunkle and L. Irving Thomas of the Standard Oil Company, he discovered that the American business man tended to be pro-Turk and anti-Armenian. Eliot G. Mears, an American economic adviser attached to Admiral Bristol's staff, suggested that American businessmen adopted this pro-Turk stance because the Turks could give Americans economic advantages, while the Armenians had little more than tales of woe and no economic advantages to offer in the form of oil or minerals.[10] Smith was pro-Armenian and profoundly anti-Turk. Being associated with the "Church lobby," as the missionary-relief element was often called, he held very strongly to the opinion that the United States should assume a mandate for Armenia. On this point, Smith wrote his sister Betty on May 19: "We are much excited here . . . by the political rumor that America will take charge of Constantinople and Armenia and other parts of the Empire. It looks as if there was truth to the report and of course sentiment is divided. For myself, I feel that the coming of American influence to the East, if it should come, can do much good. We have a mission to perform in giving good government, education, and uplift to these benighted peoples." Smith was referring to the fact that Woodrow Wilson had given the Allies on May 14 his assent to the United States' assuming mandates for Armenia and Constantinople, subject to Congressional approval. However, a proposed mandate for Armenia found little favor with the American business community who, Mears asserted, opted for "one big mandate" over the entire Ottoman Empire, because such a responsibility would offer the United States many economic benefits.[11] Smith would later involve himself in the struggle between the business lobby and the "Church lobby" as they fought to determine whether a postwar American Middle Eastern policy would favor Armenia and the missionaries or Turkey and the business man.

By suggesting that progressives also supported American imperialism, historian William E. Leuchtenburg has aroused an intense historical controversy.[12] But it cannot be said that Smith's motive for supporting the Armenian mandate was grounded on considerations of an imperial nature, for his association with the "Church lobby" placed him in juxtaposition to the business lobby which opposed the mandate but favored overseas expansion. Support for the mandate among Americans was based on a sense of mission and not on imperialism.

Smith, a devout Catholic laymen, performed a useful task for his Protestant colleagues in ACRNE. It seems that a Catholic priest, a Father Clements of the Assumptionist Order, reported that ACRNE relief personnel were discriminating against Catholics in distributing relief. There had indeed been instances where ACRNE workers had in fact discriminated in the sharing of relief, but after the Barton Commission arrived this practice ceased. Smith determined that this was the case, and he cabled his friend of long standing, James Cardinal Gibbons, the senior Catholic prelate in the United States, that relief by ACRNE "is made without distinction to race or religion."[13]

In addition to investigating discriminatory practice in the Constantinople area, Smith planned to visit Syria in order to investigate the treatment of Catholic Christians by French authorities and relief personnel. He in fact called on the papal delegate, asking him to make arrangements with the French government that he might enter Syria. But as events transpired, Smith did not make the trip.

Just as there was little time for seeing the sights, so too there was not much time for social life; but Smith did manage to attend an occasional luncheon or dinner party, always using it as a vehicle for transacting commission business and gathering information. For example, on the 21st of May he attended a dinner at the British Embassy given by Admiral Sir Richard Webb, Senior British Officer at Constantinople. At that time Smith had heard of the British plan to withdraw troops from the Transcaucasus, an event that had been rumored and one that could prove disastrous in light of the protection they gave American relief personnel. He also had tea with Sir Edwin Pears, the distinguished British lawyer-journalist and author of *Forty Years in Constantinople*, who greatly added to his storehouse of knowledge on the east and discussed with him possible solutions to the Eastern Question. On the 14th he attended a dinner party given by Dr. Patrick in honor of Reiff Bey, the Turkish Minister of Education, who gave Smith a summary of affairs in Turkey.

Following a brief week-long visit to Athens, Greece, Smith returned to Constantinople where he met Charles R. Crane and Henry Churchill King, leaders of a special commission appointed by President Wilson to investigate matters in the Middle East with a view to assigning the former subject peoples of the Ottoman Empire as mandates to the British and/or French. Crane was a personal friend of the President and head of the Board of Trustees of the Constantinople Women's College. A former president of the Crane Company, manufacturer of plumbing devices, Crane had given up his business interests and turned to philanthropy. Along with King, president of Oberlin College, they headed what was officially called the American Section, Interallied Commission on Mandates in Turkey; but since the British and French did not send representatives, the commission became known simply as the King-Crane Commission. Accompanying King and Crane were a number of advisers, including Dr. George R. Montgomery.[14] Dr. Patrick entertained members of the Commission on June 4th with a dinner at which Smith voiced his opinion on Middle Eastern affairs.

In addition to the problem posed by the forthcoming British withdrawal from the Transcaucasus, Smith also found himself involved in the complex puzzle of Armenian repatriation. One aspect of the embroglio was the question of how to repatriate the vast numbers of Turkish Armenians from the Republic of Armenia, whither they had fled at the time of Turkish persecution during the late war. It seems that the Turks would not agree to their return. But Dr. Clarence D. Ussher had drawn up a plan for their repatriation as follows: first, the relocation of refugees would be accompanied by the furnishing of adequate housing and sufficient agricultural implements to get in a new crop of grain before winter set in; second, funds for this operation would be supplied by the United States; third, a police force, made up of members of the old Ottoman gendarmerie, would be supervised by American military personnel; and fourth, the area would be placed under the administration of a joint Turkish-American team.

Events in the interior, however, determined that Smith, accompanied by Dr. Ussher, would go to Paris immediately. In addition to solving the repatriation problem, urgent steps were required to protect the Armenian Republic, because reports had been filtering in to Constantinople of the massing of Turkish troops on the border of the republic. Too, it was becoming more and more apparent that the British troop withdrawal from the Transcaucasus was imminent. Smith wrote his sister Betty Esler on June 14 of his change of plans:

"We had expected to sail for Beirut on the 20th but within forty-eight hours it has been decided by the Commission that I ought to go to Paris instead. We are to leave here tomorrow at a very early hour on a U.S. vessel and be landed at Naples." He advised that "I go in the hope of persuading high authorities to adopt some course of action that will relieve appalling conditions in the Caucasus. . . . I have no illusions as to the difficulty of my mission; but at any rate, I hope to satisfy my conscience. Plans for returning home must await the issue of this mission."

Smith's mission to the Paris Peace Conference had the stamp of officialdom; a cable from the American Relief Administration facility at Constantinople to Henry Morgenthau, an adviser on Turkish affairs attached to the American Peace Commission, declared that Smith, accompanied by Ussher, was on the way to Paris to discuss the Armenian question. Further, ARA officials advised Morgenthau that no change should be made in the administration of relief without consulting them.[15] Since his mission was of an official nature and Deemed quite urgent, Smith had little difficulty securing transportation. Getting a visa for their passports and obtaining passage on the *U.S.S. Barney*, an American destroyer assigned by Admiral Bristol to escort the battleship *Arizona* to Naples, was simply the work of a morning.

Early on the morning of the 15th the Smiths boarded the *Barney*, which got underway at 6:40 A.M. Smith noted in his "Journal" that it was the dawning of a magnificent day, one that would carry them to Naples, and then to Paris where momentous decisions were being made. They arrived at the French capital on June 22.

CHAPTER 5

The Paris Peace Conference

With his general knowledge of conditions in the Near East and his specific knowledge of those in Armenia, Smith had at his command a certain expertise which enabled him to advise the Peace Commissioners on problems pertaining to the Armenian question.[1] He thus joined the group of petitioners, many of them American, who appeared at the conference to make special representations on behalf of numerous subject peoples of the former European and Asiatic empires who were then seeking the fruits of self-determination. For example Americans representing the interests of Irishmen, Jews, Poles, Czechs, Slovaks, Italians and other minorities, were at Paris presenting petitions for their various constituencies. Some were more successful than others in achieving their respective goals.[2] As a member of this collection of petitioners Smith was well known for his professional accomplishments and for his wealth of information pertinent to the Armenian question. The American Peace Commissioners and their advisers gave Smith a good reception, realizing fully that he could facilitate their task in finding a solution. He thus had access to the sources of power then in the process of trying to formulate policy that would alleviate the distresses of the Armenians.

In his relationship with the members of the American Peace Commission and with such well-known figures as Herbert Hoover, Henry Morgenthau, Sr., and William L. Westermann, an adviser on Near Eastern affairs, Smith had some influence on the decision-making process vis-à-vis Armenia. Smith's four-fold purpose for attending the conference was: first, to convince the Peace Commissioners of the compelling urgency of the Armenian question; second, to persuade them of the need to augment and accelerate relief shipments to Armenia; third, to impress on them the obligation of repatriating the Turkish Armenian refugees to their Turkish homes from the Armenian Republic; and fourth, to convey to them the importance of one of the Great Powers assuming a mandate for the hard-pressed Armenian Republic.

THE REORGANIZATION OF ACRNE

Smith and his party obtained rooms at the Hotel Continental, and that afternoon he and Ussher conferred with Henry Morgenthau, H. C. Jaquith, the associate secretary of ACRNE, Howard Heinz, Alexander Hemphill, the chairman of the Executive Committee of ACRNE, and John Crane, son of Charles R. Crane. Smith made his report on the status of relief work in Armenia. Much to his dismay, he learned that Herbert Hoover was disturbed by what he (Hoover) considered the poor performance of ACRNE in the Caucasus. The ARA Director, Smith discovered, had decided to remove that region from the control of ACRNE and place it under a separate relief jurisidction under the aegis of the American Relief Administration. Morgenthau told Smith that Hoover's decision was based on the critical report forwarded to him (Hoover) the previous spring by Howard Heinz, who complained bitterly of the corruption of two relief workers and of slowness in dispensing supplies.[3] Smith defended the work of Major Davis Arnold, formerly of the U.S. Army and then serving as the manager of ACRNE's operations in the Constantinople region. He claimed the Barton Relief Commission had done the best possible job under the adverse circumstances. Commissioner Smith argued that, given time to develop fully, his reorganization of ACRNE's relief machinery—undertaken in Constantinople earlier in the year—would have proven effective.[3] The conference adjourned for dinner, but later in the evening Smith,

Ussher and Morgenthau resumed their talks, with Crane and Heinz present.

Smith had his initial meeting with Herbert Hoover at the Hotel Crillon on June 23, a day highlighted by the booming of cannon indicating Germany's willingness to accept the Versailles Treaty but somewhat clouded by the news of the scuttling of the German Fleet at Scapa Flow. The lawyer-diplomat recorded in his "Journal" that he was "exceedingly displeased with Hoover's manner and criticism, as well as with the conclusion to cut off the Transcaucasus into a separate jurisdiction." Hoover, the blunt, arch-administrator, was opposed to commission-type administration and was convinced the Barton Commission suffered from a "total lack of executive and business ability."[4] He told Smith that Major Joseph C. Green, U. S. Army, had been ordered to proceed to the Transcaucasus to assume temporary charge of relief work in that area. After a brief interlude for Hoover to confer with President Wilson at the latter's suite, it was determined by Hoover and Morgenthau, with Smith's acquiescence, to effect a reorganization of ACRNE's relief efforts by making a permanent separation of the Transcaucasus from the relief agency's direction. The next day Morgenthau sent dispatches to Dr. James Barton at Constantinople and to Cleveland Dodge, another of the leaders of ACRNE in New York, advising of the reorganization and pointing out that Smith had been consulted on this matter—had, indeed, taken part in the deliberations.[5]

Ultimately, the Hoover-Morgenthau plan of reorganization was carried out. Smith recorded that he called on Morgenthau on July 2. At that time he heard that Morgenthau had attended a dinner party given by A. J. Balfour, British Foreign Secretary and member of the British Peace Delegation, where he had learned of the Big Four's approval of the Hoover-Morgenthau scheme and of the appointment of Colonel William H. Haskell, U. S. Army, as permanent resident commissioner for the Caucasus with headquarters at Tiflis. Haskell was to take charge of all relief activities in the region and would be responsible to the Allied and Associated Powers at Paris.[6]

With all due respect to Hoover's administrative ability in his direction of relief work, his unqualified criticism of ACRNE is undeserved and open to question.[7] It must be remembered that the relief organization had been compelled to move swiftly. Any large organization generally runs into difficulty at the outset. Because of the enormity of the task facing ACRNE in the Transcaucasus, both

Smith and Dr. Main had recommended that government funds and agencies be requested to supplement the work of ACRNE.[8] As a corrective to Hoover's negative view of ACRNE, a report made by the American Military Mission to Armenia considered that "any criticism of unbusinesslike methods [in conducting relief work] must be accompanied with the statement of work accomplished, which has been very great and very creditable to America and her splendid citizens who have so generously contributed to the cause."[9]

Other extenuating circumstances can be offered to explain the difficulty of the task before ACRNE: Smith's efforts to revamp the relief structure at Constantinople had not been given ample time to effect a more orderly flow of supplies; Major Davis Arnold had been appointed only the preceding April and had had little time to continue the streamlining begun by Smith; the confusion at the ACRNE warehouse at Derindjé was due to improper handling by U. S. Navy officials, not relief personnel; and, finally, Hoover failed to realize that the Barton Commission was only a temporary investigating team whose primary function was fact-finding, not administration.

As for the organization and Smith's efforts to put ACRNE on a more businesslike basis, Smith's sister sheds some light on the complexities of the situation. In a letter to her brother Kilby she wrote: "If only he [Walter George] could have had everything from the beginning it would have prospered better. Dr. Barton, the President of the Commission, has been in the interior for months and when at last he came here he was taken very ill with dysentery and is now in the hospital; this left all matters in Dr. Peet's hands. He is remarkably good and intelligent," she continued, "but much occupied with the Mission Board and the affairs of the Commission were too heavy as a side issue, so they all moved slowly and when Walter came with Dr. White they had to make order. Dr. White hurried off to the Presbyterian Missions in Syria, and Walter was left to guard and guide here. He has admirable administrative ability and has helped Dr. Peet." Concluding, she said that "a strong Major Arnold has been appointed director or manager . . . and by the time Walter leaves things will be on a business issue. . . ."

ARMENIAN REPATRIATION

The second task confronting Smith and his colleague Ussher was the need to persuade the Peace Commissioners of the necessity of repatriating the Turkish Armenian refugees, one of the major problems of the Armenian Republic.[11] ACRNE was attempting to feed and clothe as many of these people as possible, but the task was immense. Ussher had devised a plan whereby the consent of certain Kurdish chiefs and the approval of the Sultan's government could be obtained to provide for peaceful repatriation. It was hoped that early resettlement of farmers would make possible the sowing of a crop of grain to help alleviate the terrible famine in the interior. Dr. Ussher had presented his plan at the initial conference attended by Smith, Morgenthau, *et al* on June 22.

On June 24 Smith and Ussher called on William Buckler, career diplomat (half-brother of Henry White and member of the Russian Division of the American Peace Delegation), to present Ussher's project. Arthur Hugh Frazier, Counsellor of the American Embassy in Paris and private secretary of Colonel Edward M. House, called and "manifested much interest" in Ussher's idea, whereupon Frazier led the group to Colonel House's room for the purpose of presenting the Ussher proposal. Unfortunately, the colonel was able to give them only a few moments, since he was awaiting an interview with Justice Louis Brandeis, recently returned from a mission to Palestine. House handed Smith a copy of the dispatch from Barton to Morgenthau (mentioned above) and made a few brief remarks. An examination of House's diary entries and of his letters relating to Armenia sheds no light on the visit; but it does indicate the Colonel's sympathy for the plight of the Armenians, and leads one to believe that he was wholly in favor of the repatriation plan espoused by Smith and Ussher.[12] Further talk with Buckler after the chat with House led Buckler to suggest that the Big Four might possibly grant Smith and Ussher an interview the next day.

Ussher and Smith did not get a hearing with the Big Four, who were very concerned at the time with the initial German reluctance to accept the terms of the Versailles Treaty.[13] In the total world picture, German problems far transcended those of tiny Armenia. However Smith, pursuing the goals of the Armenians, was not denied his day in court. On the 25th he recorded that he "subsequently had audience with Secretary Lansing, General Bliss and Henry White—fairly satisfactory." Although favoring aid to Armenia, these Peace Commissioners were very much opposed to accepting an American mandate for this tragic land.[14] They had received numerous dispatches from Admiral Mark L. Bristol at

Constantinople who had conveyed strong reservations concerning a mandate and had been swayed by Bristol's persuasive arguments.[15] Too, the Commissioners had received word from Washington—via the press, unofficial sources, and dispatches from the State Department—that many in Congress were opposed to a mandate. Moreover, Henry White had received numerous letters from Henry Cabot Lodge, chairman of the Senate Foreign Relations Commitee, expressing doubts about the wisdom of accepting a mandate for Armenia.[16] Lansing noted in his diary the talk with "Dr. Ussher and Dr. Smith (Am Bar Assn Ex-Pres) on rapatriation of Armenians" which led to his later discussion with the President about this and other pressing Turkish matters.[17]

On the afternoon of that same day, June 25, Smith and Ussher conferred with Sir Louis Mallet, Assistant Under Secretary of State for Foreign Affairs and member of the British Peace Delegation; Professor William Linn Westermann, formerly of the history department at the University of Wisconsin and at the time filling the post of chief, Near East Division, American Peace Delegation; and Eric Forbes-Adams, British Foreign Office official attending the conference as an expert on political and diplomatic questions. The topic of conversation was Ussher's repatriation measure, which Smith had hoped would go before the Big Four. Westermann recorded in his diary that the "plan was really a sound one." He noted that it called for the Peace Conference to make:

> an agreement with the Turkish govt. for the appointment of a Commission of Three for the repatriation of Armenians from Russian Armenia . . . into the Turkish Armenian vilayets. The Commission of Three was to have extensive powers—of dismissing local Turkish officials; of organizing gendarmerie from the local population; of managing all affairs of repatriation, taking over the Hoover Food Relief work, the work of the American Committee for Relief in the Near East, and all other relief work. The Peace Conference was to agree that the money loaned, by whatever government it might be, was to be regarded as a preferred loan upon the future govt. of the Armenian vilayets.[18]

On the 27th Smith continued his efforts. He conferred at an afternoon conference with Morgenthau, Westermann, Buckler,

Jaquith, and Colonel James A. Logan, Jr., the principal assistant to Hoover, and Westermann noted that the "plan for repatriation" was presented to Logan and then taken for Hoover's perusal. In the presence of Westermann, Logan, and Smith, "Hoover worked it over." There was some discussion about obtaining money to cover the work of repatriation. Westermann suggested that a loan from the U.S. Congress could be made. Hoover objected, saying it would be regarded as a scheme to get the United States to take a mandate for Armenia. Westermann replied that this was what he wanted. Smith advised that "ACRNE had enough money to install the work and take care of the immediate needs."[19] (Hoover later recorded Smith's statement in the body of his letter to President Wilson, writing ". . . I understand from the . . . Near East [Relief Committee] that they would be prepared to supply such funds as were required for incidental expenses until such other arrangements could be made.")[20] It was agreed by the conferees assembled in Hoover's suite that Morgenthau would approach General John Pershing and General J. H. Harbord to see if the latter would be available to accept the appointment as leader of a military mission to investigate conditions in the Caucasus.[21] Regarding this conference, Smith recorded on the 27th that he "approved the letter to the President providing for a military commission to the Caucasus, probably Gen. Harbord, Chief of Staff to Pershing."

Hoover reasoned that repatriation could be carried out only under the supervision of a minimum of 60,000 British or American troops. Inasmuch as congressional approval would be necessary for American supervision and for the much-discussed possibility of an American mandate, a military mission would be necessary "as a basis of determination of policy . . . even before the repatriation of refugees can be begun."[22]

From the above, it becomes apparent that Smith played a role in determining policy related to Armenia. But from a reading of Hoover's accounts of Harbord's appointment, the reader is led to conclude that his (Hoover's) efforts, and his alone, resulted in the selection of Harbord. Morgenthau observed that in the conversations leading to the appointment of the head of the mission, Hoover was actually opposed to the selection of Harbord because he (Hoover) did not wish a military man to become involved.[23] In his study of the mandate question, James Gidney concludes that "it was reports . . . from Barton and others that determined the creation of an American military mission of inquiry which should visit Armenia and inform the President of the situation there and of the problems that would confront the mandatory power."[24] On the basis of his report given at Paris, Smith would certainly qualify as one of the "others" mentioned by Gidney, because it was at Dr. James Barton's request that Smith made his journey to Paris, where his first-hand knowledge could be used to help determine policy relative to the Armenians.

Ultimately, Smith's and Ussher's efforts were fruitful, because on July 5 Buckler submitted to Secretary Lansing a recommendation pertaining to the relocation of the Turkish Armenians. It contained the essence of Ussher's plan, and called for the early return of Armenian farmers to Turkish Armenia so that they might sow a crop of grain to alleviate the severe food shortage. Lansing brought the matter before the Council of Five, suggesting that General Sir George F. Milne, Commander of British Forces in the Near East, be requested to supervise the repatriation.[25] Unfortunately, General Milne was unwilling to cooperate.

Admiral Bristol wrote Smith that Milne agreed with him about the repatriation of the Armenians. "If this is done by a military force," Bristol wrote, "there will be an explosion in the Moslem world and not only the subjugated races of Turkey will be in danger, but our own relief workers." Bristol said that the Greek landing at Smyrna on the west coast of Turkey had caused the Moslems to "lose faith in the Allied and Associated Powers. The repatriation of the Turkish Armenians by force," Bristol continued, "will appear to the Moslems as simply another Smyrna incident." Birstol said emphatically that no repatriation should be attempted until Turkey is occupied by military forces. But the Admiral suggested that if the Turks could be induced "to carry out these repatriations under their supervision, with the advice and assistance of our relief workers, it would be a most excellent scheme and could immediately be taken up without danger." In concluding, the Admiral mentioned that he had talked with the Acting President of the Armenian Republic, who said that repatriation of Turkish Armenians would be most advantageous to the Armenian Republic since it would ensure control of Turkish Armenia.[26] Smith turned Bristol's letter over to Buckler for inclusion in the Peace Conference file.

The Ussher plan of repatriation had received Smith's strongest support. But while well conceived, it had little chance of success. Major Joseph Green, the American Relief Administration director at Tiflis, sent word from Tiflis in late July that British authorities had refused to extend a credit of two million pounds sterling for the purchase of seed wheat until the political situation cleared up in Turkey.[27] However, officials at the conference placed their hope in General Harbord. Morgenthau wrote the general, "Your immediate problem would be to arrange for the migration of those horded [sic] people back to their old homesteads and farms in Turkish Armenia."[28]

An immediate end to the problem of repatriation was not achieved. General Harbord arrived in Armenia in the late summer of 1919 and surveyed conditions. His report to President Wilson stated that some 300,000 refugees from Turkish Armenia were still resident in the Armenian Republic of the Caucasus. He noted that their condition was "pitiable to the last degree" and that Colonel Haskell, the Resident Commissioner in charge of relief in the Transcaucasus, was doing all for them that was humanly possible. Some of the refugees had returned, Harbord reported, but there was little incentive for the others doing so, inasmuch as most of their property had been destroyed.[29]

In summarizing their efforts to relocate refugees, it can be said that Smith and Ussher were successful in placing the latter's plan before the proper officials at the conference and that steps were initiated to realize a successful conclusion to the refugee problem. However, conditions beyond their control prevented the implementation of the repatriation scheme.

As was the case on previous occasions when in Paris, Smith did not have a great deal of time to spare while participating in the talks on the Armenian question. During his first week in Paris, he was extremely busy, with every day devoted to conversations with Morgenthau, Hoover, and the Peace Commissioners on the Armenian problem. He wrote his brother Kilby on July 11: "It has been a steady drive with no relaxation except the delightful voyage on the Mediterranean." However, he did take out brief peiods to enjoy himself in the city he had first visited almost thirty years ago while on his wedding trip. The Smiths found numerous friends in the city and, as is the case at international conferences, there was much entertaining at which official business was often the topic of discussion.

Frequently, between talks, Smith and his sister would walk the familiar streets and broad boulevards of the city, where they would lose themselves in a sea of olive-drab uniforms. Smith must have felt very much at home, dressed in his uniform especially designed by Dr. William Peet for the members of the Barton Commission. Occasionally, the mass of olive drab would be punctuated with a "top hatted, frock," as the military referred to the diplomats, going to or from some meeting. On one occasion they happened upon Anthony Drexel, the cousin of Walter's late wife. Doubtless he was in the city looking to the family banking interests. Smith told him he and Grace had taken a trip to Greece from Constantinople aboard his old yacht, which had been turned over to the Navy for war service.

On numerous occasions Smith and his sister entertained or were entertained by some of the friends they had made while in Constantinople. Dr. Isabel Dodd and Dr. Mary Mills Patrick of Constantinople Women's College had come to Paris, where the latter presented to the Division of Western Asian Affairs of the American Peace Commission facts pertinent to the Turkish situation. After serving in the Near East for many years as president of the college, Dr. Patrick had a wealth of information to give. On several occasions she consulsted with Smith on the drawing up of her "fourteen points," as she called her statement on Turkey. Also in Paris from the American colony in Constantinople were Lieutenant Commanders Theron Damon and Hamilton Bryan, both on the staff of Rear Admiral Mark L. Bristol.

From time to time the Smiths dined with members of the Peace Commission and their advisory staff, such as Ambassador and Mrs. Morgenthau, William Westermann, William H. Buckler, Manley O. Hudson (a legal adviser), General Bliss, and Henry White, the latter two being members of the commission.

Smith also met numerous Armenian leaders in Paris. He often saw and dined with Boghus Nubar Pasha, leader of the Armenian National Delegation, which represented Turkish Armenians at the Paris Peace Conference. Several times he met with J. A. Malcolm, the official representing the Armenian National Delegation in London. These meetings proved fruitful, because subsequently Smith worked closely with the Armenian National Delegation in trying to achieve Armenian goals.

On June 28 all Paris was overcome with joy when the treaty of Versailles was signed, an event marking the end of four years of war and signaled by the firing of many guns. That evening Smith and his sister repaired to Pershing Stadium along with thousands of happy Americans to attend an athletic event in honor of the occasion. Ever the scholar and never one to enjoy field events, Smith was somewhat bored. As Grace wrote her brother Kilby on June 30, "Walter don't care much for such things."

It was customery for all persons coming to France in the immediate postwar era to visit battlefields and military cemeteries. The Smiths drove for a day's respite from the conference talks to the ancient city of Rheims to inspect the cathedral. After viewing the battle-scarred edifice—its magnificent west from pock-marked by bullets—and driving through the badly damaged city, they called on Cardinal Luçon, Archbishop of Rheims. Concerning the visit, Walter wrote his sister Betty Esler on July 6: "We went yesterday in the rain to Rheims—a dreadful scene of desolation. It is forbidden to enter the shell of the cathedral because of danger of falling stones. Enormous and irreparable damage has been done." He concluded the description of the trip, writing, "We went out into the country to where the battlelines were, and got some realization of the horror of it all." No doubt Walter George, the man, recalled the letters his father had written so many years ago describing for Walter George, the boy, the horror and destraction of another war long since committed to the history books. And there is little doubt that the scenes viewed in Northeast France spurred Smith, who later served as a member of the Advisory Committee to the Washington Disarmament Conference, to act with determination to effect disarmament and help bring an end to the horrors of war.

BRITISH EVACUATION OF THE CAUCASUS

Smith believed his mission at Paris completed and felt the need for a rest. He and his sister took a much-needed vacation. They visited friends in the south of France and stopped for a few days at Lourdes, making of their three-week journey both holiday and pilgrimage. On the whole it was beneficial and restorative. Then the Smiths returned to Paris, where they found the Armenian situation had taken a turn for the worse.

Smith arrived in the French capital on August 4. He anticipated sailing for home immediately because he hoped to arrive in time to attend a bar association meeting with his brother Kilby. But unknown to him an additional task awaited his attention. On the fifth Smith called on Buckler at the Hotel Crillon and learned of a further deterioration of the conditions in the Transcaucasus. Dispatches had arrived at Peace Commissions headquarters from Major Green and from American Vice-Consul Doolittle at Tiflis to the effect that Turks and Tartars were massing on the border of Armenia, ostensibly to launch an attack.[30] In light of the impending withdrawal of British soldiers from the Transcaucasus (made known to the American Peace Delegation on June 20 and scheduled for mid-August), this news was ominous indeed. These troops had been serving a dual purpose. First, they guarded the important rail line, from the port of Batum to the interior of Armenia, over which vitally needed supplies passed. Second, they rendered protection to the Armenian populace.

A reading of Herbert Hoover's accounts of this matter suggests the conclusion that his influence, and his alone, resulted in obtaining a British order temporarily countermading the withdrawal.[31] However, Smith added his voice to those opposed to the British evacuation, and he played no small role in helping to achieve a partial postponement and slow-down of the movement. Along with Herbert Hoover, Jaquith, and C. V. Vickrey, the General Secretary of the Executive Committee of ACRNE, the Philadelphia Commissioner signed a dispatch to ACRNE headquarters in New York, care of Cleveland Dodge, the financier-philanthropist, close friend, and Princeton classmate of Woodrow Wilson, stating: "Lloyd George insists on withdrawing British troops from Caucasus. Movement has begun. If carried out it will be fatal to Armenian cause. Massacres inevitable till complete destruction. They have already begun. We beg of you to appeal to the President to use his personal influence with George [sic] immediately to hold off withdrawal for a time longer till Congress can act on Harboards [sic] Report. Otherwise all will be lost. Daily advices show situation dark. No hope save in means proposed."[32] The following day Smith talked with Henry

White and General Bliss, exhorting them to put pressure on Lloyd George to postpone the troop removal.

To continue his efforts to gain British reconsideration of troop disposition in the Transcaucasus, Smith decided to put off his return to the United States and go instead to London to lodge a protest with British officials in Whitehall, the Cabinet, and the House of Commons. On August 8, prior to leaving Paris, he called on Philip Kerr, Lloyd George's private secretary. Kerr advised him that the planned movement of the Transcaucasus expeditionary force was irrevocable unless President Wilson would affirm his promise to accept an American mandate for Armenia. Kerr's statement suggests very strongly that British withdrawal was designed to force President Wilson to keep his May pledge to accept a mandate for Armenia.[33]

British diplomatic documents indicate that Whitehall hoped the United States would assume a protectorate for Armenia. While it cannot be proven conclusively that the withdrawal was designed specifically to elicit an immediate decision from the President, the documents do suggest that this might have been the intent. Tightly woven into the warp and woof of British Near Eastern policy was the desire for an American mandate for Armenia; such a commitment would act as a stabilizing influence in the Near East and serve to abet British imperial interests there. Fully aware of the sympathy of the American public for the Armenians, as expressed by the donation of millions of dollars for their relief, British policy-makers sought an American mandate, hoping that American humanitarian interests could be translated to serve British imperial aspirations. An American mandate for Armenia, officials in Whitehall concluded, would act as a buffer against Bolshevik incursion into the Near East where the British hoped to develop valuable oil resources in Mesopotamia. Such a buffer would also check a possible Bolshevik threat to India. And there was the added possibility, British statesmen reasoned, of a pan-Moslem movement sweeping through the Near East, depriving Britain of Mesopotamia, her holdings in Persia, and perhaps India.[34]

There is no indication in Smith's journal or letters that he thought the British were trying to bring on such an American decision, but a letter from Grace Smith to her brother Kilby indicates she was of that very opinion. *"The British,"* she wrote, *"evidently hope to force the mandate for Armenia on America,* but this way of doing it [withdrawing their Transcaucasus expeditionary force] means the extermination of the remnant of the race and soon, if they withdraw protection there will be no more Armenian question."[35] In view of Smith's influence on his sister, it seems evident that Grace Smith's letter reflects her brother's sentiments. Just as American forces would later support Greece and Turkey in carrying out the Truman Doctrine following the British pull-out in 1947, so it appears British officials in 1919 hoped that their withdrawal from the Transcaucasus would produce a vacuum into which American troops would pour to contain Bolshevism.

Smith dined on August 8 with Henry White, General Bliss, Buckler and Dr. Patrick. Smith read to them his protest against the inpending British military movement. The *New York Herald* published it in its Paris edition on August 10. The article called attention to the dispatches from the Transcaucasus reporting the imminent danger to the Armenian Republic caused by the reported marshalling of hostile Turkish forces on the Armenian border. While Smith did not indict the British for an abrupt redeployment in order to compel Wilson's acceptance of the mandate, he did level charges at British policy-makers for permitting rank commercialism to dictate policy with respect to the Transcaucasus, when the situation clearly called for the very highest humanitarian consideration. Smith's caustically worded protest questioned the intent of British removal in light of their retention of forces in Constantinople. He maintained that "commercial advantage" was to be gained in the capital, while in the hinterland only the "cause of humanity" could be served, and "as happened so often in the past, commercialism prevails and human life is ignored." Smith pleaded with those assembled at the Peace Conference not to turn "a deaf ear to the appeals for protection of the Armenians against their assassins" and warned that American educational and philanthropic institutions were about to be destroyed after many years of effective work.[36]

Before crossing the Channel to England Smith made one last call on Lloyd George's secretary. Although Kerr could not see him, another official told Smith that Kerr had forwarded letters of introduction on his behalf to George N. Barnes and H. A. L. Fisher, members of the British Cabinet.[37]

Smith set out for London on August 11, deeply troubled by the reports of the possible annihilation of the Armenians by the Turks. But he evinced real satisfaction with his work in Paris. He wrote to his sister Betty Esler: "Our mission has been successful on the whole. Relief will probably be assured in the Caucasus. As usual I have been hard at work and seen many distinguished people, but have not seen others I should liked to have known."[38] Concerning the accomplishment of his primary mission, "which was to obtain immediate attention to the conditions of the Armenian refugees in the Caucasus," Smith wrote his sister Caroline, "it has been successful I think."[39] Regarding Smith's accomplishments, Grace wrote brother Kilby that Walter "has worked wonderfully well and achieved much, and has the full confidence of the ACRNE and I realized in Paris that Henry White and General Bliss and Mr. Buckler feel his strength and rely on his help now."[40]

The high-minded Smith arrived in London determined to continue the activities on behalf of the Armenians that he had begun at Paris. He devoted most of his time to the accomplishment of the task at hand, having little time for enjoyment of his proclivity for sightseeing. Aside from visits to Windsor and Hampton Court, he made only a brief trip to Birmingham to visit his Walter relatives (See Chapter 1).

Smith's London mission enjoyed the confidence of the Peace Commission. Frank Polk, chief of the American Peace Commission, notified Secretary Lansing, who had returned to Washington, that Smith had gone to London "to try and rouse British public opinion and induce the British Government to countermand the withdrawal of . . . troops."[41]

On August 12 Smith called on United States Ambassador John W. Davis. He related a brief account of his activities at Paris and, finding the Ambassador interested, "got his approval of my plan of campaign in London." To fulfill his plan Smith hoped to see British Cabinet and Parliamentary leaders to obtain a postponement of the redeployment. He also intended to use the news media to appeal to the British people's sense of fair play and create a tide of public sentiment favorable to the Armenians. Finally, he desired to meet with members of the Labor Party because it was at the party's annual conference that an attack had been mounted on the Government's retention of forces in the distant Transcaucasus and a resolution passed calling for the immediate return of these troops to their homes.[42] In addition to delineating his strategy, Smith urged the Ambassador to advise "Washington to tell British Government [that] withdrawal of troops would be considered an unfriendly act, because of danger to American workers." Smith's advice coincided with instructions that Davis had just received from Lansing, requesting him to contact the Foreign Office and urge delay of the impending troop movement.[43]

Late in the afternoon of August 12 Smith visited Sir Campbell Stuart, a director of *The Times*, and Henry Wickham Steed, its editor. Wickham Steed exhibited considerable sympathy with the Armenian cause and "intimated that tomorrow a full article would appear in *The Times*." Advised by Sir Campbell and Wickham Steed to call on Winston Churchill, Secretary of State for War and member of the British Peace Delegation, Smith set out immediately for the War Office, but found Churchill absent delivering a speech in the House of Commons.

On August 13 *The Times* carried a lengthy editorial reflecting Wickham Steed's interview with Smith,

> At this grave moment . . . the British have announced their intention of withdrawing from the Caucasus. As a consequence, the Armenians in Armenia are in danger of extinction. For them it is now, or soon will be, a choice between extermination and an abandonment, with peace in sight, of the cause to which they have been faithful through the war. This is not an alternative to which any loyal Englishman would willingly see his friends put. It is a hard thing to say, but the troops in the Caucasus, conscripts as they are, should not be withdrawn until they have been replaced by new British voluntary troops, or, better still, by troops from the mandatory Power. . . . We believe that if the facts were put to the English people—and why there should be any suppression of them we cannot conceive—many of those who feel most strongly about the retention of our compulsory service men on foreign service would be the first to say that, at any rate, they will wait until they are relieved by others who will prevent their fine work from being thrown away.[44]

That morning Smith interviewed George N. Barnes, member of the British War Cabinet, a delegate on the British Peace Commission, and a leading figure in the Labor Party. Smith noted that Barnes "listened patiently and with some degree of sympathy to my argument." The minister gave him some assurance that complete withdrawal would not be accomplished until October 15. Smith interpreted this statement to mean that the situation was not totally hopeless.[45] Postponement until October 15 amounted to a delay in the redeployment, originally set for August 15, but Smith, like others interested in the plight of Armenia, desired a longer postponement until adequate substitutes could be found.

Later that same day Smith called on Sir Ronald Graham, Under Secretary of State for Foreign Affairs. He described the gravity of the Armenian predicament and warned of the possible consequences of withdrawal. He then requested that the order be rescinded. The Under Secretary replied that he would lay the matter before Lord Curzon, Deputy Foreign Secretary and an expert on the Near Eastern Question.

Smith returned to his room and had a long interview with Raymond G. Carroll, an overseas newspaper correspondent. He had arranged for this interview as part of his attempt to pressure London on the troop deployment. Carroll's account of the interview appeared in the *Washington Post* on August 15. Smith was quoted as saying that he was in London "to reach the official ear of the mighty British Empire before it is too late." British removal from the Caucasus, Smith warned, would permit Kurds, Tartars and Turks, whose forces were massed on the Armenian border, to annihilate the Armenian populace. Smith said "he expected to continue his conferences up to the last moment . . . in an effort to secure cancellation of the order withdrawing British troops."[46]

On August 14 Smith attended a meeting of the British Armenia Committee at the House of Commons, where he met Aneurin Williams, T. P. O'Connor and Sir Charles Towle, all Members of Parliament with a keen interest in the Armenian question.[47] In the presence of the committee, Smith delivered a two-and-one-half hour summary of events in the Near East as they related to Armenia.

On the next day Smith presented his plea to H. A. L. Fisher, the Minister of Education, who had a deep concern for the Armenians. He next conferred with O'Connor and Williams. The latter told Smith he had interviewed Lloyd George and Churchill, who told him the withdrawal must continue. Smith returned to his room where he dicatated a long memorandum for O'Connor and Williams, who intended to use this statement as the basis for speeches to be delivered in the House of Commons on the evening of the 18th.

On the 18th Smith attended an emergency meeting of the British Armenia Committee at the House of Commons. His memorandum was the topic of conversation. He addressed the group, reading a few of the "salient points" of his statement, and then submitted to questions by Lord Robert Cecil, member of the British Peace Delegation, one of the drafters of the League of Nations Covenant, and an ardent Armenophile. While at the meeting Smith received word that Lord Curzon would see him that afternoon.

Smith went immediately to the Foreign Office. After a short wait he was ushered into the presence of Lord George Curzon. The Depury Foreign Secretary promptly launched into a defense of the British redeployment, saying the terms of enlistment of many of the troops had expired, that the expense of maintaining these military units was burdensome to an already heavily taxed Government, and that formal notice had been given for the move during the preceding spring.[48] He belabored President Wilson for failing to act on the Armenian mandate, thus delaying the Turkish settlement and bringing on the troubled conditions then existing in the Near East.[49] His Lordship said he had been in constant conversation with Ambassador Davis, who expressed doubt that Congress would appropriate funds to support American troops that might be sent to the Transcaucasus as replacements for the British. The ambassador had also expressed reservations about Congress' acceptance of an American mandate for Armenia.[50] Furthermore, he told Smith he had received the same information from British diplomats in the United States and at the Peace Conference.[51]

Smith presented his argument. He asserted that notice of the impending British withdrawal had not been made public in the United States,[52] nor had it been conveyed to the English people. To the latter point Curzon replied that Parliament had been informed.[53] Smith pointed out that the abruptness of the British move would jeopardize American missionary interests—schools, hospitals, colleges, orphanages—the result of over one hundred years of work. He pleaded with the Deputy Foreign Minister to keep the troops at their post for a few months longer. Lord Curzon replied that orders had already been sent out for the redeployment, which would be gradual.

Smith mentioned that a number of illustrious Americans—such as William H. Taft, Colonel House, Senators Henry Cabot Lodge, John Sharp Williams and others—were interested in the Armenian question.[54] He also told Lord Curzon of his activities on behalf of the Armenians at Paris and in London. Curzon reponded, saying he had read Smith's article in the Paris edition of the *New York Herald* and was quite aware of his work. Smith noted that at times Curzon "spoke with patience," and that he presented his argument in a constrained manner, although "occasionally I spoke with vehemence."[55] At length the interview was brought to a conclusion— after about ninety minutes.

If Lord Curzon had attended the House of Commons that evening he would have heard Smith's argument repeated, for Williams and O'Connor addressed the House, utilizing the material furnished them in Smith's memorandum. Williams declared that the intended move had been decided upon as early as March, 1919, but that the fact had been withheld from Parliament and not made known to the public. He said that "a gentleman of very great eminence [Smith] had recently told him that such a move would play havoc with American relief efforts." O'Connor's speech followed the same vein, but he added the interesting observation that President Wilson could not accept an American mandate for Armenia until such time as the League Covenant had received the approval of the United States Senate. He made a very penetrating statement, observing that the delay in the Turkish settlement was due to the dilatory tactics of Prime Minister Lloyd George and could not be attributed to President Wilson.[56]

It would appear that Smith's work in connection with postponing the British withdrawal was only partially successful. A brief delay was obtained. However, an interesting letter from E. A. Yarrow, Assistant Chief of Staff of ACRNE forces at Tiflis, sheds further light on conditions in the Transcaucasus following the British evacuation in early September. Writing to Henry Morgenthau, Sr., Yarrow said that British troops had entirely evacuated the region by September 10, except for a few soldiers left at the Port of Batum. Yarrow pointed out that when the British had arrived in the Transcaucasus they had found a state of turmoil. The area had been eventually pacified with firmness and tact. He observed that the region was much quieter at the time of his writing in October, 1919 than it had been when the British departed, but he cautioned that it was by no means stabilized. He wrote, "There must be an armed force here." The relief official noted that the force must "be ready for use if necessary." He concluded: "One might state the situation in contrary terms, *viz.* the need for an army ceases with its arrival."[57]

General J. G. Harbord's report to the President, dated October 16, 1919, covered conditions in the Caucasus. He related that after traversing the frontier of Turkey, "The Turkish Army is not massed along the border; their oganizations are reduced to skeletons; and the country shows an appalling lack of people, either military or civilian." But in justification for the American Military Mission's presence, Harbord added that "the visit of the Mission has had a considerable moral effect in securing the safety of Christian lives and property pending action by the Peace Conference."[58]

While the crisis had evidently passed without the catastrophe that Smith had feared when the British departed, Yarrow's and Harbord's reports leave no doubt that the presence of soldiers in significant numbers would have been most desirable. Thus these two reports vindicated Smith's efforts in London. Nothing concrete, unfortunately, was done for the 300,000 Turkish Armenian refugees remaining in the Armenian Republic. Following that government's collapse in 1920, the League of Nations did consider the problem of the refugees during the next year. The Soviet Union also tendered the suggestion that the refugees might be taken to the Kuban in Southern Russia. Yet in the end the dislocated people remained where they were.

Smith was encouraged by the knowledge that he had contributed to the Powers' development of an Armenian policy at Paris and London. He and his sister departed for the United States on September 3, arriving in New York on the 13th. They stopped briefly to permit Smith to transact some business at relief headquarters and then moved on to Torresdale, where the family, J. C. Bishop and Emily Rivinus met them that afternoon.

Smith's efforts for the Armenians had just begun. During the succeeding years, he devoted increasing amounts of time to their cause, attending conferences, making speeches, and writing articles—all for the Armenians. He thus became a leading American advocate for the Armenians, and one of the few progressives espousing an international cause in the postwar era.

CHAPTER 6

An Advocate for Armenia

The Armenian question colored American diplomatic relations with the Middle East between 1895 and 1927 and, indeed, during the latter part of this period dominated American relations with Turkey.[1] Although the United States Senate refused to advise and consent to an American mandate for Armenia in June, 1920—an act that seemingly laid to rest the Armenian question insofar as the United States was concerned—nevertheless the subject of Armenia haunted American relations with Turkey during much of the balance of the decade. An American unfamiliar with his country's involvement in the Middle East in the 1920s would be prompted to question the influence of the apparently unimportant topic of Armenia. The answer is simple. A number of organizations such as Near East Relief (the name adopted by ACRNE in 1919), the American Committee for the Independence of Armenia, and the Armenia-America Society were largely responsible for keeping the topic of Armenia before the eyes of the American people during the 1920s.

In the vanguard of highly articulate American Armenophiles was

Walter George Smith. He allied himself with Protestant missionaries and philanthropists in an effort to bring about the formulation of an American foreign policy in the Middle East friendly to the goals of the Armenians. He was motivated by a progressive humanitarian spirit that sought to alleviate the suffering of that unfortunate people. Moreover, Smith sincerely believed that failure to solve the Armenian question would court the possibility of further warfare in the Middle East. He worked arduously between 1919 and 1924 to find a solution for this enigma—an end he conceived as necessary to preserving world peace. As a progressive laboring for peace at the international level Smith was an exception to the rule, because most progressives shunned international pursuits to further their particular domestic reform.

In seeking to preserve peace in the Middle East Smith attempted to show that American aid to Armenia was actually in the national interest—it would give protection to American missionary and relief interests and preserve a sanctuary for American economic investment. But during the decade of the 1920s powerful American economic groups were also in the arena working to achieve the framing of an American Middle East policy more favorable to petroleum, banking, shipping, and industrial interests that would maximize the chances of American economic expansion in the Middle East via the Open Door principle. The State Department, acting as an honest broker between the two conflicting groups believed that the demands of what might be called the "merchant lobby" were more harmonious with American national interests than those of the "church lobby." It opted for a policy favorable to the American merchant and rejected the demands of the American friends of Armenia for a policy that would enable that hapless people to realize long-sought goals.

During the autumn of 1919 the situation in the Transcaucasus rapidly deteriorated and the plight of the Armenian Republic went from bad to worse. In the wake of the British troop withdrawal from the area followed reports of Turks massing on the Armenian border to subdue the shortlived republic. This turn of events caused diplomats in Paris, London, and Washington to ponder the complex problems surrounding the Armenian question, and caused individuals like Smith and others to take steps to find some remedy for the Armenians. Efforts to alleviate the Armenian crisis were soon forthcoming from the United States Senate.

THE WILLIAMS RESOLUTION

Senator John Sharp Williams, a Mississippi Democrat and one of Armenia's best friends in the Senate, was aware of the course or reported course of events in the Middle East and of the threat to Armenia. He introduced in the Senate a resolution authorizing the President to take measures to remedy the distress resulting from the impending British troop withdrawal. One of these would involve the expenditure of funds and the dispatch of American troops to the Caucasus.[2]

Because of his recent trip to Armenia and his expert knowledge of conditions prevailing in that troubled part of the world, the Senate Foreign Relations subcommittee to which the Williams resolution was referred requested Smith to testify. Accordingly, he appeared before that body and gave testimony on Friday, October 10, 1919. As if pleading a case in court, Smith comported himself ably and presented arguments for passage of the Williams measure. He related the story of his travels to the Middle East and gave details of the horrors found there. He reiterated his efforts on behalf of the Armenians at Paris and London and told of his steps to achieve postponement of the British military evacuation from the Transcaucasus. When questioned about British motives for the withdrawal, however—his questioner, Senator Warren G. Harding, tried to elicit an answer to the effect that British withdrawal was calculated to force the American President to accept the Armenian mandate and dispatch American troops to replace the British—Smith seems to have been befuddled. His answer was not straightforward. He did seem to feel that the British move was based on a lack of funds to continue financial support of these troops and also on the necessity of returning the soldiers to their homes because their time of service had expired. He requested that American replacements be dispatched to the area to preserve peace and protect the Armenian Republic, saying: ". . . I do not say it reproachfully or satirically or ironically, but it is a fact that we have made no difficulty whatever about landing our troops in Costa Rica and at other points in South America to save a sugar plantation. We have them now in Haiti. There are," Smith continued, "200 people at work on a benevolent mission in Armenia, and there are millions of American money invested there; simply on that ground" should American troops be sent to the area to protect American life and property. He closed with a peroration, calling for the use of American forces to prevent the extinction of the Armenians by massacre.[3] He later supported the position he had taken before the subcommittee in articles which appeared in the *New Armenia* and the *Catholic World*.[4]

Smith maintained an active role in ACRNE following his appearance before the Senate subcommittee, spending much of his time in New York and Washington attending to the affairs of this organization that now consumed so much of his effort. He was present at two of the organization's meetings in New York on October 14 and 15, and shortly thereafter attended an ACRNE money-raising banquet. Along with Secretary of the Navy Joseph Daniels, Abram I. Elkus, former American Ambassador to Turkey, and Dr. Barton, he spoke out for support of the Williams resolution.[5] Later that autumn, when ACRNE was incorporated by act of Congress and became known as Near East Relief, Smith was selected as a member of the Board of Trustees. In his role as Trustee, the Philadelphian had an interview in Washington with Lord Edward Grey, the British Ambassador to the United States. Smith told him what he had said to Lord Curzon, suggesting that since "the British troops were withdrawing, at least a warship could go up the Black Sea and make demonstrations for moral effect." Lord Grey reported to Lord Curzon his conversation with Smith, saying "Mr. Smith was very vehement as to our leaving that region and when I replied that we must go and have already gone replied that we were keeping our troops at Batoum and urged that we let impression spread that country would not be finally abandoned pending decision of Paris Peace Conference and that a British ship of war might cruise around the Black Sea and occasionally drill a few marines on shore."[6]

Smith also made speeches on behalf of the Armenians, appearing in Philadelphia on November 18, in Washington on Deceber 2, and in Albany, Kenwood, and Troy, New York in mid-December. On December 20 he addressed an elect group at the Philadelphia residence of E. T. Stotesbury, a partner of Drexel and Company, and on January 13, 1920, he spoke to the Clerical Brotherhood, a Philadelphia group.[7]

THE ARMENIA-AMERICAN SOCIETY AND NEAR EAST RELIEF

Smith was also one of those persons instrumental in forming a new philo-Armenia pressure group known as the Armenia-America Society, a body of American citizens dedicated to aiding the Armenians. This body's organization committee consisted of Smith, who acted as its chairman; Hamilton Holt, editor of the *Independent*; R. J. Caldwell, businessman turned philanthropist; Charles S. MacFarland, the secretary of the Federal Council of the Churches of Christ in America; and W. N. Runyon, an ex-governor of New Jersey. Smith was elected president of the group. The leadership of Armenia-America included the organizing committee: Dr. Stanley White, secretary of the Presbyterian Board of Missions and Smith's old friend from the days at Constantinople; the versatile George R. Montgomery, the Yale Ph.D., missionary, lawyer, diplomat, and publicist whom Smith had also met at Constantinople; and Henry S. Huntington, editor of *Christian Work*. The Society consisted of a large cross-section of American Armenophiles who were anxious to further political and material goals of the peoples of the land of Ararat. Included on the National Committee were such outstanding Americans as Jane Addams of Hull House; James Gerard, former American Ambassador to Germany; Oscar S. Straus, former American Ambassador to Turkey; Senator John Sharp Williams; Rabbi Stephen Wise, a leader of the American Jewish community; William Cardinal O'Connell, the Catholic Archbishop of Boston; and General Leonard Wood, the American soldier who organized the American Expeditionary Force that went to France during the late war.

According to its charter, the Society was created to "unite in cooperation the many friends of Armenia for the purpose of ascertaining the needs of Armenia, of bringing these needs before the American people and securing satisfaction of these needs through American assistance."[8]

While the Society did not exert a great amount of influence during the latter part of 1919, it steadily grew in size and became an effective pressure group by 1920. It later rivalled the powerful American Committee for the Independence of Armenia, an organization chaired by James W. Gerard who was the group's president, and Vahan Cardashian, its spokesman. By the spring of 1922, Armenia-America had grown to sixty chapters in the United States. It maintained close ties with the Near East Relief, the American Committee for the Independence of Armenia, and the International Philarmenia League, with headquarters in Switzerland.

Smith was also a member of the American Committee for the Independence of Armenia. He was a staunch supporter of its efforts to educate the American people and influence the Congress with respect to Armenian goals. He frequently called on Vahan Cardashian, a New York lawyer and spokesman for ACIA, while in New York on business for Near East Relief and the Armenia-America Society.[9]

Following the Senate hearing on Armenia and the organization of Armenia-America, there was a hiatus of several months on the Armenian question. During this time President Wilson embarked on his tour of the West to tout the League of Nations and collapsed at Pueblo,[10] the Senate rejected the Treaty of Versailles in November, the Allies met at San Remo in April and requested Wilson to accept a mandate for Armenia, and the Senate Foreign Relations Committee rejected the Williams resolution and substituted one submitted by Senator Warren G. Harding, calling on the President to send an American warship to Batoum to protect the lives of American relief workers. The Harding resolution and the constant pressure of pro-Armenia groups caused the President to feel that the time was ripe to request Senate permission to accept a mandate for Armenia, pursuant to the San Remo communication. His request to the Senate on May 24 was duly turned over to the Senate Foreign Relations Committee for consideration, and defeated on June 1st.

Smith frequently stayed in Washington for brief periods in order to carry on his activities for the Armenians. At such times he stopped over at the Cosmos Club where he was a member. On one such occasion late in June he joined R. J. Caldwell and Hamilton Holt in pressing Secretary of State Colby to plead with the President to extend the protection to Armenia that had been accorded to the little African Republic of Liberia. Their urgency is readily understood, because the Armenian situation had deteriorated sharply since his last visit to Washington.

Simultaneous with his endeavors for the Armenians as president of Armenia-America, Smith was also active on behalf of these unfortunate people as a member of the local Philadelphia branch of the nation-wide Near East Relief. Formerly known as the Philadelphia Committee for Armenian Relief,[11] this group had affiliated with Near East Relief in the postwar era, and it was largely through Smith's efforts that this realignment was brought about. Its primary purpose was to champion the political goals of the Armenians in the Philadelphia area and to hold public meetings in order to solicit funds from area residents for the aid of the Armenian refugees. The committee frequently met in Smith's law offices in the Witherspoon Building; it was from here that a resolution in favor of accepting an American mandate for Armenia was forwarded to President Wilson in the spring of 1920.[12] As a member of the executive committee of this Philadelphia organization, Smith was one of those instrumental in organizing a state-wide Pennsylvania conference for Near East Relief.[13] He served for a while as vice-chairman of this conference. The Philadelphia branch also selected him as chairman of a special fund-raising committee "composed of men and women in all fields of civic activity" to collect Philadelphia's quota of Near East Relief's national money-raising effort.[14]

While most of his Protestant missionary-relief colleagues took a moralistic view of the Armenian question, Smith took a new approach. To be sure, he did cast much of his pro-Armenian rhetoric in the Wilsonian mold of morality, but he began to exhort his readers and American foreign policy-makers to consider American national interests in the Middle East, which also required protection. He declared that the United States had "interests" such as colleges, schools, hospitals, and other institutions of an eleemosynary nature in the area that needed government shielding.[15] One can read between the lines of the thrust of Smith's argument: American forces had been used in the past to police the Caribbean and the Philippines to protect American commercial interests, and Smith wanted American troops to be used to protect and secure American philanthropic interests in the Middle East. At a later date, the Philadelphia attorney did adopt this very line of attack in his many writings and speeches for the Armenians.

Smith continued acting as president of the Armenia-America Society. It was as the Society's president that he attended the Geneva meeting of the International Philarmenian League in the autumn of 1920.

Sympathy for the Armenian cause resulted in the formation of phil-Armenia groups in the United States, England, and Switzerland. But as these organizations lacked the unity of purpose that could be achieved by an international organization, they were often ineffective in working for Armenian goals at the international level where important decisions affecting Armenia were made.

To remedy this lack of direction among pro-Armenian groups, the Central Committee of the Federation of Swiss Committees of the Friends of the Armenians formed in 1920 a pan-Armenian group known as the International Philarmenian League for the purpose of championing the rights of Armenians and for arousing sentiment in the Western world for the goals of Armenian peoples.[16] The League elected Edouard Naville, the outstanding Swiss Egyptologist then serving as president of the Red Cross, as its president and selected an executive committee consisting of delegates from the United States, England, and Switzerland.[17] To aid the Armenian Republic, Philarmenian officers drew up a plan of action as follows: first, to issue an appeal to the Great Powers, requesting aid for the beleaguered Armenian state; second, to introduce the Armenian question to the League of Nations; and third, to coordinate efforts of pro-Armenian groups in Europe and the United States.

ARMENIA AND THE LEAGUE OF NATIONS

By late autumn of 1920 the future of the Armenian Republic was in jeopardy. None of the powers had accepted a mandate for Armenia, and a combined Bolshevik-Turkish onslaught threatened to extinguish the light of freedom in the shortlived state. At this juncture, Philarmenian League officials called an emergency meeting of its executive committee to meet in Geneva on November 11 to consider various avenues leading to a solution for the Armenian problem.

As one of the members of this executive committee Smith, along with fellow members Kilby Smith and H. C. Jaquith, traveled to Geneva.[18] The trio arrived on November 10 and, as he was one of the principal members of the pan-Armenian body, Smith immediately joined President Naville and the Buxton brothers, Harold and Noel, to draft the appeal to the Great Powers. Written that evening and approved in full committee the following day, the petition took cognizance of the joint Bolshevik-Kemalist attack on the Armenians and noted that the fall of the newly-created republic was imminent. To safeguard the continued existence of the state it implored the powers to dispatch military forces to the Transcaucasus.[19]

In urging the Great Powers to action the Philarmenian League achieved a degree of concert among the friends of Armenia seldom attained in the past. It remained only for officials of the Geneva-based league to issue a petition to the League of Nations to fulfill its third purpose.

Convening on the morning of November 12 at the Hotel Metropole, Philarmenian members selected a committee to draft the petition to the League of Nations: Smith, chairman, J. H. Harris, Herbert Ward, and Noel Buxton, all members of the British Armenia Committee. The "dominating figure in the international conference," as Kilby Smith described his brother,[20] went to work immediately, and with the aid of Harris completed the assigned task that evening. The executive committee discussed and approved Smith's work on the 13th, and requested him to deliver the plea to Fridtjof Nansen, the Norwegian delegate who acted as League of Nations High Commissioner for Refugees.[21] The petition urged the League of Nations to appoint a suitable mandatory power for Armenia; requested adequate military assistance to drive out the Turks; asked for the establishment of a viable government in keeping with the treaties of Versailles and Sevres; and suggested that a loan, guaranteed by League members, would greatly ameliorate conditions in the hard-pressed republic.[22]

Two days later the League of Nations took action at the ninth plenary meeting of the Assembly, when two resolutions were passed.[23] The initial measure was submitted by Lord Robert Cecil, delegate from South Africa, as amended by Henry LaFontaine, a Belgian delegate. It urged the selection of a committee of six to make a study with a view to ending hostilities between the Turks and Armenians.[24] The second motion, introduced by René Viviani, urged the League Council to secure the assistance of one of the Great Powers in order to use its good offices to mediate the conflict between Kemalists and Armenians.[25]

Believing the Cecil-LaFontaine motion to be the more effective of the two, Smith frequented the League of Nations hall for the express purpose of lobbying for the motion. He approached Canadian delegates Charles Doherty and Sir George Foster, Ignace Paderewski of Poland, Thomasso Tittoni of Italy, and Nansen, seeking support for this motion.[26]

Its three-fold purpose accomplished, the International Philarmenian league adjourned on November 22. This group was successful, because League action followed promptly. On November 23 the League Council, pursuant to the Viviani motion, communicated to all League members and to the United States the need for one or more of the powers to act as mediator in the conflict then raging in Armenia.[27] This cable found a ready acceptance in Washington.

Although concerned at the outcome of the 1920 election with its "solemn referendum" on the League of Nations, Wilson was not too burdened to overlook the Armenian question, long dear to his Presbyterian heart. The month of November found him completing the delineation of the Armeno-Turkish boundary pursuant to the San Remo request of the preceding April.[28] To the Council request for mediation, Wilson replied that he would willingly accept the responsibility and would soon appoint an official for the purpose of mediating the dispute.[29] On December 2 Paul Hymans, the League Council's president, advised Wilson of Spanish and Brazilian readiness to participate in the mediation effort.[30] Conferring with his Secretary of State, Wilson accepted his suggestion that Henry Morgenthau be selected for the task,[31] and the State Department promptly notified the League of the President's choice.[32]

All of this activity was for naught. Even though the treaty of Sevres, signed on August 10, 1920, guaranteed the independence of the Armenian Republic, the Turks invaded that state on September 13, 1920. Prodded by their Pan-Turanian ambitions, the Turks sought the return of Kars and Ardahan. The Armenian leaders appealed to the League of Nations, requesting membership in that organization, the defense of the Armenian nation, and enforcement of the Treaty of Sevres. These pleas fell on deaf ears. A badly beaten Armenia signed a peace with Turkey giving up the districts of Kars and Ardahan. The Turks and Russians then made an agreement that settled the destiny of the independent Armenian Republic: what Turkey had not annexed was incorporated into Russia as a Soviet Republic.

Given the Pan-Turanian ambitions of the Turks and the thrust to the south by the Bolsheviks, and given the accord by Turk and Bolshevik, the Armenians had little chance of survival as an independent state. The Armenians had to make a choice. They opted for incorporation into the Soviet state rather than face sure annihilation by the Turks. Thus Armenia did not disappear from the map, but still exists as an autonomous entity within the Soviet Union.

On December 26 Hymans notified Wilson that Armenia had been overrun by Soviet and Turkish forces, and that he should now work through the Allied Commissioners in Constantinople on the Armenian question.[33] His term of office was running out and Wilson took little further interest in the matter. But the League Committee of Six was still active.

Before the Soviet-Turkish victory was completed,[34] Lord Robert Cecil, as spokesman for the Six, asserted that a loan of $20 million would greatly enhance the chances for the survival of Armenia. Smith supported the work of this committee; he cabled his endorsement of it to the President and implored him to ask Congress for the money to fulfill the recommendations of the Committee of Six.[35] With the support of Senator Lodge, Wilson requested Congress to appropriate the funds. No money was forthcoming. A Soviet state established in Armenia settled the matter, for the Bolsheviks repudiated all foreign loans in late December.[36]

A NEW ARMENIAN STATE

The Philarmenian League's effort to save Armenia proved futile. Friends of Armenia and Allied statesmen began to seek a new solution to the Armenian question almost at once.

George Montgomery, the able secretary of Armenia-America, working in conjunction with members of the Armenian National Delegation, hoped to create an autonomous, national Armenian home within the Turkish state.[37] He pressed upon the Secretary of State the idea of setting aside territory "principally in Turkish Armenia . . . under proper protection" to be used as "an Armenian Home with the expectation that it will develop into an Armenian Commonwealth and ultimately be reunited with the liberated Caucasian Armenian Republic."[38] Realization of an Armenian national home now became the chief goal of Armenia-America. Montgomery communicated this fact to Smith while the latter was still in Euopre[39]; and when in january, 1921, the Catholic inter-nationalist returned to the United States from his toils in Geneva, he immediately joined the new crusade for an Armenian national home.

In pursuing this worthy goal Smith and the leadership of the Armenia-America Society worked in conjunction with Boghos Nubar Pasha and the Armenian National Delegation. Smith had first met Nubar in Paris in 1919 while attending the Paris Peace Conference and had renewed his acquaintance with him in 1920 while en route home from Geneva. Lunching with Nubar and H. E. Noradunghian, a former member of the Turkish cabinet and also a member of the Armenian National Delegation, the trio discussed ways and means to implement the national home plan.

The scheme for a national foyer now became a primary concern for Smith. He attended a mass meeting sponsored by Armenia-America in the Synod Hall of the Cathedral of St. John the Divine in New York City on February 6, 1921. In an address to the body he reviewed the past history of the Armenians and exhorted his listeners to consider the pathetic plight of some 250,000 of them then living in Cilicia and of approximately 50,000 residing in the three Turkish Armenian vilayets of Van, Erzerum and Bitlis. He declared that these peoples had been removed during the time of the 1915 Turkish massacre and deportation, but had been returned to their homes by the Allies following the cessation of hostilities. Until some better plan for an Armenian national home could be worked out, the Philadelphia attorney argued, some stop-gap measure must be adopted.

These Armenians were then under the protection of the French, within whose sphere Cilicia had fallen when the Allies partitioned Turkey. Smith warned that the French hold on Cilicia was tenuous, because the aroused Turkish nationalist sentiment was violently opposed to it. He submitted that "the immediate problem" which friends of Armenia must consider was "the saving of the lives of the Armenians in Cilicia and Turkey." He importuned his Armenophile audience to direct their attention to the London Conference, where the national home proposal would be proffered by George Montgomery, and to concentrate their efforts on influencing the deliberations of the ministers soon to assemble for the purpose of deciding the fate of many of the people in the Near East. Smith then restated his solution; "The French," he earnestly declared, "should be aided in their effort to hold Cilicia and as it is a question of finance, it would not be difficult to work out a plan whereby a Congressional loan would enable them to do so." The French, then, would serve as a stop-gap until a more permanent plan materialized for the establishment of a national home.

In his speech Smith also utilized a new approach—an approach quite novel, given his milieu. He proposed that the State Department consider American national interests in the Near East which were endangered by the Kemalist forces. Smith was speaking during the waning days of the Wilson era when morality and mission were the watchwords of American diplomacy. He exhorted the foreign policy makers to participate in the negotiations leading to a settlement with Turkey. Such participation, Smith said, would render protection to American interests in the Near East and at the same time afford effective aid to the Armenians. In closing his argument, Smith pleaded that the government give the same protection to American "benevolent interests . . . as it will surely make for commercial interests."[40]

Henceforth, from this time on Smith couched his advocacy of the Armenian cause in terms that coupled a moral imperative to pursue a humane course that would save the Armenians with the need to protect American national interests in the Near East that included investments in educational and philanthropic institutions. This avenue was obviously calculated to appeal both to the high-minded American, motivated by humanitarian considerations, and to investment-conscious, property-minded Americans concerned about the more material aspects of American Near East interests.

In addition to hearing speeches, members of Armenia-America passed a resolution supporting Montgomery's proposed national home. They implored the powers, soon to convene in London on February 21, to preserve the "advantages alloted [the Armenians] in the Treaty of Sèvres," to set aside a protectorate or national home in the territories delimited by the President, and to provide for "the safety of Armenians who were encouraged to settle in Cilicia after the Armistice." By subtle implication the resolution suggested that the Allies permitted commercial interests to guide their hands in making Near Eastern policy; the resolution boldly asserted that "the recent course of events in the Ottoman territory has aroused a suspicion that the cause of the Armenians is being abandoned for other reasons." Stated quite clearly was the hope that Turkish and Soviet Armenia would be joined together with "the expectation that they will develop utlimately into an Armenian commonwealth."[41]

Not content simply with making speeches and affirming resolutions, Smith tried to bring political influence to bear on the London Conference via the State Department. He wrote Roland S. Morris, a Philadelphia lawyer and Democrat of national standing on close terms with the Wilson administration, to use his position to bring home to the State Department the necessity of helping Armenia: "I would urge that a strong statement should be made through the proper diplomatic channels to the Allied Powers in Conference in London, that the American people are watching with deep concern for the outcome of their deliberations and it is earnestly hoped that whatever settlement they may reach will include proper guarantees for the safety and repatriation of the Armenians."[42] Forwarding Smith's missive under a letter of transmittal, Morris notified Arthur Bullard, Chief, Division of Russian Affairs, State Department, that he would see him personally in the near future about the Armenian problem. In the meantime, Morris suggested he take it up with Robert Craigie, the British Chargé d'Affairs in Washington, urging the British to take official notice of the concern of the American government and people for the well-being of the Armenians.[43]

Thus, prior to the London conference at which the national home solution would be considered, Smith had done all in his power to create a climate conducive to the new proposal. At long last, proponents of the Armenian cause could hope for an end to the Armenian problem, which the Great Powers of Europe had been sadly neglecting since the Congress of Berlin. The London Conference offered much to those who had seen the hopes of the Armenians dashed more than once.

Deliberations at London opened in late February, 1921. Representing the Armenia-America Society, George Montgomery filed a statement of the views of the members. He asserted that the American society of Armenophiles had "certain justifications" for intervening in the discussions of the conference because of the vast financial outlays made by American philanthropic institutions in the Near East for the aid of the Armenians and other indigents. Recalling the aid rendered by the Armenians on the Caucasus front during the late war, the Armenia-America spokesman pressed upon the premiers the need to reward these people by considering the creation of an Armenian state. He suggested the territories delimited by the President should be "earmarked" expressly for the "future of the Armenian people."[44]

But once again Armenian aspirations were jettisoned. On March 12, 1921, the London conferees rejected the proposal for an integral Armenian state consisting of Turkish and Russian Armenia. The Wilson award to Armenia was thus cast aside. In so doing, however, the premiers merely acknowledged an accomplished fact: the Bolsheviks controlled the Armenian Republic, while the Kemalists held Turkish Armenia. Instead, the premiers decided to set aside a national home for the Armenians in Cilicia. The League of Nations Council would have the responsibility for drawing the boundaries. However, this new solution would constitute only a short-lived victory, because the premiers were already discussing possible French withdrawal from Cilicia. Without French protection, an Armenian home in Cilicia would be meaningless. To the Turks, an Armenian Cilica would be just as objectionable as the Greek enclave at Smyrna.

Smith expressed his disappointment at the outcome of the London Conference, writing caustically of the Allied statesmen: "Could there be a greater example of political cynicism than is shown by the Council of Premiers which has so lately adjourned in London?"[45] Despondent, but nevertheless keeping his hope alive, Smith wrote Secretary of State Charles Evans Hughes, calling attention to the impending French withdrawal from Cilicia: "I feel sure that you and President Harding will do whatever in your wisdom seems expedient to save those poor Cilician Armenians who, after years of exile, were recalled to their homes by the Allies only to be exposed to their present dangers."[46]

Along with other members of Armenia-America, Smith had hoped to influence Harding and Huges with respect to Armenia. He had met the President in October, 1919, while Harding was serving as chairman of the Senate subcommittee which had held hearings on the Williams resolution. Harding had evinced then a more than passing interest in the Armenian question and, although firmly opposed to American acceptance of a mandate, had introduced the resolution urging the dispatch of an American battleship to the Near East to protect American lives and property. The President's sympathy for the plight of the Armenians of Cilicia was real. He wrote the Secretary of State, expressing the wish to find some way "in which to utter the admonition of the five great powers to restrain the hands of the assassins in that unfortunate land."[47]

Armenia-America Society leaders reasoned that Hughes was an active member of the American Committee for the Independence of Armenia and had shown real interest. Hughes's biographer observed that his inability to help the Armenians left him in an "embarrassing position" because, prior to his appointment as Secretary of State, Hughes had been the "principal supporting pillar" of the articulate American Committee for the Independence of Armenia. Since an Armenian homeland would have required the presence of American occupation troops, "Secretary Hughes thus found it necessary to abandon a cause that Citizen Hughes had earnestly fought for."[48] In summary Smith had hoped to accomplish his goals through influence on Harding and Hughes. The former was sympathetic but passed the problem along to Hughes. Hughes, as a private citizen, had been and probably still was sympathetic, but as Secretary of State his major concern was that of the United States as a whole. Moreover, it is certain that Secretary Hughes was influenced toward another course of action by Admiral Bristol, whose views on the Near East did not coincide with those of Smith.

Research in the Department of State records and in Bristol's papers indicates that he influenced postwar American Near East policy and reshaped the Secretary's thinking on Armenia.[49] The admiral favored the open door policy but was opposed to American support for the Armenian cause. The High Commissioner urged the resumption of normal American diplomatic relations with Turkey to gain new markets for American merchants and new opportunities for American investment capital in the Near East. Support for an Armenian homeland would, in Bristol's eyes, constitute a hindrance to extension of commercial operations. In short, Admiral Bristol concluded that American backing for an Armenian home would require American troops to enforce a decision completely at variance with the aspirations of the ultra-nationalist Kemalists. He had so persuaded the State Department of the validity of this position, and he was so highly regarded by Department officials that the "church lobby's" later efforts to remove him from office came to naught.[50]

Smith and his Armenia-America colleagues were unsuccessful in obtaining the endorsement of Harding and Hughes for a national home, because missionary-relief control of American Near East foreign policy was giving way to control by the advocates of the open door policy. These men espoused the cause of American economic penetration and looked with disfavor on the use of military force to champion philanthropic causes that in the long run would only jeopardize American economic advancement.

FINANCIAL SUPPORT FOR ARMENIA

While working for the national homeland, leaders of Armenia-America were busy on another front. They also lent their backing to the achievement of financial support for the Armenians in the form of a loan. Efforts to achieve financial help for Armenia had originated in 1920 with Dr. James Barton, who asked President Wilson and Senator Lodge of the Foreign Relations Committee to make funds available to the Armenian Republic. Unfortunately, the 1920 endeavor to obtain funds was fruitless because, even though Senator Lodge and President Wilson joined forces, Congress would grant no money.

In 1921 Armenia-America leaders resumed efforts to secure a loan, thinking financial assistance might induce the French to remain in Cilicia in spite of the growing Turkish pressure. The society's officials hoped an American loan to France would enable that country to maintain a protectorate over the Armenians who had returned to Cilicia. This expedient would serve as a temporary measure until such time as a more permanent solution could be arranged. At the society's mass meeting on February 6, 1921, at the Cathedral of St. John the Divine, Smith addressed an open appeal to the audience and called upon the Allied premiers assembled in London to arrive at an equitable solution to the Armenian enigma once and for all, saying: "The French are in Cilicia. They are likely to remain there if money can be found to maintain them. Perhaps in the wisdom of our State Department some recommendation can be made to Congress whereby a loan could be made to France upon her assuming the responsibility of keeping order in Cilicia."[51]

As so frequently happened, leaders of Near East Relief joined those of Armenia-America in this new attempt to find financial assistance. Dr. Barton wrote Senator Lodge, pointing out the efficacy of an American loan to the French. The redoubtable missionary leader requested Lodge's opinion on the possibility of congressional approval of such a measure.[52] The Senator was sympathetic with the plight of the hapless Armenians but replied that a loan was not feasible.[53] Lodge also wrote Secretary Hughes, saying he had done all he could to secure money for the Armenians, "but I think you will agree with me that it is very unlikely that Congress will at present . . . undertake to lend more money to establish any government anywhere."[54] The Secretary's reply corroborated Lodges's assumption.[55] Once more the attempt to gain financial assistance had failed, but this fact did not seem to dismay Smith.

While devoting most of his energy to securing Armenian goals under the aegis of the Armenia-America Society, Smith did not neglect cooperation with Near East Relief. Although the society did not enjoy the cooperation of the American Committee for the Independence of Armenia on the Armenian homeland effort and several other Armenian goals, it did always seem to work closely with Near East Relief. Doubtless Smith's commanding position in the society and his presence on the board of trustees of Near East Relief added that measure of harmony necessary to cooperation between the two organizations. Dr. Barton also took an interest in the two groups and exerted his influence to ensure harmony. At any rate, Smith dutifully attended Near East Relief's executive committee meetings in New York, and in May, 1921, he joined Near East Relief officials to put pressure on Congress on behalf of the Armenians. In company with Dr. Barton and Dr. Stanley White, his fellow commissioner from the Barton Commission days, Smith helped draw up a resolution which was presented to Congress. This proposal implored the legislators to exert pressure upon the Allies and the Turks to put an end to the "state of anarchy" in the Near East and to avert a possible disaster as a result of Turkish mistreatment of Armenians in Cilicia. It asked them to insist that the English, French, and Italian governments restore order in Asia Minor and also ensure protection of the Christian minorities in Anatolia. Sent to Congress in late May, 1921, the proposal also solicited protection for the American philanthropic institutions in the region.[56] Smith supported this resolution in the *New Armenia*, writing, "We have large interests there, not commercial, but educational and religious. We have a right to know what our Allies in the recent war, Great Britain, France, and Italy, intend to do now that they have tacitly admitted that the Treaty of Sèvres is not a final settlement." Continuing, Smith declared, "We have a right to insist in the name of humanity, as well as for our imperiled interests, that peace be brought about, and with it justice for the almost destroyed Christian peoples from Chaldea to the coast."[57]

In order to put additional pressure on Congress and to revive the flagging interest of the American public in the Armenian question, Smith, Barton, and White mounted a propaganda campaign on behalf of the Armenians perhaps unequalled in all of the years that the Armenian question was before the American people. On June 3, 1921, the trio addressed a circular letter to a very large number of people who had made contributions to the Near East Relief charity chest. The circular read in part: "You are earnestly requested to read carefully the enclosed statement, and if your judgement concurs, to act promptly and with a vigorous message to your Senators and Congressmen, getting as many other influential citizens, societies and organizations as possible to send similar communications."[58] Attached to the appeal was an enclosure entitled "The Tragedy in the Near East." After reviewing briefly the efforts of Near East Relief and protesting profusely any political aims or aspirations, the circular advised the reader that the forthcoming French withdrawal from Cilicia would be followed by further massacres of the Armenians. Moreover, that unless the American and Allied governments took steps to protect the threatened Armenians, all of the hard work, all of the monetary contributions of the last five years would "come to nothing." Finally, the circular reminded supporters of Near East Relief that the most effective means of abetting the cause of the Armenians was to make "a personal expression" of concern to members of Congress in order that "official Washington" might "realize that the brain and heart of America expect that prompt and effective steps will be taken in the direction here indicated."[59]

The campaign was successful to the extent that it created a climate of opinion more favorable to Armenia. Congressmen and senators, in the words of Senator Frank B. Brandegee, Connecticut Republican, were "flooded with letters" requesting the United States government to urge the European powers to take "some sort of joint action to prevent the Turks from massacreing [sic] the Armenians."[60] Congressional, reaction to the letters varied. One congressman, L. T. McFadden, wrote Secretary Hughes requesting information that he might send to his constitutents. The stock answer sent out by the State Department to this congressman, to others who had submitted similar queries, and to the hundreds of letters submitted by private citizens, was that the United States had no diplomatic relations with either Turkey or Russia and that it would be difficult to make any representations on behalf of the Armenians to safeguard them from the iniquitous Turks.[61]

Many representatives and senators harbored strong opposition to American involvement in the Armenian question and wrongly advised their constituents about the American commitment to Armenia.[62] Leaders of Armenia-America found it necessary to correct this faulty information.[63] To do this society officials sent out a "Memorandum to Senators and Representatives on the Armenian Situation," advising of the situation with respect to the Middle East.[64]

In addition to correcting false reports circulated by congressmen, Armenia-America officials turned their attention to rectifying untruths emanating from another source. There appeared in the December, 1919 issue of *Catholic Missions* an extract from a letter by the Roman Catholic Archbishop of Beirut, claiming that personnel in Near East Relief had discriminated against his flock. He also maintained that relief workers used supplies as a means of proselytizing among the Catholic community, withholding aid from Catholics unless they converted.[65]

Smith was concerned about the archbishop's charges because he was the lone Catholic on the Barton Commission and he felt it incumbent upon himself to correct them. He gave an interview to a reporter of the *Catholic Standard and Times* in which he refuted allegations of discrimination, and the paper later published an open letter from Smith which said that his investigations showed charges of discrimination and proselytizing to be unwarranted.[66] Smith also wrote Monseigneur Freri, repudiating all allegations, and engaged in a long exchange with Cardinal Gibbons which persuaded the Catholic prelate that Near East Relief was fair in handing out relief and that its efforts should receive his continued endorsement.[67]

Smith was successful, for Catholics continued to contribute to Near East Relief and the secretary of the Apostolic Delegate in Syria assured Smith that the issue could be closed satisfactorily.[68]

FRANCE, CILICIA, AND THE UNITED STATES

Having corrected misconceptions originating from members of Congress and from sources in far-away Syria, Smith and the other leaders of Near East Relief and Armenia-America were soon faced with other troubles in the autumn of 1921. Ultimately, the event Armenia-America leaders feared came to pass: the French agreed to withdraw their forces from Cilicia, the area which Society officials and others had hoped to set aside as a national home for the Armenians. In return for this October, 1921, agreement with the Turks the French received valuable economic concessions. When they finally departed Cilicia in the autumn of 1921, some 150,000 Greeks and Armenians fled with them, for these Christians, despite Turkish assurances for their protection, were in no mood to trust the Turks, whose past record belied their stated good intentions.

Mistrust of the Turks prompted Smith to write Henry P. Fletcher, Under Secretary of State, in December, 1921. He warned that the French announcement of intended evacuation had thrown the "Armenian population of Cilicia . . . in terror." The attorney declared that there is in the United States "a deep and widespread interest in the fate of the Armenians," as evidenced by their contribution of $60 million to the Near East Relief fund. The Philadelphia Armenophile pleaded his cause with force, writing: ". . . in behalf of the Armenia-America Society, I appeal to the State Department to make a public protest to the Kemalist government to abstain from further violence to the Armenians under their jurisdiction and especially in Cilicia." Smith observed; "There are abundant precedents for such a moral protest and it will be effective action to the extent of showing to Mustafa Kemal that the American Government is interested in the fate of the Christian peoples of the Near East." He anticipated that a European conference would be called in the immediate future for the purpose of discussing the Near Eastern Question, and he utilized the most persuasive argument in urging American participation in the forthcoming talks: "It is to be expected that in the future the Allies will take up the question of a permanent settlement, and when they do, we feel that the United States should participate in the discussions, because *American interests are vitally affected.* When that times comes," Smith continued, "the Administration will doubtless bear in mind the sentiment of the American people, and by friendly suggestion may advise a course that will lead to a satisfactory and permanent settlement." Concluding, Smith wrote: "This may come about by the appointment of a Christian governor for Cilicia, or by the delimitation of some part of Turkey which might be regarded as an Armenian national home. Cilicia, by reason of its large native Armenian population, would naturally suggest itself as a proper place for such a home."[69]

Smith used less temperate language in an article in the *New Armenia.* He referred to the evacuation as the "cowardly duplicity of the French Government in surrendering Cilicia." He declared that this move was motivated by the French hope for a "promise of free commerce." However, he seems to have hurled his sharpest barbs of criticism at the British: "Great Britain, after all she has suffered for the Allied cause, has become through her own lack of vision and sordid commercialism an object of suspicion and hatred so great that even the Turk is supported against her. Greece," Smith continued, "has no friend but Great Britain, and Great Britain is too hard pressed to save her from her misfortune. Out of such a welter of duplicity, cruelty and horror it is hard to find a way towards peace and justice."[70]

But the American State Department, while willing to listen to the importunings of the Armenia-America Society, Near East Relief, the Philadelphia branch of Near East Relief, and other pro-Armenian organizations, was not disposed to take effective action to obtain security for the Armenians. The campaign launched by Near East Relief and Armenia-America to induce Congress to urge the State Department to make representations to the Allied governments on behalf of the Armenians was not immediately effective. Warren Robbins of the Near East Division at State, for example, advised Fletcher that he was emphatically opposed to intervening with the Allied Powers.[71]

Later in the year Robbins changed his tune when the President took an active interest in the question of Cilicia. On November 21, 1921, a Committee of Armenians called on President Harding with four requests. They asked that the United States government exhort the Quai d'Orsay to call a halt to the evacuation of Cilicia; second, the delegation suggested the Allies place the Cilician area under a joint commission; third, it recommended that American warships steam to a port in Cilicia to protect American lives and property; and, fourth, the Armenians raised the possibility of an American official being delegated to supervise American relief activities in Cilicia.[72] Aware that the Naval Disarmament Conference was then meeting in Washington, the members of the Armenian Delegation apparently hoped that Harding would confront visiting British, French, and Italian diplomats with the rapidly deteriorating situation of the Armenians of Cilicia. Both Near East Relief and Armenia-America favored introducing the Armenian question before the Washington Conference. At any rate, a lengthy memorandum of conversation in the State Department file related to the Armenian question suggested that this was exactly the course of action that Smith wanted.[73]

Harding wrote Secretary Hughes about the Armenian delegation's visit and suggested that some action be taken. He stated he would not want the question of the Cilician Armenians "intruded into the Conference program", rather, he preferred that the matter be put to Arthur Balfour, British delegate to the Naval Conference, and French Premier and delegate Aristide Briand.[74] The Secretary referred the President's letter to Robbins at the State Department, who advised that either the Secretary or the President might contact Balfour and Briand. But he adhered to the hard line, saying: ". . . no active plan of action could be taken by the Government of the United States in Cilicia," but that a "joint warning on the part of the United States, France and Great Britain to the Porte would appear to be advisable."[75]

The State Department remained unmoved by the efforts of the Armenophiles. It was one thing to take the Armenian question up with Balfour and Briand verbally but quite another to make formal representations to Whitehall and the Quai d'Orsay through diplomatic channels. But the American friends of Armenia did not despair.

On December 17, a committee composed of Smith, James Barton, Charles Vickrey, and George Montgomery called at the State Department. Fletcher was not available and Smith left a note requesting that he meet with the group on the 21st in connection with the "immediate crisis in the Near East."[76] On that date Smith, accompanied by Montgomery and Vickrey, again called on Under Secretary Fletcher. Smith acted as spokesman and called attention to the situation in Cilicia, which he regarded as "agonizing." He said that the lack of "genuine assurance for the protection of the Armenians" had caused a "genuine panic" among the peoples of Cilicia.[77] In addition, he read Fletcher a memorandum with respect to the situation in the Near East, which he left with him. Drawn up in seven parts, it urged that Admiral Bristol, the American High Commissioner in Constantinople, be requested to make a "public protest against the persecution of the Christians, and to insist upon non-interference by Turkish officials with American philanthropic work." Second, it urged the State Department to make some indication of what steps, if any, had been taken to secure the safety of the Armenians and other Christians in Cilicia. It also asked if an American commissioner could be placed in Cilicia. Smith's fifth point inquired whether a new treaty with Turkey might be forthcoming. Then he raised the possibility of American participation in an international conference on the Near East. Finally his memorandum asked whether the American Ambassador in London would be instructed to attend the conference of the Supreme Allied Council soon to meet.[78]

In replying to Smith, Fletcher said that his memorandum would be given careful consideration but that no answers could be given at this time with respect to the questions raised in it. Fletcher concluded by saying the time was not yet ripe for action.[79]

While Admiral Bristol at Ankara was quite willing to protest the Turkish treatment of the Armenians, he was unwilling to act in concert with the Allies on this matter. He felt quite correctly that the United States would only earn Turkish disfavor if it associated with those powers then subjecting Turkey to their collective will.[80]

There seems to have been a hiatus of some months before steps were initiated to look into matters in Anatolia. During the period from November, 1921, to March, 1922, the President and his Secretary of State were more concerned with the Naval Disarmament Conference and with Senate ratification of the treaties stemming from them. Furthermore, as President Harding wrote Secretary Hughes, there was "no American support for a proposal to send an armed force there [to Turkey] to correct any abuses which are proven."[81] Yet in May, 1922, when Whitehall initiated a plan for a joint commission of Allied and American officers to investigate conditions in Anatolia, American acceptance came after only a brief hesitation.[82] In time, Generals James J. Harbord and Henry T. Allen were selected as American representatives on the joint commission.[83] Eventually, however, the French persuaded the British to let the Red Cross hold the investigation, because the state of war existing between Turkey and the Allies might create an awkward situation.[84] Ultimately, no commission was sent by the Allies. While the United States was quite willing to use diplomatic pressure to moderate Ankara's policy with respect to Christian minorities, it was adamantly opposed to the use of American forces to put down disturbances in Anatolia.

There was, however, a good possibility that a European conference would be called in the near future to discuss the Near Eastern Question. According to Ralph E. Cook, Smith was one of the very first to advocate that the United States' participation in an international settlement would be advantageous to the protection of American interests and those of the Armenian people.[85] Smith and Montgomery advocated American participation in the treaty revision thought to be forthcoming and addressed a joint letter to the President. In order to achieve their goal the pair employed a new twist. Both were aware that the idealism of the American people during the first two decades of the century had given way to the materialism of the decade of the 1920s. Further, they realized that the missionary feature of Wilsonian diplomacy had given way to the stress on economic expansion via the open door policy. As a lever to gain American participation in a Near Eastern settlement, Armenia-America's leaders pointed to the economic advantages that might accrue to the United States should she become signatory to the treaty.

They wrote: "America's commercial and philanthropic investments and their probable developments in Turkey are of such a character, and of such an importance, as to give by themselves a warrant for America's taking official part in the Near East talks. Our interest is second to those of no other power."[86] Continuing in the same vein, the note read: "Aside from our moral obligations toward the Armenians . . . we believe it to be the general American public sentiment that settlements involving our interests . . . should not be made with our Government outside the council halls."[87] That Smith realized again the need to combine protection of American national interests with the protection of Armenian interests as an inducement to obtain official government action on behalf of the Armenians is to his credit as an advocate for the Armenians. Unfortunately for Smith and the Armenians, American foreign policy-makers did not agree with his line of reasoning.

The conference alluded to by Smith and Montgomery was held in March, 1922, but since an end to the hostilities between Greece and Turkey was not forthcoming, the conference goal of a revised Treaty of Sèvres was not achieved.

Nevertheless, leaders of Armenia-America had other trump cards to play. Montgomery and Ernest Riggs of Armenia-America drew up a resolution and prevailed upon Representative John J. Rogers of Massachusetts to introduce it in Congress on December 21, 1921. This measure urged the President to "express to the *de facto* Government at Ankara the moral protest of the United States against the persecution of the Armenians . . . and to take up with Great Britain, France, and Italy the question of calling a conference for the purpose of considering methods by which the Armenians may be given an opportunity to establish themselves as a nation."[88] The House Committee on Foreign Affairs held hearings on the Rogers resolution and, Smith testified before this body on March 7, 1922. He reiterated for the committee the valiant efforts of the Armenian soldiers on the Caucasus front during the war. For their reward, Smith said, the Armenians were being persecuted and the Turks were perpetrating a "reign of terror indescribable." The Armenia-America president couched his argument in practical terms: ". . . there are vast economic interests in that country. . . . There are to a certain extent American commercial interests there." He reviewed his efforts as an advocate for the Armenians at the Paris Peace Conference, before members of the British Cabinet and Parliament, and at the Geneva meeting of the Philarmenian League. He said the resolution under consideration was simply a moral protest against the Turkish atrocities and he called on the Allies to put an end to those atrocities. Like a lawyer making a closing argument in court, Smith, pleaded: "But gentlemen, eliminating from this case, if you can, all who have passed judgment on Armenia, eliminating humanity, or benevolence, is it not a loss to the world and a loss to the United States that these people are being slowly eliminated when they can be saved? It comes now simply to begging you," Smith continued, "so far as you represent the sentiment of the people, and it is the last appeal we have, as far as I can see, to say to the world that you disapproved of it. Is it not your duty to end this sandal?"[89]

Unfortunately, the State Department could find little to recommend the Rogers resolution, President Harding's sympathetic attitude notwithstanding. Moreover, when Armenian National Union officials urged Senator Lodge to introduce the Rogers proposal in the Senate, he sought the advice of Secretary Hughes, who advised him to refrain from doing so. The Secretary maintained that support of the measure would require the use of military force and would also require the United States to deal with the Angora regime and the Bolsheviks, neither of whom had received official recognition from Washington.[90] Once again the Secretary was apparently following the advice and reasoning of Admiral Bristol.

Because he regarded Admiral Bristol as inimical to the Armenians and obdurate in his attitude toward protecting the interests of American missionaries in the Near East, Dr. Barton and others initiated a movement to have Bristol removed from his post.[91] With regard to this matter, Bristol wrote L. I. Thomas, a friend and official with the Standard Oil Company, that "the missionaries are taking a crack at me" and "you know the principal leaders in the missionary work . . . Dr. James. L. Barton, Dr. Stanley White, Mr. Walter George Smith . . . a lawyer who was at one time head of the Bar Association, and Charles E. Vickrey, the Executive Secretary of Near East Relief."[92] Bristol, considered by many to be pro-Turk and anti-Armenian, had no fear of removal, for his position with the State Department was secure. Bristol was important in helping to shape an American Near East policy; however, it was American economic interests, not the missionaries, that exerted the greatest influence on the admiral.

During the summer of 1922 Smith was extremely pessimistic. Writing Montgomery, he told the secretary of his discouragement and of his inability to come up with some solution to the Armenian problem. "For the moment," Smith wrote, "my mind is barren of suggestions. We must keep our flag flying, however, to the end."[93]

THE TREATY OF LAUSANNE

The final chapter in the Armenian story—at least as far as Smith was

concerned—opened at Lausanne, November, 1922, where representatives of the Allies and Turkey met to revise the defunct Treaty of
Sèvres. Richard Washburn Child, Joseph Grew, and Admiral Bristol represented the United States as observers, while Dr. Barton,
George Montgomery, and Dr. Peet journeyed to the Swiss city to
represent Armenia-America. Montgomery was spokesman for the
group. He had drawn up a plan for the creation of a national home for
the Armenians in Cilicia.[94] However, observers Grew and Child
noted that the Turks were adamantly opposed to the creation of such
a home on Turkish soil.[95] To make matters worse, neither the
French nor the Italian delegates favored this plan; to add insult to
injury, Grew and Child themselves, at the outset, opposed this
solution.[96]

The minorities question came before the conference on December
12. On the 14th, conference leaders organized a subcommittee to
handle the problem of the Armenians.[97] On December 30,
Montgomery presented the plan for the creation of an Armenian
national home to the subcommittee.[98] But nothing came of this
proposal during the first session of the conference.

During the interim between the first and second phases, Smith
urged the Allies not to sign a treaty without some provision for the
Armenians. He realized that a treaty between the United States and
Turkey would be forthcoming in the second round of the conference, and wrote: ". . . the moral influence of the United States is
very great. The public would applaud its exercise by the Government, even though we have not been at war with Turkey. Let us
hope that the new Congress, under the wise advice of the present
Administration, will bear in mind the traditional sympathy of the
American people for the oppressed throughout the world, and the
Senate will approve no new treaty which does not guarantee an
independent State of the Armenians. We owe that much at least to
these victims of Eastern cruelty and Western ingratitude."[99] Smith
thus became the first Armenophile to urge the Senate to withhold its
consent to a treaty containing no provision for an Armenian national
home.

The second round of the Lausanne talks witnessed both the sign-
ing of the international accord between the Allies and the Turks and
the conclusion of the Turco-American Treaty of Lausanne. Neither
treaty included provision for the much-desired national home. While
the Turkish treaty with the Allies provided for protection of minor-

ity peoples, the accord with the United States contained no such provision. Lausanne was clearly a victory for the Turks.

Smith joined critics of the treaty in charging that the Armenian national home was bartered away for valuable oil concessions and the lucrative Chester Concession. He failed to realize that the Allied and American negotiators could not under any circumstances short of military intervention have obtained a provision for an Armenian homeland. He castigated the statesmen responsible for the Lausanne agreements: the "philosophy of Machiavelli" and the "modern spirit of commercialism," guided and motivated these statesmen who have forgotten the past. "A great international amnesty," Smith continued, "is granted to the allies of Germany, to the victors of Gallipoli, to the perpetrators of the massacres and deportations of Armenians."[100] A short time after writing this criticism of the American negotiators Smith added his name to a list of prominent Americans who had endorsed a "Memorandum Against Ratification by the Senate of the Lausanne Treaty," issued by the American Committee for the Indpendence of Armenia: Governor Al Smith of New York, Josephus Daniels, Herbert Croly of the *New Republic*, Bishop Thomas J. Shahan, and J. G. Hibben, president of Princeton University. The signatories of the memorandum opposed the treaty primarily because it was claimed the United States government had traded Armenian rights for commercial concessions from the Turkish government at the Lausanne Conference. In addition to this accusation, five other reasons were given for opposition: surrender of the capitulations; placement of missionary institutions under Turkish control; failure to gain archaeological rights for American citizens equal to those granted others; lack of proper indemnity for property damage sustained during the war by American missionary institutions; and failure to obtain the national home for the Armenians.[101]

Of the setting aside of the Armenian national home, Secretary Hughes wrote Senator Lodge that no "Turkish territory could in any probability be obtained for this purpose without an intervention by force of arms on the part of some power and the maintenance by force of any territory which might thus be obtained."[102] As to the accusation that America had traded "Armenian rights" for material benefits, Joseph Grew wrote Hughes that there was not "any connection whatever between the Armenian question and the principle of the Open Door or the Chester or any other economic concession, whether dubious or not. There was no trading, and by the nature of things there have been no trading, in these entirely disassociated issues." Grew asserted: "The project of any Armenian national home failed to succeed owing to the insurmountable opposition of the Turkish Government. No effort was left unmade, no argument left unused, but the Powers represented at Lausanne were obliged to deal with the facts."[103]

Not having been privy to the negotiations at Lausanne, critics of the Lausanne Treaty could not be blamed for having drawn the conclusions they did. They failed to realize that American diplomacy in the Near East was being shaped by a different set of men according to a different set of principles. Morality no longer formed the basis of an American Near East policy. It was simply not in the American national interest to send American soldiers there to defend an Armenian homeland. Unfortunately for the Armenians, Admiral Bristol had a clearer vision of the national interest of the United States than did Walter George Smith. Too, Turkey was no longer a defeated nation. It had defeated the Greeks and the French and now could and did throw off the yoke imposed by the victorious Allies following the war. A vaunted Turkish nationalism could not be expected to bow to the wishes of the Protestant missionaries and relief workers in their quest for an Armenian homeland.[104]

The Turco-American Treaty of Lausanne was signed on August 6, 1923, a treaty which created immediate opposition. Writing in the *New Armenia* what proved to be his last effort on behalf of the Armenians, Smith warned that "should our own country put the stamp of its approval on the pending treaty, it will be a confession that we too place the favor of the Turk in commercial transactions above all other considerations."[105] To the end Smith argued that the "gallant Armenians" were being sacrificed on the altar of mammon for "commercial advantages."

Although an Armenian homeland was not realized, Smith and a large number of like-minded men and women kept the Armenian issue before the American people for over a decade. Although merchants, industrialists, oil men and bankers now controlled American Near East policy, nevertheless missionaries, educators, philanthropists, and others having eleemosynary associations with the Near East continued to exert a pronounced influence on foreign policy makers. For while it might be construed an empty victory, the friends of Armenia were able successfully to oppose Senate approval of the Turkish-American Treaty of Lausanne because it contained no provision for the Armenian homeland. True, Smith had died shortly before, in April, 1924, but his expressed sentiments were those of the treaty opponents and his work undoubtedly contributed to the defeat of the treaty in 1927.

Although devoted in the main to the Armenian question during the international phase of his public career, Smith was also busy on another front. President Harding appointed him to a twenty-one member Advisory Committee in November, 1921. Its purpose was to assist the American Delegation to the Washington Naval Conference. Smith continued to devote himself to finding a solution to the Armenian question during the period November 1921 to February 1922, but he turned his attention largely to the deliberations of the Naval Conference.

CHAPTER 7

The Washington Naval Conference

The period of the 1920s was highlighted in the United States by a search for world peace. Although the country did not join the League of Nations, many individuals and organizations proposed numerous schemes to ensure that a war of the magnitude of World War I would not be repeated. Internationalists vied with isolationists to capture the attention of the American public, hoping to generate a ground swell of public opinion for a particular peace nostrum. Collective security, disarmament, outlawry of war, isolation, and adherence to the World Court were panaceas proposed by 1920-style "peaceniks." There was a real need for an effective peace movement because economic rivalry and navalism produced tension among several powers.

Following World War I American diplomatic relations with Britain and Japan deteriorated. At the conclusion of the war Britain had gained access to large oil reserves in the Middle East. She denied American oil companies access to these sources of oil, thus violating the American principle of the Open Door. For her part, Japan had embarked on a policy that aimed at shutting the Open Door in China. Other factors also exacerbated American-Japanese relations: American reluctance at the Paris Peace Conference to grant the

Japanese racial equality; the Japanese occupation of Siberia; and Japanese reluctance to grant cable rights to the United States on the island of Yap. To compound a bad situation, a three-way naval race among the United States, Britain, and Japan created an environment making war a distinct possibility. Given this development, American naval and diplomatic experts viewed with horror the Anglo-Japanese treaty of alliance which was still in force.

Administration leaders were very much concerned. Republican senators who had opposed American membership in the League of Nations—at least on the terms specified by President Wilson—looked aghast as war clouds loomed on the horizon. At length one of their number proffered a possible remedy. Senator William E. Borah, the Idaho Republican who had staunchly opposed American membership in the League of Nations, presented on December 14, 1920, a resolution calling for an international conference to limit naval armament. It was opposed by President Harding but the Borah measure immediately elicited enthusiastic public support. Senate passage of the resolution in mid-1921 forced the President's hand.

After some delay the President authorized Secretary of State Charles Evans Hughes to act. He queried London, Paris, Rome, and Tokyo about the feasibility of such a conference, and decided to broaden the aims of the conference to include not only disarmament but also problems related to the Pacific and Far East as well. He sent out invitations to these capitals and also to Belgium, China, Portugal, and the Netherlands.

The calling of the Washington Conference indicated the importance of Senate influence on the shaping of American foreign policy in the 1920s, and the Administration's selection of delegates took this factor into consideration. In addition to Hughes, government officials selected Oscar W. Underwood, senate minority leader; Henry Cabot Lodge, Senate majority leader; and Elihu Root, lawyer-elder statesman.

THE ADVISORY COMMITTEE

As an aroused American public played a role in forcing President Harding to call the disarmament conference, administration leaders thought it wise to appoint an Advisory Committee of twenty-one members for the purpose of assisting the American Delegation.[1] In addition to sampling public opinion, the committee also served as liaison between the government and the public at large. State Department officials selected Walter George Smith and other outstanding persons in the fields of the military, government, finance, agriculture, commerce, law, and women's groups;[2] the three great religious faiths of Protestantism, Catholicism, and Judaism were also represented. Thus the committee served to reflect the feelings of large interest groups in the country.

Smith's selection to the committee was due to several reasons. First, as a former president of the American Bar Association he was one of the nation's most prominent attorneys. Second, he had achieved a reputation as a proponent of world peace. (At the time of his appointment to the committee, he was at Geneva pleading with the League of Nations to use its influence to keep the peace in the Caucasus.) Third, due to his opposition to President Wilson's domestic policies, Smith had converted to the Republican Party, was known to President Harding, and was a prominent Catholic layman. All of these qualities would enable him to sway lawyers and Catholics on the question of disarmament. Smith was pleased to receive this appointment and his letter of acceptance expressed his enthusiam.[3]

In accepting this honor, Smith joined a group consisting of leading members of the nation's Protestant, Anglo-Saxon establishment. Membership associated him with some of the nation's leaders and made it possible for him to participate in the Washington Naval Conference, the major American effort to guarantee peace by disarmament. An internationalist, Smith believed in the disarmament approach to peace. As a lawyer his legal mind easily accepted the idea of maintaining peace by international treaties. As a progressive who had worked for order on the domestic scene he gladly accepted the responsibility to work with leading advocates of peace to keep world order. However, his Catholic and progressive background made his presence on the committee somewhat novel, because most progressives during the decade of the '20s eschewed internationalism and large numbers of Catholic of Irish and German background turned to isolationism.

At all events Smith brought a measure of prestige to the committee for, with the exception of Herbert Hoover, he was the only member that had participated in the deliberations of the Paris Peace Conference, and the only one who had taken part in an effort to sway the League of Nations. Smith was not out of his element. He already knew a number of his committee colleagues. He had met Samuel Gompers, Herbert Hoover, and Mrs. E.F. Egan while attending the Paris Peace Conference in 1919. He had come to know Fletcher while making representations on behalf of the Armenians to the State Department. He had known Senator George Sutherland and Willard Saulsbury, both prominent members of the American Bar Association. The former had defeated him for the presidency of that organization in 1916.

Although the role of the Advisory Committee at the Confrence had been characterized as mere "stage scenery" or as "window dressing,"[4] the report of the American Delegation, submitted to the President by the Secretary of State, stated that the "Advisory Committee made careful studies of all the problems before the Conference and its reports and advice were of the greatest value."[5] Hughes had said that the committee was one that would "give complete expert assistance" and "create a special body of dignity."[6] The record indicated that the Advisory Committee's efforts did amount to more than mere "window dressing" or "stage scenery." At any rate, several of the committee members recorded that they did in fact consider their efforts to be worthwhile, inasmuch as the aim was the preservation of world peace. For example, Smith wrote his friend Dr. Lawrence Flick, a Philadelphia physcian, that he felt his work to be of great import.[7] Samuel Gompers wrote Arthur Sweetster of the International Labor Organization in Geneva that it was the consensus of the committee that it "has very important work to perform and it is thoroughly capable of meeting the necessities of the occasion."[8] At all events Smith found his participation on the committee stimulating.

The minutes of the Advisory Committee show that it met a total of ten times between November 9, 1921, and January 6, 1922,[9] and that Smith was present at all but one, at which time he was "laid up with a cold." Concerning his work and his state of health Smith, aged 67, wrote that he found his work for peace and disarmament to be "gratifying" but that his health "was not up to par."[10] The elderly Smith found the work demanding. In fact, his colleague Samuel Gompers wrote that committee members were not even permitted to leave town because they "were subject to call at any moment," because the chairman or the Secretary of State might desire their services.[11] Although diligent in his committee obligations, Smith was not a dominant figure in the committee deliberations, but he did participate regularly in the discussions.[12]

The first three sessions of the Advisory Committee were devoted in the main to matters of organization. At the initial meeting the American Delegation, consisting of Secretary Hughes, Senators Lodge and Underwood, and Mr. Root, joined the larger Advisory Committee for a joint session. The Secretary of State made a short address to those assembled, saying he was pleased to have the support of "such a distinguished and representative committee." He dwelt upon the serious nature of the conference and expressed the hope that the committee would support the delegation by presenting it with a "well-informed opinion."[13] At the close of the Secretary's address Under Secretary of State Fletcher nominated Senator Sutherland, Smith's old bar association adversary, as permanent chairman of the committee. The nomination was passed by unanimous vote. After hearing some instructions from Hughes, Chairman Sutherland announced the appointment of a Committee on Organization. At a subsequent session this committee appointed an Executive Committee of seven members and four special subcommittees, one to deal with each of the four topics outlined in the conference agenda: Limitation of Naval Armament; Limitation of Land Armament; Pacific and Far East Questions; and New Agencies of Warfare. Smith was assigned to the subcommittees on Naval Armament, Land Armament, and Far East Questions.

For the purpose of this study it is deemed best to examine the contribution of each subcommittee Smith was on rather than to focus on the individual sessions of the Advisory Committee sitting as a whole. Since the subcommittee on Naval Limitation, made the most important contribution, and in so doing aroused the greatest public interest, the work of that subcommittee will be discussed first.

THE SUBCOMMITTEE ON NAVAL LIMITATION

In response to the Secretary of State's request, Chairman Sutherland introduced the subject of limitation of naval armament first. He advised the committee to enter into discussion on this matter in preparation for the Secretary's calling for an advisory opinion on it.

He asked Assistant Secretary of the Navy Roosevelt to outline the context within which the discussions should take place. Roosevelt complied and, following an additional exchange, the chairman urged Admiral Rodgers to take up the report on naval limitation, using Roosevelt's talk as a guideline. In addition to his initial charge to the subcommittee on naval limitation, Sutherland also charged Admiral Rodgers to determine popular feeling on the question: Should the submarine be abolished? Accordingly, the Admiral's subcommittee sent out two hundred letters to newspapers, requesting an expression of opinion on the use of the submarine as a weapon of war.[14]

After several subcommittee meetings, Admiral Rodgers gave the report on naval limitation at the sixth meeting of the Advisory Committee on November 30. It accepted Roger's report and approved a "naval holiday of ten years in the construction of capital ships."[15] Next, the Admiral presented the report on the submarine. This was the most controversial report presented by any of the subcommittees because, although the Admiral's subcommittee had determined by poll the American public's opposition to continued use of the submarine, the report did not take into account this expression of American public sentiment. In strict compliance with the recommendation of the General Board of the Navy, the subcommittee opted for the employment of the submarine as a vital component of the ships of the line against merchant vessels and warships. However, it opposed unlimited submarine warfare.[16] Speaking for his subcommittee as well as for the General Board, Admiral Rodgers said the United States needed the submarine for defense as it was not usually well prepared for war. He declared that the nation required a boat with a great radius because, having first repulsed the enemy's initial attack, the submarine could then strike an offensive blow.[17] After an extended discussion the committee, at Smith's suggestion, elected to postpone final vote on the submarine report until next day, at which time the report was unanimously accepted.[18]

Assistant Secretary Roosevelt consulted with the Secretary of State, seeking to win approval of the submarine report. He was successful.[19] Hughes regarded the report as an "able, illuminating and conservative" document, one that "set forth" the American government's position very well.[20] At a subsequent meeting of the Advisory Committee Chairman Sutherland presented the secretary's views on the report, saying: "He spoke again this morning about the report on submarines and complimented us again very highly. We said exactly what he wanted and he said it would be of great use to him."[21]

Hughes did make use of the Advisory Committee's submarine report when a controversy between Britain and France over the use of submarines caused him to bring the statement before the conference of delegates. France threatened to break up the conference by demanding a large quota for submarines to compensate for its lower quota of capital ships. It demanded at least 90,000 tons, or about four and one-half times what it already had. Britain viewed the submarine as a distinct threat to the vital communication lines of its empire and favored total their abolition. The American delegates wanted to apply the capital-ship ratios to auxiliary ships and submarines, and American naval experts, stressing the need for the submarine, were caught in the middle of the controversy.

On December 22 British delegate Lord Lee sought to bring the submarine issue to a head. He favored "total and final abolition" of the undersea weapon. Undoubtedly aware of the strong American sentiment favoring abolition, his Lordship was appealing to American public opinion to support the British position. Although he did not gain the British aim he did succeed in arousing the ire of the American public.

One can only sympathize with anglophile Smith. With his strong feeling for Great Britain, he undoubtedly accepted abolition as a point of departure on the submarine.

Actually, Hughes had hoped to keep the submarine issue behind closed doors, but failing this, he introduced the Advisory Committee report to the conference in open session. This document represented a middle position, but all efforts to conciliate the French on the submarine issue failed. On December 26 French delegate Albert Sarraut announced France would accept the 175,000 ton limit for capital ships, but it would accept nothing less than 330,000 tons for auxiliary vessels and 90,000 tons for submarines.

The American Delegation had failed in its effort to apply quotas to submarines. It then tried to restrict the use of this under-sea weapon by the same set of rules that apply to surface warships. Embodied in a set of resolutions drawn up by Elihu Root, the principles were set forth in a treaty drafted by Chandler Anderson and James Brown

Scott, legal advisers to the American Delegation. The treaty called for submarine captains to visit and search merchant vessels before attacking, otherwise an attack would be construed as an act of piracy. Provision was also to be made for the removal of the crew before proceeding with the destruction of the vessel.[22]

Secretary Hughes's disclosure of the Advisory Committee report on submarines created a sensation in the United States. The American public, never forgetting the *Lusitania*, favored total abolition of the submarine. The Advisory Committee received a total of 422,488 appeals calling for removal of the submarine from the high seas. The press criticized the Advisory Committee for failing to note in its report the wide tide of public sentiment in favor of abolition.

At its penultimate meeting on January 4, 1922, Chairman Sutherland took cognizance of the furor created by the submarine report. In an address to the full committee he said he was aware of the many appeals protesting the report. He declared that, although there was a strong feeling in the country against the continued use of the submarine, he was "inclined to think . . . that it is an emotional view, very largely the result of deliberate propaganda. Societies," the chairman continued, "have sent out postal cards to be returned, expressing the view of the society rather than the individual."[23] He said he had asked Admiral Rodgers to call his subcommittee together to consider the matter. Rodgers told the assembly that submarines were a vital weapon. The British had used it effectively in home waters for scouting and reporting the movements of the German fleet in the late war. In short, he concluded, it was an admirable defensive weapon.[24]

His Quaker anti-war sensitivities aroused, Secretary of Commerce Hoover joined the discussion, saying that a most embarrassing situation had arisen in which the committee appeared to be in favor of "expanded military activity." He asserted that the committee's submarine report "carries the impression of belligerency and increased armament." After further discussion of the report the committee accepted the need to prvace it with a statement based on four of the points presented by Hoover: first, that the submarine has a vital role to play in defense against offensive warships; second, that the committee does not condone the misuse of the submarine and strongly urges the drafting of rules to govern the continued use of the submarine; third, that the committee recognizes the need for prohibiting the employment of armed merchantmen; and fourth, that the committee declares that disarmament and eventual abandonment of the submarine is the ultimate goal but, given the world situation, realizes that this aim is impossible; and it therefore declares that arms limitation is a good first step in the direction of total disarmament.[25]

At the final meeting Chairman Sutherland presented the Advisory Committee's "Additional Report on Submarines," dated January 6, 1922. It took cognizance of widespread public condemnation of the submarine in response to the initial report of December 1, and it incorporated the four previously discussed ideas of Hoover. It also noted with satisfaction that the Conference had taken under consideration the drawing up of rules governing the use of the submarine as a weapon of war.[26]

Thus, given the adamant feeling of the French, the American Delegation and Advisory Committee failed to realize restrictions on the submarine. The American team had to be content with a treaty embodying the Root resolutions. Although this treaty was signed by a number of the powers at the conference, it did not become valid until all had ratified. Since France did not ratify, it never became effective.[27]

PACIFIC AND FAR EAST QUESTIONS

The subcommittee on Pacific and Far East Questions, of which Smith was also a member, presented its report at the eighth session on December 19, 1921. As the spokesman for the subcommittee, Chairman Porter told those assembled that the report consisted of four parts: first, the Japanese occupation of Siberia and Sakhalin; second, regulation of the Chinese tariff; third, Chinese leases such as that at Shantung; and fourth, the question of Korea. The Advisory Committee approved the first three sections of the report with little discussion. However, part four, dealing with Korea, caused a lenghty exchange. Under Secretary of State Fletcher observed that the subject of Korea was not on the agenda of the conference. Smith replied Korea was a possible *casus belli* in the Pacific. To this Fletcher declared that this section would be of no use to the American Delegation because as it was not on the agenda, it would not come up for deliberation. Smith replied, saying the subcommittee had devoted five or six meetings to the topic. Casting aside the purely legalistic claim of Japan to Korea, the Philadelphia attorney asserted that Japan acquired the Hermit Kingdom in a "highly immoral" manner.

Smith conceded Fletcher's point that the subject was not on the agenda, but he noted that the conference is "endevering to remove causes of war in the Far East. Our Advisory Committee," the lawyer continued, "has been given a free hand to express any views we might think wise to our plenipotentiaries." He maintained that the Korean question was likely to produce friction in the Far East. Smith closed with a rhetorical flourish reminiscent of his defense of the Armenians: "It seems to me the whole spirit, as far as I can gather from the utterances that have been made by our plenipotentiaries at least, has been to restore to China her full sovereignty, which has been sadly impaired by force and duress. Korea is not a part of China but an independent nation which has been ravished by military forces and presents a grievance that is likely to remain until settled and settled justly, if the present spirit of the world prevails."[28] Fletcher, a diplomatic pragmatist, said that the discussion was anti-Japanese and, although he did not say it, he implied that it might jeopardize the other negotiations. Chairman Sutherland declared that Japanese control of Korea was "an established fact." The committee voted to lay the matter of Korea aside.

Although the American Delegation did not utilize the report of the subcommittee on Pacific and Far East Questions, it did present a resolution based on the work of the subcommittee on the Limitation of Land Armaments, the third committee on which Smith served. Smith's presence on this committee proved of some benefit.

LAND ARMAMENTS

Actually, the question of the limitation of land armament at the conference hung on the French attitude. France would not accept the limitation of her army unless she could obtain some form of guarantee of her security against German aggression. Since France received no guarantee from the United States or Britain, limitation of land armament was out of the question.

However, General Pershing of the Land Armament subcommittee made his report on November 30. The general bluntly spoke against the use of chemicals in warfare, saying: "I would rather see us undertake to limit the means of destroying our fellow man than to extend it. I believe that a strong statement by this Conference . . . would have a far-reaching effect on the attitude of the peoples of the world in that regard."[28] There was an additional exchange on the subject of gas warefare. Carmi Thompson, chairman of the subcommittee on New Agencies of Warfare, interjected that the subject of gasses came within the purview of his group, and he questioned how the Advisory Committee should treat the subject. At this point Smith intervened, suggesting that General Pershing and Thompson agree to a joint meeting of their two groups on the following day at the general's office at the War Department to settle the matter there.

As a result of Smith's timely suggestion a joint meeting between the two subcommittees was held at 10:15 on December 1 in the general's office. Pershing's group drew up a resolution calling for the "total abolition of chemical warfare."[29] That afternoon the Advisory Committee reconvened at 3:15 P.M. Carmi Thompson presented the report of his subcommittee. This report urged that an international agreement be drawn up to prohibit the utilization of gasses in warfare. This report was unanimously accepted by the committee.[30]

The latter report, signed by General Pershing of the Land Armament subcommittee, urged that "Chemical warfare should be abolished among nations, as abhorrent to civilization. It is a cruel, unfair, and improper use of science. It is fraught with the gravest danger to noncombatants and demoralizes the better instincts of humanity."[31] Chairman Hughes received the report and introduced it at a general meeting of the conference on January 5, 1922. He said the report had received the approval of the Navy's General Board, and he therefore asked Root to draft a resolution along the lines of the subcommittee report on New Agencies of Warfare. This was done with the aid of Chandler Anderson and James Brown Scott,[32] and the resolution was adopted unanimously by the Committee on Limitation of Armament, and incorporated into Article V of the Five-Power Treaty, "In Relation to the Use of Submarines and Noxious Gasses in Warfare."[33]

The Land Armament and New Agencies of Warefare subcommittees had done their work well. Unfortunately, their work never went into effect, since the French failed to ratify the treaty.

The work of the fifth subcommittee, the Committee on General Information, related to the sampling of the nation's press on topics on the conference agenda and the preparation of news summaries for the American Delegation. In addition this group also did yeoman service for the other four subcommittees by preparing assessments of public opinion on such issues as naval disarmament, the use of the submarine, and the employment of gas warfare. In so doing it provided a means by which public reaction to the various topics on the agenda could be measured so that the Delegation might sense the drift of public sentiment.

That the Advisory Committee provided more than "window dressing" is apparent from the record. The records of the conference show that two of the subcommittee reports on submarines and gas warfare were translated into meaningful parts of the Five-Power Treaty. The Secretary of State was most appreciative of its work. Addressing the Sixth Plenary Session of the Conference on February 4, 1922, he expressed his debt of gratitude to the committee which had supported the delegation by providing it with "careful monographs and studies upon the various problems" which have come before the conference. He also commended the committee for providing information that "greatly contributed to our understanding of public opinion in this country."[34]

While Smith did not play a dominant role in the deliberations of the Advisory Committee—this role having been assumed by Sutherland, Hoover, Roosevelt, and Rodgers—he did nevertheless participate in its discussions in an informed and intelligent manner. That he had a thorough grasp of the major points under consideration is indicated by his publication of an article entitled "Disarmament Conference in Washington" in the *American Bar Association Journal* in January, 1922. In this piece he set forth clearly and concisely the purposes of the conference, some of the major problems encountered by the conferees, and its major accomplishments.[35]

Smith derived a great deal of satisfaction from his work on the Advisory Committee, believing sincerely that the work of the conference would serve to preserve world peace.[36] He had traveled through the desolate region of Armenia and witnessed the horror of war on every hand, and had visited the French battlefields and seen the graves of countless thousands of American soldiers. Undoubtedly these travels in Asia and Europe contributed greatly to his sense of urgency to carry out disarmament that the threat of war might not occur again in the future.

Smith's expression of concern for the plight of the Koreans and his willingness for the subcommittee on Pacific and Far East Questions to make some recommendation to the delegation with respect to this people should come as no surprise. By the time of the Washington Conference he had devoted three years to defending the cause of another hapless people—the Armenians. Within eighteen months of the conclusion of the Naval Conference, President Harding would call on Smith to undertake a mission to aid still another disadvantaged people—the American Indian.

CHAPTER 8

Pleading for the Pueblos

In the years following World War I a resurgence of nativism caused many Americans to forsake the melting pot concept, long the traditional response to the waves of immigrants from Europe. Many now believed that only immigrants from Northern Europe were acceptable; while others, interested in promoting cultural pluralism, began to feel that those already here should retain their separate cultural identity. Just after World War I some white Americans organized a movement to deprive the Pueblo Indians of New Mexico and Arizona of their lands—a movement that would virtually destroy a culture old when the first Spaniards arrived four hundred years ago. Many reform-minded Americans joined with older organizations that had been associated for many years with the defense of Indian rights to save the Pueblos, a people Theodore Roosevelt has described as "one of America's most precious possessions."[1] The Spanish had arrived in the region of the American Southwest in the sixteenth century. They considered the Pueblos as wards of the government and had given these Indians large grants of land. Following the Mexican Revolution, the Pueblos became citizens of Mexio, but not for long. The Treaty of Guadalupe Hidalgo had concluded the American war with Mexico. It ceded the Southwest (containing

162

the Pueblo lands) and California to the United States and bound the American government to honor the land grants of the Pueblo as former Mexican citizens. But the citizens of New Mexico and Arizona took the position that the Pueblos' Mexican citizenship entitled them to sell or otherwise dispose of their lands as they saw fit. This view was held by the territorial government and confirmed by the United States Supreme Court in 1876.

Over the years, many Hispano- and Anglo-Americans bought land from the Indians and held it under clear title, while others settled on Indian lands as squatters. Settlers, whether title-holders or squatters, thus encroached on Indian lands and gradually assumed control of Indian water rights, with a resulting deprivation of the Pueblo systems of irrigation. But in 1913, after statehood had been granted New Mexico and Arizona, the Supreme Court reversed its earlier decision, saying the Pueblos were "uninformed and inferior people."[2] This, the Sandoval decision, gave the Indians the irrevocable right to reclaim land taken from them. It also created a feeling of uncertainty among those who had taken up land from the Indians.

The Harding administration's Indian policy aimed to clarify this ambiguity. Secretary of the Interior Albert Fall was a former United States Senator from New Mexico. He gave his support to a bill sponsored by Senator H. O. Bursom of New Mexico in 1921 that would deprive the Pueblos of large portions of their lands and hand them over to the white citizens. In the following year Fall ruled that "Executive Order Reservations" (those set aside for the Indians by order of the president) were only temporarily withdrawn and could be placed at the disposal of corporations desiring to develop oil and gas deposits in the region.[3] This ruling would remove from the Indians approximately twenty-two million acres which they felt rightfully belonged to their domian.

The Harding administration's policy on Indians not only sought to remove lands from them but it extended to cultural matters as well. In 1923 the Commissioner of Indian Affairs issued a Dance Order designed to prevent the Indians from enjoying certain ritualistic dances because the Indian agents of the federal government considered them immoral and indecent. This order received the support of missionaries and others who regarded many of the secret Indian dances as pagan and not in the Indians' best interests. Although pro-Indian groups were divided on the question raised by the

Dance Order, they were all of one mind that the administration's land policy would virtually destroy the Pueblo Indian culture. A militant opposition to this policy was soon forthcoming.

By early 1923 an aroused American public evinced anxiety that the government was in the process of perpetrating what Senator William E. Borah of Idaho described as "one of the boldest raids on Indian lands ever attempted in Congress."[4] Long established Indian defense organizations such as the Indian Rights Association and the General Federation of Women's Clubs heeded the public outcry, and they became increasingly active in their efforts to protect Indian lands. To these ranks came reformers like Walter George Smith who had in the past only been peripherally interested in the Indian question.

THE BOARD OF INDIAN COMMISSIONERS

For many years Smith had aided the cause of the American Indian through the work of Mother Katherine Drexel. But in 1923, at a time when the American public showed great concern over the Bursum bill and the Fall ruling on Executive Order Reservations, he became more directly involved in the move to preserve the Pueblos, who had become a symbol of American injustice to the Indians. Governor Al Smith of New York resigned from the Board of Indian Commissioners on December 30, 1922. To fill this vacancy, Dennis Cardinal Dougherty of Philadelphia and Senators Frank B. Kellogg and Selden Spencer recommended to Secretary Fall that Smith receive the appointment. Fall accepted this recommendation and on January 9 he requested the President to sign Smith's commission to the board, saying he had "no doubt of his eminent ability."[5] In his letter of acceptance to Malcolm McDowell, Secretary of the Board of Indian Commissioners, Smith advised of his intention to attend the Board's January meeting at the Department of the Interior in Washington.[6]

Speculation on reasons for Smith's appointment to the Board of Indian Commissioners leads one to the conclusion that his long association with Mother Katherine and the work of the Sisters of the Blessed Sacrament among the Indians, his cooperation with Monseigneur Joseph Stephan, director of the Catholic Indian Bureau, and his work in the field of education such as his membership on the Philadelphia Board of Public Education influenced his selection.

And there can be little doubt that Smith's status as a past president of the American Bar Association and his knowledge of the law pertaining to real estate titles, deeds, and the like also influenced the choice. Too, he was well known for his affiliation with Near East Relief and its effort to aid the Armenians, a work that admirably prepared him for his work among the Indians as a member of the government's Indian board.

President Ulysses S. Grant had instituted the Board of Indian Commissioners in 1869, pursuant to an act of Congress. In the early days of its history, members of the board performed a variety of services no longer required of them. For example, they approved vouchers for supplies for the Indian Service, a task that helped prevent graft and corruption in a service that was plagued with the greed of unscrupulous men. Board members spent much time in the field investgating causes for Indian wars and concluding treaties— tasks that were fraught with danger. The Indians were still hostile and members often found it necessary to have military escort to accomplish their assigned tasks. In the modern era members made inspections of Indian reservations and made an annual report to the Secretary of the Interior. Commissioners received no salary, but Congress did make an annual appropriation to defray the costs of commisioners' inspection tours. The board met three times a year, and it consisted of ten members, each from a different section of the country. One of them, George Vaux, Jr., the chairman of the board and a Philadelphia lawyer, was a friend of Smith.

In the course of the January, 1923, meeting Smith discussed with McDowell the necessity of fulfilling his obligation to the board by making a tour of investigation. Shortly after returning home from the Washington meeting, he wrote Secretary McDowell of his intention to visit the Chippewa reservation in August, after his attendance at the American Bar Association's annual meeting in Minneapolis. Smith also advised that he would be available for a tour of inspection in the Southwest during the late spring.[7] McDowell accepted Smith's offer to make an inspection of the Pueblo and Chippewa Indians, saying the board would like very much for him to visit the Pueblo country with a view to looking into the question of land titles, water rights, etc. "I think if you were to go down there as a lawyer," he wrote, "you would be able to give to the Board . . . some very valuable advice and suggestions."[8] To this the attorney replied that he was "quite taken with the idea of spending a fortnight on such a matter in New Mexico and Arizona."[9]

SMITH AMONG THE PUEBLOS

Following McDowell's suggestion, Smith made preparations for the forthcoming trip. First, he familiarized himself with the problems pertaining to the Pueblo land question by reading the reports of two congressional committees on the matter. Next, he informed many friends along his anticipated route of his upcoming trip. Finally, he applied for government funds for the journey, and McDowell wrote him that $350.00 had been alloted to cover his expenses.

In addition to providing the necessary funds McDowell also gave Smith detailed instructions covering his trip. He advised the atttorney that it was not necessary for him to visit all of the pueblos, but that visits to a few representative establishments would suffice. He suggested that Smith "drop in on them casually and talk with the head men." In this way, he declared, "you will be better able to arrive at a definite conclusion on Pueblo land titles and irrigation needs if you see these Indians in their homes and at work on their little farms." He also urged Smith to visit the Navajo, a non-reservation tribe.[10] Thus it becomes clear from McDowell's letters to Smith that the board hoped to take advantage of Smith's talents as a lawyer to help find a solution to the Pueblo land enigma.

While he was making his plans for the western tour of the Pueblo and Chippewa Indians, Congress put the Indian lands question in a new light. Senator Holm O. Bursum's bill to quiet titles to lands within the Pueblo holdings had been amended on February 28, 1923, by Senator Irvine L. Lenroot of Wisconsin. The Lenroot amendment had as its salient provision the establishment of a special land board which would be responsibile for investigating and reporting upon the lands confirmed to the Pueblo Indians. The board would have to rule for the white settlers in cases where they or their predecessors had had land in their possession under color of title for 20 years, or 30 years' possession without color of title. In either case the white settler would be entitled to a quit-claim deed to the land from the United States government and from the Pueblo Indians.[11] This amendment put a new complexion on the matter. Now the Indians would at least have their day in court. Aware of the thrust of the Lenroot amendment and convinced that it would give justice to both Indian and settler alike, Smith approached his task with the judicious temperament of the lawyer, hoping to achieve a just end to the problem.

Well supplied with letters of introduction to various officials in the Indian Service and accompanied by his sister Grace who acted as his secretary, Smith set out from Torresdale on May 12 for a tour of the Pueblo Indians.[12] They arrived in New York and promptly boarded the S. S. *Momus* for the first leg of their journey, New Orleans. After a delightful six-day voyage, during which Smith read and made an address to the passengers regarding the Near Eastern situation, they arrived in the Crescent City on May 18. Following a two-day sojourn the Smiths made their way by train to El Paso, and by automobile to Albuquerque.

Smith immediately reported to H. P. Marble, Superintendent for Indian Agencies, to familiarize himself with the problems of the Pueblos. He learned that in all there were nineteen pueblos. The majority were located north of Albuquerque in the Rio Grande valley, while four lay directly west of that city. The Hopi inhabited eastern Arizona. There were approximately 9,000 Indians in the villages living a sedentary, agricultural life. Unfortunately for the Indians, approximately 3,000 settlers, with color of title or without, laid claim to lands formerly belonging to the Pueblos.

The Philadelphia commissioner wasted little time in gaining a grasp of the problem. Marble introduced him to Herbert F. Robinson, supervising engineer of the irrigation division of the Indian service of the Albuquerque district. After briefings from Marble and Robinson, Smith began his tour on May 24 and completed his fact-finding mission on June 25. During this period he and his sister Grace visited fourteen of the Pueblos: Zuni, Isleta, Acoma, Laguna, Santa Ana, Sandia, Zia, Tesuque, San Ildefonso, Nambe, Santa Clara, Jemez, San Juan, and Taos. He also visited the Navajo Indians. Now 68 years of age, Smith found the trip trying at first. He frequently complained of the intense heat which brought on fatigue. The tour often required travel over poor, unimproved roads. An occasional dust storm marred the journey. In many respects his tour of the Indians was similar to the one he had made to Armenia some four years earlier. But gradually he became acclimated to the environment and he soon found the dry heat a tonic for his chronic respiratory ailment.

While on the inspection he met with four Indian councils at the

Isleta, Santa Ana, Laguna, and San Juan pueblos. The council consisted of the leading men and the governor who was elected annually. In each of the meetings Smith tried to explain the purpose of the Lenroot amendment to the Bursum bill in an effort to overcome the Indian's patent mistrust of the government's intentions on the question of land titles. But he also listened to the Indian complaints which, for the most part, dealt with encroachment on their lands, irrigation problems, loss of water rights, unfulfilled government promises on work improvement projects, and health problems. He also took note of a host of other problems related to education, religion, and disease and sanitation.

Smith used every opportunity to familiarize himself with Indian life. He had many talks with Catholic missionaries about their experiences with the Indians. From these nuns and priests he gained a better insight into the Indian question. He met with officials in the Indian Service from whom he obtained many details relative to Indian mores and folkways. On several occasions he met with artists who devoted themselves to portraying the American Indian on canvas. He exhibited great interest in Indian pottery, silverware, and weaving. Not only did he see Indian craftsmen at work making pottery (the Pueblos do not use the potter's wheel), at the forge and the loom, but he also visited a museum where Indian arts and crafts were on display. And he availed himself of the opportunity to talk with members of an archaeological expedition who were then working in the region of the Pueblos.

With his fourteen visits to Indian pueblos, his talks with the Indians, missionaries, artists, archaeologists, and Indian Service personnel, Smith spent his time well. To his brother Kilby he wrote: "I have motored for many miles through the country, looking at Pueblos, conversing with Indians and others and feel I have a fair knowledge of the problems, which all relate to water—irrigation ditches."[13] To his sister Betty he noted that the "fresh, fine air and the total change of mental occupation has been good for both of us."[14] Considering his advanced age and the rigors of the climate, Smith drove himself intensely to accomplish his task. While on the tour he used the services of his sister to write up the report which he duly submitted to Secretary McDowell in Washington.[15]

THE REPORT ON THE PUEBLOS

Smith's report was comprehensive. In the main he addressed himself to the encroachment of settlers on Indian lands and the matter of water rights. He was very disturbed about the loss of Pueblo Indian lands to white settlers. With his lawyer's sense of justice and fair play he did not feel that they had always been aboveboard in their dealings with the Indians. With respect to the Navajos, whom he visited only briefly, his report took on an ominous note: "If the Government," Smith warned, "continues the present policy of leaving this land open to homesteaders, the fate of these Indians is gloomy. There is but little water and little pasturage, probably not more than enough to afford a range for the Indian's flocks and herds."[16]

As he showed concern in his report for the loss of Navajo Indian lands, he also evinced anxiety for the loss of Pueblo water rights: "the main question in all these pueblos, needless to say, is water. Gradually they have lost or alienated a large portion" of their water rights.[17] For example, he reported that the San Ildefonso pueblo has been "robbed of practically all irrigation water." He observed that where water was in short supply crops and animals suffered greatly.[18] His awareness that water was necessary to the life of the agrarian Pueblos led Smith to make numerous recommendations that the Indian Service carry out its promises to make improvements on the Indian irrigation systems. He also called attention to problems that had arisen to impair the efficiency of the water ways. For example, he asserted that among the Zuñi Indians there was great need for the Indian Service to provide funds to dredge out a water reservoir that was gradually filling up with silt.[19]

With respect to land titles Smith's report indicates the judicious temperament of a Solomon. He hoped that the Lenroot amendment would provide justice for both white settler and Indian alike. He was very much in favor of the Pueblos retaining their unique way of life. To this end he believed that they must retain sufficient land and water to support their special form of habitation. On this point he wrote: "When the subject of land titles is investigated it is much to be hoped that without doing injustice to those white intruders they may be eliminated from the village."[20] Yet he was also very sympathetic with the plight of the white settlers, "who have been in good faith in the enjoyment of Pueblo lands."[21] Knowing that the Indians would surely lose some of the land, Smith recommended that Congress provide a fund for their just compensation.[22]

Smith was also of the opinion that the Pueblos should retain their cultural identity. He viewed the Indian, perhaps through the eyes of Jean Jacques Rousseau, as the proud red man who lived in close proximity to nature. He expressed the hope that the government would protect him from the more vile elements of the white civilization which might corrupt him. Of the Taos Indians he declared in terms not unlike Tacitus' description of the Germans: "This is the most beautifully situated and picturesque of all the pueblos. Its people are handsome and intelligent. They should be carefully guarded against the demoralization that is threatened by certain white influences."[23]

While visiting the Tesuque and San Juan pueblos, Smith had the opportunity to witness the beautiful Buffalo and Eagle dances, dances that had long been an integral part of the Pueblo way of life. Of this "universal custom" he wrote, "I was profoundly impressed by the picturesque character of these unique performances. I can see no reason why they should be discouraged, when they are merely symbolical and historical." Smith declared that he did not favor the ban of these dances. But accepting the Catholic missionaries' opinion that some of the other dances were pagan, immoral, and certainly detrimental to the Indians, Smith urged a halt to these secret dances which made for promiscuity, idleness, and neglect of crops.[24]

Although he did not desire the Pueblo culture obliterated by white civilization, he did feel that the Indian could benefit from the educational, medical, and engineering services made available by the government. With his long background of interest and service in the cause of education, Smith took every care to look into the educational opportunities provided the Indians. Not only did he look into the educational institutions provided by Catholic missionary orders, but he also visited the United States Indian schools at Albuquerque and Santa Fe. He believed that the Indians, following their graduation, would return to the pueblos and there "be an influence for good in overcoming ancient superstitions and pagan practices."[25]

Smith's views on the Indian's education, dances, and religion lead one to the inescapable conclusion that, although he did believe in preserving the Indian way of life in the midst of modern, industrialized America, he felt that the white man's culture was vastly superior to the Indian's and that white men should determine what facets of Indian life were good and hence worth preserving, and what was bad and not worthy of retention. For example, he found the Taos Indians making increased use of the drug from the peyote bean. He learned from Santiago Sandoval, the governor, that the Indians obtained peyote through the mail. The governor told Smith the drug had a deleterous effect on the habits of the Indians. Smith recommended that proper medical methods be used to determine the effect of peyote and, if necessary, that Congress should adopt measures to put an end to the use of this drug.[26]

In addition to his concern for the education of the Pueblos, Smith addressed himself to their medical needs. He believed that the dreaded trachoma, "the dangerous and contagious disease of the eyes," existed in all of the pueblos that he visited. He recommended the establishment of a trachoma hospital. He took note of one serious drawback in the Indian Service's care for the Indian medical problems, asserting that the low salaries paid to physicians in the Service made it difficult to secure adequate medical personnel to see to their health care.[27]

SMITH'S LAST JOURNEY

He completed his tour of the Pueblo and Navajo Indians in early July. Accompanied by his sister, he took an extended trip with frequent stops along the way. They made their way to Los Angeles, and from there to Riverside, where he consulted with Mrs. Stella Atwood, chairman of the General Federation of Women's Clubs, an organization devoted to the defense of Indian rights. The Smiths moved on to San Mateo to visit Miss Francis O'Connor, the daughter of James Kent Stone who, following his wife's death, had entered the religious life, taking the name Father Fidelis of the Cross.[28] While stopping at San Mateo for the month of July, Smith began to write a biography of Father Fidelis of the Cross. They traveled on to Spokane where Smith visited friends and then journeyed to Browning, Montana, where he visited a reservation of the Blackfeet Indians. At the invitation of F. C. Campbell, the Indian agent, Smith made a rather hurried inspection of the government school and hospital. From there they traveled to Minneapolis, arriving on August 22 for the annual meeting of the American Bar Assocation. After the convention Smith visited the Chippewa Indians at Cass Lake, approximately 200 miles from Minneapolis. Here too he made only a perfunctory inspection, as time did not permit a more extended visit.

Smith then proceeded to Philadelphia, with intermittent stops along the way. To collect information for his biography he visited Kenyon College, Gambier, Ohio, and Hobart College, Geneva, New York. He also stayed for a few days in Milton, Massachusetts with his niece Amabel Eshleman and her husband. The Smiths arrived in Philadelphia on September 25.

Smith continued to devote himself to the work of the Board of Indian Commissioners. During the autumn he had hoped to return to Montana for a more lengthy inspection of the Blackfeet Indians, but such a trip was out of the question because it was necessary that he attend the Board's fall meeting at Lake Mohonk, New York, and also confer with Commisioner of Indian Affairs Charles H. Burke and Secretary of the Interior Herbert Work.[29] At the latter meeting Smith presented orally a summation of the report he had formally submitted at the conclusion of his western tour the previous summer. He also contacted New Mexico senators A. A. Jones and H. O. Bursum, to urge them to seek a congressional appropriation for the erection of two bridges across the Rio Grande at Cochiti and San Juan that the Indians might have easier access to their fields on the other side of the river. During the late autumn Smith and McDowell began to discuss plans for Smith to visit the Navajo in Southern California during the month of June, 1924. In late March Smith attended the Board's Lake Mohonk meeting at which arrangements were completed for his June tour.

Smith returned to Torresdale from the Lake Mohonk meeting on March 31 in the midst of a late winter blizzard. The following morning he did not go in to Philadelphia to his office. The ground was covered with a deep snow. Telephone wires were down, trees had toppled over, and trains were running late. Grace persuaded her brother that inclement weather was liable to bring on a cold and that he needed to remain at home to complete a speech for delivery at Georgetown University. Smith reluctantly acquiesced. From ten to twelve on the morning of April 1 he paced up and down, dictating the speech as the faithful Grace typed it. As the Angelus was tolled at Eden Hall at the noon hour he stopped, and together brother and sister recited the Angelus. They then went in to luncheon. After luncheon Smith retired to his room, as was his custom while at home.

At 3:00 he had not returned to finish his speech. Grace went to his room, thinking he might have been writing a letter for the late mail. She found him slumped over in an arm chair, his rosary in his hand. She aroused him, saying: "Brother, do you want to send anything out in the mail?" He murmured, "I must have slept." Realizing that he was ill, she sent Dora to fetch Father Lawrence Wall, rector of St. Dominic's, and called the local physician who, on arrival, announced that Smith had suffered a cerebral hemorrhage. Father Wall administered Extreme Unction and Holy Viaticum. Smith lapsed into unconsciousness.

During the three days that he lingered there were many visitors to his room. The Sisters of the Blessed Sacrament came frequently to pray. They would have noticed that his room was that of a religious man. With the exception of the oil painting and marble bust of his wife, the room was adorned with religious pictures and a large crucifix, with a well-worn prieu dieu at the foot of the bed. They would have observed that the room was really more the bedroom of a monastic than that of a successful Philadelphia attorney.

Walter George Smith died at 1:30 on the afternoon of April 4. Present were members of the family and Bishop Shahan of Catholic University, who recited the prayers for the dead.[30] Smith's funeral was held in the chapel at Eden Hall. There in the presence of family and friends, priests and religious of the Philadelphia area, Cardinal Dougherty presided at the solemn pontifical requiem mass. Bishop Shahan celebrated, and delivered the sermon. Following the funeral, the crypt directly beneath the Lady Chapel was opened and Smith was laid to rest beside his wife.[31]

CHAPTER 9

The Summing Up

In the papers of Walter George Smith there are numerous memorials and letters of condolence from people who shared many of the varied interests that Smith pursued during the three phases of his long and interesting life. The American Bar Association, the Philadelphia Bar, the Philadelphia Contributionship, the Board of Indian Commissioners, the Catholic Bureau of Indian Affairs, Near East Relief, the Sisters of the Blessed Sacrament, the National Conference of Commissioners of Uniform State Laws, the City of Philadelphia, these and many others are represented. In essence they all carry the theme that Smith was a citizen who gave of himself to his fellowman and did his duty where he saw it. Perhaps the most significant of these memorials is one that appeared in the *Christian Work*, a Protestant periodical, because it touches on the main theme of Smith's life. Entitled "A Roman Catholic Who Co-Operated," the article describes Smith as a "convinced Roman Catholic" who accepted the teachings of the Church and yet found the time to work "with multitudinous good movements beyond the confines of his own church." The memorialist noted, for example, that he had worked with Protestant missionaries in the Near East, where he "marveled to find in them a devotion like that displayed by men and women of his own faith."[1] It is indeed a tribute to the ecumenical and tolerant spirit that Smith carried to his work with his associates in the various pursuits of his well-spent life. While Smith could not be considered a lovable character, it can be said that he was highly respected by those who knew him. He did his duty by his family and by his fellowman. Undoubtedly this attribute explains, in part at least, the remarkable success that he enjoyed in each of his three careers.

Ever since Philadelphian Andrew Hamilton had ably defended John Peter Zenger in the famous libel suit in New York in 1736, the term "Philadelphia lawyer" has carried the special connotation of erudition, perception, ability, and success. Smith exhibited to a marked degree the first three traits, thereby ensuring success in his legal career. One indication of this success is his last will and testament which documents an estate valued at $202,429.96—a sum that certainly points to material success.[2] Also indicative of Smith's success in terms of income was his ability to devote much uncompensated time to various interests such as the uniform state law movement, the Armenian cause, and the Pueblo land problem. His accomplishments in his profession are also clear from the tribute paid him by members of the Philadelphia, Pennsylvania, and American bar associations.

Smith was aware of his responsibility as a lawyer not only to his profession but to his city of Philadelphia, his state, and the nation. He never lost sight of the need to keep the good of the community in mind in conducting his affairs. He firmly believed, as he asserted on more than one occasion, that by virtue of his professional background the lawyer should not only act as a conservative check on the passions of those in the community who would act hastily and irresponsibly, but that he must also maintain a constant vigilance to ensure that those in public office should work for the good of the public weal and not to line their pockets. It was with this finely honed social conscience and conservative political credo that Smith approached the progressive era.

As a reformer Smith's rural birth and rearing, his staunchly held Catholic faith, his rise to Philadelphia's upper social strata, and his opposition to a number of progressive aims, make him atypical of any profile hitherto established by historians of the progressive era—a fact that tends to substantiate the recent scholarly writing which questions the existence of any clearly defined progressive typology.

Smith affiliated with those in the late 1880s and the last decade of the century who espoused the cause of urban reform. His membership on the Committee of Nine in the 1901 Union Party effort to unseat machine politicians placed him in the ranks of those advocates of good government who laid the foundation in Philadelphia in urban reform that led to the emergence of the City Party in 1905, when reformers soundly trounced the Philadelphia machine.

Although active in urban reform in Philadelphia, Smith's greatest contribution in the progressive era came in the movement to create uniform state commercial and divorce laws—laws making for efficiency in the economic sphere and for social control in the social realm. While he deplored the growth of commercialism in the legal profession in his adopted city—a trend in which lawyers increasingly flocked to the service of the large corporation—Smith nevertheless realized certain realities about the economic life of modern, industrial America: first, he recognized that on the welfare of the business community depended the welfare of the majority of the citizenry; second, that the diverse nature of the state commercial laws in the United States greatly hindered any business enterprise that sought a national market transcending state borders; and third, that it was expedient to aid these corporate giants. With this in mind, Smith joined the movement to rationalize the inefficient system of state commercial codes so that the business community might function more efficiently, thereby benefitting the nation's economy and the American community. In so doing he proved to be a valuable servant to the American business man, because the movement resulted in the passage of a host of commercial laws. This movement, it might be noted, has largely been overlooked by scholars of the progressive era.

The Philadelphia lawyer's success in achieving uniformity in state commercial laws did not obtain in his quest to bring about the passage of uniform state divorce legislation. Smith realized that the family was one of the basic social institutions threatened by the pressures of the industrial revolution and the forces of modernism. He was also convinced that the strengthening of state divorce laws would do much to protect the family and ensure greater social control. Therefore he cooperated with the Protestant leadership to fight the divorce evil by achieving stricter, more uniform divorce laws in the several states. The movement was unsuccessful. But by engaging in this type of response to the divorce problem Smith revealed that he had not clearly broken from the traditionally conservative matrix of the Gilded Age.

Smith's progressivism also compelled him during the 1920s to join those working to defend Indian land titles and cultural patterns and outlets. His work with the Board of Indian Comissioners was part of the movement to give a square deal to the Indians. Although he died in April, 1924, his efforts nevertheless contributed in a small measure to the passage of legislation that greatly ameliorated the condition of the Pueblo Indians. The Bursum bill, with the Lenroot amendment attached, passed the Senate on May 13, 1924, the House on June 5, and received Presidential approval on June 7.[3] The bill provided for the establishment of a Pueblo Lands Board with headquarters in Santa Fe. The board's duty was to investigate the land question between Indian and settler. In early test cases before a federal court in New Mexico the claims of 24 settlers on the San Juan Pueblo were rejected, thereby dispossessing the non-Indian occupants and restoring the land to the Pueblos.[4]

Smith's efforts as an internationalist, while not as successful as his efforts as a progressive domestic reformer, certainly had wider impact. His relief work among the Armenians was a facet of the progressive era, for he and his co-workers sought to bring order where there was chaos and to bring food and clothing where there was starvation. He did participate in the decision-making process at the Paris Peace Conference, a type of activity that is attracting greater attention from scholars of the Peace Conference. In advocating the Armenian cause during the decade of the 'twenties, he and his co-workers managed to keep the Armenian question before the public eye and, in so doing, to influence the course of American diplomacy with Turkey. As a member of the "church lobby" Smith engaged in the struggle against those who were boosting American economic interests in the Near East. State Department officials determined that American post-war policy in the Near East called for economic expansion. They regarded the "church lobby" as motivated by a sense of morality but as fostering a cause wholly at odds with American national interests. Smith is to be commended, however, for trying to gain State Department endorsement of the proposals of the "church lobby" for Armenia by claiming that such action would be in the scope of American national interests because it would result in greater protection for American missionary investments in Turkey and Armenia and could lead to American exploitation of raw materials in that region.

Although he and his contemporaries in the pro-Armenia movement did not achieve all of their goals, they at least publicized the great physical need of the war-ravaged Armenians; if they could not help them fulfill their political goals, they certainly did fulfill their material needs by supplying food, clothing, shelter, and medical care.

It appears that two factors gave central meaning to Smith's life. First, he was a product of the times in which he lived. The social awareness that emanated from his Roman Catholic faith, his family and educational background, first led him to work for the welfare of his family during its time of need. It was sharpened and honed to a fine edge by the experiences of his era. This awareness developed into a progressive consciousness that permeated and influenced all three of his careers. It manifested itself in the young lawyer who exercised his talents in numerous activities that benefitted the indigent. It is apparent in the reformer who diligently tried to restore political power to the people. He believed that divorce resulted in undue social dislocation and was convinced of the benefits that the cohesive family rendered the individual member. He strove to curb the rising divorce rate to protect individuals from the trauma that accompanies divorce, and in so doing adhered to the teaching of the Catholic Church. This progressive consciousness can also be seen in Smith the internationalist, who keenly felt the distress of the devastated Armenians and sought to remedy their sad plight by speeding up relief supplies and working for their political independence. Second, the ambition that led Smith to achieve success in all phases of his life was in large measure due to his realization at an early age of the necessity to interact successfully with the dominant Anglo-Saxon, Protestant elite in American social, political, and economic life. He was convinced that this was an important social asset through his early contacts with neighbors in suburban Philadelphia and with friends at preparatory school and university, and Smith used this valuable social grace in all three phases of his life.

Ultimately, one must raise the question: How would Smith, the progressive liberal of 1900 vintage compare to a liberal American in the last quarter of the twentieth century? On the one hand, his conservative views on education, religion, and marriage, his paternal attitude toward American Indians, and his apparent neglect of Blacks would put him out of step with his modern counterpart. On the other hand, his concern for world peace and for civil rights, as expressed in his 1918 presidential address to the American Bar Association, would align him with liberals today. But on balance it would be difficult to place Smith, with his fastidious attitude toward the social niceties, his elitist, paternal view of minorities, and his skepticism about big federal government, among the ranks of today's liberals.

Smith's life can be summed up as somewhat of a paradox in five senses. First, he combined in his person two divergent tendencies: one, genteel, conservative and backward-looking, that hoped to preserve that which was; the second, a forward-looking tendency that aimed at change and reform. Smith managed to reconcile these and the result was a conservative progressivism frequently found among those Northeastern lawyers who strove to manage change, prevent excess, and control the social, economic, and political milieu.

Second, he enjoyed a successful law practice that led him to a position of national eminence in the country's legal profession. However, like Sir Thomas More, the English lawyer with whom he has been compared, the causes that Smith suported were for the most part lost causes. His efforts in politics, his championing of the uniform divorce law, his support for the Armenians, his participation in the Washington Naval Conference, and his work for the Indians did not lead to far-reaching success. The uniform divorce law was accepted by only a few states, and even his own state of Pennsylvania rejected it. The Armenians did not gain independence as a sovereign state, but today make up one of the fifteen republics in the Soviet Union. Although the Washington Conference was highly regarded as a peace-keeping device in the 1920s, it cannot be regarded as wholly successful since the treaties emanating from it did not deter Japanese navalism or Japanese aggression in the Far East during the succeeding period. And while the Pueblo Indians did receive immediate benefits from the work of Smith and his colleagues on the Board of Indian Commissioners nevertheless, in the final analysis, the plight of the American Indian is today far from good.

Third, while Smith earnestly worked for worldly success, he also exhibited traits of a genuine monastic vocation. Although he greatly admired those with the sacerdotal vocation, secular or religious, he nevertheless tried to deter his brother from entering the religious life. This irony is easily explained: Smith's mother imbued him with a deeply religious nature, while his father passed on to him a desire for temporal success.

Fourth, Smith supported Armenian and Indian aspirations, but there is little in his manuscript collection indicating that he had any real concern for the welfare of the American Negro and other indigent ethnic groups in his immediate surroundings. Of course he did aid and assist the work of the Sisters of the Blessed Sacrament who were involved in helping the Negroes, and there is evidence in his 1918 presidential address to the American Bar Association that he deplored discrimination against Negroes and favored strong guarantees of their civil liberties.[5] But there is no indication that he actively supported the cause of Blacks as he did for Armenians and Indians. One cannot be too critical of Smith for this neglect as most progressives of his day, aside from such people as Ray Stannard Baker and Jane Addams of Hull House, showed little concern for the rights of black people and other poverty-stricken ethnic groups. It would be many years following his death before Americans would adopt such causes.

Fifth, Smith was a devout practicing Catholic, who adhered to the letter and spirit of the Church's teaching. But he spent much of his adult life working with Protestants, both lay and clerical—a practice not common among American Catholics of that era. Indeed, during the Armenian years he worked with Protestant leaders almost exclusively in serving the cause of the peoples of the land of Ararat. To be sure, he did cooperate with Cardinal Gibbons in this effort but, in the main, his work was with Protestants. In one sense of the word Smith was an ecumenicist. In another, he was the product of his rearing, which abhorred narrowminded bigotry. Certainly, this son of a Catholic mother and a Protestant father seems to have reached that happy state in which he could live his faith and yet enjoy fruitful relationships with those not of his creed.

Most biographical studies end with a short concluding chapter relating the subject's activities in retirement. This is not necessary with Smith because he continued to engage in useful pursuits until death struck him down. When he died he was still active in his law chamber fulfilling professional responsibilities; he continued to work for the Armenians, and he anticipated making at least one more tour of investigation of Indian reservations. Smith's was a life well lived.

Notes

Preface

1. As used in this sense, the term "Philadelphia lawyer" simply identifies Smith as an attorney who practiced law in the city of Philadelphia. But the term also carries a special connotation of erudition, ability, perception, and success. (See chapter 9).

2. Richard Hofstadter, *The Age of Reform from Bryan to F.D.R.* (New York, 1955), p. 163.

Chapter 1

1. Numerous allusions in letters throughout his life attest to this. Except where otherwise indicated, this chapter is based on the unpublished "Autobiography" of Walter George Smith and on a number of biographical sketches in the Walter George Smith Manuscript Collection, American Catholic Historical Society, Philadelphia, Pa.

2. For a sketch of Smith's ancestry and early family background, see Walter George Smith, *The Life and Letters of Thomas Kilby Smith* (New York, 1898), pp. 1-10.

3. Thomas Kilby Smith's promotion to Brigadier General came in 1863, following a recommendation by General Grant. Smith, *Life and Letters*, p. 80.

4. Personal interviews with Mrs. Jean Bullitt Darlington, a neighbor of the Smith family for many years, and Sister M. Francisca, a religious of the Congregation of the Sisters of the Blessed Sacrament.

5. T. K. Smith to W. G. Smith, Jan. 17, 1867, Smith, *Life and Letters*, p. 414.

6. T. K. Smith to W. G. Smith, Dec. 13, 1868, *ibid*, p. 446.

7. The University of Pennsylvania, *The University Record*, (Philadelphia, 1873), p. 2

8. *Ibid.*, pp. 5-6.

Chapter 2

1. Unless otherwise indicated, material for this chapter was drawn from sources in Smith's manuscript collection such as his unpublished "Autobiography" and from several typed biographical sketches also in the collection.

2. *Weekly Notes of Cases Argued and Determined in the Supreme Court of Pennsylavania, the County Courts of Philadelphia, and the United States District and Circuit Courts for the Eastern District of Pennsylvania.* VII (1879), 57-59.

3. *Ibid .,* IX (1881), 402-03; X (1881), 53-55 and *Pennsylvania State Reports,* I (1882), 211-15.

4. Concerning the Lunch Club, see large scrapbook in Smith Collection, pp.13, 17 and George Wharton Pepper, *Philadelphia Lawyer: An Autobiography* (Philadelphia, 1944), pp.66-67.

5. *Philadelphia Public Ledger*, October 1, 1886.

6. See Walter George Smith, "The Proposed Amendments to the National Constitution: An Address to the Lawyer's Club of Buffalo, March 30, 1918," *Addresses of Walter George Smith*, Smith Collection. Hereafter cited as *Addresses*.

7. For these letters see Sheppard to Pattison, Oct. 15, 1886; Price to Pattison, Oct. 26, 1886; and Robb to Pattison, Oct. 13, 1886, Smith Collection.

8. Interview with Hubert Horan, Dec. 14, 1969.

9. 114 *U. S. Reports*, 149-158.

10. See Thomas A. Bryson, "Walter George Smith and General Grant's Memoirs," *Pennsylvania Magazine of History and Biography*, XCIV, No. 2 (April, 1970), pp.233-44. Portions of this article are reproduced by permission of the editor. Also see H. C. V. Feinstein, "Mark Twain's Lawsuits," unpublished doctoral dissertation, University of California at Berkeley, 1968.

11. For Smith and Rawle's initial argument, see the *Philadelphia Inquirer*, July 22, 1886, p. 8. Also see 27 *Federal Reporter*, 914.

12. Feinstein, "Mark Twain," p. 271.

13. *Ibid.,*pp. 257-58; 296-97; and 313b.

14. See Thomas A, Bryson, "A Lawsuit concerning the Publication of Jefferson Davis's *The Rise and Fall of the Confederate Government,*" *Georgia*

Historical Quarterly, LIV, No. 4 (Winter, 1970), pp. 540-52. Portions of this article are here reproduced by permission of the editor.

15. Interview with Sister M. Francisca, Sisters of the Blessed Sacrament, Dec. 12, 1970.

16. There were three Drexel girls. Elizabeth Langstroth, the eldest was born August 25, 1855. Her middle name was her mother's maiden name. Katherine Drexel was Elizabeth's younger sister and was born in 1858, at which time their mother Hannah Langstroth died. On April 10, 1860, Drexel married Emma Mary Bouvier and by her had one daughter, Louise, born in 1863.

17. Smith to Sister Katherine, Nov. 11, 1889, Papers of the Rev. Mother Katherine Drexel, Sisters of the Blessed Sacrament, St. Elizabeth's Convent, Cornwells Heights, Pa. Hereafter cited as SBS.

18. GWC to KMD, Christmas, 1889, Sister Dolores Letterhouse, *The Francis A. Drexel Family* (Cornwells Heights, Pa. 1939), p. 375.

19. ELD to KMD, Advent, I, 1889, *ibid.,* pp.382-83.

20. ELD to KMD, Sunday, Dec. 21, 1889, *ibid.*

21, EDS to GS, Feb. 23, 1890, *ibid.,* p. 397.

22. EDS to LDM, May 18, 1890, SBS; and EDS to Miss Mary Anne Cassidy, Jun. 9, 1890, SBS; and EDS to LDM, Jun. 8, 1890, Letterhouse, *Drexel Family,* p. 398.

23. EDS to Miss Cassidy, Jul. 26, 1890, Letterhouse, *Drexel Family,* pp.403-05.

24. Smith to KMD, Oct. 25, 1890, SBS.

25. Smith to KMD, Dec. 27, 1890, SBS.

26. Interview with Miss Dora O'Malley, May 31, 1971.

27. Wills of Francis A. Drexel and Elizabeth Drexel Smith, City Hall, Philadelphia, Pa; Sister Consuela Marie Duffy, *Katherine Drexel: A Biography* (Philadelphia, 1966), pp.72-75, and John H. Davis, *The Bouviers: Portrait of an American Family* (New York, 1969), pp.133-36.

28. Smith to KMD, Oct. 25, 1890, SBS.

29. See Walter Geo. Smith, "Uniform Marraige and Divorce Laws: Paper Read before the Ohio Bar Association, Jul. 8, 1909,"*Addresses.*

30. See Walter Geo. Smith, "The Lawyer as a Citizen: Paper Read to the Rhode Island Bar Association, Dec. 2, 1912," *ibid.*

Chapter 3

1. Except where noted this chapter is based on the unpublished "Autobiography" of Walter George Smith.

2. See George E. Mowry, *The Era of Theodore Roosevelt and the Birth of Modern America, 1900-1912* (New York, 1958), pp. 85-88; Richard Hofstadter, *The Age of Reform from Bryan to F. D. R.* (New York, 1955), pp. 131-73; Afred D. Chandler, Jr., "The Origins of Progressive Leadership," in Elting Morison, et al, ed. *Letters of Theodore Roosevelt* (Cambridge, 1951-54), VIII, Appendix III. pp. 1462-64. For a comprehensive essay on the progressive

era, see David M. Kennedy, "Overview: The Progressive Era," *Historian*, 37 (May 1975), 453-468.

3. G. E. Mowry, *Era of Theodore Roosevelt*, ch. V and Hofstadter, *Age of Reform*, pp. 135-66.

4. Samuel P. Hays, "The Politics of Reform in Municipal Government in the Progressive Era," *Pacific Northwest Quarterly*, LV (Oct. 1964) pp. 157-69.

5. Otis L. Graham, Jr., *An Encore for Reform* (New York, 1967), p. 201.

6. Peter G. Filene, "An Obituary for 'The Progressive Movement,' " *American Quarterly*, XXII (Spring, 1970), pp. 29, 30.

7. *Ibid.*, p. 30.

8. *Ibid.*, pp. 21-23.

9. *Ibid.*, pp. 24-26.

10. Robert H. Wiebe, *The Search for Order*, 1877-1920 (New York, 1967), pp. 165, 129, 146, 153, 155, 169.

11. Mowry, *Era of Theodore Roosevelt*, p. 103.

12. Hofstadter, *Age of Reform*, pp. 138, 143.

13. George E. Mowry, *The California Progressives* (Berkeley, 1951), pp. 87-89; James B. Crooks, *Politics & Progress: The Rise of Urban Progressivism in Baltimore, 1895 to 1911* (Baton Rouge, 1968) pp. 198-199; E. Daniel Potts, "The Progressive Profile in Iowa," *Mid-America*, XLVII (Oct. 1965), p. 261; William T. Kerr, Jr., "The Progressives of Washington, 1910-1912," *Pacific Northwest Quarterly*, LV (Jan. 1964), pp. 16-27; and Richard B. Sherman, "The Status Revolution and Massachusetts Progressive Leadership," *Political Science Quarterly* LXXVIII (Mar. 1963), pp. 59-65.

14. Hofstadter, *Age of Reform* p. 163.

15. Letter to author from William Barclay Lex, dtd. Jul 21 1972. Interviews with Hubert Horan, Dec. 14, 1969, and with Charles J. Biddle, Mar. 17, 1970. Moses King listed Smith among the most "notable Philadelphia lawyers." See Moses King, *Philadelphia and Notable Philadelphians* (New York, 1901). p. 26.

16. See James Grafton Rogers, *American Bar Leaders*, 1878-1928 (Chicago, 1932), pp. 194-97; obituary notice on Walter George Smith, *American Bar Journal*, X (Apr. 1924), pp. 241-42; "Walter George Smith: An Appreciation," *Ibid.*, X (June 1924), pp. 425-26; Minute Adopted by Conference of Commissioners on Uniform Divorce Laws, 1924, on Death of Walter George Smith, Smith Collection; obituary of Walter George Smith (1854-1924) in *Report of the Thirtieth Annual Meeting of the Pennsylvania Bar Association* (Philadelphia, 1924), pp. 108-111; and letter from William Barclay Lex to author, July 21, 1972.

17. Walter George Smith, "Uniform Commercial Law: An Address before the North Carolina Bar Assocation, June 28, 1916," *Addresses*.

18. See *Report of the Thirty-fifth Annual Meeting of the American Bar Association* (Baltimore, 1913), pp. 756-766.

19. Esther Lucile Brown, *Lawyers and the Promotion of Justice* (New York; 1938), p. 129.

20. Hofstadter, *Age of Reform*, p. 157. These goals constituted an effort by richer lawyers to raise the standards of the professional at the expense of those colleagues not so fortunate.

21. See "Address of Chairman" (Legal Education Committee), in *Report of the Thirty-fifth Annual Meeting of the American Bar Association;* pp. 756-766.

22. James Willard Hurst, *Growth of American Law* (Boston, 1950), p. 290.

23. *Report of the Thirty-ninth Annual Meeting of the American Bar Association* (Baltimore, 1917), p. 98. For sketches of the American Bar Association, see Rogers, *American Bar Leaders*, pp. iii-ix, Brown, *Promotion of Justice* p. 128; and Hurst, *Growth of American Law*, pp. 287-290.

24. Robert H. Wiebe, *Businessmen and Reform: A Study of the Progressive Movement* (Chicago, 1962), Chap. II, and *Search for Order*, p. 112; Graham, *Great Campaigns*, p. 24; and Hofstadter, *Age of Reform*, Chap. IV.

25. *Report of the Thirtieth Annual Meeting*, p. 111.

26. Graham, *The Great Campaigns*, p. 26.

27. Walter George Smith, "World War and the Scientific Theory of Education," *Catholic World*, 108 (Mar. 1919), pp. 721-30.

28. E. Digby Baltzell, *Philadelphia Gentlemen* (New York, 1958), pp. 323, 324. For information on the University of Pennsylvania in this period, see Frances Newton Thorpe, *William Pepper* (Philadelphia, 1904) and Edward Potts Cheyney, *History of the University of Pennsylvania, 1740-1940* (Philadelphia, 1940).

29. See the collection of letters from Smith to Bishop Shahan, Thomas Shahan Collection, ACHS Archive, St. Charles Borromeo Seminary, Philadelphia, Pa.

30. For a study of Catholics in the progressive era, see Aaron I. Abell, *American Catholicism and Social Action* (South Bend, 1963).

31. Smith to Drexel, Nov. 11, 1889, SBS.

32. See Letters from Smith to Mother Katherine Drexel in the SBS collection.

33. Interview with Sister M. Francisca, Dec. 12, 1970, St. Elizabeth's Convent, Cornwells Heights, Pa.

34. These letters are in the Smith collection.

35. *Philadelphia Evening Bulletin*, April 9, 1921.

36. See list of Smith's speeches in *Addresses*.

37. There are a number of letters in the Smith Collection from Repplier, Mitchell, and Furness to Smith. There are also a number of letters from Grace Smith to Agnes Repplier, dated after Smith's death.

38. See Nicholas B. Wainwright, *A Philadelphia Story, The Philadelphia Contributionship* (Philadelphia, 1952) for an interesting study of this old company.

39. Baltzell, *Philadelphia Gentlemen*, p. 244.

40. Memorial to Walter George Smith by J. Rodman Paul, chairman of the Philadelphia Contributionship, Smith collection.

41. Maisie Ward, *Unfinished Business* (New York, 1964), pp. 214, 140.

42. Interview with Mrs. Kate Loughran Sands and Miss Dora O'Malley, May 30, 1971, Torresdale, Pa.

43. Lincoln Steffens, *The Shame of the Cities* (New York, 1902), p. 134.

44. See Clinton Rogers Woodruff, "Philadelphia's Republican Tammany," *Outlook*, 69 (Sep. 21, 1901), p. 169 and "Philadelphia's Election Frauds," *Arena*, 24 (Oct., 1900), pp. 397-404.

45. For a discussion of Philadelphia politics during the period, see A. K. McClure, *Old Time Notes of Pennsylvania* (Philadelphia, 1905), II; Robert Douglas Bowden, *Boies Penrose: Symbol of an Era* (New York, 1937); Donald W. Disbrow, "The Progressive Movement in Philadelphia, 1910-16," unpublished Ph.D. dissertation, University of Rochester, 1956; and Paul S. George, "Philadelphia's Municipal Affairs During the Latter part of the 19th Century with Emphasis on the Mayoralty Contest of 1896," unpublished master's thesis, Florida State University, 1968. Giving full treatment to this period is Joel Mustin's doctoral dissertation, "Philadelphia Politics, 1885-1910," in progress at the Case-Western Reserve University, Cleveland, Ohio.

46. It is worth noting that reformers played a role in this episode, for Rudolph Blankenburg, a Philadelphia merchant long associated with reform movements, claims that he brought about the dropping of Penrose by threatening to publish a photograph of him leaving one of the city's well-known brothels. This combination of boss and reformer making common cause to achieve a political end is pointed out to highlight an all too common occurrence in Philadelphia politics—the cooperation of the advocates of machine rule with those of good government.

47. See Donald W. Disbrow, "Herbert Welsh, Editor of *City and State*, 1895-1904," *The Pennsylvania Magazine of History and Biography*, XCIV (Jan. 1970) 62-74 and Herbert Adams Gibbons, *John Wanamaker* (New York, 1926), I, pp. 350-58.

48. *Philadelphia Evening Bulletin*, Sept. 22, 1898.

49. Francis F. Kane to Herbert Welsh, undated, Herbert Welsh Collection, Historical Society of Pennsylvania, Philadelphia.

50. Baltzell, *Philadelphia Gentlemen*, 131.

51. *City and State*, V (Sept. 29, 1898), pp. 193, 196; (Aug. 25, 1898), p. 113; and (Oct. 6, 1898), p. 213.

52. *Philadelphia Evening Bulletin*, Nov. 5, 1898. Reformers won in Philadelphia, but Quay was successful in obtaining the governor's mansion for his candidate Stone. Wanamaker's efforts were not in vain, because the state legislature chosen in that year did not re-elect Quay some two months after the gubernatorial race. This fact accomplished little good, for Governor William Stone, Quay's handpicked man, appointed him to fill the vacancy that occurred when the legislature failed to re-elect him.

53. Lincoln Steffens, *The Autobiography of Lincoln Steffens* (New York, 1931), p. 410.

54. Clinton Rogers Woodruff, "The Philadelphia Campaigns against Machine Rule," *Review of Reviews*, XXIV (Nov. 1901), pp. 556-58.

55. Pepper to Welsh, June 28, 1901, Welsh Collection.

56. McClure, *Old Time Notes*, II, pp. 620-24.

57. Woodruff, "Philadelphia Campaigns," p. 558.

58. *Philadelpha Inquirer*, Jun. 20, 1901. Concerning Rothermel's performance, Pepper said, "The volume of business in the D. A.'s office in this city is very great. It is so great that the office is said to be behind in its work." See Pepper nominating speech, George Wharton Pepper Collection, Van Pelt Library, University of Pennsylvania.

59. *Philadelphia Inquirer*, Jun. 28, 1901 and Jun. 29, 1901.

60. *Ibid.*, Jul. 19, 1901 and *Philadelphia Public Ledger*, Jul. 19, 1901.

61. *Philadelphia Public Ledger*, Jul. 19, 1901.

62. *Ibid.*, Jul. 20, 1901.

63. *City and State*, XI (Jul. 25, 1901), p. 50.

64. *Philadelphia Public Ledger*, Jul. 23, and Jul. 24, 1901.

65. *Ibid.*, Jul. 24, and Jul. 30, 1901.

66. See Rudolph Blankenburg's series of reform-oriented articles entitled "Forty Years in the Wilderness," in the *Arena* from 1905 to 1906, for the reformer's viewpoint. Also see Lucretia Blankenburg, *The Blankenburgs of Philadelphia* (Philadelphia, 1928).

67. *Philadelphia Public Ledger*, Aug. 6, 1901.

68. *Ibid.* Aug. 16, 1901 and Aug. 27, 1901. Blankenburg was also chairman of the party finance committee, which included George Burnham, Charles E. Cadwalder, M. D., Maurice Fels, William T. Tilden, Mahlon N. Kline, John T. Bailey, Charles B. Harding, Henry M. Steel, J. R. Keim, and Finley Acker. This latter committee sent out a flyer, asking for contributions. It estimated that the party would need $80,000.00 to finance a proper campaign. See undated flyer over Rudolph Blankenburg's signature, Rudolph Blankenburg Collection, Historical Society of Pennsylvania.

69. *City and State*, XI (Aug. 1, 1901), p. 65 and (Oct. 31, 1901), p. 272.

70. *Philadelphia Public Ledger*, Jul. 26, 1901.

71. *New York Times*, Aug. 1 and Aug. 25, 1901.

72. *Ibid.*, Sep. 25, 1901 and *Philadelphia Inquirer*, Sep. 25, 1901.

73. *Philadelphia Public Ledger*, Sept. 25, 1901.

74. *Ibid.*, Sep. 25, 1901.

75. *Philadelphia Inquirer*, Oct. 2, 1901 and *City and State*, XI (Aug. 15, 1901), p. 96.

76. McClure, *Old Time Notes*, II, p. 622,

77. *Philadelphia Inquirer*, Sept. 25, 1901 and Oct. 30, 1901. Concerning Rothermel's performance of his duties, Hampton Carson, in a letter endorsing Rothermel, wrote Ernest L. Tustin, chairman of the City Committee, Union Party: "He has performed his duties during the past three years with such conspicuous ability and fidelity as to deserve not only commendation but the open support of all those who believe that a faithful public servant should be sustained by an overwhelming vote of confidence." Carson to Tustin, October 8, 1901, Hampton Carson Collection, Historical Society of Pennsylvania.

78. *Philadelphia Public Ledger* clipping (undated), Scrapbook of Walter George Smith, Smith Collection.

79. *City and State*, XI (Nov. 7, 1901), p. 286.

80. William S. Vare, *My Forty Years in Politics* (Philadelphia, 1933), p. 82.

81. *Philadelphia Inquirer*, Oct. 23, 1901.

82. *City and State*, XI (Oct. 31, 1901), p. 272.

83. Concerning the proposed debate, see Weaver to Moore, Oct. 8, 1901; Moore to Weaver, Oct. 11, 1901; Weaver to Moore, Oct. 14, 1901; Moore to Blankenburg, Oct. 14, 1901; and Blankenburg to Moore, Oct. 15, 1901. J. Hampton Moore Collection, Historical Society of Pennsylvania.

84. *Philadelphia Inquirer*, Nov. 7, 1901.

85. *City and State*, XI (Nov. 14, 1901), p. 305; McClure, *Old Time Notes*, II, p. 622.

86. *Philadelphia Public Ledger*, Nov. 7, 1901.

87. McClure, *Old Time Notes*, II, p. 623.

88. See Lloyd M. Abernethy, "Insurgency in Philadelphia, 1905," *Pennsylvania Magazine of History and Biography*, LXXXVII (Oct. 1960), pp. 379-96.

89. See William L. O'Neill, *Divorce in the Progressive Era* (New Haven, 1967), p. ix.

90. *Ibid.*, Chapter II.

91. *Ibid.*, p. 54.

92. Smith to Dike, Nov. 27, 1906, Samuel Dike Collection, Library of Congress.

93. Walter George Smith, "Divorce in Civil Jurisprudence," *Catholic Encyclopedia* (1912), V, pp. 64-69.

94. Walter George Smith, "The National Divorce Congress," *Addresses*.

95. Smith to Dike, Dec. 6, 1906, Dike Collection.

96. *Loc. Cit.*

97. Speech to Social Science Section of the New Century Club, Philadelphia, Pa., Mar. 21, 1906, Smith Scrapbook, p. 110.

98. Smith to Dike, Feb. 8 and 27, 1906, Dike Collection.

99. *Proceedings of the National Congress on Uniform Divorce Laws Held at Washington, D. C., February 19, 1906* (Harrisburg, 1906).

100. *Ibid.*, p. 199. Also see Nelson Manfred Blake, *The Road to Reno: A History of Divorce* (New York, 1962), pp. 140-45.

101. *Proceedings of the Adjourned Meeting of the National Congress on Uniform Divorce Laws Held at Philadelphia, Pa., Nov. 13, 1906* (Harrisburg, 1907), pp. 13-14.

102. O'Neill, *Divorce in the Progressive Era*, p. 243.

103. Smith to Dike, Oct. 28, 1908 and Dec. 9, 1908, Dike Collection.

104. *Papers and Proceedings of the American Sociological Society*, III (1909), pp. 150-160.

105. *Ibid.*, pp. 169-73.

106. *Ibid.*, pp. 173-77.

107. *Ibid.*, pp. 179-80.

108. Smith to Dike, Jan. 2, 1909, Dike Collection.

109. Smith to Dike, Jan. 15, 1909, Dike Collection.

110. Smith to Dike, Mar. 22, 1910, *ibid.*

111. Smith to Harrison, May 16, 1909, Smith Collection.

112. Harrison to Smith, May 19, 1909, *ibid.*

113. Smith to Harrison, May 26, 1909, *ibid.*

114. Harrison to Smith, Jun. 8, 1909, *ibid.*

115. Smith to Harrison, Nov. 8, 1909, *ibid*

116. Robbins to Smith, Nov. 9, 1909, *ibid.*

117. *Philadelphia Evening Telegraph*, Dec. 3, 1909.

118. *Ibid.*, Dec. 3, 1909.

119. *Philadelphia Inquirer*, and *Evening Telegraph*, Dec. 4, 1909.

120. A marble bust of Smith with the medal affixed to his lapel is in the foyer at St. Francis's Industrial School, Eddington, Pa.

121. This speech is reprinted in Julia E. Johnsen, ed., *Selected Articles on Marriage and Divorce* (New York, 1925), pp. 280-84.

122. Samuel Haber, *Efficiency and Uplift: Scientific Management in the Progressive Era, 1890-1920* (Chicago 1964), p. ix.

123. Graham, *The Great Campaigns*, p. 23.

124. See National Conference of Commissioners on Uniform State Laws, *American Uniform Commercial Acts*, (Cincinnati, 1910), pp. 11-13. Concerning this movement, see also Emerson D. Fite, *Government by Cooperation* (New York, 1932) and W. Brooke Graves, *Uniform State Action: A Possible Substitute for Centralization* (Chapel Hill, 1934).

125. See "Uniform Commercial Laws: An Address Before the North Carolina Bar Assocation by Walter George Smith, June 28 1916." "Uniformity of Legislation: An Address to the Maryland State Bar Assocation, Atlantic City, New Jersey, June 28, 1918, by Walter George Smith, Esq." "Uniform State Legislation," delivered to the New Hampshire Bar Association on July 6, 1918 *Addresses*. See also "Present Status of Workmen's Compensation Laws," *The Annals of the American Academy of Political and Social Science* (July, 1911), pp. 128-43.

126. *Philadelphia Evening Bulletin*, Sep. 11 and 16, 1916 and *Philadelphia Evening Telegraph*, Sep. 16, 1916.

127. Donald Disbrow, "Reform in Philadelphia Under Mayor Blankenburg, 1912-1916," *Pennsylvania History*, XXVII (Oct. 1960), pp. 379-96.

128. See Harold Quicksale, "Political Crime in Philadelphia," *New Republic*, XII (Sep. 29, 1917), pp. 246-48; "Government by Murder: The Unhappy Plight of Philadelphia," *Outlook*, 117 (Oct. 24, 1917), pp. 283-84; and "Philadelphia's Deplorable Murder," *Literary Digest*, 55 (Oct. 13, 1917), pp. 48-52.

129. Speech by R. Blankenburg, Blankenburg Collection.

130. *Philadelphia Evening Bulletin, Oct. 12, 1917.*

131. *Loc. Cit.*

132. *Philadelphia Inquirer*, Oct. 13, 1917.

133. Bowden, *Boies Penrose*, p. 192.

134. *Philadelphia Inquirer*, Oct. 15, 1917.

135. *Ibid.*, Oct. 23, 1917, and *Philadelphia Evening Bulletin*, Oct. 23, 1917.

136. Clipping from Smith Scrapbook, Smith Collection.

137. Interview with Miss Dora O'Malley, May 30, 1971, and Mr. Hubert Horan, Dec. 12, 1970, Smith Scrapbook, Smith Collection. *Philadelphia Inquirer*, Oct. 22, 1917.

138. *Ibid.*, Nov. 6, 1917.

139. *Ibid.*, Nov. 7 and 8, 1917.

140. *ibid.*, Nov. 9, 1917.

141. *Ibid.*, Nov. 24, 1917.

142. *Ibid.*, Nov. 24, 27, and 28, 1917.

Chapter 4

1. Unless otherwise noted, this chapter is based on the manuscript "Journal of a Journey to the Near East," by Walter George Smith. The author has edited this journal which appears in six parts in the *Armenian Review*, XXIV (Spring, Summer, Autumn, Winter, 1971) and XXV (Spring, Summer, 1972). The letters cited in the text are in the Smith Collection.

2. Robert H. Wiebe, suggests in his study, *The Search for Order, 1877-1920* (New York, 1967), p. 169 that the central theme of humanitarian progressivism was the child who was "the carrier of tomorrow's hope. . . ." Joseph L. Grabill maintains in his work, *Protestant Diplomacy and the Near East: Missionary Influence on American Policy, 1810-1927* (Minneapolis, 1971), pp. 70-71, 80-89, 117, and 290 that overseas philanthropy was a natural concomitant. of domestic progressivism and that both Crane and Dodge were examples of men who served in the areas of domestic reform and philanthropy abroad.

3. See James L. Barton, *The Story of Near East Relief* (New York, 1930), pp. 107-137.

4. Armenian Christians constitute one of the oldest branches of Christendom, having accepted the Christian faith *as their state religion* as early as 301 through the efforts of St. Gregory the Illuminator. The autocephalic Armenian Church, often called the "Gregorian Armenian Church" after its chief founder, is headed by a catholicos who resides in the monestery-see at Etchmiadzin. The patriarch of the Catholic Armenians, who are in communion with the Holy See in Rome, resided in Constantinople, as did the autocephalic Armenian patriarch. The Latin patriarch traveled frequently to Rome on official duties. The autocephalic patriarch, the religio-political head of the great majority of Armenians in the Ottoman Empire, rarely traveled outside the country.

5. Unpublished Diary of Charles T. Riggs, Marc 9, 1919. By permission of Mrs. Charles MacNeal, Hightstown, N. J.

6. Diary of Mark Lambert Bristol Collection, the Library of Congress, Washington, D. C.

7. On the emergency of Armenia, see Rochard G. Hovannisian, *Ar-*

menia on the Road to Independence, 1918 (Berkeley, 1969), and *The Republic of Armenia* (Berkeley, 1971).

8. John Elder, "Memories of the Armenian Republic," *Armenian Review*, VI (Mar. 1953), pp. 3-27.

9. Herbert Hoover, *The Memoirs of Herbert Hoover* (3 vols., New York, 1952), I, 386. On May 8, 1919, Heinz presented an ARA check for $100,000.00 to ACRNE, Constantinople. Riggs Diary, May 8, 1919.

10. Eliot G. Mears, *Modern Turkey* (New York, 1924), p. 515.

11. *Ibid.*, p. 515.

12. See William E. Leuchtenburg, "Progressivism and Imperialism: The Progressive Movement and American Foreign Policy, 1898-1916," *Mississippi Valley Historical Review*, XXXIX (December 1952), 483-504; Barton J. Bernstein and Franklin A. Leib, "Progressive Republican Senators and American Imperialism, 1898-1916: A Re-appraisal," *Mid-America*, 50 (July 1968), 163-205; and John M. Cooper, "Progressivism and American Foreign Policy: A Reconsideration," *Mid-America*, 51 (October 1969), 260-277.

13. Smith to Gibbons (undated), James Cardinal Gibbons Collection, Catholic Archdiocesan Center, Baltimore, Md.

14. Smith and Montgomery later organized the Armenia-America Society, an effective pro-Armenia pressure group.

15. ARA to Morgenthau, June 20, 1919, Henry Morgenthau, Sr. Collection, Library of Congress, Washington, D. C.

Chapter 5

1. This chapter is based primarily on Smith's unpublished "Journal of a Journey to the Near East," and in part on a previously published paper by the author, entitled "Walter George Smith and the Armenian Question at the Paris Peace Conference, 1919," *Records of the American Catholic Historical Society of Philadelphia*, 81 (Mar., 1970), pp. 3-26. Portions of this article are here reproduced by permission of the editor. See also Thomas A. Bryson, *American Diplomatic Relations with the Middle East, 1784-1975: A Survey* (Metuchen, N. J., 1977), p. 69. Also see Grabill, *Protestant Diplomacy*, pp. 206-208.

2. See Joseph P. O'Grady, ed., *The Immigrants' Influence on Wilson's Peace Policies* (Lexington, 1967). Lawrence Gelfand delivered a paper entitled "The American Mission to Negotiate Peace, 1919: Fifty Years of Historiography in Review," at the 1969 meeting of the Organization of American Historians. In this paper Gelfand suggested the need to investigate the role of persons like W. G. Smith at the Paris Conference to determine if they did, in fact, play a role in the decision-making process.

3. Diary of Henry Morgenthau, Sr., Jun. 22, 1919, Henry Morgenthau, Sr. Manuscript Collection, Library of Congress, Washington, D. C.

4. Hoover to ARA, Jun. 14, 1919, copy in the Morgenthau Collection.

5. Morgenthau to Barton and Dodge, Jun. 24, 1919, *ibid*. Although he acquiesced in this matter, Morgenthau reports that Smith was somewhat

"perplexed" at first. The following day Barton replied that he could neither approve nor disapprove the Hoover-Morgenthau plan. He thought no real advantages would result and that confusion would surely follow. Barton to Morgenthau, Jun. 25, 1919, *ibid.*

6. Morgenthau Diary, Jul. 2, 1919. Also see U. S. State Department, *The Papers Relating to the Foreign Relations of the United States, 1919, II, 827.* Hereafter cited as *FRUS.*

7. Herbert Hoover, *An American Epic: Famine in Forty-five Nations* (3 vols., Chicago, 1961), III, p. 201; *The Ordeal of Woodrow Wilson* (New York, 1958), p. 142; and *Memoirs,* I, p. 386.

8. U. S. Senate, Senate Document, unnumbered, 66th Cong, 1st Sess, 1919. *Maintenance of Peace in Armenia* (Washington, 1919), pp. 67, 84.

9. *FRUS,* 1919, II, p. 850.

10. G. Smith to K. Smith, Jun. 9, 1919, Smith Collection.

11. Some 300,000 Armenian refugees from Turkey fled the Turkish persecution of 1915 to the Armenian Republic in Russian Armenia.

12. Edward M. House Manuscrupt Collection, Yale University Library, New Haven, Conn. There is little of importance on the Armenian question in Charles Seymour, ed., *The Intimate papers of Colonel House* (4 vols., Boston, 1928).

13. Initial German reluctance to accept the Treaty stemmed from the violent German reaction to what was considered a harsh treaty.

14. For Lansing's opposition to a mandate, see the Desk Diary of Robert Lansing and his Memoranda in the Lansing Collection; General Tasker Bliss also expressed hesitancy about such a responsibility. See Diary of Tasker Bliss, Tasker Bliss Manuscript Collection, Library of Congress, Washington, D. C. and David Trask, *General Tasker Howard Bliss and the "Sessions of the world,"* (Philadelphia, 1966), p. 56; White's views are recorded in the extensive correspondence with Senator Henry Cabot Lodge, copies of which are in the Elihu Root Manuscript Collection, Library of Congress, Washington, D. C. and in Allan Nevins, *Henry White* (New York, 1930).

15. For Bristol's influence on this matter, see Thomas A. Bryson, "Mark Lambert Bristol, U. S. Navy, Admiral Diplomat: His Influence on the Armenian Mandate Question," *The Armenian Review,* XXI (Winter, 1968), pp. 3-22.

16. Copies of these letters from Lodge to White are in the Root Collection and in Nevins, *Henry White.*

17. Lansing Desk Diary, Jun. 25, 1919, Lansing Collection.

18. Diary of William Linn Westermann, p. 95. William Linn Westermann Manuscript Collection, Columbia University, New York City.

19. *Ibid.,* 96.

20. Hoover to Wilson, Jun. 27, 1919, Hoover, *An American Epic,* III, 397-98.

21. Westermann Diary, p. 96.

22. Hoover, *Ordeal of Woodrow Wilson,* p. 144 and *An American Epic,* III, pp. 397-98.

23. Morgenthau Diary, Jun. 22, 1919.

24. James Gidney, *A Mandate for Armenia* (Kent University Press, Ohio, 1967), p. 167.

25. *FRUS, Paris Peace Conference*, 1919, VII, pp. 40-44.

26. Bristol to Smith, Jun. 28, 1919, National Archives, RG 59, 867B.00/55. A memorandum in David Hunter Miller's *Diary* indicates that Ferid Pasha, Grand Vizier of the Sultan's Government, was quite willing to move the Armenians remaining in Turkish Armenia to the Armenian Republic, but nothing was said about repatriation of Turkish Armenians from the Caucasus to their homeland in Turkey. David Hunter Miller, *My Diary at the Conference of Paris* (21 vols., New York, 1924), XVI, 482. It goes without saying that Mustapha Kemal's regime in Angora would hardly have approved repatriation of the Armenians from the Caucasus to Turkey, for they would have constituted a virtual Trojan Horse inside the Turkish state. Concerning the question of population in Turkish and Russian Armenia, see Richard Hovannisian, *Armenia on the Road to Independence, 1918* (Berkeley, 1969), Chapters 1 and 2.

27. Green to American Mission, (undated) copy in Miller, *Diary* XX, 374.

28. Morgenthau to Harbord, Jun. 25, 1919, Morgenthau Collection.

29. Report from Maj. Gen. J. G. Harbord to President Wilson, Oct. 16, 1919, *FRUS*, 1919, II, p. 850.

30. John Philip Richardson, "The American Military Mission to Armenia," Master's thesis, George Washington Univ., 1964, p. 24.

31. Hoover, *The Ordeal of Wilson*, pp. 143-4 and *American Epic* III, p. 206.

32. Hoover, Smith, *et al* to Dodge, (undated) NA, 867B.00/205A.

33. At a meeting of the Council of Four on May 24, 1919, President Wilson agreed, subject to the approval and consent of the Senate, to accept a mandate for Armenia, Constantinople, and the Straits of the Bosporus and Dardanelles. *FRUS, Paris Peace Conference*, 1919, V, 622. See Grabill, *Protestant Diplomacy*, pp. 210-11.

34. See Thomas A. Bryson, "An American Mandate for Armenia: A Link in British Near Eastern policy," *The Armenian Review*, XXI (Summer, 1968), pp. 23-41 for a discussion of British motives for suggesting the mandate to the United States. Frederick G. Howe commented on this point, writing that at a buffet breakfast with Philip Kerr, Arnold Toynbee and others, Howe was told that America had a debt to Britian and could pay it off by accepting a mandate for Armenia. Frederick G. Howe, *Confessions of a Reformer* (New York, 1925), p. 296. Howe was a Cleveland lawyer and friend of President Wilson.

35. G. Smith to K. Smith, Aug. 12, 1919, Smith Collection. My italics are added.

36. *New York Herald*, (Paris edition), Aug. 10, 1919.

37. There was also in the National Archives collection on Armenia an unsigned letter dated Aug. 6, 1919, to Lord Bryce, the patriarch of British Armenophiles, advising of Smith's trip to London "with a view to persuading your government not to withdraw the troops from Georgia and Ar-

menia. . . ." This letter requested that he see Smith on his arrival. NA 867B.00/206A.

38. Smith to Mrs. E. B. Esler, Jul. 6, 1919, Smith Collection. Included in the personages seen by Smith were the American career diplomat Bellamy Storer and members of the Benois D'Azy family. But among those not seen was Frank Polk, State Department official.

39. W. G. Smith to C. Smith, July 8, 1919, Smith Collection.

40. G. Smith to K. Smith, Aug. 12, 1919, *ibid.*

41. Polk to Lansing, Aug. 12, 1919, NA 860J.01/45.

42. *The Annual Register: A Review of Public Events at Home and Abroad for the Year 1919.* (London, 1920), pp. 78-80.

43. *FRUS,* 1919, II, p. 828.

44. *The Times,* Aug. 13, 1919.

45. Actually all British troops were withdrawn by Sept. 10, 1919.

46. *Washington Post,* Aug. 15, 1919.

47. The British Armenia Committee was not a parliamentary body; it consisted of many English religious, political, military, and commercial leaders who were concerned about the fate of Armenia.

48. The British Army was indeed having troubles with mutinies, riots, and general discontent. See A. J. P. Taylor, *English History, 1914-45* (London, 1965), pp. 120-50.

49. See Thomas A. Bryson, "Woodrow Wilson and the Armenian Mandate: A Reassessment," *Armenian Review,* XXI (Autumn, 1968), pp. 10-29 in which is refuted the argument that Wilson delayed the settlement. It is posited in this paper that British and French policy-makers delayed the settlement by following a devious policy in the Middle East.

50. Davis to Curzon, Aug. 12, 1919, *FRUS,* 1919, II, pp. 829-30.

51. On Aug. 16, 1919, Curzon received word from the British Chargé in Washington that American acceptance of the mandate "was most unlikely." E. L. Woodward and Rohan Butler, eds., *Documents on British Foreign Policy, 1919-1939,* 1st Series, IV, p. 730. Balfour had sent word from Paris along the same line on that very date *(ibid.,* p. 734). The Washington official in the British Embassy sent a second warning on the 25th. *(Ibid.,* p. 738, hereafter cited as *British Documents.)*

52. Smith later testified on this point before the Senate Foreign Relations subcommittee on Armenia. U. S. Senate, Senate Document, 66th Cong, 1st Sess, 1919. *Maintenance of Peace in Armenia.* (Washington, 1919).

53. On Parliament's cognizance of this move, Arthur A. Ponsonby and Aneurin Williams spoke out in Parliament and claimed that the Government had not made the matter known. Great Britain, *Parliamentary Debates, House of Commons,* 1919, 5s, 2057-63 and 110, 5s, pp. 3260-61. Hereafter cited as *Parl. Deb.*

54. These men were members of the American Committee for the Independence of Armenia, an American pressure group that Smith later joined.

55. A later dispatch from Curzon to the British Chargé in Washington

implied that a heated exchange had taken place. He wrote: "Having barely recovered from a conversation lasting an hour and a half with Mr. Walter Smith, an American gentleman officially interested in the American effort in Armenia, and deeply concerned at the risk to the American people involved by our intended evacuation. . . ." Curzon to Lindsay, Aug. 18, 1919, *British Documents*, 1st Ser, III, pp. 511-12.

56. *Parl. Deb. H. Com.*, 119, 5s, pp. 2057-63 and 2063-66.

57. Yarrow to Morgenthau, Oct. 14, 1919, Morgenthau Collection.

58. *FRUS*, 1919, II, pp. 867-68.

Chapter 6

1. This chapter is based in part on a paper previously published by the author. See Thomas A. Bryson, "The Armenia-America Society: A Factor in American-Turkish Relations, 1919-1924," *Records of the American Catholic Historical Society*, 82 (June 1971), pp. 83-105 and Bryson, *American Diplomatic Relations with the Middle East*. pp. 71-83.

2. *Congressional Record*, 66 Cong, 1 Sess, p. 5067.

3. U. S. Congress, Senate Document, unnumbered, 66 Cong, 1 Sess, 1919. *Maintenance of Peace in Armenia*, p. 76. Smith saw to it that copies of the committee hearing were sent to Near East Relief. See Vickrey to Williams, Nov. 19, 1919, John Sharp Williams Collection, Library of Congress.

4. Walter George Smith, "The Williams Resolution," *New Armenia*, XI, (Nov. 1919), pp. 161-63 and "The Armenian Crisis," *Catholic World*, CVIII (Dec. 1919), pp. 305-16.

5. E. David Cronin, ed., *The Cabinet Diaries of Josephus Daniels, 1913-1921* (Lincoln, 1963), p. 449.

6. Grey to Curzon, Oct. 23, 1919, in E. L. Woodward and Rohan Butler, eds., *Documents on British Foreign Policy, 1919-1939*, 1st Series, (London, 1947-50), IV, p. 843. Concerning British intentions, Dr. Peet had written Dr. Barton—with a copy to Smith—that "A long conference with Admiral Webb convinced me that it will be impossible to change the British position by any representation that can be made. . . ." Peet to Barton, Sep. 20, 1919, Records of the American Board of Commissioners for Foreign Missions, Harvard University. By permission.

7. *Philadelphia Evening Bulletin*, Nov. 18, 1919; Cronon, *Cabinet Diaries*, p. 466; and *Philadelphia Evening Bulletin*, Jan. 13, 1920.

8. Ralph Elliott Cook, "The United States and the Armenian Question, 1884-1924," unpublished Ph.D. dissertation, Fletcher School of Law and Diplomacy, 1957, p. 304 and Grabill, *Protestant Diplomacy*, p. 249.

9. Smith to Cardashian, March 30, 1920, Vahan Cardashian Collection, Hairenik Association, Boston, Mass. Smith attended an ACIA rally at Carnegie Hall on March 20, 1920 and addressed the group. See James Gerard to Senator Lodge, Mar. 17, 1920, Henry Cabot Lodge Collection, Massachusetts Historical Society, Boston, Mass; Gerard to Colby, Apr. 3, 1920, NA 860J.01/234.

10. Wilson felt it unwise at the time to ask for a mandate as it might hurt the chances of the League to pass the Senate. See Wilson to Lansing, Aug. 4, 1919, NA 860J.01/262. Regarding the mandate, Lansing's successor Bainbridge Colby wrote Richard Olney, Member of Congress, that no action could be taken until "final disposition of the Treaty with Germany including the Covenant of the League of Nations which, as you are aware, controls the creation of the mandates." Colby to Olney, Apr. 12, 1920, NA 860J.01/242.

11. See the Herbert Welsh Collection for the papers pertaining to this organization. Historical Society of Penna., Philadelphia.

12. Haig Y. Yardumian, Field Secretary to the Philadelphia Committee, to Colby, May 25, 1920, NA 860J.01/269.

13. G. E. Silloway, State Director of the Pennsylvania Conference of Near East Relief, to Herbert Welsh, Jan. 17, 1920, Welsh Collection.

14. Smith to Welsh, Mar. 20, 1920, *ibid.*

15. Walter George Smith, "The Armenian Tragedy," *Catholic world*, CXI (July, 1920), pp. 485-92.

16. This was one of the oldest organizations devoted to the Armenian cause. It was formed in 1895 and had operated since that date. It was instrumental in keeping the Armenian question before a world public. See "Memorial from the Swiss Federal Committee of Relief for the Armenians to the Paris Peace Conference," (undated) in the House Collection.

17. This committee consisted of Smith and his brother Kilby, H. C. Jaquith, and Dr. W. W. Peet for the United States; John Harris, Noel Buxton, Harold Buxton, and Herbert Ward for Great Britain; Auguste de Morsier, Paul Moriard, James Valloton, A. Krafft-Bonnard, Leopold Favre, William Rappard, Jules Breitenstein, and Anton Vallemon for Switzerland. See Memorandum from H. Gary of American Legation, Berne to Sec. State, Nov. 21, 1920, NA 860J.01/369.

18. See the "Diary of a Journey of Walter George Smith to the International Philarmenian League, Nov. 2, 1920-Jan. 31, 1921," edited by Thomas A. Bryson, in *Armenian Review*, XXV (Summer, 1972), 55-75 and by the same author, "Walter George Smith and the International Philarmenian League: A Note on the Armenian Question before the League of Nations," in Robert W. Thomson, ed., *Papers on Modern Armenian History* (Cambridge: Armenian Heritage Press, 1972), 71-82.

19. *Ibid.*, Nov. 10, 1920, For a copy of the appeal see *New York Times*, Nov. 13, 1920.

20. K. Smith to Mrs. E. B. Esler, Nov. 12, 1920, Smith Collection.

21. Smith Diary, Nov. 20, 1920, *ibid.*

22. A copy of this appeal to the League of Nations is contained in a letter from Gary to Sec. State, Nov. 24, 1920, NA 860J.01/371.

23. League of Nations, *The Records of the First Assembly Plenary Meetings* (Geneva, 1920), p. 202.

24. *Ibid.*, pp. 184-96.

25. *Ibid.*, pp. 189-91.

26. Smith Diary, Nov. 16, 17, and 18, 1920, Smith Collection.

27. *Records of the First Assembly*, pp. 242-43.

28. *FRUS*, 1920, III, p. 789-804.

29. *Ibid.*, pp. 804-05.

30. *Records of the First Assembly*, p. 244.

31. Colby to Wilson, Nov. 26, 1920, Woodrow Wilson Collection, Library of Congress.

32. *FRUS*, 1920, III, p. 807.

33. *Ibid.*, p. 809.

34. *New York Times*, Nov. 27, 1920.

35. Smith to Wilson, Nov. 19, 1920, Wilson Collection.

36. Robert L. Daniel, "The Armenian Question and American-Turkish Relations, 1914-1927," *Mississippi Valley Historical Review*, XLVI (Sep. 1959), p. 265 and *New York Times*, Dec. 23, 1920.

37. Martin Halabian, "The Life and Times of James A. Malcolm: Armenian Patriot and Gentile Zionist," unpublished Ph.D. dissertation, Braindeis University, 1971.

38. Montgomery to Colby, Jan. 20, 1921, NA 860J.01/378.

39. Smith Diary, Jan. 4, 1921, Smith Collection.

40. *New York Times*, Feb. 7, 1921. For a copy of Smith's speech, see Walter George Smith, "The Forthcoming Conference at London and the Armenians," *Christian Work* (Feb. 19, 1921), pp. 233-34.

41. *New York Times*, Feb. 7, 1921.

42. Smith to Morris, Feb. 11, 1921, NA 860J.48/78.

43. Morris to Bullard, Feb. 12, 1921, *ibid*.

44. *New York Times*, Feb. 25. , 1921.

45. Walter George Smith, "History Repeats Itself," *New Armenia*, (Mar. 1921), pp. 17-18.

46. Smith to Hughes, Apr. 14, 1921, NA 860J.01/422.

47. Harding to Hughes, Apr. 21, 1921, NA 860J.4016/96.

48. Merlo J. Pusey, *Charles Evans Hughes* (2 vols, New York, 1951), II, p. 574. Concerning Hughes's feelings on Armenia, an unsigned, undated memorandum in the Hughes manuscript collection, probably prepared by Henry C. Beeritz, the Secretary's private secretary, read: "Although Secretary Hughes had since his college days at Colgate felt considerable sympathy for the persecuted Armenians, he realized the futility of advocating the creation of an Armenian State. . . ." Charles Evans Hughes Collection, Library of Congress.

49. See Thomas A. Bryson, "Mark Lambert Bristol, U.S. Navy, Admiral-Diplomat: His Influence on the Armenian Mandate Question," *Armenian Review*, XXI (Winter, 1968), pp. 3-22.

50. See Thomas A. Bryson, "Admiral Mark L. Bristol: An Open Door Diplomat," *International Journal of Middle East Studies*, V (1974), pp. 454-457.

51. *New York Times*, Feb. 7, 1921 and Smith, "The Forthcoming Conference at London and the Armenians," p. 233.

52. Barton to Lodge, Apr. 22, 1921, Lodge Collection.

53. Lodge to Barton, Apr. 25, 1921, *ibid*.

54. Lodge to Hughes, Apr. 25, 1921, *ibid.*

55. Hughes to Lodge, May 9, 1921, *ibid.*

56. *New York Times*, May 26, 1921.

57. Walter George Smith, "Armenian Independence," *New Armenia*, XIII (Jul. 1921), p. 52.

58. The circular, addressed to "Dear Friend," signed by James Barton, Walter George Smith, and Stanley White, and dated June 3, 1921, was sent out to over 110,000 subscribers and contributors to Armenian relief work in the Middle East. Clipping from the *Buffalo Commercial*, (undated), Scrapbook in the Hamilton Holt Collection, Rollins College, A copy of the circular is in the packet under NA 860J.4016/P81/196.

59. Near East Relief circular, *ibid.*

60. Brandegee to Hughes, Jun. 13, 1921, NA 860J.4016/P81/196.

61. These queries were answered by stock replies over Secretary Hughes's signature. For example, See Hughes to McFadden, July 18, 1921, NA 860J. 4016/P81/288.

62. For example, Cong. A. M. Free wrote that American aid was being misappropriated. A copy of Free's letter to his constitutents, dated Aug. 27, 1921, is attached to NA 860J.48/104.

63. Montgomery to Robbins, *ibid.*

64. Copy of this is attached to Montgomery to Hughes, June 25, 1921, NA 860J.01/449.

65. An excerpt from this letter appeared in Smith's letter to Monseigneur Joseph Freri, editor of *Catholic Missions*, Dec. 22, 1919, Gibbons Collection.

66. *Catholic Standard and Times*, July 26, 1919 and Aug. 30, 1919.

67. Smith to Gibbons, Jan. 24, 1920, Feb. 10, 1920; Feb. 15, 1920; May 13, 1920. Gibbons to Smith, Feb. 12, 1920; May 14, 1920, Gibbons Collection. Also see Thomas A. Bryson. "A Note on Near East Relief: Walter George Smith and Cardinal Gibbons and the Question of Catholic Discrimination;" *Muslim World*, LXI (July 1971), pp. 202-209.

68. A copy of the letter from Cyrille Coussa to Smith was found in the Gibbons Collection. Coussa to Smith, May 24, 1920. As a sad note to the episode, Near East Relief officials requested Smith to represent the organization at the Cardinal's funeral in 1922 and to memorialize His Eminence in its official journal. C. V. Vickrey to the Rt. Rev. O. B. Corrigon, Mar. 30, 1921, Smith Collection. Walter George Smith, Memorial to "His Eminence James Cardinal Gibbons," *Near East Relief* (May, 1921), p. 8.

69. Smith to Fletcher, undated, but received on Dec. 6, 1921, NA 860J.4016/107. Smith was referring to the much discussed plan of revising the Treaty of Sevres at an international conference. My italics are added.

70. Walter George Smith, "The Discredited Allies," *New Armenia*, XIV (Nov. 1922), pp. 83-84.

71. Robbins to Fletcher, June 22, 1921, NA 860J.4016/77.

72. The committee, made up of Raphael Constantian, Vahan Kurkjian, M. Varton Malcom, and G. H. Papazian, presumably wanted the

President to present the matter to the Washington Naval Conference. See *Appeal to the President of the United States on behalf of the Armenians in Cilicia,* Nov. 21, 1921, NA 860J.4016/96. The memorandum of conversation is attached to NA 870J.01/466.

73. See Montgomery to Harding, Aug. 18, 1921, NA 860J.01/466 and the joint letter signed by Vickrey and Montgomery to Hughes, Nov. 10, 1921, NA 860J.01/477.

74. Harding to Hughes, Nov. 21, 1921, NA 860J.4016/96, President Harding had appointed Smith on November 1, 1921, to a committee of twenty-one members, known officially as the Advisory Committee, for the express purpose of gaining public affirmation of the government's policies at the Naval Conference and to act as a liaison group between the people and the government (see chapter 7).

75. Robbins to Fletcher, Nov. 22, 1921 and to Hughes, Nov. 23, 1921. *ibid.*

76. Smith to Fletcher, Dec. 17, 1921, NA 4016/135.

77. Memorandum of Conversation between Smith and Fletcher, Dec. 21, 1921, NA 860J.4016/114.

78. Memorandum with respect to the situation in Asia Minor from Smith to Fletcher, *ibid.*

79. *Loc. Cit.*

80. Cook, "United States and the Armenian Question," p. 310.

81. Harding to Hughes, May 20, 1922, *FRUS,* 1923, II, P. 922.

82. Memorandum from Hughes to Harding, May 25, 1922, *ibid.*

83. Hughes to Harding, June 16, 1922, *ibid.,* p. 929.

84. British Chargé, Jul. 19, 1922, *ibid.* Also see Laurence Evans, *United States Policy and the Partition of Turkey, 1914-1924* (Baltimore, 1965), pp. 343-43.

85. Cook, "United States and the Armenian Question," p. 307.

86. While it is true that American missionary and philanthropic interests were dominant, the same cannot be said of American economic investments which lagged well behind those of other nations. Oddly enough, American philanthropic or "good will" investments exceeded that of American commercial investment. But it is true that in 1920 there was a tremendous upsurge of American exports to Turkey, chiefly due to the vast outpouring of millions of dollars in American relief. For this reason, many Americans hoped Turkey would become a lucrative market for American products. Leland James Gordon, *American Relations with Turkey, 1830-1930* (Philadelphia, 1932), p. 246.

87. Smith and Montgomery to Harding, Feb. 11, 1922, NA711.67119/2.

88. U. S. Congress, *House Hearings before the Committee on Foreign Affairs, In Behalf of the Armenians,* 67 Cong, 2 Sess, on H. Res. 244 (Washington, 1922), pp. 1-13. Hereafter cited as *House Hearing.*

89. *Ibid.,* p. 13.

90. Cook, "United States and the Armenian Question," pp. 297-98.

91. Grabill, *Protestant Diplomacy,* p. 260 and Peter M. Buzansky, "Ad-

miral Mark L. Bristol and Turkish-American Relations, 1919-1922," un-published PhD dissertation, University of Calif., Berkeley, 1960.

92. Bristol to Thomas, July 24, 1922, Bristol collection.

93. Montgomery to Phillips, May 31, 1922, NA 860J.48/187.

94. *New York Times*, Nov. 18, 1922 and Dec. 8, 1922.

95. Diary of Joseph Grew, Nov. 22, 1922, Joseph Grew Collection, Harvard University.

96. *Ibid.*, Nov. 22, 1922; Cook, "United States and the Armenian Question," p. 321; and Richard Washburn Child, *A Diplomat Looks at Europe* (New York, 1924), p. 116.

97. Harold Nicolson, *Curzon, The Last Phase 1919-1925* (Boston, 1934), pp. 316-18.

98. *FRUS*, 1923, II, pp. 940-41; 944-45.

99. Walter George Smith, "The Kuban Proposition," *New Armenia*, XV, (Mar. 1923), pp. 21-22.

100. Walter George Smith, "The Lausanne Treaties," *Ibid.*, XV, (Sept. 1923), pp. 67-68.

101. Gerard to Hughes, Nov. 19, 1923, NA 711.672/207.

102. Hughes to Lodge, Dec. 9, 1922, Lodge Collection.

103. Gordon, *American Relations With Turkey*, p. 33.

104. See Roger R. Trask, *The United States Response to Turkish Nationalism and Reform, 1914-1939* (Minneapolis, 1971).

105. Walter George Smith, "The Outlook for Armenia," *New Armenia*, XVI (Jan. 1924), p. 5.

Chapter 7

1. See John Chalmers Vinson, *The Parchment Peace*, (Athens, 1955), p. 130 and C. Leonard Hoag, *Preface to Preparedness*, (Washington, 1941), Ch. VII.

2. The Advisory Committee consisted of George Sutherland, former U. S. Senator from Utah; Herbert C. Hoover, Secretary of Commerce; General John J. Pershing, Chief of Staff of the Army; Rear Admiral W. L. Rodgers, U. S. Navy; Congressman Stephen G. Porter of Pennsylvania; Governor John M. Parker of Louisiana; Henry P. Fletcher, Under Secretary of State; J. M. Wainwright, Assistant Secretary of War; Theodore Roosevelt, Jr., Assistant Secretary of the Navy; Mrs. Charles Sumner Bird of Massachusetts; Mrs. Katherine Phillips Edson of California; Mrs Eleanor Franklin Eagan, of New York; Mrs. Thomas G. Winter of Minnesota; William Boyce Thompson, New York financier; Willard Saulsbury, ex-Senator from Delaware; Samuel Gompers of the American Federation of Labor; John L. Lewis of the United Mine Workers; Walter George Smith; Carmi Thompson, former Treasurer of the United States; Charles S, Barrett, President of the National Farm Bureau; and Harold M. Sewell, former Minister to Hawaii. See the list of committee members in Department of State, Conference on Limitation of Armaments, U. S. Delegation (Advisory Committee), Record Group #43, National Archives.

3. Smith to Hughes, Nov. 3, 1921, NA 500, 41c/10.

4. See Herbert Hoover, *The Memoirs of Herbert Hoover* (New York, 1952), II, 179; the manuscript diary of Chandler Anderson, Oct. 28, 1921, Chandler Anderson Collection, Library of Congress; The Hearst Press contrasted the American Advisory Committee with the Japanese diplomats and said the Japanese used trained diplomats while the United States sent only "laymen." Cited in Hoag, *Preface to Preparedness*, p. 156-57.

5. U. S. Senate, *Conference on the Limitation of Armament.* Senate Documents, Vol. 10, 67 Cong, 2 Sess, 1921-1922, p. 785.

6. Hughes to Ambassador Geo. Harvey, cited in Hoag, *Preface to Preparedness*, p. 126.

7. Smith to Flick, Nov. 4, 1921, Lawrence Flick Collection, Catholic University, Washington, D. C.

8. Gompers to Sweetster, Nov. 8, 1921, Samuel Gompers Collection, Library of Congress.

9. See Minutes of the Advisory Committee, Conference on Limitation of Armaments, Record Group #43. Hereafter cited as Ad Com.

10. Smith to Flick, Nov. 4, 1921, Flick Collection.

11. Gompers to F. J. Conigan, Dec. 2, 1921, Gompers Collection.

12. Of the Advisory Committee members, only Chairman Sutherland, Under Secretary Fletcher, and Assistant Secretaries Wainwright and Roosevelt had access to the confidential files of the American Delegation. Anderson Diary, Oct. 28, 1921.

13. AdCom I.

14. AdCom IV, Hoag, *Preface to Preparedness*, p. 110.

15. AdCom VI.

16. *Ibid.*

17. *Ibid.*

18. AdCom VII.

19. See the manuscript diary of Theodore Roosevelt, Jr., Dec. 21, 1921, Theodore Roosevelt, Jr. Collection, Library of Congress.

20. Hoag, *Preface to Preparedness*, p. 133.

21. AdCom VIII.

22. See Anderson Diary, Dec. 21-29, 1921; for a copy of this treaty see Yamato Ichihashi, *Washington Conference and After* (Stanford, 1928), pp. 386-88.

23. AdCom IX.

24. *Ibid.*

25. *Ibid.*

26. AdCom X.

27. Fortunately, the United States was free to employ the submarine for scouting purposes in Far Eastern waters where American undersea craft were effecting in crippling the Japanese forward thrust in the early days of World War II.

28. AdCom IX.

29. AdCom VI.

30 *Loc. Cit.* See also Hoag, *Preface to Preparedness*, p. 139, and Diary of

John J. Pershing, Dec. 1, 1921, John J. Pershing Collection, Library of Congress. Unfortunately, the Pershing Diary gives only superficial references to the conference.

31. AdCom VII.

32. U. S. Senate, *Conference on Limitation of Armament*, p. 386.

33. Anderson Diary, Dec. 21-29, 1921, Anderson Collection.

34. U. S. Senate, *Conference on Limitation of Armament*, p. 394.

35. Walter George Smith, "Disarmament Conference in Washington," *American Bar Association Journal*, VIII (Jan. 1922), pp. 71-76.

36. Personal Interview with Miss Dora O'Malley.

Chapter 8

1. "Pueblos Plea for Justice," *Literary Digest*, 76 (Feb. 17, 1923), p. 17. The word "pueblo" is Spanish for town or village.

2. Quoted in Edward P. Dozier, *The Pueblo Indians of North America* (New York, 1970), p. 107.

3. Hazel W. Hertzberg, *The Search for an American Indian Identity* (Syracuse, 1971), pp. 200-201.

4. "Are the Pueblo Indians to be Robbed of Their Heritage? Bursum Bill," *Current Opinion*, 74 (Feb. 1923), p. 213.

5. Fall to Harding, Jan.9, 1923, Records of the Bureau of Indian Affairs, Board of Indian Commissioners, Record Group #75, National Archives. Hereafter cited as BICNA.

6. Smith to McDowell, Jan. 5, 1923, *ibid.*

7. Smith to McDowell, 1923, *ibid.*

8. McDowell to Smith, Feb. 15, 1923, *ibid.*

9. Smith to McDowell, Feb. 19, 1923, *ibid.*

10. McDowell to Smith, Apr. 20, 1923, *ibid.*

11. *Congressional Record*, 67 Cong, 4 Sess, p. 4876. Also see the memorandum on the Lenroot amendment by A. A. Berle, Jr. dated Apr. 28, 1923, BICNA. Although this bill is referred to as the "Lenroot substitute bill," it is properly called the Bursum bill in the *Congressional Record*, because Senator Lenroot merely made an amendment to the original Bursum Bill.

12. Unless otherwise indicated, this chapter is based on Smith's manuscript "Journal of a Western Tour of 1923." Smith Collection.

13. Smith, to K. Smith, Jun. 10, 1923, *ibid.*

14. Smith to Mrs. E. B. Esler, Jun. 23, 1923, *ibid.*

15. See *Fifty-Fourth Annual Report of the Board of Indian Commissioners for the Year Ended June 30, 1923* (Washington, 1923), pp. 12-18.

16. *Ibid.*, p. 17.

17. *Ibid.*, p. 16.

18. *Ibid.*, p. 16.

19. *Ibid.*, p. 19.

20. *Ibid.*, p. 16.

21. *Ibid.*, p. 12.

22. *Ibid.*, p. 12.

23. *Ibid.*, p. 16.

24. *Ibid.*, p. 13.

25. *Ibid.*, p. 17.

26. *Ibid.*, p. 16.

27. *Ibid.*, p. 13.

28. James Kent Stone, known as Father Fidelis of the Cross in religion, had been a married clergyman of the Episcopal Church. At his wife's death, he converted to the Roman Catholic Church, placed his children in foster homes, and entered the Passionist Order.

29. See Herbert W. Work, *Indian Policies: Comments on the Resolutions of the Advisory Council on Indian Affairs* (Washington, 1924).

30. For a description of the illness and death of Smith, see the letter from Mother M. Mercedes, SBS, to Mother Katherine Drexel, Apr. 3, 1923, SBS, and the memorial entitled, "The Death of a Catholic Layman," *Records of the American Catholic Historical Society*, LX (1949), pp. 110-15.

31. When Eden Hall was closed in 1969, the remains of Smith and his wife, along with those of Mr. and Mrs. Drexel, were translated to the crypt beneath the Chapel of the True Cross, St. Michel, Torresdale. See *Register*, Sisters of the Blessed Sacrament, St. Michel, Torresdale, Pa.

Chapter 9

1. "A Roman Catholic Who Co-Operated," *Christian Work*, (Apr. 19, 1924), clipping in Smith's scrapbook.

2. Will of Walter George Smith, City Hall, Philadelphia, Pa.

3. *Congressional Record*, 67 Cong, 4 Sess, p. 4876; 68 Cong, 1 Sess, p. 8450; p. 10,743.

4. Work, *Indian Policies*, p. 12.

5. *Report of the 41st Annual Meeting of the American Bar Association* (Baltimore, 1919), p. 219.

Bibliography

I. MANUSCRIPT SOURCES
A. *Walter George Smith:* The Smith Collection, located in the Archive of the American Catholic Historical Society, St. Charles Seminary, Philadelphia, Pa. and in private hands, spans the greater part of Smith's life. The collection consists primarily of journals of his travels, scrapbooks, miscellaneous letters, collections of Smith's speeches and articles, an autobiography, and numerous biographical sketches.
B. *Official*
Department of State, Records on Armenia and Turkey, Record group #59, National Archives, Washington, D. C. _____, Conference on the Limitation of Armaments, U. S. Delegation, Record Group #443, National Archives, Washington, D. C.
Department of the Interior, Records of the Bureau of Indian Affairs, Board of Indian Commissioners, Record Group #75, National Archives, Washington, D. C.
C. *Private*
American Board of Commissioners for Foreign Missions, Houghton Library, Harvard University, Cambridge, Mass.

Chandler Anderson MSS*

Rudolph Blankenburg MSS, Historical Society of Pennsylvania, Philadelphia, Pa.

Tasker Bliss MSS*

Mark L. Bristol MSS*

Vahan Cardashian MSS, Hairenik Association, Boston, Mass.

Hampton Carson MSS, Historical Society of Pennsylvania, Philadelphia, Pa.

Samuel W. Dike MSS*

Katherine Drexel MSS, St. Elizabeth's Convent, Cornwells Heights, Pa.

Henry P. Fletcher, MSS*

Lawrence Flick MSS, Catholic University, Washington, D. C.

Herbert Adams Gibbons MSS, Princeton University, Princeton, N.J.

James Cardinal Gibbons MSS, Catholic Archdiocesan Center, Baltimore, Md.

Samuel Gompers MSS*

Joseph Grew MSS, Houghton Library, Harvard University, Cambridge, Mass.

Hamilton Holt MSS, Rollins College, Winter Park, Fla.

Edward M. House MSS, Yale University, New Haven, Conn.

Charles Evans Hughes MSS*

Robert Lansing MSS*

Henry Cabot Lodge MSS, Massachusetts Historical Society, Boston, Mass.

J. Hampton Moore MSS, Historical Society of Pennsylvania, Philadelphia, Pa.

Henry Morgenthau, Sr. MSS*

George Wharton Pepper MSS, University of Pennsylvania, Philadelphia, Pa.

John J. Pershing MSS*

Theodore Roosevelt, Jr. MSS*

Charles Riggs MSS, Hightstown, N.J.

Elihu Root MSS*

Thomas Shahan MSS, ACHS, St. Charles Seminary, Philadelphia, Pa.

Herbert Welsh MSS, Historical Society of Pennsylvania, Philadelphia, Pa.

William L. Westermann MSS, Columbia University, New York, N.Y.

Henry White MSS*

John Sharp Williams MSS*

Woodrow Wilson MSS*

*Library of Congress, Washington, D. C.

II. PRINTED SOURCES
A. *Official*
Congressional Record, 1919, 1922, 1923

Grt. Britain: Parl. Debates., *House of Commons*, 1919

League of Nations, *Record of the First Assembly Plenary Meetings.* (Geneva, 1920).

U. S. Congress, House Document, 67th Congress, 2nd Session, 1922. *Hearings before the Committee on Foreign Affairs on H. Res. 244 in Behalf of the Armenians.*

U. S. Department of the Interior, *Fifty-Fourth Annual Report of the Board of Indian Commissioners to the Secretary of the Interior for the Fiscal Year Ended June 30, 1923.* Washington, 1923.

U. S. Department of State, *Conference on the Limitation of Armament.* Washington, 1926
, *Papers Relating to the Foreign Relations of the United States, 1919-1923.*

U. S. Senate, Senate Document, 67th Congress, 2nd Session, 1921-1922. *Conference on the Limitation of Armament.* Washington, 1922.

U. S. Senate, Senate Document, 66th Congress, 1st Session, 1919. *Maintenance of Peace in Armenia.* Washington, 1919

Woodward, Edward L. and Rohan Butler, eds., *Documents on British Foreign Policy, 1919-1939.* 1st Series, London: Her Majesty's Stationery Office, London.

B. *Unofficial*
American Bar Association, *Reports of the American Bar Association.* Baltimore: Lord Baltimore Press, 1897-1924.

Annual Register: A Review of Public Events at Home and Abroad for the year 1919. London, 1920.

Dooley, Dennis A., ed., *Index to State Bar Associations and Proceedings.* New York, 1942.

National Conf. of Commissioners on Uniform State Laws, *American Uniform Commercial Acts Including Uniform Sales Act.*

Papers and Proceedings of the American Sociological Society Proceedings of the Adjourned Meeting of the National Congress on Uniform Divorce Laws Held at Philadelphia, Pa., Nov. 13, 1906. Harrisburg, 1907.

Proceedings of the National Congress on Uniform Divorce Laws Held at Washington, D. C., Feb. 19, 1906, Harrisburg, 1906.

III. MEMOIRS, AUTOBIOGRAPHIES, BIOGRAPHIES, LETTERS & DIARIES
Barnes, George Nicoll, *From Workshop to War Cabinet,* London: H. Jenkins, 1923.

Blankenburg, Lucretia L., *The Blankenburgs of Philadelphia.* Philadelphia: John C. Winston Co., 1928.

Bowden, Robert Douglas, *Boies Penrose: Symbol of an Era.* New York: Greenberg, 1937.

Bradley, Edward Scully, *Henry Charles Lea*. Philadelphia: University of Pennsylvania Press, 1931.

Burton, Katherine, *The Golden Door: The Life of Katherine Drexel*. New York: Kennedy and Sons, 1957.

Child, Richard W., *A Diplomat Looks at Europe*. New York: Duffield & Co., 1925.

Childs, George W., *Recollections*, Philadelphia, 1890.

Cronon, E. David, ed., *The Cabinet Diaries of Josephus Daniels, 1913-1921*. Lincoln: Univ. of Nebraska Press, 1963.

Davis, John H., *The Bouviers: Portrait of an American Family*. New York: Avon Books, 1969.

Duffy, Sister Consuela Marie, *Katherine Drexel: A Biography*. Philadelphia: Peter Reilly Co., 1966.

Dugdale, Blanche, *Arthur James Balfour: First Earl of Balfour*. 2 vols. New York: Putnams & Sons, 1937.

Earnest, Ernest, *S. Weir Mitchell, Novelist and Physician* Philadelphia: University of Pennsylvania Press, 1950.

Egan, Maurice Francis, *Recollections of a Happy Life*. New York: Doren Co., 1924.

Ellis, John Tracy, *The Life of James Cardinal Gibbons, 1834-1921*. 2 vols. Milwaukee: Bruce Pub. Co., 1952.

Fisher, H. A. L., *James Bryce*. 2 vols. New York: Macmillan, 1927.

Gates, Caleb Frank, *Not to Me Only*. Princeton: Princeton University Press, 1940.

Gerard, James W., *My First Eighty-three Years in America: The Memoirs of James W. Gerard*. New York: Doubleday, 1951.

Gibbons, Herbert Adams, *John Wanamaker*. 2 vols. New York: Harper & Bros., 1926.

Gompers, Samuel, *Seventy Years of Life and Labor: An Autobiography of Samuel Gompers*. 2 vols. New York: E. P. Dutton, 1952.

Hoover, Herbert, *The Memoirs of Herbert Hoover*. 3 vols. New York: Macmillan Co., 1952.

Howe, Frederick Clemson, *Confessions of a Reformer*. New York: Chas. Scribner's Sons, 1925.

Kuehl, Warren, *Hamilton Holt: Journalist, Internationalist, Educationist*. Gainesville: University of Florida Press, 1960.

Lansing, Robert, *The Peace Negotiations: A Personal Narrative*. Boston: Houghton, Mifflin Co., 1921.

Letterhouse, Sister Dolores. *The Francis A. Drexel Family*. Cornwells Heights, Pa. Sisters of the Blessed Sacrament, 1939.

Lloyd George, David, *Memoirs of the Peace Conference*. 2 vols. New Haven: Yale University Press, 1939.

Love, Donald M., *Henry Churchill King of Oberlin*. New Haven: Yale University Press, 1956.

McClure, A.K., *Old Time Notes of Pennsylvania*. 2 vols. Philadelphia: John C. Winston Co., 1905.

Miller, David Hunter, *My Diary at the Conference of Paris.* 21 vols. New York: Appeal Printing Co., 1924.

Morgenthau, Henry, *All in a Lifetime.* New York: Doubleday, 1922

Nicolson, Harold, *Curzon: The Last Phase, 1919-1924: A Study in Post-War Diplomacy.* Boston: Houghton Mifflin Co., 1934.

Nevins, Allan, *Henry White: Thirty Years of American Diplomacy.* New York: Harper and Bros. 1930.

Palmer, Frederick, *Bliss, Peacemaker.* New York: Dodd, Mead., 1934.

Patrick, Mary Mills, *Under Five Sultans.* New York: Century Co., 1929.
———, *A Bosporus Adventure: Istanbul Women's College, 1871-1924.* Stanford: Stanford Univ. Press, 1934.

Peet, Louise, *No Less Honor: The Biography of William W. Peet.* Chattanooga: Private Printing, 1939.

Pepper, George Wharton, *Philadelphia Lawyer: An Autobiography* Philadelphia: J. B. Lippincott Co. 1941.

Pusey, Merlo, *Charles Evans Hughes,* 2 vols. New York: Macmillan Co., 1951.

Rowland, Dunbar, ed., *Jefferson Davis, Constitutionalist: His Letters, Papers, and Speeches.* 10 vols. Jackson: 1923.

Scipio, Lynn A., *My Thirty Years in Turkey,* Rindge: Richard R. Smith Pub. Co., 1955.

Smith, Walter George, *Life and Letters of Thomas Kilby Smith.* New York: Putnams Sons, 1898.

Steed, Henry Wickham, *Through Thirty Years, 1892-1922: A Personal Narrative.* 2 vols. Garden City: Doubleday, 1925.

Steffens, Lincoln, *The Autobiography of Lincoln Steffens.* New York: Harcourt, Brace & Co., 1931.

Thorpe, Francis Newton, *William Pepper.* Philadelphia: J. B. Lippincott Co., 1904.

Trask, David F., *General Tasker Howard Bliss and the "Sessions of the World," 1919.* Philadelphia: American Philosophical Society, 1966.

Vare, William S., *My Forty Years in Politics.* Philadelphia: Roland Swain Co., 1933.

Ward, Maisie, *Unfinished Business.* New York: Sheed & Ward, 1964

IV. GENERAL

Abell, Aaron I., *American Catholicism and Social Action: A Search for Social Justice, 1865-1950.* South Bend: University of Notre Dame Press 1963.

Baltzell, E. Digby, *Philadelphia Gentlemen: The Making of a National Upper Class.* New York: Free Press, 1958.

Bane, Suda, *Organization of American Relief in Europe, 1918-19.* Stanford: Stanford Univ. Press. 1943.

Barton, James L., *Story of Near East Relief (1915-1930): An Interpretation.* New York: Macmillan Co. 1930.

Bierstadt, Edward Hale, *The Great Betrayal: A Survey of the Near East Problem.* New York: R. M. McBride Co., 1924.

Blake, Nelson Manfred, *The Road to Reno: A History of Divorce.* New York:

Macmillan Co., 1962.

Bonsal, Stephen, *Suitors and Suppliants: The Little Nations at Versailles*. New York: Prentice Hall Co., 1946.

Braisted, William Reynolds, *The United States Navy in the Pacific, 1909-1922*. Austin: University of Tex. Press, 1971.

Brown, Esther Lucile, *Lawyers and the Promotion of Justice*. New York: Russell Sage Foundation, 1938.

Bryson, Thomas A., *American Diplomatic Relations with the Middle East, 1784-1975: A Survey*. Metuchen, N.J.: The Scarecrow Press, Inc., 1977.

Buckley, Thomas H., *The United States and the Washington Conference, 1921-22*. Knoxville: University of Tenn. Press, 1970.

Buell, Raymond Leslie, *The Washington Conference*. New York: Russell & Russell Co., 1922.

Burt, Nathaniel, *The Perennial Philadelphians: The Anatomy of an American Aristocracy*. Boston: Little, Brown, 1963.

Chamberlain, Joshua L., ed., *The University of Pennsylvania*. 2 vols. Boston: R. Herndon Co., 1901.

Chandler, Alfred D., "The Origins of Progrssive Leadership," in Elting Morison, et al, ed., Letters of *Theodore Roosevlt*. 8 vols. Cambridge: Harvard University Press, 1951-54.

Cheyney, Edward Potts, *History of the University of Pennsylvania, 1740-1940*. Philadelphia: Univ. of Penna. Press, 1940.

Crooks, James B., *Politics & Progress: The Rise of Urban Progressivism in Baltimore, 1895 to 1911*. Baton Rouge: Louisiana State Univ. Press. 1968.

Debo, Angie, *A History of the Indians of the United States*. Norman: University of Oklahoma Press, 1970.

DeNovo, John A., *American Interests and Policies in the Middle East, 1900-1939*. Minneapolis: University of Minnesota Press, 1963.

Dozier, Edward P., *The Pueblo Indians of North America*. New York: Holt, Rhinehart, Winston, 1970.

Evans, Laurence, United States Policy and the Partition of Turkey, 1914-1924. Baltimore: Johns Hopkins Press, 1965.

Fite, Emerson, D., *Government by Cooperation*. New York: Macmillan Co., 1932.

Gidney, James B., *A Mandate for Armenia*. Kent: Kent University Press, 1967.

Gordon, Leland James, *American Relations with Turkey, 1830-1930*. Philadelphia: University of Pennsylvania Press, 1932.

Grabill, Joseph L., *Protestant Diplomacy and the Near East: Missionary Influence on American Policy, 1810-1927*. Minneapolis: University of Minnesota Press, 1971.

Graham, Otis L., Jr., *An Encore for Reform: The Old Progressives and the New Deal*. New York: Oxford University Press, 1967.

_____, *The Great Campaigns, Reform and War in America, 1900-1929*. Englewood Cliffs: Prentice Hall, 1971.

Graves, W. Brooke, *Uniform State Action: A Possible Substitute* for Centralization. Chapel Hill: University of North Carolina Press, 1934.

Haber, Samuel, *Efficiency and Uplift: Scientific Management in the Progressive Era, 1890-1920.* Chicago: University of Chicago Press, 1964.

Hertzberg, Hazel W., *The Search for an American Indian Identity: Modern Pan-Indian Movements.* Syracuse: Syracuse University Press, 1971.

Hoag, C. Leonard, *Preface to Preparedness: Washington Disarmament Conference and Public Opinion.* Washington: American Council on Public Affairs, 1941.

Hofstadter, Richard, *The Age of Reform from Bryan to F.D.R.* New York: Vintage Books, 1955.

Hoover, Herbert, *An American Epic: Famine in Forty-Five Nations: Organization behind the Front, 1914-1923.* 2 vols. Chicago: Henry Regnery Co., 1961.

———, *The Ordeal of Woodrow Wilson.* New York: McGraw-Hill Book Co., 1958.

Housepian, Marjorie, *The Smyrna Affair.* Harcourt, Brace, Jovanovich, 1971.

Hovannisian, Richard G., *Armenia on the Road to Independence, 1918.* Berkeley: University of California Press, 1969.

———, *The Republic of Armenia.* 3 vols. Berkeley: University of California Press, 1971.

Howard, Harry N., *An American Inquiry in the Middle East: The King-Crane Commision.* Beirut: Khayats, 1963.

Hurst, Willard, *The Growth of American Law: The Law Makers.* Boston: Little Brown & Co., 1950.

Ichihashi, Yamato, *Washington Conference and After: A Historical Survey.* Stanford: Stanford Univ. Press, 1928.

Johnsen, Julia E., ed., *Selected Articles on Marriage and Divorce.* New York: H. W. Wilson Co., 1925.

Kazemzadeh, Firuz, *The Struggle for Transcaucasia, 1917-21.* New York: Philosophical Library, 1951.

King, Moses, *Philadelphia and Notable Philadelphians.* New York: Moses King, 1901.

Kolko, Gabriel, *The Triumph of Conservatism: A Reinterpretation of American History, 1900-1916.* Chicago: Quadrangle Books, 1963.

Kurkjian, Vahan M., *A History of Armenia.* New York: Armenian General Benevolent Union of America, 1959.

Lynch, H. F. B., *Armenia: Travel and Studies.* 2 vols. Beirut: Khayats, 1965.

Marra, Harold J., *St. Dominic's 100 Years, 1849-1949.* Philadelphia: Private Printing, 1950.

Mears, Eliot Grinnell, *Modern Turkey: A Politico-Economic Interpretation, 1908-1923.* New York: Macmillan Co., 1924.

Mowry, George E., *The Era of Theodore Roosevelt and the Birth of Modern America, 1900-1912.* New York: Harper and Row, Pub., 1958.

———, *The California Progressives* (Berkeley; University of California Press, 1951.

Nansen, Friedjob, *Armenia and the Near East.* New York: Duffield and Co., 1928.

Oberholtzer, Ellis Paxson, *Philadelphia: A History of the City and Its People*. 4 vols. Philadelphia: S. J. Clarke, 1912.

O'Grady, Joseph P., ed., *The Immigrant's Influence on Wilson's Peace Policies*. Lexington: University of Ky. Press, 1967.

O'Neill, William L., *Divorce in the Progressive Era*. New Haven: Yale University Press, 1967.

The Philadelphia Club, 1834-1934. Philadelphia: Private Printing, 1934.

Repplier, Agenes, *Philadelpha: The Place and the People*. New York: Macmillan Co., 1925.

Rogers, James Grafton, *American Bar Leaders, 1878-1928*. Chicago: American Bar Association, 1932.

Scharf, J. Thomas and Thompson Westcott, *History of Philadelphia, 1609-1884*, 3 vols. Philadelphia: L. H. Everts Co., 1884.

Steffens, Lincoln, *The Shame of the Cities*. New York: Hill and Wang, 1960.

Surface, Frank M. and Raymond L. Bland, *American Food in the World War and Reconstruction Period*. Stanford: Stanford University Press, 1931.

Taylor, A. J. P., *English History, 1914-45*. London: Oxford University Press, 1965.

Tillman, Seth P., *Anglo-American Relations at the Paris Peace Conference of 1919*. Princeton: Princeton University Press, 1961.

Trask, Roger R., *The United States Response to Turkish Nationalism and Reform, 1914-1939*. Minneapolis: Univ. of Minnesota Press, 1971.

Vinson, John Chalmers, *The Parchment Peace: The United States and the Washington Conference, 1921-1922*. Athens: University of Georgia Press, 1955.

Vratzian, Simon, *Armenia and the Armenian Question*. Boston: Hairenik Publishing Co., 1943.

Wainwright, Nicholas B., *A Philadelphia Story, The Philadelphia Contributionship for the Insurance of Houses from Loss by Fire*. Philadelphia: Wm. Fell Co., 1952.

Westermann, William Linn, "The Armenian Problem and the Disruption of Turkey," in Edward Mandell House and Charles Seymour, eds., *What Really Happened at Paris: The Story of the Peace Conference, 1918-1919*. New York: Scribner's, 1921.

Wiebe, Robert H., *Businessmen and Reform: A Study of the Progressive Movement*. Chicago: Quadrangle Books, 1968.

_____, *The Search for Order, 1877-1920*. New York: Hill and Wang, 1967.

Wilson, R. Jackson, *Reform, Crisis, and Confusion, 1900-1929*. New York: Random House, 1970.

Windrich, Elaine, *British Labour's Foreign Policy*. Stanford: Stanford University Press, 1952.

Work, Herbert W., *Indian Policies: Comments on the Resolutions of the Advisory Council on Indian Affairs*. Washington, GPO, 1924.

V. DISSERTATIONS & THESES

Bryson, Thomas A., "Woodrow Wilson, the Senate, Public Opinion, and the Armenian Mandate Question, 1919-20," Unpublished Ph.D. dissertation, University of Georgia, 1965.

Buzanski, Peter M., "Admiral Mark L. Bristol and Turkish-America Relations, 1919-1922," Unpublished Ph.D. dissertation, University of California, 1960.

Cook, Ralph Elliott, "The United States and the Armenian Question, 1884-1924," Unpublished Ph.D. dissertation, Fletcher School of Law and Diplomacy, 1957.

Disbrow, Donald W., "The Progressive Movement in Philadelphia, 1910-16," Unpublished Ph.D. dissertation, Rochester University, 1956.

Feinstein, H.C.V., "Mark Twain's Lawsuits," Unpublished Ph.D. dissertation, University of California, 1968.

George, Paul S., "Philadelphia's Municipal Affairs During the Latter Part of the 19th Century," Unpublished master's thesis, Florida State University, 1968.

Halabian, Martin H., "The Life and Times of James A. Malcolm: Armenian Patriot and Gentile Zionist," Unpublished Ph.D. dissertation, Brandeis University, 1971.

Richardson, John Philip, "The American Military Mission to Turkey," Unpublished master's thesis, George Washington University, 1964.

Index

A

Abbott, Louis, 9
Abbott, Mr. and Mrs. Rodman, 9, 13
Academy of Music, 21, 56, 59, 60
Acker, Finley, 188n. 68
Acoma, 167
Adams, John, 2
Adams family, 2, 39
Adamson Act, 74
Addams, Jane, 122, 180
Advisory Committee (see Washington Naval Conference), xi, 108, 150-161, 201n. 2
"Age of Organization", 45
Albany Argus, 26
Alexander v. Green, 26
Alex. Manoogian, xiii
Allen, Henry T., 142
Allied Organizations for Good Government, 59
American Bar Association, 15, 19, 42, 43, 44, 45, 64, 66, 72, 78, 90, 103, 151, 152, 165, 172, 174, 180
American Bar Association Journal, 160, 179
American Board of Commissioners for Foreign Missions (ABCFM), 81, 83
American Committee for the Independence of Armenia (ACIA), 118, 123, 133, 135, 146
American Committee for Relief in the Near East (ACRNE), see also Near East Relief, xi, 78, 79, 80-85, 90-95, 99, 100, 101, 102, 103, 112, 116, 121
American Expeditionary Force, 122
American Indians, 48, 167, 179
American mandate for Armenia, 94, 103, 110, 115, 116, 118, 123, 124
American Military Mission to Armenia, see Harbord Mission, 101, 117
American Negro, 180
American Peace Commissioners, 98, 99, 101, 106, 107, 109, 112
American Relief Administration, 84, 90, 93, 97, 99, 106
American Sociological Society, 67, 69, 70
Anabasis, 86
Anatolia College, 83
Andalusia, 27
Anderson, Chandler, 155, 159
Andranik, General
Anglo-Japanese Treaty, 150

214

Appleton, D. & Co., 28

Arizona, 162, 163, 166, 167

Arizona, U.S.S., 97

Armenia, American Loan for, 134-135

Armenia, American Society, 118, 122-125, 128, 130, 131, 132, 133, 134, 135, 137, 138, 139, 140, 142, 143, 145

Armenia, Provisional Government of, 87, 88, 89, 90

Armenia, Republic of, 87, 88, 89, 96, 99, 106, 119, 120, 125, 127, 132

Armenia, mandate for, 99, 102, 103, 123; British motives for, 110

Armenian Christians, 191n. 4

Armenian National Delegation, 107-108, 128, 129

Armenian National Home, 128, 129, 131, 133, 135

Armenian National Union, 144, 145, 146

Armenian Patriarch, 82

Armenian Review, xii

Armenians, xi, 79, 82, 83, 84, 85, 87, 88, 89, 91, 92, 93, 94, 96, 97, 101, 102, 105, 106, 112, 113, 114, 115, 116, 117, 121, 122, 124, 125, 126-130, 131-134, 136-138, 140, 145, 148, 165, 177

Armenians, repatriation of, 96, 99, 101-108

Armstrong, Thomas F., 75, 77

Arnold, Major David G., 92, 93, 99, 101

Arroll, James, 90, 91

Ashbridge, Samuel H., 52

Assumptionist Order, 95

Astor, John J., 85

Astor, Vincent, 85

Atwood, Mrs. Stella, 171

Azerbaijanis, 88, 89

B

Bailey, John T., 188n. 68

Baker, Ray Stannard, 180

Balfour, A. J., 100, 140

Baltzell, Digby, 46

Barnes, George N., 111, 113

Barnes, J. Hampton, 58

Barney, U.S.S., 97

Barrett, Charles S., 201n. 2

Barton, James L., 81, 100, 101, 102, 104, 105, 121, 134, 135, 136, 140, 144, 145

Barton Relief Commission, 81, 95, 99, 100, 101, 107, 135, 137

Beck, James M., 55

Beeber, Dimner, 54

Beeritz, Henry C., 198n. 48

Belford's Magazine, 22, 27

Bellevue-Stratford Hotel, 66

Bellfounder, 77

Benedict XV, 81

Bible House, 82, 93

Biddle, Charles, 18, 27, 58

Biddle, Charles J., xi, 42

Biddle, Colonel Charles J., 27

Biddle, Judge Craig, 14, 16, 17, 55

Biddle, George N., 17, 27

Biddle, Nicholas, 27

Big Four, 100, 102, 103

Bird, Mrs. Charles S., 201n. 2

Birkenbine, John, 27

Bishop, J. C., 117

Bispham, George Tucker, 59

Blackfeet Indians, 171, 172

Blankenburg, Rudolph, 58, 61, 74, 75

Bliss, General Tasker, 102, 107, 110, 111, 112

Board of Indian Commissioners, 48, 164, 165, 172, 174, 177, 179

Board of Tax Assessors, 58

Bodine, Samuel T., 9

Bodleian Library, 33

Bolsheviks, 89, 125-126, 127-128, 132

Borah, William E., 150, 164

Borie, Edward R., 75

Bourne, Francis Cardinal, 82

Bouvier's Law Dictionary, 15

Boyle, James S., 75

Brandegee, Frank B., 136

Brandeis, Louis, 102

Bregy, F. Amedée, 22

Breitenstein, Jules, 127n. 17

Briand, Aristide, 140

Bristol, Admiral Mark L., 84, 85, 94, 97, 102, 103, 105, 107, 133, 141, 144, 145, 147

British Near Eastern Policy, 110-111, 115

British Armenia Committee, 114, 115, 126

Bromley, John H., 57

Brown, David Paul, 23

Brown, John P., 76

Browne, Louis Edgar, 85

Bryan, Hamilton, 107

Bryan, William Jennings, 54

Buckler, William M., 102, 103, 105, 107, 109, 110, 112

Budd, George, 4
Budd, Henry, 60, 61
Buffalo dance, 170
Bullard, Arthur, 131
Bullitt, Bill, 52
Bullitt, John D., 17, 46
Burk, Henry, 60
Burke, Charles H., 127
Burnham, George, 58, 59
Bursom, H. O., 163, 164, 172
Bursom bill, 166, 168, 177
Businessmen's League, 54, 59
Butler, Judge William, 23, 25
Buxton, Rev. Harold J., 126, 197n. 17
Buxton, Noel, 126, 197n. 17

C

Cadwalder, Charles E., 188n. 68
Caldwell, R. J., 122, 123
Calef, Hannah, 2
Cameron, J. Donald, 52
Cameron, Simon, 52
Camp Dennison, Ohio, 3
Campbell, F. C., 171
Campbell, John M., 55
Cardashian, Vahan, 123
Carr, W. Wilkins, 9, 61
Carroll, Raymond G., 114
Carson, Hampton L., 15, 44, 58
Carville, Kate, 3
Cassidy, Miss Mary Anne, 33
Catholic Congress, 49
Catholic Encyclopedia, 63
Catholic Federation, 41
Catholic Indian Bureau, 164, 174
Catholic Missions, 137
Catholic Standard and Times, 137
Catholic University of America, xii, 45, 47, 173
Catholic World, 121
Catholicox, 89
Cecil, Lord Robert, 115, 126
Cecil-LaFontaine motion, 126
Centennial Exhibition, 1876, 11
Central Committee of the Federation of Swiss Committees of the Friends of the Armenians, 125
Chambers, Moreau B. C., xii
Chase, Salmon, 2, 28
Chester Concession, 146, 147
Chicago Daily News, 85

Chicago Herald, 26
Child, Richard Washburn, 145
Childs, George W., 26, 31
Chippewa Indians, 165, 166, 172
Christian Work, 122, 174
"Church lobby," 94, 119, 133, 117
Churchill, Winston, 113, 114
Cilicia, 129, 130, 132, 133, 134, 135, 136, 138, 139, 140, 141
Cincinnati, 2
City and State, 55, 56, 57, 61
City Party, 62, 74, 176
Clemens, Samuel L., see Mark Twain, 24, 25
Clement, Samuel, 57
Clements, Colin C., 85
Clements, Father, 95
Cleveland, Grover, 22, 23
Colby, Bainbridge, 123
College Hall, 9
Committee of Nine, 57, 58, 59, 74, 176
Committee on Legal Education of American Bar Association, 43
Committee on Uniform State Laws, 44
Congregation of the Sisters of the Blessed Sacrament for Indians and Colored People, 31, 48, 164, 173, 174, 180
Congress of Berlin, 131
Conference of Commissioners of Uniform State Laws, 44, 45, 72, 174
Constantinople, 81, 82, 93, 94, 96
Constantinople College for Women, 82, 92, 107
Cook, Ralph E., 142
Coray, E. A., 60
Cosmos Club, 123
Costello, Peter F., 78
Craigie, Robert, 131
Crane, Charles R., 79, 95, 96, 99
Crane, John, 99, 100
Crocker, William D., 66
Croly, Herbert, 146
Curzon, Lord George N., 114, 115, 116, 121

D

Dale, Richard C., 46
Damad Ferid Pasha, 194n. 26
Damon, Theron, 107
Dance Order, 163, 164
Daniels, 121, 146

Darlington, Mrs. Jean B., xi
Davis, George H., 60
Davis, Jefferson, 24, 27, 28, 29
Davis, John W., 112, 115
Davis, Mollie Camp, xii
Davis, Sussex, 18
Delaware River, 5
Department of Interior, 164
Derindje, 83, 101
DeVillier, Mary Anne, xii
Dickinson, D. M., 23
Dickson, Samuel, 17, 46
Dike, Dr. Samuel W., 63, 65, 67, 68, 69, 70
Dillon, Justice John F., 23
Divorce: A Study in Social Causation, 67
Dodd, Isabel Frances, 107
Dodge, Cleveland H., 79, 84, 100, 109
Doherty, Charles, 127
Dolci, Mgr., 83
Dom Pedro, Emperor of Brazil, 12
Donnelly-Ryan Democrats, 62
Doolittle, Vice Consul, 109
Dougherty, Dennis Cardinal, 49, 164, 173
Drexel, Anthony, 32, 33, 47, 107
Drexel, Elizabeth L., x, 29, 30, 31, 32, 33,
    34, 35
Drexel, Emma Bouvier, 30
Drexel, Francis Anthony, x, 29, 30, 31, 34
Drexel, Katherine, 31, 32, 34, 35, 48, 164
Drexel, Louise, 31, 32
Drexel Institute, 47
Drinker, Biddle, Reath, 42
Duponceau, Peter S., 17
Durham, Israel, 52, 56, 60

E

Eagle Dance, 170
Eckhoff, xii
Eden Hall, 5, 6, 34, 51, 173
Edgar, Police Chief, 60
Edson, Mrs. Katherine P., 201n. 2
Egan, Mrs. E. F., 152
Eisenbrown, William, 75
Elcock, Thomas R., 16
Elder, John, 90
Elkins, William, 53
Elkus, Abram, 121
Emery, John R., 66
Episcopal Academy, 6
Eshleman, Amabel, 172
Eshleman, Bettina, 91

Esler, Mrs. E. B., 34, 89, 96, 108, 168
Etchmiadzin, 89
Executive Order Reservations, 164
Extreme Unction, 173

F

Fair, Rev. Bartholomew, xii
Fall, Senator Albert, 163, 164
Fant, Handy Bruce, xii
Favre, Leopold, 197n. 17
Federal Council of Churches of Christ, 122
Fels, Maurice, 188n. 68
Fidelis of the Cross, Father, see James Kent
    Stone, 171
"50-50" ticket, 75
54th Ohio Volunteers
Filene, Peter, 38
Finnie, Gordon, xii
Fish, Asa Israel, 14
Fisher, H. A. L., 111, 114
Flether, Henry P., 138, 139, 140, 152, 153,
    158
Flick, Dr. Lawrence, 152
Folk, Joseph, 56
Folk, Richard N., xii
Folwell, Nathan T., 57
Forbes-Adams, Eric, 103
Forty Years in Constantinople, 95
Foster, Sir George, 127
Fraley, Joseph C., 18
France, 128-138, 138-142
Francisca, Sister M., xi
Franklin, Benjamin, 49, 50
Frazier, Arthur H., 102
French, H. B., 59
Freri, Monsignor, 137
Furness, Horace Howard, 49

G

Gardener, G. Clinton, 10
Garland, A. H., 23
Gasparri, Cardinal, 82
Gasquet, Cardinal Francis Aidan, 49
Gates, Caleb Frank, 84
General Board of the Navy, 154, 159
General Federation of Women's Clubs,
    164, 171
George Washington University, 67
Georgetown University, 172
Georgians, 88, 89
Gerard, James W., 122, 123

Gibbons, James Cardinal, 49, 63, 95, 137, 180
Gidney, James B., xii, 104, 105
Girrard Trust Co., 16
Gompers, Samuel, 152
"Goo Goos", 59, 75
Goodwin, Harold, 58
Gordon, James Gay, 53, 58, 59
Grabill, Joseph L., xii
Graham, George S., 53, 58
Graham, Otis L., Jr., 38, 71
Graham, Sir Ronald, 114
Grant, Ulysses S., 1, 10, 24, 25, 28, 76, 77, 165
Gratz, Simon, 60
Great Awakening, 71
Gregorian Armenian Church, 191n. 4
Grelis, J. J., 75
Green, Major Joseph, 100, 106, 109
Grew, Joseph C., 145, 146, 147
Grey, Lord Edward, 121
Grinnell College, 45
Guadalupe Hidalgo, Treaty of, 162
Gunkle, Oscar, 95

H

Haber, Samuel, 71
Halsey, Rev. Edmund, xii
Hamilton, Andrew, 175
Hamilton County, Ohio, 3
Hancock, General Winfield Scott, 7, 19
Hand-in-Hand, 50
Harbord, Maj. Gen. James G., 104, 106, 109, 117, 142
Hardin, Charles, 188n. 68
Harding, Warren G., 120, 123, 132, 133, 134, 139, 140, 141, 144, 150, 151
Harding administration, 163, 165
Harmer, A. C., 21
Harper, Clarence, 58
Harris, John H., 126, 197n. 17
Harrison, Charles Custis, 69
Harvard University, xii
Haskell, Colonel William, 100, 106
Hatch, Harold, 81, 83
Hawes, Mrs. Lilla Mills, xii
Hays, Samuel P., 38
Heins, Lieutenant, 85
Heinz, Howard, 84, 85, 86, 87, 90, 91, 92, 93, 99, 100
Hemphill, Alexander, 99

Henry, Bayard, 15, 18
Hersch, Jane, xii
Hibben, John G., 146
Hispano-Americans, 163
Historical Society of Pennsylvania, xii
Hoadly, George, 28
Hoadly, Lauterbach, Johnson, 28
Hobart College, 172
Hofstadter, Richard, 38, 39, 41
Holt, Hamilton, 122, 123
Holy Ghost Fathers, 70
Holy Viaticum, 173
Honest Government Party, 53
Hoover, Herbert, 84, 93, 99, 100, 101, 104, 106, 109, 151, 152-157
Hopi Indians, 167
Horan, Hubert, xi, 42
Hotel Continental, 99
Hotel Crillon, 100, 109
Hotel Metropole, 126
House, Colonel Edward M., 102
Howard, George E., 67, 68, 69
Howe, Frederick, 194n. 34
Hubbard Brothers, 27
Hudson, Manley O., 107
Hughes, Charles Evans, 44, 73, 132, 133, 134, 135, 137, 140, 141, 144, 146, 150, 152, 153, 154, 155, 159, 160
Hull House, 122, 180
Hunter, George W., 4
Huntington, Dr. George H., 84
Huntington, Henry S., 122
Hymans, Paul, 127

I

Igdir, 89
Independent, 122
India, 110
Indian Affairs, Commission of, 163
Indian Rights Association, 164
Indian Service, 165, 168, 169, 171
Indians, see chapter 8
Interallied Commission on Mandates in Turkey, see King-Crane Commission, 96
International Labor Organization, 152
International Philarmenian League, 123, 125, 126, 127, 138
Isleta, 167, 168

J

Jackson, George, 14

James, Arthur Curtis, 81, 92
Jaquith, H. C., 99, 109, 125, 197n. 17
Jeffersonian Society, 59
Jemez, 167
Jobson, Betty, xii
Johnson, John Graver, 17, 59
Jones, Senator A. A., 172
Jones, J. Levering, 46, 69
Junkin, Joseph DeF., 58
Justice, Thio., 58

K

Kachaznuni, Hovhannes, 88
Keating, Percy, 18
Keating-Owen Act, 74
Keim, J. R., 188n. 68
Keith, Charles P., 9
Kellogg, Frank, 44, 164
Kemal, Mustafa, 138
Kemalists, 128-132, 133, 138
Kenyon College, 172
Kerr, Philip, 110, 111, 194n. 34
Keystone Party, 74
King, Henry Churchill, 95
King, Samuel, 52
King-Crane Commission, 96
Kinsey, 54
Kline, Mahlon N., 188n. 68
Krafft-Bonnard, A., 197n. 17
Krauskopf, Joseph, 67

L

Labor Party, 112
Ladner, Albert D., 57
Laetare Medal, 47
Lafayette Hotel, 57
LaFontaine, Henry, 126
Laguna, 167, 168
Lake Mohonk, 172
Land Title Co., 75
Langstroth, Hannah, 184n. 16
Lansing, Robert, 102, 105, 112
Lausanne, Treaty of, 144-148
Law Academy, 17
Law Association of Philadelphia, 18
Law Association Library, 14, 18
League of Nations, xi, 117, 123, 125, 126, 127, 132, 149, 150, 151
Leake, Frank, 58
Lee, Lord, 155
LeHavre, 81

Lenrott, Senator I. L., 166
Lenroot amendment, 166, 168, 169, 177
Leuchtenburg, William, 94
Lex, William Barclay, xii, 42
Lewis, John L., 201n. 2
Lichtenberger, Dr. James P., 63, 67, 68, 69, 70
Lincoln, Preston S., 85
Linden, Robert J., 58
Lloyd George, David, 109, 110, 111, 114
Lodge, Senator Henry Cabot, 103, 115, 116, 134, 135, 144, 146, 150, 153
London Conference, 129, 130, 131, 132
Lucon, Cardinal, 108
Ludlow, James R., 16, 17
Lukens, R. A., 60
Lunch Club, 18
Lusitania, 74, 156

M

McCall, Peter, 17
McClure, Colonel Alexander, 53, 59, 60, 62
McCullough, Elizabeth Budd, 2
McCullough, Dr. William Budd, 2
McDonough, John xii
McDowell, Malcolm, 164, 165, 166, 168, 172
McFadden, L. T., 137
MacFarland, Charles S., 122
McFaul, Bishop James, 49, 70
McGurk, Joseph, 16, 17
McMurtrie, Richard G., 17
MacNeal, Mrs. Charles, xii
McNeille, Mrs. Martha, 91
Mac-O-Cheek, 2, 3
Machinists Union, 59
Main, Dr. J. H. T., 81, 83, 87, 92, 93, 101
Malcom, James A., 107
Mallet, Sir Louis, 103
Marble, H. P., 167
Martin, David, 52
Matthews, Justice Stanley, 23
Maurice, Father, see Theodore D. Smith, 25, 32, 34
Mears, Dr. Elliott, 94
Meldrim, Peter, 44
"Memorandum Against Ratification by the Senate of the Lausanne Treaty," 146
"merchant lobby," 119
Mercur, Ulysses, 17

Merry del Val, Rafael Cardinal, 82
Mesopotamia, 110
Mexico, 162
Milne, General Sir George F., 91, 105
Mitchell, Lt. M. M., 91
Mitchell, Dr. Silas W., 46, 49
Momus, S. S., 167
Montgomery, Rev. George R., 96, 122, 127, 128, 129, 130, 131, 140, 141, 144, 145
Moore, Prof. Edward C., 81, 83, 92, 93
Moore, H. Hampton, 61
More, Sir Thomas, 179
Morgan, Junius S., 33
Morgan, Randall, 9, 46, 69
Morgenthau, Henry, 97, 98, 99, 100, 102, 104, 106, 107, 116, 127
Moriard, Paul, 197n. 17
Morrell, Edward, 31
Morrell, Louise Bouvier Drexel, 34
Morris, Effingham B., 16, 17
Morris, Roland S., 131
Morsier, Auguste de, 197n. 17
Mowry, George E., 38, 39
Muckrakers, 37
Munson, C. LaRue, 65, 66
Mustin, Joel, xii

N

Nambe, 167
Nansen, Frithjob, 126, 127
National Armenian Church, 89
National Association for Armenian Studies and Research, xiii
National Divorce Congress, 64, 65, 66
National League for the Protection of the Family, 69
nativism, 162
Navajo Indians, 166, 167, 169
Naville, Eduard, 125, 126
Near East Relief, 118, 121, 123, 124, 134, 135, 136, 137, 138, 139, 140, 144, 165, 174
Neff, Dr. Joseph S., 9
Negroes, 48
New Armenia, 121, 135, 139, 147
New England Divorce Reform League, 63
New Mexico, 162, 163, 166
New Republic, 146
New York Herald, 111, 116
New York Post, 26

New York Record, 26
New York School of Philanthropy, 68
New York Tribune, 26
Nicholson, William R., 75, 77
Noma, U.S.S., 85, 86, 92
Noradounghian, Gabriel, 129
Notre Dame University, 47
Nubar, Boghos Pasha, 107, 129

O

Oberlin College, 95
O'Connell, William Cardinal, 122
O'Connor, Miss Francis, 171
O'Connor, T. P., 114, 116
Ogden, Robert C., 24
O'Hara, Constance, xii
O'Malley, Flora, xi, 76
Open Door Policy, 119, 133, 134, 142, 146, 149
O'Sullivan, Dennis, 15-16
Ottoman Empire, 79, 84, 88, 94, 96

P

Packard, Charles S. W., 46
Paderewski, Ignace, 127
Palestine, 102
Panama, 7
Pan-Turanian movement, 88, 127
Paris Peace Conference, xi, 85, 88, 89, 93, 96, 97, 98, 116, 117, 129, 149, 152, 177
Parker, John M., 201n. 2
Passionist, 12
Patrick, Dr. Mary M., 82, 84, 92, 95, 96, 107, 111
Patterson, Stuart, 18
Pattison, Robert E., 21, 57, 59
Paul, A. J. Drexel, xii
Paul, J. Rodman, 18, 50
Paul Pierre III Terzian, 82
Pears, Sir Edwin, 95
Peet, Dr. William W., 81, 83, 92, 93, 101, 106, 145, 197n. 17
Pennsylvania Bar Association, 19, 44
Pennsylvania Commission on Uniform State Laws, 44
Pennsylvania Globe Gas Light Co., 53
Pennsylvania, Supreme Court of, 43
Pennsylvania, University of, 7
Pennypacker, Samuel W., 47, 64, 65, 66, 67
Penrose, Boies, 53, 75, 76

Penrose Club, 60, 61
People's Bank of Philadelphia, 52, 53
Pepper, George Wharton, 56, 70
Pershing, General John J., 104, 158, 159
peyote, 171
philarmenia groups, 125
Philadelphia, 20, 21, 39-40, 74-78
Philadelphia, City of, 174
Philadelphia Armenian Relief, 124
Philadelphia Bar, 174
Philadelphia Bar Association, 18
Philadelphia Board of Public Education, 47, 164
Philadelphia Branch of Near East Relief, 124, 139
Philadelphia Contributionship, 46, 50, 174
Philadelphia Evening Bulletin, 26, 54, 75
Philadelphia Evening Star, 26
Philadelphia Evening Telegraph, 70
Philadelphia Herald, 26
Philadelphia Inquirer, 26, 60, 61, 75
Philadelphia Law Academy, 12
"Philadelphia lawyer," 175
Philadelphia Municipal League, 56, 59
Philadelphia News, 26
Philadelphia political machine, 51-53, 56-57
Philadelphia Press, 26
Philadelphia Public Ledger, 19, 26, 57, 62
Philadelphia Times, 53
Philadelphia Traction Co., 53
Piatt, Benjamin M., 2
Piatt, Donn, 2, 22, 27, 28
Piatt, Elizabeth, 2
Pittsburgh Dispatch, 26
Pleasants, Henry, 9
Polk, Frank, 112
Ponsonby, Arthur A., 195n. 53
Porter, Stephen G., 159
Potter, Bishop Henry, 63
Potts, Charles W., 57
Price, J. Sergeant, 22
progressive profile, 37-38
Pueblo Indians, x, 162, 163, 164, 165, 166, 167, 168; report on, 169-71
Pueblo Lands Board, 177
Purcell, Archbishop John B., 2

Q

Quay, Matthew S., 52, 53, 55, 56

R

Rappard, William, 197n. 17
Rawle, Francis, 14, 15, 23, 24, 25, 26, 27, 44
Rawle, William, 18
Rawle, William H., 17, 18
Read, John R., 23
Reed, Henry, 22
Records of the American Catholic Historical Society of Philadelphia, xii
Reiff Bey, 95
Repplier, Agnes, 49
Richberg, John C., 65, 66
Rigg, Sarah, xii
Riggs, Charles T., xii, 83
Riggs, Ernest, 143
Riley, Stephen T., xii
Rise and Fall of the Confederate Government
Riter, Frank, 59
Rivinus, Emily, 117
Robb, Samuel, 14, 22
Robbins, Edward, 70
Robbins, Dr. James W., 11
Robbins, Warren, 139, 140
Robert College, 84
Robinson, Herbert F., 167
Rodgers, Admiral W. L., 154, 156, 160
Rogers, John J., 143
Rogers resolution, 143, 144
Roosevelt, President Theodore, 162
Roosevelt, Theodore, Jr., 154, 160
Root, Elihu, 44, 150, 153, 155, 159
Root resolution, 159
Rotan, Samuel P., 75, 77
Rothermel, Peter F., 53, 54, 55, 56, 57, 59, 60, 61, 62, 75
Rousseau, Jean Jacques, 170
Rugovitch, Capt. V., 85
Runyan, William N., 122
Ruskell, Jan, xii
Russian Volunteer Army, 85
Ryan, Archbishop Patrick, 32, 49, 70

S

Sacred Heart, Order, 5, 30
St. Dominic's Church, 32, 173
St. Elizabeth's Convent, 48
St. Francis's Industrial School, 34, 51
St. Gregory the Great, Order of, 70
St. Gregory the Illuminator, 191n. 4

St. Helen's, 30
St. John the Divine, Cathedral of, 129, 134
St. Louis Globe Democrat, 26
St. Michel, 30, 32, 33, 34
San Ildefonso, 167, 169
San José, 33
San Juan, 167, 168, 170, 177
San Remo Conference, 123, 127
Sandia, 167
Sandoval, Santiago, 171
Sandoval decision, 163
Sands, Kate Loughran, xi
Santa Ana, 167, 168
Santa Clara, 167
Saratoga Springs, N.Y., 44
Sarrut, Albert, 155
Saulsbury, Willard, 152
Savannah Morning News, 26
Schmandt, Raymond H., xii
Schmidt, Dr. Gottfried Christian, 1
Scott, James Brown, 156, 159
Sellers, William, 58
Senate Foreign Relations Committee, 103
Servell, Harold M., 201n. 2
Sèvres, Treaty of, 127, 130, 136, 143, 144
Shahan, Thomas J., 47, 70, 146, 173
Sharswood, George, 12, 14, 16, 44
Shaw, Marti, xii
Sheehan, James B., 76, 77
Shellem, Rev. John J., xii
Sheppard, Franklin L., 57
Sheppard, Furman, 10, 22
Sheppard, H. R., 75, 77
Sherman, General William T., 1
Shippen, Edward, 56
Smith, Adrian (brother of WGS), 3, 5, 50
Smith, Alfred E., 146, 164
Smith, Arabella "Belle" (sister of W. G. S.), 2, 3, 5
Smith, Caroline "Caleen" (sister of W. G. S.), 5, 50, 112
Smith, Elizabeth (mother of W. G. S.), 2, 3, 5
Smith, Elizabeth "Betty", see Mrs. Esler, 2, 3
Smith, Elizabeth Drexel (wife of W. G. S.), 29-35
Smith, George (grandfather of W. G. S.), 2
Smith, Helen Grace (sister of W. G. S.), 5, 33, 49, 50, 81, 85, 92, 95, 101, 107, 108, 110, 112, 167, 172, 173

Smith, Henry Austie, 27
Smith, Robert Meade, 9
Smith, Theodore Dehon, see Father Maurice, (brother of W. G. S.), 3, 6, 12, 25
Smith, Thomas Duncan (brother of W. G. S.), 3, 5, 50
Smith, Thomas Kilby (father of W. G. S.), 1, 2, 3, 4, 6, 7, 23
Smith, Thomas Kilby (brother of W. G. S.), 5, 50, 51, 83, 89, 90, 101, 106, 108, 109, 110, 172, 125, 126, 168, 197n. 17
Smith, Walter George, Adamson Act, opposition to, 74; Advisory Committee of Washington Naval Conference, 151-161; Alexandropol, 87; Altoona, 10; American Bar Association, joins, 19, 78; American Committee for the Independence of Armenia, member of, 123; American Committee for Relief in the Near East, xi, 79, 81, 99-101; American Sociological Society, 67-68; ancestry, 1-3; Armenia-America Society, 122-125; 128-135; 137-148; Armenia, loan for, 134-138; Armenian government, thoughts on, 89; Armenian national home, and, 129-130; Armenians, repatriation of, 103-108; Armenians, speeches for, 121, 129; bar, admitted to, 12; Batoum, 86; Benedict XV, audience with, 33; Beneficial Savings Fund Society, and, 50; beneficiary of wife's will, 34; birth, 1, 3; Board of Indian Commissioners, x, 48; Ch. 8; *Bouvier's Law Dictionary*, and, 15; British troop withdrawal from Transcaucasus, and, 91, 96, 99, 108-119; William Jennings Bryan, and, 54; business, and, 72-73; career of, 24, 35, 36, 42-43; Catholic Church's influence on, 40-41; Catholic Congress, 49; Catholic Federation, 41; Catholic University of America, 47; child labor laws, and, 74; Civil War years, 3-5; Class Day, 9; Constantinople, 82; Commissioner for Uniform State Laws, 44; Committee on High Schools and Discipline, 47; Committee of Nine, 57-59; Committee on Legal Education, 43; Committee on Resolutions at National Divorce Congress, 65 66; Committee on Uniform State Law:

44; Conference of Commissioners of Uniform State Laws, 44, 45, 72; Congress, runs for, 19; Constitutional Club, 12; E. A. Coray, and, 60; Court of Common Pleas, seeks appointment to, 21; Lord Curzon, and, 115-116; Davis case, 74; death of, 173; description of, 29, 32; U.S. District Attorney, seeks appointment as, 22; divorce, ideas on; 41, 63-64; Doctor of Laws Degree, 46; Katherine Drexel, aid to, 48; Drexel Institute, and, 47; education, 3, 6; educator and religionist, 46-51; engagement, 31; Episcopal Academy, 6, 11; family, supports, 14; father, death of, 23; Asa I. Fish, practices law with, 14; Geneva, visits, 125-127; Grant case, 24; General Winfield S. Hancock, and, 19; Hubbard case, 27; income tax, and, 73-74; Ivy Day, 9; Middle East, mission to, xi, 94; Knight of the Order of St. Gregory the Great, 70; Laetare Medal, 47; Latin Club, 9; Lausanne Treaty, and, 145-46; Law Class of 1877, 12; Law Oration, 12; Law School, 11-12; League of Nations, lobbys at, 127; League of Nations, petitions, 126; Legal Club 51; legal profession, views on, 40, 43; legal reforms, and, 42-46; literary interests, 49; Leo XIII, audience with, 81; London, visits, 111-117; Lourdes, 108; Lunch Club, 18; McGurk case, 16; Mac-O-Cheek, 3; memorials to on death of, 174; National Divorce Congress, 64; political machines, fear of, 40; oratory, permission to have, 70; O'Sullivan case, 15-16; Paris Peace Conference, at, xi, 98-119; Pennsylvania Club, 51; Pennsylvania Railroad, works at, 10; Philadelphia Club, and, 51; Pennsylvania Commission on Uniform State Laws, 44; Phi Kappa Sigma fraternity, 9; Philadelphia Company for Guaranteeing Mortgages, 50; Philadelphia Contributionship for the Insurance of Houses from Loss by Fire, 50; Philadelphia Law Academy, 12; Board of Public Education of Philadelphia, 47; political creed, 20; political reformer, 51, 54, 55; progressive profile of, 39; progressive reformer, xi, Ch. 3; progressive values 9; Pueblo Indians, and, x, 162-173; reform, motives for, 39-40; relief in the Middle East, 79; reports for court, 14; Register of Wills, seeks election to, 75-77; Republican Party, joins, 151; Rheims, visits, 108; Rogers resolution, and, 143-144; P. F. Rothermel, and, 57-62; Rittenhouse Club, 51; rural life in Ohio, 4; Stoddart case, 26, 27; Tiflis, 87; Torresdale, 5, 35; Town Meeting Party, and, 76; to Transcaucasus, 85-92; trial lawyer, 15; Underwood Tariff, 73; uniform divorce bill, and, 62, 64-70; uniform commercial laws, and, 41, 43, 71-73; U.S. Supreme Court, and, 23; University Club, 51; University of Pennsylvania, student at, 4-10; Board of Trustees, 46-47, 69; Washington Naval Conference, xi, 148-161; WASP syndrome, Ch. 3; wedding trip, 33; White House, 25; wife, death of, 34-35; will of, 175; Williams resolution, testimony on, 120; Woodrow Wilson, and, 73; Yellow Springs, 3; Zelosophic Literary Society, 9

Smith, William Duncan (brother of W. G. S.), 5
Smith, William Rudolph, 27
Soviet Armenia, 131
Soviet Union, 117, 179
Spencer, Selden, 164
Staake, William H., 65, 66
Stamboul, 82
Standard Oil Co., 94, 144
Stapleton, Dr. Robert, 92
State House, 74
"status revolution," 38
Steed, Henry Wickham, 113
Steel, Henry M., 188n. 68
Steffens, Lincoln, 51, 56
Stehr, George, 14
Stenger, William, 57
Stephan, Monsignor Joseph, 164
Stephenson, John, 23
Stephenson v. Brooklyn Cross-Town Railroad Co., 23
Stoddart, Joseph M. and Co., 26, 27
Stone, Charles W., 53
Stone, James Kent (See Father Fidelis of the Cross), 171

Stone, William A., 53
Stork, Theodore B., 9
Straus, Oscar S., 122
Stotesbury, Edward T., 122
Stuart, Sir Campbell, 113
Stuart, Edward B., 22
Sutherland, George, 44, 152, 153, 154, 156, 157, 158, 160
Swallow, Dr. Silas, 53
Sweetster, Arthur, 152

T

Taft, William H., 44, 115
Taos, 167, 170, 171
Tashjian, James, xii
Teitlebaum, Rabbi Aaron, 81, 83
Tesuque, 167, 170
Thomas, L. Irving, 94, 144
Thompson, Carmi, 159
Thompson, William Boyce, 201n. 2
Thomson, General Sir William, 91
Thucydides, 86
Tilden, Samuel J., 12
Tilden, William T., 58, 188n. 68
Times, The, 113
Tittoni, Thomasso, 127
de Tocqueville, Alexis, 43
Torresdale, Pa., 5, 30, 34, 35, 50
Towle, Sir Charles, 114
Town Meeting Party, 75, 76, 77
Toynbee, Arnold, 194n. 34
trachoma, 171
Transcaucasian Federative Republic, 88
Transcaucasus, 84, 85, 86, 87, 88, 91, 92, 93, 96, 100, 109, 110, 111, 112, 119, 126
Trebizond, 92
Triple Entente, 88
Truman Doctrine, 111
Turco-American Treaty of Lausanne, 147, 148
Turks, 88, 89, 90, 94, 96, 105, 125-126, 127, 129, 135, 138, 144
Tustin, E. L., 188f. 77
Twain, Mark, 24, 25, 26

U

Underwood, Oscar W., 150-153
Underwood Tariff, 74
uniform state commercial laws, 71-73
uniform state divorce laws, 62-71
Union Party, 56, 57, 59, 60, 61, 62, 74, 176

United Gas Improvement Co., 46
U.S. Supreme Court, 163
University of Pennsylvania, 8, 46, 47, 67, 69
University Record, The, 8, 9
Ussher, Dr. Clarence D., 87, 96, 99, 100, 102, 103, 105, 106

V

Valleman, Antone, 197n. 17
Vallotton, Joseph, 197n. 17
Vare, Edwin H., 75
Vare, William S., 61, 175
Vaux, George, 165
Vaux, Richard, 17
Veditz, C. W. A., 67
de Vere, Aubrey, 49
Versailles Treaty, 100, 102, 108, 123
Vickrey, C. V., 109, 140, 141, 144
Vinson, J. Chal, xii
Virginian, The, 49
Vivianni, René, 126, 127

W

Wainwright, J. M., 201n. 2
Wainwright, Nicholas Biddle, xii
Wall, Rev. Lawrence, 173
Walter, Eliza Bicker, 2
Walthall, Maj. W. T., 28
Walton, J. M., 60
Wanamaker, John, 24, 25, 26, 27, 53, 55, 59
Wanamaker, Thomas, 24
Ward, Henry Galbraith, 18, 46
Ward, Herbert, 126, 197n. 17
Ward, Maisie, 50
Ward, Wilfrid, 49
Warwick, John F., 52
Washburn, Dr. G. H., 81, 83, 93
Washington Naval Conference, xi, 108, 140, 148, 149-161; Advisory Committee, 150-161, 201n. 2; American Delegation, 150, 152, 155, 157, 158, 160; Committee on Organization, 153; Executive Committee, 153; subcommittee on Limitation of Naval Armament, 153, 154-157; subcommittee on Limitation of Land Armament, 153, 158-161; subcommittee on Pacific and Far East Questions, 153, 157-158; subcommittee on New Agencies of Warfare, 153, 159; Five-Power Treaty, 159, 160; France,

155; Great Britain, 155; gas warfare, 159; Japan, 149; Korea, 157; public opinion, 159-160; Sakhalin, 157; Siberia, 150; Shantung, 157; Smith, and, 150-161; submarines, 154, 155, 156, 157; Yap, 150

Washington Post, 114

Weaver, John, 56, 61

Webb, Admiral Sir Richard, 95

Webster, Charles L., 24, 25

Welsh, Herbert, 55, 56, 57, 58, 61

Westermann, William L., 99, 103, 107

Wharton, H. R., 9

Wharton School, 69

White, Dr. George E., 83

White, Henry, 102, 103, 107, 110. 111, 112

White, Dr. Stanley, 81, 83, 93, 101, 122, 135, 136, 144

Widener, Peter A. B., 53

Wiebe, Robert H., 38, 45

Williams, Aneurin I., 114, 116

Williams, Senator John Sharp, 115, 120, 122

Williams resolution, 120-122, 132

Wilson, Woodrow, 73, 74, 80, 84, 94, 96, 100, 103, 105, 106, 109, 110, 111, 115, 116, 117, 120, 123, 124, 127, 131, 132, 134, 150-151

Winter, Mrs. Thomas G., 201n. 2

Wise, Rabbi Stephen S., 122

Wister, Owen, 49

Witherspoon Building, 124

Wood, General Leonard, 122

Woodruff, Clinton Rogers, 51, 52, 56, 59

Woodward High School, 2

Work, Herbert, 172

World Court, 149

X

Xenophon, 86

Y

Yarrow, Ernest, 116, 117

Yellow Springs, 3, 4

Yerkes, Harman, 60

Young Democracy, 59

Young Men's Democratic Association, 19

Z

Zenger, John Peter, 175

Zia, 167

Zuni, 167, 169